Editors

STANLEY W. STANDAL, Ph.D.

*Consulting Psychotherapist and
Marriage Counselor; Co-Director,
The Clinic for Counseling and
Psychotherapy, Honolulu, Hawaii*

RAYMOND J. CORSINI, Ph.D.

*Associate Director
Daniel D. Howard Associates
Counselor, Chicago Community
Child Guidance Centers*

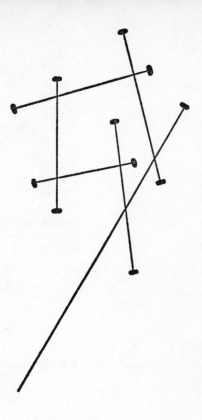

CRITICAL

INCIDENTS IN

PSYCHOTHERAPY

Englewood Cliffs, N.J.
PRENTICE-HALL, INC.
1959

PRENTICE-HALL PSYCHOLOGY SERIES

Paul E. Meehl, Editor

Library of Congress Catalog Card No.: 59–10111

If names of persons in this book bear any similarity to those of
actual persons, the similarity is purely fortuitous.

Printed in the United States of America
19382

Preface

Practicing psychotherapists frequently cite interesting cases. Eminent authorities often use such cases as vehicles for discussion of theoretical and procedural points. We seldom have an opportunity to hear *several* well-known persons with variant points of view simultaneously discuss *one* specific instance taken from actual psychotherapy. This book attempts to approximate that desirable situation with many instances. In it you will find twenty-three anonymous "critical incidents," accounts of events which therapists in the field thought worthy of procedural, theoretical, or ethical comment. After each critical incident you will find the opinions of several eminent "consultants" on such issues as ways the case should have been handled, implications for theory and practice, and ethical and legal ramifications. In the last chapter the editors have analyzed, summarized, and drawn conclusions from the discussions by twenty-eight consultants about twenty-three distinct critical incidents.

The book serves a variety of readers. The professional psychotherapist or counselor will find a wealth of concrete instances which will parallel those of his own work, along with many viewpoints on dynamics and procedural matters relating to them. The student psychotherapist who wishes to broaden his purview of psychotherapy will discover startling similarities among authors whose isolated writings may appear poles apart. A very gratifying feature of the book is the number of "off-beat" speculations which the informal nature of the discussion has encouraged. Experimentalists and theoreticians will find these speculative flights thought-provoking. The editors have discovered that lay readers find the material fascinating. It has even been used with considerable success as adjunctive bibliotherapy with less disturbed cases.

The process of constructing the book went as follows: Approximately four hundred practicing psychotherapists were invited to submit "critical incidents" of theoretical, procedural, or ethical interest. They also were asked to suggest "consultants" they would like to have comment on the critical incidents. Forty-one incidents were selected from those submitted.

The various consultants suggested by the contributors, as well as a number of people in related disciplines, such as theoretical psychology, sociology, semantics, theology, and anthropology, were invited to participate. Those who agreed to do so were sent, for the most part, ten critical incidents from which they were asked to comment on as many as they wished and in any way they deemed pertinent. Incidents which received fewer than five comments were not included in the book.

The editors wish to extend their appreciation to all the contributors and consultants, whose names follow this preface, for their generous help. We have an even deeper indebtedness to a number of individuals who helped in various special ways, primarily with encouragement during the early phases of the work. Specifically, we acknowledge the efforts of Rudolf Dreikurs, Abraham Maslow, O. Hobart Mowrer, and Carl Rogers. Both Frieda Fromm-Reichmann and Robert M. Lindner, who very early accepted our invitation to serve as consultants, died before they could participate. We wish also to thank Josephine Standal and Lucy Corsini for their forbearance and encouragement. Valuable editorial assistance was given by Louis Segaloff. Finally, we thank Polly Welch for her many extra hours of patient typing and retyping.

STANLEY W. STANDAL
RAYMOND J. CORSINI

Commenting
Consultants

The authorities in the social and biological sciences who are listed below have all made significant contributions to the understanding of human personality. Each of them has also thereby given something to the complex task of helping that personality attain greater harmony. In this book their experience and wisdom is pooled in such a way that we can observe and pinpoint their similarities and differences as these are operative in real-life issues.

Nathan W. Ackerman, M.D., is Associate Clinical Professor of Psychiatry at Columbia University and Attending Psychoanalyst at the Psychoanalytic Clinic for Training and Research in New York City. He is also Clinical Director of the Family Mental Health Clinic. He is president of the Association for Psychoanalytic Medicine, and has been a psychiatrist at the Menninger Clinic in Topeka, Kansas, and Director of The Child Development Center in New York City. His special interests are psychosomatic medicine, child psychiatry, and interdisciplinary research. His books include *Personality in Arterial Hypertension* (1945), *Antisemitism and Emotional Disorder* (1950), and *The Psychodynamics of Family Life* (1958).

C. Knight Aldrich, M.D., is Professor and Chairman of the Department of Psychiatry at the University of Chicago School of Medicine. Formerly he was Associate Professor of Psychiatry at the University of Minnesota Medical School where he established a liaison service between the departments of psychiatry and internal medicine. Dr. Aldrich began his medical career with the United States Public Health Service. He has published *Psychiatry for the Family Physician* (1955) and various articles, chiefly relating to the interpretation of dynamic psychiatry to physicians.

Robert R. Blake, Ph.D., is Professor of Psychology at the University of Texas and Director of the Human Relations Training Laboratory. In 1949–50 he was Honorary Clinical Psychologist, Tavistock Clinic, London, and Visiting Professor of Psychology, University of Reading, Reading, England. From 1950–51 he was Research Associate at Harvard University. His primary interest is the laboratory method of training in social psychology. Dr. Blake is co-author of *Perception: An Approach to Personality* (1951).

Rudolf Dreikurs, M.D., is Professor of Psychiatry of the Chicago Medical School and Director of the Alfred Adler Institute, Chicago. Past President of the American Society of Adlerian Psychology and of the American Society of Group Psychotherapy and Psychodrama, Dr. Dreikurs is also founder and first editor of the *Journal of Individual Psychology*. A student and collaborator of Alfred Adler, he is a leading exponent of Adlerian Psychology and Group Psychotherapy. His major publications are *The Challenge of Marriage* (1946), *The Challenge of Parenthood* (1947), *Fundamentals of Adlerian Psychology* (1950), *Character Education and Spiritual Values in an Anxious Age* (1952), and *Psychology in the Classroom* (1957).

Wladimir G. Eliasberg, M.D., Ph.D., is in the private practice of psychiatry in New York City. He was the founder and general secretary of the German Congress for Psychotherapy, editor of the *Allg. Aertztl Ztschrft. f. Psychother.*, and Visiting Professor, Academy of Political Sciences, Prague. He is now the Associate Editor of *Group Psychotherapy*. Among his numerous writings are *Psychologie und Pathologie der Abstraktion* (1925) and *Multitudes, Moguls and Mind Healers* (1957).

Albert Ellis, Ph.D., practices psychotherapy and marriage counseling in New York City. Formerly, he was Chief Psychologist of the New Jersey Department of Institutions and Agencies and the New Jersey State Diagnostic Center, Menlo Park. He is past Chairman of the New York Association of Psychologists in Private Practice. Dr. Ellis is founder (*circa* 1955) of the approach to psychotherapeutic technique known as *rational psychotherapy*. His major books are *An Introduction to the Principles of Scientific Psychoanalysis* (1950), *The American Sexual Tragedy* (1954), *New Approaches to Psychotherapy Techniques* (1955), *How to Live with a Neurotic* (1957), and *Sex without Guilt* (1958).

Jerome D. Frank, M.D., Ph.D., is Associate Professor of Psychiatry at Johns Hopkins University School of Medicine and Psychiatrist-in-Charge of the Psychiatric Out-Patient Department at Johns Hopkins Hospital. Dr. Frank was strongly influenced by Kurt Lewin, and did research on self-esteem, level of aspiration, and social influence. His current research interest is in group psychotherapy and the "placebo" effect. He is the co-author of *Group Psychotherapy: Studies in Methodology of Research and Therapy* (1953).

Viktor Frankl, M.D., Ph.D., is Professor of Psychiatry and Neurology at the University of Vienna Medical School and Chief of the Neurological Department of the Vienna Polyclinic. He is President of the Austrian Medical Society for Psychotherapy. He was formerly Chief of the Neurological Department at the Rothschild Hospital in Vienna. He has lectured at the University of Buenos Aires, Harvard, Princeton, Yale and Columbia Universities. Dr. Frankl is the founder of a school of psychotherapy known as *logotherapy* or *existential analysis*. He is the editor of *Handbuch der Neurosenlehre und Psychotherapie* (five volumes). Among his books are *The Doctor and the Soul: An Introduction to Logotherapy* (1955), and *A Psychologist Experiences Life in a Concentration Camp* (1958).

Iago Galdston, M.D., has been in psychiatric practice since 1925. He is the Executive Secretary of the Medical Information Bureau of The New York Academy of Medicine, and was formerly Director of Health Activities of the Community Councils of Greater New York and Consultant in Health Education, National Tuberculosis Association. He is associated with New York Medical College, Fordham University, and New York University School of Education. Dr. Galdston is the author of *Progress in Medicine* (1940), *Behind the Sulfa Drugs* (1943), *The Meaning of Social Medicine* (1954), and co-author of *Modern Attitudes in Psychiatry* (1946) and *Freud and Contemporary Culture* (1957).

Vincent Victor Herr, Ph.D., S.J., is Chairman of the Department of Psychology at Loyola University, Chicago. Prior to this he was Professor of Philosophy at West Baden College and Assistant Professor of Biology at Xavier University. He is a former president of the American Catholic Psychological Association. He has done research in physiological changes in treatment for neuroses and psychoses, and is the author of *How We Influence One Another* (1945).

Ernest R. Hilgard, Ph.D., is Professor of Psychology and Education at Stanford University. He has been an instructor at Yale University, Executive Head of the Department of Psychology at Stanford, and later Dean of the Graduate Division. He is past President of the American Psychological Association and past President of the Society for the Psychological Study of Social Issues. Dr. Hilgard is identified primarily with experimental psychology, especially the psychology of learning (he was awarded the Warren Medal in 1940). Now Associate Director of the Laboratory of Human Development at Stanford, Dr. Hilgard is doing research on human motivation. He is co-author of *Conditioning and Learning* (1940) and *Psychoanalysis as Science* (1952); and author of *Theories of Learning* (1956), and *Introduction to Psychology* (rev. ed. 1957).

J. McV. Hunt, Ph.D., is Professor of Psychology and Coordinator of Training and Research in Clinical and Counseling Psychology at the University of Illinois. He was formerly the Director of the Institute of Welfare Research for the Community Service Society of New York, Associate Professor at Brown University, and Psychological Consultant at Butler Hospital. His interests have been in psychotherapy and experimental psychology. He is a past president of the American Psychological Association, and former editor of the *Journal of Abnormal and Social Psychology*. He is the editor of *Personality and Behavior Disorders* (2 vols., 1944); and the author of *Measuring Results in Social Casework* (1950), *Testing the Results of Social Casework* (1950), and *A Followup Study of the Results of Social Casework* (1953).

Fay B. Karpf, Ph.D., is in private practice in Beverly Hills, California. She was formerly a faculty member at the Graduate School for Jewish Social Work, New York City. Her approach to psychotherapy is neo-Rankian, psycho-social, and interdisciplinary. Dr. Karpf was analyzed by Dr. Otto Rank and was associated with him for several years. She is the author of *American Social Psychology, Its Origins, Development, and European Background* (1932), *Dynamic Relationship Therapy* (1937), *Personality from the Standpoint of Rankian "Will" or "Dynamic Relationship" Psychology* (1940), and *The Psychology and Psychotherapy of Otto Rank* (1953).

J. W. Klapman, M.D., is on the staff of the Chicago State Hospital and Consultant at the Downey Veterans Hospital. He was formerly on the faculty of Northwestern University Medical School. Dr. Klapman is President of the Physicians Association and former President of the National Mental Hospital and Clinic Physicians Association. His publications include *Group Psychotherapy; Theory and Practice* (1946), and *Social Adjustment: a Textbook for Patients in Group Psychotherapy* (1950).

Ashley Montagu, Ph.D., is the Chairman of the Department of Anthropology at Rutgers University; Associate Professor of Anatomy at Hahnemann Medical College and Hospital, Philadelphia; Consultant to Unesco; and Visiting Lecturer, Department of Social Relations at Harvard University. Dr. Montagu was formerly Senior Lecturer, Veterans Administration Postgraduate Training Program in Psychiatry, Philadelphia, and Curator of Physical Anthropology, Wellcome Historical Medical Museum, London. Among his many books are *The Natural Superiority of Women* (1953), *On Being Human* (1953), *The Direction of Human Development* (1955), *The Biosocial Nature of Man* (1956), and *Anthropology and Human Nature* (1957).

Jacob L. Moreno, M.D., is Physician-in-charge of the Moreno Sanitarium and Director of the Moreno Institute. He is also editor of *Group Psychotherapy*, and Adjunct Professor at New York University. He is a past President of the American Society of Group Psychotherapy and Psychodrama. He is the originator of *psychodrama*, a method of spontaneity psychotherapy, and of *sociometry*, a technique for measuring social dynamics. Dr. Moreno has been Visiting Lecturer at twenty-two universities throughout Europe and Asia and at eleven universities in the United States. Among his major publications are: *Group Psychotherapy* (1932), *First Book of Group Psychotherapy* (1945), *Psychodrama Volume I* (1946), *Who Shall Survive* (rev. ed. 1953), and *Sociometry and the Science of Man* (1955).

O. Hobart Mowrer, Ph.D., is Research Professor of Psychology at the University of Illinois. He has held positions at Northwestern University, Princeton and Yale, and from 1940 to 1948 was Assistant and then Associate Professor of Education in the Graduate School of Education at Harvard. He is a past President of the American Psychological Association. Dr. Mowrer's main professional interests are learning, personality, and language. His books include *Learning Theory and Personality Dynamics* (1950), *Patterns of Modern Living* (1950), *Psychotherapy—Theory and Research* (with others) (1953), and *Learning Theory and Behavior* (1958).

Ruth L. Munroe, Ph.D., is in private practice of psychotherapy and personality diagnosis in New York City, and a Visiting Professor at the City College of New York. She was formerly Psychologist at Sarah Lawrence College. She is the co-author of *The Happy Family* (1938), and author of *Teaching the Individual* (1942) and *Schools of Psychoanalytic Thought* (1955).

Elias H. Porter, Ph.D., is Assistant Head of the Human Factors Department of the Rand Corporation. Previously, Dr. Porter was Research Associate at the University of Chicago, and Director of Psychological Service for Science Research Associates. He was the first to quantify therapeutic protocols for research purposes. At present he is engaged in research and development in the area of man-machine systems and the newly developed area of system training. Dr. Porter is the author of *An Introduction to Therapeutic Counseling* (1950).

David Riesman, LL.D., is Professor of the Social Sciences, University of Chicago and Harvard University. Under a grant from the Ford Foundation Fund for Research in Psychiatry, he is working on an investigation of the therapeutic and survey interview. He is an editor of *The American Journal of Sociology* and *The Journal of Nervous and Mental Diseases*. Among his books are *Civil Liberties in a Period of Transition* (1942), *The Lonely Crowd* (1950), *Faces in the Crowd* (1952), *Thorstein Veblen* (1953), and *Individualism Reconsidered* (1954).

Carl R. Rogers, Ph.D., is Professor in the Departments of Psychology and Psychiatry at the University of Wisconsin. He was formerly Professor of Psychology and Executive Secretary of the Counseling Center, University of Chicago. He is President of the American Academy of Psychotherapy and past President of the American Psychological Association. Dr. Rogers is the founder (*circa* 1940) of the approach to psychotherapy known variously as *nondirective* or *client-centered*. He and the "Chicago group" were among the vanguard of research workers who helped bring empirical methods of research to counseling and psychotherapy. An active psychotherapist for nearly thirty years, his publications include *Clinical Treatment of the Problem Child* (1939), *Counseling and Psychotherapy* (1942), *Client-Centered Therapy* (1951), and *Psychotherapy and Personality Change* (1954), of which he was co-editor.

William U. Snyder, Ph.D., is Professor of Psychology and Director of the Psychology Clinic at Pennsylvania State University. He was formerly Director of the Des Moines Child Guidance Clinic, and Assistant Professor of Psychology and Co-Director of the Psychology Clinic at Ohio State University. Dr. Snyder is the author of *Casebook of Nondirective Counseling* (1947), and *Current Status of Psychotherapeutic Counseling* (1947).

Bess Sondel, Ph.D., is Professorial Lecturer in Communication at the University of Chicago. She is interested in the application of field theory of communication in industry, and is a consultant to several large industrial organizations. Among her publications are *Everyday Speech*

(1950), *Speak Up! A New Approach to Communication* (1952), and *The Humanity of Words: A Primer of Semantics* (1958).

Pitirim A. Sorokin, Ph.D., is Director of the Harvard Research Center in Creative Altruism. He is founder and former chairman of the Sociology Department at Harvard University and was formerly Professor of Sociology and Law at the University of St. Petersburg. Past President of the International Institute of Sociology, Dr. Sorokin is a member of the Royal Academy of Arts and Sciences of Belgium, of Roumania, and of the American Academy of Arts and Sciences. The author of more than thirty volumes in sociology, social philosophy, and psychology, his works include *The Ways and Power of Love* (1954), *Symposium, Forms and Techniques of Altruistic and Spiritual Growth* (1954), and *Fads and Foibles in Modern Sociology and Related Sciences* (1956).

Clara Thompson, M.D., is a Fellow of the Washington School of Psychiatry, Fellow and Executive Director of the William Alanson White Institute of Psychiatry, Psychoanalysis and Psychology, and teaches courses in psychiatry and psychoanalysis in Washington, D.C., and New York. Dr. Thompson has been an instructor in psychiatry at Johns Hopkins Medical School and Assistant Clinical Professor of Psychiatry at New York Medical College. She is the author of *Psychoanalysis: Evolution and Development* (1950), and an editor of *Outline of Psychoanalysis* (1955).

Frederick C. Thorne, M.D., Ph.D., is in the private practice of psychiatry and clinical psychology, and is the editor and publisher of *The Journal of Clinical Psychology*. He was formerly the Director of the Brandon State School, and Assistant Professor of Psychiatry at the University of Vermont Medical College. Dr. Thorne's major interest is the promulgation of an eclectic approach to psychological diagnosis and therapy. He is the author of *Principles of Personality Counseling* (1950), and *Principles of Psychological Examining* (1955).

Carl A. Whitaker, M.D., is in the private practice of psychiatry in Atlanta, Georgia. He was formerly Professor and Chairman of the Department of Psychiatry at Emory University College of Medicine, and before that, an instructor at the University of Louisville College of Medicine. He is interested in research and group psychotherapy, especially in multiple group therapy. He is the co-author of *Roots of Psychotherapy* (1953), and *Psychotherapy of Chronic Schizophrenic Patients* (1958).

Werner Wolff, Ph.D., was Professor of Psychology at Bard College before his recent death. He was formerly Professor at the Psychological Laboratory in Barcelona, and for many years was Visiting Lecturer in Psychology and Child Study at Vassar College. Among his many books are *The Expression of Personality: Experimental Depth Psychology* (1943), *Diagrams of the Unconscious* (1946), *The Threshold of the Abnormal* (1950), *Values and Personality: An Existential Psychology of Crisis* (1950), and *Contemporary Psychotherapists Examine Themselves* (1956).

Contributors
of Critical Incidents

All the psychotherapists who are listed below submitted critical incidents to this project. All of them, that is, offered their "accounts of events in therapeutic practice deemed significant or worthy of practical, theoretical, or ethical comment." Since a spirit of mutual cooperation is intended as the keynote of this book, the following list includes every such contributor whether or not his account drew sufficient comment to be included.

Joseph Andriola, Ph.D. Chief Social Worker, Atascadero State Hospital, Atascadero, California, and part-time private practice of family casework. *Eclectic.*

Eduard Ascher, M.D. Private practice, Baltimore, Md.; Assistant Professor of Psychiatry, Johns Hopkins Hospital, Baltimore. *Modified psychoanalytic.*

Bill J. Barkley, Ph.D. Private practice, Cleveland, Ohio. Instructor, Department of Psychology, Western Reserve University, Ohio. *Gestalt therapy.*

Ruth Berenda, Ph.D. Private practice, New York City. *Emphasis on the interpersonal aspect of the analytic situation.*

Maxwell Boverman, M.D. Private practice, Washington, D.C. Clinical Assistant Professor of Psychiatry, Georgetown University School of Medicine, Washington, D.C. *Psychoanalytic framework.*

A. H. Chapman, M.D. Consulting Psychiatrist, the Children's Mercy Hospital, Kansas City. *Eclectic.*

Raymond J. Corsini, Ph.D. Associate Director, Daniel D. Howard Associates; Counselor, Chicago Community Child Guidance Centers. *Eclectic.*

Marjorie B. Creelman, Ph.D. Private practice, Cleveland, Ohio. *Gestalt therapy.*

Rogelio Diaz-Guerrera, M.D., Ph.D. Professor, National University of Mexico, School of Higher Studies; private practice of psychiatry. *Systematic eclectic.*

Lawrence A. Dombrose, Ph.D. Private practice, Cleveland, Ohio. *Gestalt therapy.*

Albert Ellis, Ph.D. Private practice, New York City. *Unorthodox Psychoanalytically oriented.*

Jerome D. Frank, M.D. Associate Professor of Psychiatry, Johns Hopkins Hospital, Baltimore, Maryland. *Eclectic.*

Iago Galdston, M.D. Private practice, New York City. *Psychoanalytically oriented active psychotherapy.*

George Genn, Ph.D. Private practice, Englewood, New Jersey. Attending psychologist, Englewood Hospital; Lecturer, Rutgers University. *Eclectic with a heavy weighting toward analytic.*

Zoltan Gross, Ph.D. Private practice, Los Angeles; Consultant, City of Hope. *Neo-analytic.*

Gerald Haigh, Ph.D. Post-doctoral Fellow, Menninger Foundation, Topeka, Kansas. *Client-centered.*

Verda Heisler, Ph.D. Private practice, San Diego, Calif. *Psychoanalytically oriented psychotherapy.*

J. McV. Hunt, Ph.D. Professor of Psychology, University of Illinois, Urbana. *Essential nondirective.*

Elizabeth M. Junken, Ph.D. Director, Morrow Educational Center, Englewood, New Jersey; private practice. *Intra- and inter-personality study.*

Fay B. Karpf, Ph.D. Private practice, Beverly Hills, Calif. *Rankian.*

Lawrence Kaufman, Ph.D. Private practice, New York City. Clinical psychologist, Bellevue Hospital. *Eclectic.*

J. W. Klapman, M.D. Private practice, Chicago. Psychiatrist II, Department Public Welfare, Chicago. Psychiatrist, Northwestern University Medical School. *Eclectic.*

H.C. Kramer, M.D. Supervising psychiatrist, Pilgrim State Hospital, West Brentwood, Long Island, New York. *Eclectic.*

Arthur Lerner, Ph.D. Instructor, Los Angeles City College; private practice. *Eclectic.*

Helene Papanek, M.D. Private practice, New York City. Director of Training Institute for Individual Psychology, New York City; Supervising Psychiatrist and Lecturer, Post-graduate Center for Psychotherapy, New York City. Adjunct Attending Psychiatrist, Hillside Hospital, Glen Oaks, New York. *Adlerian.*

Gerald Perman, M.D. Private practice, Washington, D.C. Instructor in Psychiatry, Georgetown University Medical School. *Psychoanalytically oriented.*

Bina Rosenberg, M.D. Private practice, Chicago. Counselor, Community Child Guidance Centers, Chicago. *Adlerian.*

Robert Schaef, Ph.D. Chief Psychologist, Columbus Psychiatric Clinic, Columbus, Ohio. *Psychoanalytically oriented.*

Lydia Sicher, M.D. Private practice, Los Angeles. Associate Clinical Psychiatrist, Los Angeles Psychiatric Service. Counselor, Counseling Service of the Institute for Individual Psychology. *Adlerian.*

Stanley W. Standal, Ph.D. Private practice, Honolulu, Hawaii. Co-Director, The Clinic for Counseling and Psychotherapy. *Client-centered.*

Frederick C. Thorne, M.D. Private practice, Brandon, Vt. Assistant Professor of Psychiatry, University of Vermont College of Medicine. Editor and publisher, *Journal of Clinical Psychology. Eclectic.*

Contents

"Don't Give
Me Up!"

1

History

The patient, Tom, was referred to the writer, then clinical psychologist in a prison, by a social worker who characterized the patient as "probably the most hopeless individual I have ever seen." Tom's personal history certainly bore out the contention.

His mother was fourteen when he was born out of wedlock. His early youth was spent shuttling between his mother (who became a prostitute) and his grandparents (the step-grandfather actively rejecting him, and reminding him of his illegitimacy). He began correctional institutionalization at the age of ten for truancy, and at twenty-five, when first seen by the writer, had already accumulated thirteen years of correctional institutional experience. At the age of eighteen, on one of his rare releases from a reformatory, he enlisted in the Navy, but even before his record could be located, he received a dishonorable discharge for stealing a pistol. At the time seen by the writer, he had just been transferred to the present institution from a prison in another state together with four members of his gang.

Although his formal education went only as far as the sixth grade, he had an IQ of 137, and a scholastic achievement of 13 (first year college). In appearance he was tall and thin, with a characteristically defiant expression.

Tom was called in to the writer's office and was told without any prologue that the social worker had mentioned him as a person who seemed to be almost hopelessly incorrigible, and that he had been referred to the writer for possible help, even though it seemed to be useless. The writer stated that while he knew nothing of Tom except what was in the prison record and from the social worker, he maintained a theory that the "worst" people were the "best" ones. That is to say, he explained, that people who have the most terrible records are often the people with the greatest capacities, which have been turned the wrong way. In any case, the therapist said, if Tom were interested, he (the therapist) would be glad to work with him.

Tom wanted to know what therapy would be like, and the writer explained that a group would be the best solution. In a mocking spirit Tom accepted the invitation, and entered the writer's therapeutic group.

The group consisted of approximately ten prisoners, charged with diverse crimes, and of various ages, who had been in the group from one to eight months. The prisoners were probably somewhat superior to the average of the institution in intelligence. Up to the entry of Tom, the group atmosphere had been one of cautious exploration, but with the entry of Tom, things changed. He immediately began to dominate the group, attacking the therapist, the institution, and the group members in such violent and immoderate terms that other members began to complain in and out of the group that Tom should be removed, since "no progress" was being made. The writer, however, insisted that Tom had a right to belong, and refused to remove him. But things went from bad to worse, and Tom continued his behavior. Several members actually did quit, stating that they could not take him. Some new members were recruited but they too began to complain about Tom, and wanted to quit. Within eight weeks, the group dropped to six people and there seemed to be almost every indication that this one person would destroy the group.

In desperation, the writer called Tom into his office and put the question to him. Should the writer go on, keep Tom in the group, or should Tom go? Still in a mocking manner, Tom stated he had gotten nothing out of the group, that it was all an evident farce, that the other prisoners were giving me a "snow job" (that is, were dishonestly pulling my leg), and that if I preferred I should send him out of the group.

We sparred for some time about this issue. I tried to make clear to him that while his statements about the truthfulness of the other members might have had some validity, they were nevertheless struggling to find themselves and he was preventing them. Since he would not make the decision, I would make it for him. He would have to go. I was sorry, but the situation was such that I had to make a decision: him or the others, and I chose to have the group maintain its existence.

Incident A

At this point, Tom looked me in the eye and very clearly and slowly said, "If you give me up, then there is no hope for me."

At this moment I was overwhelmed with a complex and powerful set of emotions composed of sorrow, hatred, pity, and inadequacy. This sentence of Tom's became a "critical incident" for me. I was at that moment closer to him than I had ever been to any person on earth. I realized clearly that this human being was in trouble and that he trusted me, no matter how it may have looked. But, because I did not want to go back on my decision, I said, "You will have to leave the group. There is no question about that. If you remain, the group will come to consist of only you and me. So, let us make it a group of two. I will see you individually, but with this agreement: that we will meet for only ten hours, one hour a week. The reason for this is that I have many obligations and it is institutional policy that no long-term psychotherapy be attempted with any prisoner."

Tom agreed. I explained to him how we would work. He was to talk with me for one hour at a time for ten consecutive weeks. I would make notes as he talked. Whatever he said would be privileged, that is to say there would be no information transmitted from me to the institution. (He had to believe that or the ten weeks would be lost.) He accepted the conditions, and we set the hour and day for the first session.

At the end of the ten weeks, I knew a great deal more about Tom. I found him a profoundly disillusioned and morbidly cynical person who was obsessed with thoughts of death. He had absolutely no hope: "Life is a windblown tree. . . . Whoever would marry me would have to be insane or mentally defective. . . . One is born in pain and one dies in pain and in between, one suffers." Such were his ideas.

Following the tenth session, I had an eleventh session with him to discuss what we had achieved. The reason for the eleventh session was that at that time I held on to a somewhat naive concept of client-centered therapy and did not want to contaminate my "therapeutic" sessions with any opinions of my own. The eleventh session was a post-therapy session to over-view the therapy.

We came to a full and complete agreement that the therapy seemed to be an evident failure. I commented that some people needed years of treatment and that no magic could be expected in ten weeks. It had been a most interesting and valuable experience for me, and I personally was sorry that it had not continued further, and while I would like to, in view of the department's policy, I just could not go on with it.

He accepted, as far as I could tell, my statements, shook hands with me, and left. As far as I was concerned, the whole relationship was terminated.

Incident B

About four months later I received a request from Tom to interview him, and I sent for him immediately.

He came to the point at once.

"The funniest thing happened to me Saturday. I don't know if I am crazy or what. Nothing like this ever happened before. I was walking across the big yard, going over to a group of people I knew, and as I was walking I suddenly experienced something. It came over me like a cloud. I couldn't move. Suddenly I felt peaceful and happy. I felt clean, pure, good, and wonderful. I never experienced such a feeling of happiness. I don't know how long it lasted. Maybe a second, maybe a minute. I have only a memory of it, but I do know that this feeling had something to do with you."

We discussed the experience, which he likened to Saul's conversion on the road to Damascus, and continued in a friendly chat, and when I suggested that we have another round of therapy, he assented eagerly.

Once again we went through ten weeks of therapy, and once again on an eleventh session we discussed the therapy and came to an agreement that as far as could be told, little had been done, although I had the feeling that I had become a "significant other" in this young man's mind. After the therapy he rejoined the group, and remained in it for about a year, until the writer left the institution.

There is a sequel to the therapy, or two of them, which may be of some interest. The first one occurred in an interview with a prisoner, one of Tom's gang that had committed some six years earlier a series of crimes in two states. The gang as a whole had served four years in the first institution, and then had been transferred to the second institution. Tom had belonged to this gang, the members of which were all in their twenties and all of superior mental ability.

I do not think that this particular individual knew of my relationship with Tom, so I began to ask him about his various crime partners, and what he thought of them. He had a high regard for three of them, but of Tom he said something as follows: "He is a different kind of person. He used to be a nice guy, crazy as they come, but now he is funny. I can't understand him. I don't have much to do with him anymore. The others also feel there is something wrong with him."

The second sequel has to do with Tom's later behavior on release. He left the institution about a year after the writer did, and on the invitation of the writer, who got him a job, took up residence some two thousand miles from his original state. He began to work, and after six months married. At the present time, six years after release, he is the father of a child, owns a new car, is buying a house, and is in all ways a substantial citizen. We correspond irregularly. He seems to be making a good, uneventful adjustment.

The four other members of the original gang were also subsequently released. Every one of them is now back in prison for new crimes.

Discussion

I would like to consider the first incident, the one that involved me. At the time I tried to take the attitude that every person was equally important, and that in the manner of the parable of the shepherd and the lost sheep, I would make sacrifices for one individual if necessary. But actually I was somewhat disturbed by the fact that Tom was killing my group with his behavior. I was willing to face the other members and refuse to throw Tom out, but secretly I hoped that Tom would leave. When I discussed the problem with him, I really gave him no alternative. When he said, "If you give me up, there is no hope for me," I grew up as it were. I understood that something had been lacking in me, that I was going through motions and following formulas, but that if things got too difficult for me, I was willing to let the lost sheep perish. I also got a glimpse of the importance that I had for him, in terms of a personal relationship. In short, I felt disgusted with myself, and realized that I was willing to sacrifice him to my own convenience. The realization that I was *really* important to someone else was a profound shock.

The second incident is still not understandable, and one reason that I bring it up is that I have had at least four cases in some 15 years of prison experience of similar "conversion" reactions, in which individuals "felt" something of a mystic kind. In all cases, the individuals were hard-headed persons, and in all cases these "conversions" presaged complete behavioral changes. Whether Tom "made it up," whether it was a dodge to get me to see him again, whether it was a "real" experience, or what, I do not know.

The last point I want to discuss is probably the most important. As I see it, Tom became a good citizen partly as a result of our interaction, and I wonder to what extent it was due to my being his therapist and to what extent it was due to my being his friend. Before one states it is the latter, let me indicate that subsequent to his release, while I did offer him an opportunity and gave him money (which he returned), we were not friends in any sense of the word. He formed acquaintances of his own, and when we met our relationships were more or less perfunctory. That is, we never were intimates, in any sense of the word.

What I want to ask others is this: What meaning, if any, does this experience have in terms of penology? Would Tom probably have gone straight anyway? Did I turn him from a life of crime? If so, what was the element of change? How can this be formalized so that other Toms can be helped?

ROBERT BLAKE . . .

Two aspects of social perception and personal adjustment can be isolated for analytical purposes in understanding Tom's behavior change. One deals with reactions to authority. The other relates to his perception and acceptance of membership in peer groups.

Authority Relations

Tom is confronted with problems of adjustment to authority from the beginning: repudiation by his mother and step-grandfather for illegitimacy, rejection by school authority for truancy, and rejection by military authority for stealing. Tom can say something like this to himself, "Confronted with the dilemma my behavior creates for them (family, school, military, society) they take recourse in action against me, but I won't bend to them." The dynamic elements of these three examples of rejection are similar when viewed from Tom's frame of reference: "To accept authority and to conform with its behavioral requirements is to admit one's own inadequacies. I will challenge them even if it results in being repudiated. To be caught is preferable to bowing to authority by conforming with its requirements."

Here, in a sense, is the contra-authority position that Tom also brings to the therapy group and which, in my view, was finally altered when he was confronted with rejection by both his peers and the therapist.

Peer Relations

Actual ability to establish and to maintain peer relationships is evidenced in his gang memberships. This fact also is critical in understanding Tom's change, for peers (other prisoners) perhaps unwittingly aided the therapist in administering the *coup de grace* by leaving the group themselves in preference to association with him. Here again is a powerful motivating force toward self-confrontation and change.

At the time of the therapist's decision to remove him from the therapy group, at least three factors are present in his experience, and all point to personal unacceptability and to the untenability of his position. Tom is confronted with evidences of his personal and social unacceptability by society through imprisonment, by a therapist who rejects him even while seeking to act helpfully, and by his peers, who have also suffered the repudiation of society.

The two critical factors in Tom's behavior change are rejection by an authority he had finally decided to trust, and repudiation by peers, with whom he was usually able to relate well. They demand an agonizing reappraisal of self as a social member. This is particularly so for that aspect involving personal repudiation by the therapist within a prison situation which already constitutes social repudiation. The therapist can't punish in an *active* way. His real source of power in this situation is to *withhold* help; to take away any opportunity of acceptance through change. The therapist's repudiation in this context constitutes a double rejection and, perhaps, defines the most powerful possible definition of personal unacceptability. Tom's behavior in the group therapy situation implies that he did not realize the full impact of his aggressive, hostile attacks on the therapist and others. Yet when he suffered this repudiation the ground work was laid for him to appreciate his untenable position: within a prison situation his behavior was unacceptable even to an accepting, help-giving person. He had, in a sense, gone beyond the point of no return and could return only by some unusual route, in this case, a "conversion" experience.

Significant here is the invitation to two-person therapy—further offer of help in the face of double repudiation. Would behavior change have occurred without it? Perhaps so. At least one can imagine that Tom sought readmission to the group on terms which he later came to accept outside prison—terms which involved conforming with the behavioral requirements of social and legal authority.

Also significant is the fact that Tom already possessed and therefore had no need to learn the basic social skills of establishing and maintaining group membership. His earlier gang membership is evidence of this. His situation, in other words, is not one of being *unable* to perform within a group frame of reference and according to a set of prescribed codes, but is rather one of being unwilling to do so where a representative of social and legal authority also is present. In my view, the massing of compelling evidences of unacceptability compelled Tom in a constructive direction.

VIKTOR E. FRANKL . . .

In the beginning of this account there is a discussion concerning the requirement that a therapist help a patient develop his abilities. At this point, for me, this question arises: What does it mean "to help"—and for which purposes are "abilities" to be used? From which standpoint are they to be considered "abilities"? In short, there is a question of a frame of reference, within which one can talk about "help" or "abilities." It is remarkable to see how this frame of reference became altered in the course of the depicted therapy.

The first shock to this frame of reference (or as we could say, of this value system, or orientation to a personal world of meaning and value) consisted of the separation of the patient from the therapy group. This occurred in an entirely proper manner since such a group is comparable to a genuine democracy. A therapy group, as a democracy, exists for all the members—except for those who deny the democracy itself. Such people do not deserve to receive the advantages of democracy. The democracy must fulfill its obligation to protect itself. This concept is transferable to a therapeutic group. If the patient had not been transferred from the group, it would have meant that the group would not have represented reality as it is. Realistically oriented psychotherapy overcomes *the monadologism which is inherent in a one-sided, exclusively psychodynamically and psychogenetically oriented psychotherapy*. I shall discuss the problems in this case in a manner consistent with my discussion of the case in Chapter 3.

Separation from the group was a disappointment for the patient. But at the same time he had the experience of being taken seriously as a responsible human being—in other words, as a person. In this way the personal disappointment became a personal shock. The shock itself—a shock of the man's existence—became at the same time the basis of what followed: the offer of individual therapy.

This individual therapy demonstrated what in *logotherapy* we call *"existential vacuum,"* namely the apparent emptiness of a concrete life—an abysmal nothingness of human existence—a meaninglessness which so often—as in this case, too—is interpreted as hopelessness. The patient was disillusioned. He had experienced the dwindling of all values to a mere illusion: he had never been lucky—the world seemed to him to be full of pain, suffering, and shattered hopes. No one had ever taught him that even suffering is of potential value, and not only creative work or love. He did not realize that suffering may actualize even the greatest value. He did not realize that *facing an unavoidable and inescapable suffering offers a possible, nay, even the highest meaning to human existence*. Dostoevski, in the sense of my words, once said that he had only one desire—to be worthy of his suffering. (See my book on concentration camps for further elaboration of this point.[1]) It can thus be understood that in reading the therapist's account of his therapy, I thought I might have preferred that the patient read Dostoevski rather than giving him therapeutic instructions or explanations; did not the patient experience a "Dostoevskian" adventure, as seems evident from the discussion? However, it was an irrational adventure, one that hardly could be verbalized or rationalized.

What evolved in him was a happy feeling, which is found in apparently (consciously) atheistic patients who repressed their religiosity into the realm of the subconscious from which they ascend as dreams in symbolically masked form. Anyhow, those happy feelings are characterized by a typically religious feature, even when not understandable as such to the patient. Justifiably so, the author of this incident calls the patient's adventure "conversion." In actual fact, one deals here with a "reversion"—to be precise, a return to a connection—the return to "religio." This religion was subconsciously existent, although repressed. Finally, *any cynicism is frustrated idealism*.

[1] Viktor E. Frankl, *From Death Camp to Existentialism, A Psychiatrist's Path to a New Therapy* (Boston: Beacon Press, 1959), Foreword by Gordon W. Allport.

In my *Theorie und Therapie der Neurosen*[2] I wrote: "The pathos of atheism is based on an implicit religious ethos; and the passion of the un-religious includes a hidden love of God." Moreover, we have passed the stage of accepting repressed instinctuality alone. There also exists a sub-conscious spirituality, morality, and religiosity.[3] But this religiosity was repressed—the patient had grown up in the contemporary nihilism, materialism, and naturalism. What logotherapy does is to go one step beyond Freud. Did not Freud once say that the human being is not only subconsciously more immoral than he believes himself to be—but also more moral than he thinks himself to be?—and we dare to add: occasionally, *man is also more religious than he supposes himself.*

The author asks himself and the reader whether or not the patient was using some trick or "dodge." I must ask: what is truth and what is trick? Something may be empirically unreal and yet existentially true. I remember in this connection the story of a chassidic rabbi to whom I have referred in a previous book.[4] Once a rabbi was asked how to tell whether or not heaven had forgiven a sinner. The rabbi said: "If the sinner will not sin again."

The writer of this incident asks how much his role was that of a therapist and how much that of a friend. I believe both coincided at the right moment—in a highly "fruitful moment" (Lessing). The relationships of the therapist to the patient grew to a human feeling—to a fully human encounter which was not a mere emotional but a totally existential relationship between two persons—two partners. I do not think the writer's assertion that they were never, and in no way, intimate friends is very important. In a certain higher sense, they were intimates—in the sense of spiritual proximity. One can be very close spiritually to another person. Such full-human relationships and partnerships need not be long lasting, nor need they be externally evident. Such a partnership can be "instantaneous"—limited to one moment—just as conversion is an instantaneous experience confined to a moment.

We turn now again to the conversion; that was the second shock, after the first personal one. It was, so to speak, a transpersonal and transpsychological shock. Indeed, such an experience cannot be included in the realm of psychology. Psychology is a science and as such has its proper objects and special methods. The concern of psychology is with human affairs, and not suprahuman matters; the anthropological and not the theological; the personal and not the transpersonal. As far as method is concerned,

---

[2] Viktor E. Frankl, *Theorie und Therapie der Neurosen* (Wien: Urban & Schwarzenberg, 1956).

[3] Viktor E. Frankl, *Der Unbewusste Gott* (Wien: Auflage, 1948), 1st ed.

[4] Viktor E. Frankl, *The Doctor and the Soul: An Introduction to Logotherapy* (New York: Alfred A. Knopf, Inc., 1955).

psychology, not unlike other sciences, is concerned with generalization. Science as such is concerned only with what can be generalized, what can be raised to a general law. The single—the unique—must be excluded.

Therefore, the ultimate reason for the conversion and the return to religiosity cannot be explained scientifically, nor can it be resolved in the manner of an explanation; rather, it must remain as an historical report, a unique example—like a story. I find it especially gratifying that the writer has cited this case because such reports of single experiences make it possible—despite the utter impossibility of *psychologizing the transpsychological* and generalizing the unique—to *extend psychotherapy beyond the psychical to the spiritual dimension*—or, as I prefer to call it to avoid any *primarily* religious connotations, the noetic dimension—in a word: *to extend psychotherapy to logotherapy.*

Vincent Herr . . .

This particular incident is a tough case of an apparent conflict between the common value versus the individual good. The therapist believed that he had to decide whether he would keep Tom in the group, and thus possibly affect negatively the other members, or to let Tom out. Actually, this dichotomous thinking was false, and this was borne out by the therapist's later decision to see Tom privately. And yet it is possible that had there not been the possibility of this alternate solution, the therapist would have been forced to make this decision. We come here to a knotty problem, that of the primacy of the common over the individual good. One may think of the parable of the lost sheep. Should the shepherd have gone to search for this lost sheep if this might have meant the possibility of harm for the rest of the flock? At this point one can only say that a responsible therapist must not only decide that two is more than one, but that the importance of a single individual, at least in a spiritual sense, can not be so easily assessed against the importance of two or more individuals. Common sense tells us that one who wants to help other people wants to help individuals, whether singly or in groups. It is a tribute both to Tom and to the therapist that after that soul-moving realization "If you give me up, then there is no hope for me," an answer was found.

I believe the "conversion" experience can be explained simply in this fashion. It was a dynamically clear and conscious reaction to an unconscious or vaguely felt decision. All men are made in the image of their Creator and are therefore fundamentally good. Those who are misled by evil under the guise of good cannot be thoroughly happy, even though they may revile the good life and enjoy apparent pleasure. Tom was a fundamentally unhappy youth; of that there can be no question. He had lived a particular type of life and held particular concepts in contrast to the essential message of morality. Via the therapist's intercession, he must have been re-awakened to consciousness of another life which meant love, regard, consideration, hope, and positive accomplishment; and it was consequent upon his vague and perhaps inarticulate determination to leave a life of evil and live a life of good that he experienced this dynamic conversion. This new experience was the consequence of his movement in a new direction. It was the *momentum crucis* of his new existence. And so, he had a feeling of peace. We priests have seen this peace many times on death-beds when a sinner finally put himself in mystical communion with God and his laws.

A third comment has to do with the therapist himself. I get the impression that Tom's statement (how much courage may have gone into that heart-rending plea, "If you give me up . . .") shook the therapist. This may have been because psychotherapy had perhaps been for the therapist merely a game in which one deals with visible human objects rather than with realities that transcend the sensible and material; this direct meeting between the two, in which both individuals become humans communicating, made the therapist grow up. He realized he had a real responsibility for people and that psychotherapy was not a mere exchange of words. All people who are in the helping areas face this type of problem. It is so easy to become hardened, to obtain false impressions of one's own importance, to perform duties perfunctorily, to type and classify humans, forgetting in therapy their eminent uniqueness and inherent value. The therapist bravely and humbly realized the magnitude of the forces he was dealing with, and as he says himself, grew up. He realized, I would put it, that he was the humble instrumentality of forces greater than himself.

Finally, I think it is necessary to discuss the importance of the subsequent behavior of the therapist to this individual. His concrete evidence of faith and love, lending money, getting him a job, befriending him, it seems to me, gave irrefutable evidence to Tom that his prior conception of the world was false, that this therapist did value him; and thus points out a doctrine of Saint Paul that salvation is not obtained by faith alone, but that it is also necessary to do good works.

I would submit that the deep personal interchange between these two individuals might not have had a favorable result if the therapist had been content to limit his behavior to the exchange of fine words. It was this other behavior—the love and kindness shown in giving, that possibly had much more meaning to Tom than did the formal therapy. One is forced to think of the episode in *Les Misérables* when the abbé showed by his actions that he really loved the criminal Jean Val Jean, which in turn induced Val Jean to reorganize his distorted perceptions of social reality.

ERNEST HILGARD . . .

The reform of the "hopeless criminal" raises many questions about our conception of the psychopathic or sociopathic personality and our interpretation of therapy in such cases.

The bad social background and the quarrel against society stands out; but even the cruel grandfather who rejected the boy and reminded him of his illegitimacy may have done something to establish standards: he represented society, with its taboos, and he was the important male in the boy's environment. While he must have aroused negative attitudes—hate and resentment—he must also have aroused some envy as a staunch citizen, and there may have been some "identification with the aggressor." This gives us one hypothesis with respect to the origins of enough social conscience to supply the lack when the opportunity came later on.

From a learning point of view we would say that the grandfather reinforced at once both sides of a conflict: he reinforced defiant and antisocial behavior, but he reinforced also conforming and socially acceptable behavior. This statement in itself is, of course, too empty; if it is true, it would be interesting to know *how* both of these were reinforced, and what aspects of them *could* be learned at once, or on the separate occasions when he was with his grandfather.

The behavior in the group therapy sessions is not unlike that found among Aichhorn's incorrigibles,[5] or among the children who hate as studied by Redl[6] and his collaborators. The active protest is probably better than apathy, just as the violent schizophrenic is a better therapeutic risk than the hebephrenic one. Many sociopathic individuals are disarmingly pleasant and affable in a relationship in which such behavior achieves their ends; that this patient was fighting what he thought to be "leg-pulling" behavior was, in a sense, to his credit. If we accept the interpretations of Aichhorn and Redl, he was in some sense "testing the limits," all the while becoming attached to the therapist as someone who was really trying to understand. (He was really protecting the therapist from the deceptions of the other prisoners, as he perceived the sessions.)

How can we state "testing the limits" in the terminology of learning? It is really a form of hypothesis testing. It goes something like this: "Someone says he is your friend, and he gets you to tell him intimate things about yourself; he really doesn't care about you, but is just using you to try out some of his ideas; in the end he'll throw you out, the way everybody else has done. I'll try this guy out; I won't give him anything that he can hurt me with, and I'll see how much he can take before he really shows himself up."

[5] August Aichhorn, *Wayward Youth* (New York: The Viking Press, 1935).
[6] F. Redl, and D. Wineman, *Children Who Hate* (Glencoe, Ill.: The Free Press, 1951).

The probabilities in the situation turn out to be different from those previously experienced; this then sets the stage for possible change.

The patient here had just about come to believe that the therapist was "O.K." when he did try to throw him out. One can read several meanings into his statement "If you give me up, then there is no hope for me." One interpretation, coherent with the hypothesis-testing notion, would go something like this. "You brought me nearer to believing that there was someone willing to tolerate me than I have ever come before; if you now fail me, I doubt if I'll have the strength to give anyone else the chance I have given you to help me."

Fortunately the therapist had a way of accepting his own "countertransference" by offering a contained proposal for limited individual psychotherapeutic sessions. We know practically nothing about these sessions; apparently the therapist was at that time too inexperienced to detect such progress as there must have been.

Now the conversion experience, four months later. Things started in therapy go on outside the therapeutic hours. We don't know what was happening, but we do have an account of the experience itself. "Suddenly I felt peaceful and happy. I felt clean, pure, good, and wonderful." These are feelings he treasured; they must already have been within his value system; possibly the envied side of his grandfather, brought into focus by a relationship with a therapist who to him embodied these same values. He rightly related them to the experience that changed Saul into Paul.

Conversion experiences have gone out of style within our culture, although it was not so many years ago that they were considered a normal part of adolescent development. When circumstances are right, there is no reason to be surprised at their occurrence today. A possible interpretation is that the conversion resolves ambivalence and brings to the fore a fairly well integrated value system that was held in abeyance by a superimposed one. Most "converts" at revival meetings are those with religious backgrounds in early life who later accepted more superficial social values to the neglect of the deeper ones associated with religion. Thus conversion is not really a very great change in personality structure, but a bringing to light of another set of behavior patterns (values) that had been there all along. Even a learning theorist such as Guthrie, who argues that the organism always does what it last did, finds that there are alternative types of habit in the behavior repertory. When one habit has been used over and over again, another one previously used may come to the fore.

The argument here is that the conforming personality (represented by conjecture in the grandfather) was there all the time, ready to be used when the social opportunity was right for rewarding this behavior and not making the person feel belittled. The nonconforming personality was engendered perhaps by this same grandfather but reinforced by the peer-culture of other protesting young men with whom he felt comfortable and by whom he was liked. It is difficult to relinquish this culture; the prison community makes them his peers also, and to begin to change makes him seem "crazy" to them. It takes almost a dramatic occasion to provide commitment to change; this came in the "conversion" experience.

The experience was undoubtedly related in some manner to the therapy sessions. For one thing, they provided reinforcement from a conforming culture by a representative of that culture, set against the peer culture of his friends among the prisoners. Perhaps the therapist's inexperience at the time made it impossible for the patient to report all that was going on; at that time client-centered counselors were probably not prepared to handle the transference problems involved. He would find it hard to say properly: "I want to be like you instead of like my friends." If he did say this, we don't quite know what the response would have been, but it is doubtful if it would have led then and there to something like a conversion experience. Even in the interviews following the "conversion," the therapist does not see his own role, except as in some vague sense a "significant other."

Let us be careful not to interpret what I have said as critical of either the therapist or of client-centered therapy. This patient made a good adjustment, and he fits the "type" for whom a successful outcome is not usually predicted. One must respect these facts; one wishes only that the steps were more clearly understood.

O. HOBART MOWRER . . .

In their book, *Psychoanalytic Therapy,* Alexander and French[7] refer to the episode in Victor Hugo's *Les Misérables* in which a confirmed criminal robs a priest, but the priest deals with the situation in such a surprisingly benign way that the robber is converted from his life of crime to one of integrity and responsibility. Though fictional, this incident portrays a phenomenon which, while perhaps rare, is none the less real and, if better understood, might also be commoner.

Now that we have pretty thoroughly explored and apparently exhausted the therapeutic possibilities of transference as psychoanalytically conceived, there seems to be a growing impression that genuine, realistically deserved *gratitude* can be therapeutically powerful. Until recently it was assumed, at least by some analysts, that the therapist does not need to be good to the patient in any commonly accepted meaning of that term. As an analyst friend of the present writer once put the matter some 20 years ago, "You assume that the patient is always *wrong.*" How different was the

[7] F. Alexander, and T. M. French, *Psychoanalytic Therapy* (New York: The Ronald Press, 1946).

assumption of Tom's therapist. Certainly a great deal was, in truth, "wrong" with Tom; but the therapist approached him with the theory that sometimes the "worst" people are the "best" people and said that he would be glad to work with him. Tom accepted this overture mockingly, but he did accept it, and it could hardly have been without positive impact.

The therapist bore Tom's mockery and even his destructiveness in group therapy until its devastating effects upon others were unmistakable. The result was that, when confronted by the realities of the situation, Tom threw himself upon the therapist's mercy: "If you give me up, then there is no hope for me." And it is interesting to note that in speaking of his own powerful feelings about Tom at this point, the therapist did not try to analyze them away as "countertransference." He accepted them as very real and important: "I realized clearly that this human being was in trouble and that he trusted me, no matter how it may have looked." And, once again, he made a personal sacrifice to "stay with" Tom.

Then, a little later, came Tom's strange and remarkable feelings of peace and wholeness. It is not inappropriate that he should have thought of Saul's Damascus road experience; for others have also seen conversion-like reactions take place in therapy.[8] Why such personality alterations occur suddenly in some persons, rather than gradually, is a very puzzling question. And there is even a question as to whether or not they are always constructive and healthy. For example, the present writer recalls a former patient who, early in therapy, referred repeatedly to a similar experience she had had some years before. It *sounded* psychotic. The patient, who was in no formal sense religious, said that while washing the dishes one evening she suddenly felt ". . . just wonderful, as if God had spoken to me. I felt, for that moment, as if I could do anything. It was *wonderful*, but the feeling soon passed away."

Tom, too, was puzzled by his experience: "I don't know if I am crazy or what." But might not such experiences have great therapeutic potential if we only knew how to handle them properly? Can it be that such "flashes" of good feeling come to people as a token of what a different way of living could lead to? Certainly from this point on Tom started changing: somehow he had a new conception of life. And if it were to do over again, the present writer, instead of ignoring the "vision" of the woman patient, would give it very careful and sympathetic consideration.

The experience of allowing himself to become deeply involved with another person, instead of "following formulas," the therapist says, came as "a profound shock," a result confirmed by others in *Progress in Psycho-*

---

[8] See, for example, Paul Bergman, "A Religious Conversion in the Course of Psychoanalysis," *American Journal of Psychotherapy*, VII, (1953), pp. 41–58. See also Harold Begbie, *Broken Earthenware* (London: Hodden and Staughton, 1910). (Also published under the title: *Twice-born Men*.)

therapy.[9] Psychologists and psychiatrists, with their scientific training and background, are understandably distrustful of anything that savors of mysticism. But perhaps there are certain "experiments" which we have been unwilling to perform, so that our distrust is alloyed with inexperience. We cannot but be grateful to Tom's therapist for his courage in submitting himself to this ordeal and, equally, for his courage in so candidly reporting it.

Some rather remarkable and quite independent confirmations of this way of thinking may be found in a manuscript by A. H. Maslow[10] which is recommended to the reader in its entirety. Here the author says:

"Peak experiences have some therapeutic effects, in the strict sense of removing symptoms. I have at least two reports—one from a psychologist, one from an anthropologist—of mystic or oceanic experiences so profound as to remove certain neurotic symptoms forever after. Such conversion experiences are of course plentifully recorded in human history, but so far as I know have never received the attention of psychologists and psychiatrists. . . .

"The person is more apt to feel that life in general is worthwhile, even if it is usually drab, pedestrian, painful, or ungratifying, since beauty, excitement, honesty, truth, and meaningfulness have been demonstrated to him to exist."

E. H. PORTER . . .

It has always struck me as obvious that a child does not have to be instructed in learning how to feel guilty or useless or unloved. If there is any instruction involved, it is the way his world acts toward him. It seems obvious enough in this case that this man had a childhood world that clearly taught him how utterly unwanted a person he was; he simply wasn't wanted and he learned it well.

This does not in any way mean that he *thought* of himself as an unwanted person or that he *thought* of others as rejecting people who could accept him only if they were "insane or mentally defective." The crucial fact is that he didn't *think* of himself or others as being any particular way at all. For him people *symbolized* unwanting and his self *symbolized* unwantedness.

It is a trap we fall into when we presume that these perceptual habits (habits in the sense of highly stable and consistent perceptual responses) can become altered only through interpretation or reflection or Socratic

---

[9] Frieda Fromm-Reichmann, and J. L. Moreno, *Progress in Psychotherapy* (New York: Grune & Stratton, 1956).

[10] A. H. Maslow, "Cognition of Being in Peak Experience," Presidential Address for the Division of Personality and Social Psychology, annual meeting of the American Psychological Association, Chicago (1956), p. 31.

teaching or traumatic confirmation or adherence to a limit or any other single variable.

In my view, we are still poverty-stricken in concepts which encompass what happens in psychotherapy. We still are shackled by the perception of psychotherapy as a situation in which (1) the patient comes for help, (2) the therapist must do something, and (3) there must be best techniques of doing that something. We are often honestly puzzled by the fact that another therapist does the most damned-fool things (from our point of view) and yet gets results. Moreover, we know they are damned-fool things because we do something different and get good results. Yes, we may even perceive the results he gets as bad because they can be only temporary or because there remain residual neurotic symptoms and so on. Of course we recognize that our own patients seldom stay long enough for the complete cure.

What if we were to take the position that the individual is just as active a conceptualizer and symbolizer in adulthood as in childhood—and at the same level of unawareness or unthoughtfulness of what he is being taught? What if we take the position that it is not any one technique or incident which produces a change, but that evidences of new learnings will become expressed sooner or later, sometimes around an incident apparently critical and sometimes in the prison yard in absence of any external stimulus?

If we are to take these positions, we must ask ourselves not, "What technique should I use?" *nor* "What does the patient need in view of his neurosis?" but, "How do I really feel about this person and how do I act it out?" "What is my behavior teaching this individual about the kind of person he is—and the kind of person I am?"

I guess that I have seen too many clients or patients get help from me during periods when I was personally distressed, and have seen too many clients or patients get help from others when they were personally distressed, to believe any longer that the therapist must be a model of personal adjustment, exuding only the most wholesome of attitudes.

It seems to me that when a therapist (1) has a genuine respect, although not necessarily a complete respect, for what the patient can be, (2) is sufficiently self-confident to act freely rather than be bound by technique, and (3) has pretty well learned that no matter how the patient acts toward him, it represents the patient's view and does not necessarily have implications for the kind of person he, the therapist, is—then the therapist will present a climate in which the patient can begin to develop new concepts of himself and others.

Even monkeys learn how to learn. Conceivably, human patients do also. Maybe therapy is essentially the promotion of a learning how to relearn rather than a process of curing a neurosis or a psychosis.

DAVID RIESMAN . . .

In this consultant's opinion, people cling most ferociously—perhaps especially people underprivileged in other respects—to their map of the world: their map which gives them the feeling that the world makes sense even if it is very painful sense. Tom had such a map, clarifying and in that sense protective in its cynicism. To begin to help him, one had to challenge the map, in spite of Tom's frantic efforts (analogous to those a paranoid person makes) to confirm his map by the vice and devise of his own behavior with the therapist in the group. At least he wanted to conclude that the therapist was soft and therefore among those to be exploited.

Who knows how much hope, how much desperation, and how much exploitativeness were combined in Tom's first comment to the therapist (that is, the first critical incident): possibly Tom half hoped that the therapist would give him up and thereby support and solidify his map. The therapist had fitted the map before, by virtue, as he candidly says, of behavior that followed formulae and presented Tom with little unmanageable novelty. But here something unexpected happened. The therapist was confronted with at least potential novelty and in turn, by offering to help Tom in unanticipated ways while not responding to his blackmail about rejoining the group, he first confronted Tom with something the latter could not cynically interpret or misinterpret.

It is my criticism of many formula-grounded therapies that they fail to confront particular patients with behavior so novel and so "unmanageable" that they cannot go on as before. One is reminded here of *Les Misérables* and the incident of Jean Val Jean. Undeviatingly nondirective therapy might have struck Tom as either a critical game or a sign of softness, but the new flexibility of which the therapist found himself capable was perhaps able to convey to Tom that Tom could matter to somebody—that something human could get through from beneath his own thick protective covering of cynicism. A delayed reaction to that encounter which, in our limited vocabulary, we may term "conversion" is no more and no less a miracle than any human encounter which escapes previous determinisms.

WILLIAM SNYDER . . .

Several aspects of this case, with its two critical incidents strike me as important. First, with regard to the question of whether Tom should have been excluded from the group, it seems to me that the therapist had little familiarity with the literature on group therapy, or he would have removed Tom from the group much earlier than he did. He would also likely have offered Tom the privilege of individual therapy at the time he excluded him from the group. It seems a well accepted tenet of group therapists that highly destructive criticism of group members by one person in the group is extremely injurious to group progress, and to the eventual therapeutic progress of the individuals. Slavson makes this point many times. The therapist's great reluctance to exclude Tom not only reveals his lack of familiarity with good handling of group therapy situations, but more importantly it probably reveals signs of a strong countertransference. The therapist appeared willing to sacrifice a whole group of clients for the welfare of a single one. There is nothing reasoned about such a willingness; it is purely emotional, and thus is probably proof of the countertransference.

The evidence of countertransference that appears in the first critical incident also gives the clue to the significance of the second one. The therapist's sudden realization that he was "at that moment closer to him (client) than I had ever been to any person on earth" closely parallels Tom's experience that "Suddenly I felt peaceful and happy. I felt clean, pure, good, and wonderful. . . . I do know that this feeling had something to do with you."

With no implication of censure, it is entirely legitimate to point out that these two people, therapist and client, were each giving voice to an experiencing of a strongly affective interest in the other. Both were mystified by it, but this merely reveals understandable naiveté on the part of the client, and somewhat excusable repression on the part of the therapist. These experiences of what analysts call transference and countertransference are, in the writer's opinion, the very heart of effective therapeutic relationships, as they are, in fact, the heart of most satisfying human relationships. The client compared his experience to the conversion of Saul at Damascus, and the comparison may be quite apt. The realization that one is the recipient of a deep and sincere "love" has been demonstrated many times to be an experience that is entirely capable of modifying one's life-style. This writer has pointed out elsewhere[11] that the need to be loved is so basic a human need that it drives many people into therapy, because they are insufficiently loved outside of therapy. Tom's conversion of life-style, his becoming a "good" citizen after an unbelievably delinquent childhood and youth, is the parallel of similar conversions throughout recorded history; Saul, Augustine, and many members of Alcoholics Anonymous have made identical changes, and for the same reason. There can be little doubt that it was the result of the therapeutic relationship.

It seems unfortunate that the therapist felt himself limited by the arbitrary time limit on individual therapy in the prison where he worked. He obviously found it easy to double the duration of the treatment by the use of

[11] William Snyder, "Comment on Donald Walker's 'Carl Rogers and the Nature of Man.'" *Journal of Counseling Psychology*, II (1956), pp. 91–92.

the expedient of two different periods of therapy, separated by a time lapse. Had the therapist been able to recognize the significance of the relationship that had developed between himself and his client, and to have interpreted this relationship and its significance to the client, it is probable that the therapy would not have had to be judged unsuccessful by the client. Both therapist and client could have recognized the very normal course of a transference relationship. It is not surprising that Tom did not find it necessary to prolong a close after-therapy relationship. He had experienced the "love" that the average person experiences as coming from a parent, and the therapist was in this case a typical benevolent father-surrogate. Tom was able to grow normally out of the therapy transference relationship, and to develop normal channels of libidinal expression. The average person goes through the same metamorphosis with regard to his own parents. Experienced therapists are quite accustomed to having their clients, who were at one time deeply "in love" with them, grow away from them. Properly, they prefer it to be that way. An occasional letter or card, arriving at decreasingly frequent intervals is a typical sign of the continued maturation of the client into a self-dependent adult.

BESS SONDEL . . .

"If you give me up, then there is no hope for me."

When the patient made this statement to the therapist, the therapist knew, of course, that this is not a bona fide causal hypothesis but, rather, an imputed relationship that is a matter of opinion and not of fact. This statement calls for prediction. Something the therapist may do, the patient says, could affect him irrevocably. This hypothesis places all of the potency in the therapist; none in the patient. This hypothesis assumes that the environment plays no part whatsoever over and beyond that played by the therapist. This hypothesis assumes infallible knowledge of the consequences of human actions. On all these grounds the hypothesis is questionable, as the therapist knows.

But the statement provides information under semantic analysis:

It is an implicit affirmation by the patient of his desire to remain with the group (much as he denies identification with the group on intellectual and social grounds).

This statement, is, also, implicitly valuative in that it implies: *You can help me.*

But this statement is primarily incitive in that the patient desires a specific action response—a reconsideration, probably, of removal from the group and, hence, *dissociation with the therapist.*

The therapist made a significant decision; he removed the patient from

the group (a source of conflict) and agreed to treat him as an "individual"
—as someone separate and apart from the group. This was probably the
"cause" of the "transformation" in the patient. His seemingly sudden experience of peace and well-being was, I believe, a final reaction of cumu-
lative experience which provided the patient the desired intellectual and
personal experience.

I believe this procedure can be generalized. A patient with an IQ of 137
who suffers from lack of self-actualization probably experiences great
"hopelessness," for this is the very negation of his human potential. Identification of such an individual with others of low potential—ethical and intellectual—is thwarting and the occasion for rebellion against society as a
whole. I believe the therapy was directly responsible for his regeneration
since it provided both intellectual and social contact of a kind desired by
the patient.

Pitirim Sorokin . . .

So far as I can tell from the description of this "critical incident," two
factors appear to be particularly instrumental in the successful reintegra-
tion of Tom. The first is real concern, friendship, or altruistic love on the
part of the therapist for Tom. Tom became convinced of this, and he felt it
with his total personality, especially after Incident A.

According to my own investigations, and the investigations of an ever
increasing number of psychiatrists, psychologists, and real educators, the
factor of genuine love, roughly speaking, in 80 per cent of the cases reported exerts its beneficial effects upon normal as well as abnormal human
beings.

The second important factor is the regrouping of social affiliations of
Tom which resulted in his separation from members of his gang, from other
persons, and in an establishment of affiliation with new groups after he had
received a job at a place some 2,000 miles from the prison.

In my humble opinion, psychiatrists do not generally give sufficient
importance to this factor of group affiliation, and often do not study carefully with what groups and persons an individual has been affiliated, and
what changes can take place in these affiliations. Often, when the patient
establishes a truly friendly relationship with the therapist, and the therapist becomes one of the important centers of affiliation of the patient, the
patient (returning back to his other groups which have been partly responsible for his disintegration) is subjected again to the disintegrating
effects of these groups.

In these brief comments I cannot go into the full development of this
idea, but in several of my works, particularly in *The Ways and Power of*

Love,[12] and then in *Society, Culture and Personality,*[13] the importance of this factor is analyzed in considerable detail. It is an important factor because the total structure of personality of everyone of us is in a way a microcosm reflecting the total social macrocosm amidst which everyone is placed. In a most humble way I would plead that the psychiatrists, psychologists, and all persons in charge of molding and educating or instructing human beings should be paying much greater attention to this factor of social affiliations of the individual. As my own and other studies of striking moral and religious conversions of individuals show, this factor is always one of the most important factors of success or failure of re-integration and therapeutic cure of individuals.

Clara Thompson . . .

The last question raised in this case is the one upon which the significance of the other experiences depends. "Would Tom have gone straight anyway?" Obviously no control experiment can be conducted to prove or disprove the importance of the therapy in Tom's life. It seems clear, however, that the therapy was of importance to Tom. Although at no point did he acknowledge any specific insight gained, there is no doubt in my mind that the therapist reached and influenced some basic emotion. Here is a rejected boy of more than average intellect, tossed about by life, without guidance. After thirteen years of correctional institution experience, he expected nothing from anybody. He dared not believe there was hope, and so accepted the prospect of therapy in a mocking spirit, probably to forestall possible disappointment.

The therapist did what I have recommended in Chapter 16. He told him that he knew he was a tough case, but that he was willing to work with him. The patient obviously did not dare believe this, having no similar experience in his life, so he proceeded to test the therapist to the point of despair. Tom knew the underworld, and probably was correct in thinking that many in the group were lying, but, more importantly, Tom needed special attention. He wanted someone all to himself. It seems likely that most of his criminal behavior had been strongly motivated by the need to get attention and be understood. At any rate, I am sure there was something in the therapist's character which Tom sensed and respected—some genuine interest in him. I say this because if there had not been genuine interest I doubt that the therapist would have responded to, "If you give me up, then there is no hope for me."

I think his decision to take the patient out of the group and see him alone

[12] Pitirim A. Sorokin, *The Ways and Power of Love* (Boston: Beacon Press, 1954).
[13] Pitirim A. Sorokin, *Society, Culture and Personality* (New York: Harper & Bros., Inc., 1947).

was the correct one. It stated, "You are a real problem, but I am interested in you." To have kept him in the group at this point would probably not have worked. Therefore, I wonder why the therapist felt disgusted with himself. A test situation was set up by the patient, and he met it intuitively. This points to a real relationship with the patient. The therapist seems to have had some doubts of his own importance, some neurotic humility. He says he was ready to sacrifice him (Tom) to his own convenience. I do not see it this way. As the patient had played it up to this point, the natural conclusion for the therapist to draw was that Tom intended to destroy the group. So it was a question of sacrificing Tom or the group—not sacrificing for the therapist's convenience.

Anyway, he recognized and responded to a note of sincerity in the patient, and there followed ten weeks of individual therapy. But Tom had been too hurt by life to admit easily any gain. It was only after he had left and was alone that, in a moment of revery perhaps, he was able to experience the feeling that he had found a friend. Again it had to be tested with the report of no gain. But what is meant by no gain? We are told that after the second ten weeks, he was able to work in the group for a year. Isn't the therapist trying to be too theoretical here? A man has gone from disrupting a group to being able to work in it. This is gain, whether it can be verbalized or not.

So finally the question is raised whether he helped him as friend or therapist. Here again, I think the therapist is seeing therapy in terms of some verbal theoretical insight. The relationship to the therapist is an essential part of any cure. I believe in this case the relationship was probably more important than any verbal insight acquired. For the first time in his life, Tom had the experience of having someone show real concern for him, and when he had tested it enough, he knew it to be genuine. I am ready to say that, without doubt, something in the doctor-patient relationship changed Tom's life.

This raises the question of Tom's diagnosis. We are very quick to think of delinquents and criminals as psychopaths; that is, people without a shred of integrity on which to build. Tom obviously had something—some desire to "go straight." We do not know enough of his history to trace its origins. Perhaps many more of our alleged psychopaths also have this "something," but, not having the same kind of dedication as this therapist, we fail to awaken it. Of course, it is not easy to awaken. In the criminal group, we are dealing with desperately damaged people.

FREDERICK C. THORNE . . .

This incident illustrates a point which has not been well understood among nondirective therapists, namely that a strongly rejecting directive action taken by a therapist does not inevitably disrupt rapport or cause a breakdown in therapy. While the client may react intensely at the moment when a painful interpretation or administrative action is given, it is not the immediate reaction but the long term result which is significant. Nondirective therapists in their research have given too much attention to short-term results of directive actions which arouse antipathy in the client, while largely disregarding long term reactions which occur after the client has had opportunity to assimilate the directive action. Quite often the client will later come to accept and thank the therapist for having taken directive action which was immediately painful but which had positive long term results.

This incident illustrates how even a most refractory patient can be influenced therapeutically even during long periods of negativism and overt hostility. Here the client was told that even though most others rejected him as hopeless, the therapist believed that he had positive personality resources and might eventually straighten out. Even though the patient displayed intense hostility during the initial period of group therapy, and in the first series of 11 interviews could report no progress, at least he had developed enough confidence in the therapist to request later another series of 11 interviews following his "conversion" experience. This conversion experience may be regarded as an attitudinal reorientation which took place spontaneously as the client gradually assimilated the implications of (1) the new hope that he could do something with himself, (2) the core attitude that "If you give me up, then there is no hope for me," (3) the clear realization that he would be ostracized from all worthwhile social groups if he continued his antisocial behavior, and (4) the reorganization of his mental context to resolve the inconsistencies among his conflicted personality tendencies.

CARL WHITAKER . . .

Without the described therapeutic effort, Tom would not have gone on to a successful adjustment in living but would have continued in his criminal behavior.

The structuring of the therapeutic relationship is conspicuously significant here. The therapist challenged the patient by his honest admission that the outcome would probably be a failure. He was able and willing to join in the power struggle with the patient, and by forcing the patient to lose he induced the beginning of the therapeutic regression.

The friendship aspect of the relationship between the therapist and the patient was of little importance. The impelling force that changed his behavior was the symbolic experience of psychotherapy. It seems apparent that the therapist's personal growth is the *sine qua non* for the patient's therapeutic experience. In a very clear way the therapist defines the fact that the patient helped produce a change in him. In fact he says, "I felt disgusted with myself and I felt that I was growing." When the therapist's "growing edge" is expanding, the patient can be sure his own regression is protected. If the therapist is unwilling to break with his previous adjustment patterns and move into a new area of unknown adjustment, then the patient dares not move into a new type of adjustment himself.

It is a mistake to call this transformation a conversion since the implication of this word is hysterical. To say this in another way, all transference cures are not temporary. It may be that transference cures are solid and will continue to be effective if the transference is bilateral; that is, if the therapist himself has grown because of his "countertransference" to the patient.

In the second therapeutic series the therapist was doing what we call "staying for breakfast," that is, after the emotional intercourse of the night before, he was willing to reassert and, before the world, validate the sense of oneness that had been present in their previous episode. To say it more formally, this was a reality integration of the fantasy (symbolic) relationship.

The episode which we would describe as a therapeutic psychosis and which took place in the yard was precipitated by the patient's voluntarily permitting himself to use fantasy for fantasy satisfaction, in place of his years of using reality for fantasy satisfaction. That is, for once he did not project his fantasy out into the world but was able to perceive it as it took place within him. This, it seems, was a crucial point of change. He then moved from being a delinquent or an acting-outward person to becoming a neurotic or an acting-inward person.

Is it true, as might be deduced from this incident, that crime is a form of psychosis with reality actually functioning as a type of distorted perception? If so, then the recovery, or the so-called adjustment, is merely the fact that the patient is now able to attain fantasy satisfaction in fantasy and reality need not be used as fantasy. Reality can become merely real living and crime is unnecessary as an expression or a method of acting out fantasy.

WERNER WOLFF . . .

This incident invites a discussion on the orbit and the depth of psychotherapy. At the surface, the patient seemed to be "the most hopeless individual I have ever seen," and each of the two therapeutic series was understood by therapist and patient to be "an evident failure." Nevertheless, after a sudden revelation which, as the patient explained, had something to do with the therapist, healing processes set in. These processes, however, did not appear in the subsequent therapy.

It seems to me that the therapist, without formalizing it, used what I call existential psychotherapy. I distinguish three basic therapeutic approaches:

1. *Structural psychotherapy,* dealing, like the various psychoanalytic schools, with the psychic structure in its ego, superego, and id aspects and its formation by past events and future goals.
2. *Social psychotherapy,* dealing with the individual's adjustment to his present social environment, as advanced by counseling and group therapy.
3. *Existential psychotherapy* which, client-centered, stimulates the unfolding of the many aspects of personality focusing upon the patient's self-evaluation of the meaning of his existence. The deep disillusionment in the present case was laid bare: "Life is a wind-blown tree . . . One is born in pain and one dies in pain and in between, one suffers."

I distinguish three basic aspects in the transference response of the therapist: that of *empathy,* feeling with the patient up to the point of identification; that of *ecpathy,* by which the therapist discovers his own problems as general life problems in the patient; and that of *sympathy,* in which a warm but detached relationship is formed. Structural psychotherapy mobilizes sympathy, social psychotherapy points toward empathy, while the existential approach seems to involve ecpathy.

In the present case, the therapist set an existential approach by his value statement that "people who have the most terrible records are often the people with the greatest capacities, which have been turned the wrong way." The therapist was moved by self-evaluations which triggered his emotions of "sorrow, hatred, pity, and inadequacy;" and by the feeling: "I was at that moment closer to him than I had ever been to any person on earth." At this moment the therapy and the transference became an existential problem for the therapist himself: "I realized clearly that this human being was in trouble and that he trusted me." The patient answered with the existential insight: "If you give me up, there is no hope for me."

According to my observations, existential psychotherapy may, more than other approaches, trigger "critical incidents," which bring about revelations and conversions as described by the patient: "Suddenly I felt peaceful and happy. I felt clean, pure, good, and wonderful. Maybe a second, maybe a minute." The conversion is experienced like a seizure, as Dostoevsky described it and as William James refers to it in his *Varieties of Religious Experience.*

Existential psychotherapy seems to penetrate to those unconscious processes in which superego and id converge, as it becomes manifest in existential dreams where impulses and drives fuse with values. In one of my books,[14] I have tried to point out that therapy proceeds on various levels of consciousness and unconsciousness, and that the therapist should be careful not to bind and to limit the patient unto one single level such as the sexual or the social one.

Concerning the specific questions of the therapist in the present case I should like to offer the following comments:

The overpowering problem of the case should have suggested very soon that the patient was not material for a group therapy and that he needed personal challenge and a personal direction. Special cases which disrupt the level of a group should—for the sake of the individual as well as of the group—not be mixed.

The therapist's transference in this case included a friendship experience that promoted transformations and structurations in the patient, namely, stimulating self-healing processes working in the absence of a therapeutic relationship. Therefore, the present approach, in which cathartic experiences of patient and therapist converged, cannot be generalized or formalized. We can suppose, not that the patient would have gone straight anyway, but that the unconscious contact of existential processes, the "deep human element" between patient and therapist, the mutual "libido transference" gave a support through which a restructuring could take place.

[14] Werner Wolff, *Values and Personality: An Existential Psychotherapy Crisis* (New York: Grune & Stratton, 1950).

"Behave Yourself"

2

History

The patient is a girl of 27, a very attractive and talented musician and singer. She comes from a well-to-do Baptist family in Texas. A brother in his thirties is not married and is probably homosexual. The mother is the church organist in the small town in which they live (so is the brother) and has dominated the entire family.

The patient came to therapy because a very casual boyfriend suggested that she needed help. She had no clear-cut awareness of her problems or the area in which she wanted to change. She came to analysis the same way she did everything else—she was a "good little girl" and did what was expected of her. Her dream material was, from the beginning, very significant, but she would present it to the therapist like "an apple" for the teacher. She would say: "I have a dream for you—," heave a sigh, and relax. Some of her early dreams showed hostility and competitiveness with the doctor, but she would deny it on a conscious level. This general passivity was applied even to insight gained. She would report doing something and the motives which made it "wrong" (even to her), but would not bother connecting the two. One of her problems was her sexual promiscuity. She slept with every man that dated her. She would report such an event without any affect or any sense of guilt. This she would often do even when presumably in "love" with one special one. No man would know about the other, and though she picked them from the same musical circle she would really take no precautions to be discreet. She had no girl friends. She came twice a week for two years and marked reforms were noted: in greater care in her own appearance, more feminine behaviors, greater interest in the world around her, and more adult dealings with people in the orchestra and the conductors. There was still the complete flatness of effect and the passivity.

She was at all times *nice* and accommodating with me as with all other people, and I in the fear of meeting her need for dependence just went along with her.

Incident

One day, after two years of therapy, she again reported her sexual adventures. She had been on tour and really went on a "binge." She slept with married men whose wives she knew, and did not even take precautions.

I then decided to be more active and I said: "I forbid you to sleep with another man. You know now the reasons why you do it and now you must do the job—you must make the effort to stop yourself." In so doing I was still afraid that not only was I becoming authoritarian like her mother, but also I was now making the decision for her.

Discussion

The patient was relieved and accepted her responsibility. With my prohibition, I gave her a frame of reference which she lacked. In her desire to rebel against her mother, she was using one thing which to her mother would make her "unlovable" and "bad." She did not take into account the price she herself was paying and the self contempt and the acceptance of her mother's negative concept of herself that entered into this promiscuous behavior. She also began to understand how, with her promiscuous behavior, she tried to be a man and express her desire to identify with her father. She began to interpret her dreams and increased the number of sessions to five a week. Now, she is becoming aware of the fact that she has been indiscriminate and impractical and no longer feels competitive with the therapist. She is also less concerned about being liked and can, in sessions and outside, express her feelings.

C. KNIGHT ALDRICH . . .

My first question is: why did the therapist have so much "fear of meeting (the patient's) need for dependence" that he "just went along with her"? Meeting dependent needs may indeed be risky at times, but it also may be necessary, kept within reasonable limits, if treatment is to progress. Adequate personality diagnosis, not evident in this case, should have established both the degree of her deprivation and her capacity to tolerate "meeting her need for dependence."

Granted, however, that there is a risk in meeting or trying to meet her dependence needs, the therapist who "just goes along" with a patient is not avoiding the risk. By his (implied) inactivity for two years, the therapist has not only stirred up the patient's dependency needs, but he has stirred up her fantasy that her needs would be met. Furthermore, he has given indirect sanction to her acting out through promiscuity.

The sanction to her acting out is my most serious criticism of this incident. It apparently took two years for the therapist to indicate his position; meanwhile I suspect that his failure to take a stand was interpreted as permission, sanction, and even encouragement, as Johnson and Szurek[1] have clearly demonstrated in similar cases. When the therapist finally did get around to declaring himself, it could have appeared as a betrayal—he had let her get in over her head, perhaps had derived vicarious satisfaction from the recitations, and then after two years suddenly began to criticize. She was relieved, naturally, when someone (on whom she was dependent) finally made an effort to help her stop what she couldn't stop by herself.

There is much more to the problem of acting out than rebellion against the mother or identification with the father. If the super-ego defect had been handled constructively at the start of treatment, she might have had a chance much earlier to use treatment to work on her underlying neurotic disturbance. More frequent sessions, and more dream interpretations, may well have been included in this process, although the material suggests that in this case the patient used dreams as resistance and to seduce the therapist, as well as for more constructive uses.

---

[1] A. M. Johnson, and S. A. Szurek, "The Genesis of Antisocial Acting Out in Children and Adults," *Psychoanalytic Quarterly*, XXI (1952), p. 323.

ALBERT ELLIS . . .

The therapist's technique, in this case, is doubly disturbing, since he appears to have gone from one extreme to another, without for a moment considering resting on some middle ground. In the first place, out of a self-confessed fear of interfering with the patient's need for dependence, the therapist passively went along with her, and apparently for a period of two whole years of analysis made little or no attempt to show her that she was acting in an obviously over-nice manner and that she had better seriously consider some possible alternatives.

Then, after the patient has apparently spent the first two years in therapy making very little progress in her somewhat reckless and indiscreet behavior, the therapist is confronted with additional evidences of this behavior and suddenly becomes unequivocally authoritative and commands her to change her sexual ways. Fortunately, his commands seem to work; but they just as easily could have got her into still more serious difficulties with herself.

A more judicious, more middle-of-the-road approach would have been, it seems to me, for the therapist, soon after he noticed what this girl's behavior pattern was, to have started her questioning herself about it. He could have easily, when evidences of her indiscretion were reported, questioned her by saying something like: "Your sexual promiscuity may be perfectly all right for you, providing that you really want it that way and are not merely engaging in it to win approval. But do you think it entirely wise to be that indiscreet about it, or to sleep with men whose wives you know?" If the patient, after this kind of questioning, insisted on continuing her same pattern of behavior, that would be her prerogative. But at least the therapist would have raised the issue of her possibly hurting herself by this behavior, and would have given her the opportunity to give the matter serious thought.

Not, apparently, working on the matter at all, and then suddenly commanding the patient to change her behavior, seems to me to be somewhat like jumping out of the frying pan into the fire. Actually, the girl may have had important reasons, whether neurotic ones or not, for being sexually indiscreet. As it happened, some of these reasons came out after the therapist's prohibition; but it would have been much safer to explore them *before* any such prohibition was made.

This is not to contend that therapists should not, under any circumstance, insist that patients do or not do certain things. Often, they should; and often, as in this case, their doing so results in profound insight *after* a given act is commanded or prohibited. It is not, therefore, that I am in any sense opposed to the general idea of highly active, and at times quite authoritative, therapeutic procedures. It just seems to me that in this particular case the prohibition against sexual behavior was made in too abrupt and too risky a manner, largely because the therapist was (consciously or unconsciously) feeling guilty about his prior over-passivity. Direct prohibitions and commands should usually be made in therapy when more subtle forms of persuasion have been tried and failed. I do not see, in this case, where subtle persuasion was employed at all; and I feel that it should have been before the drastic step of direct prohibition was taken. Fortunately, all's well that ends well in this instance; but calamity also could have befallen.

Viktor E. Frankl . . .

There is no question whatever of authoritative interference in the case under consideration. The therapist simply verbalized what the patient already subconsciously knew. Is it not, ultimately, the task of psychotherapy to make unconscious knowledge available, so that the patient can manage it, and thereby become more aware of it? Actually what I call *existential analysis* (*Existenzanalyse*) consists of helping a person to come to an explicit understanding of one's existence.[2]

Only after this interference by the therapist did the patient begin to understand what she had done in the past. Furthermore, the patient might have continued this behavior, if the therapist had not dared to explain the meaning and result of her behavior, without embarrassment and unhampered by fears of directness. Only after the therapist became active, and even emotional, did it become clear to the patient that she had acted not only contrary to the customs and rules of society, but also against her own true wishes. This is to be understood by conceiving that she really did not initiate responsible actions but rather was drawn by circumstances, temptations, seductions, and in the last analysis, instincts.

In general, one may say that many an "epoche" (in the sense of the ancient Greek philosophers)—that is, an abstaining from any values or judgments, which is generally looked on as a basic principle of Anglo-Saxon psychotherapy—is in reality much more likely to imply a value judgment than the seeming interference that was so fortunately practiced in this case. The steps of the therapist were meant and intended to support and to strengthen the patient's already existent knowledge.

Vincent Herr . . .

This incident interests the writer because it involves questions which come up so frequently in actual practice, such as: Is it permitted for a

[2] Viktor E. Frankl, "On Logotherapy and Existential Analysis," *American Journal of Psychoanalysis, 18,* 28–37, 1958.

counselor always to be permissive to the counselee, in every conceivable kind of instance or circumstance? The question, more specifically as applied to the incident would be as follows: May a therapist wait long years, passively, and permissively, while he observes his client performing and glorying in the performance of antisocial and/or unsocial acts, in the hope that the eventual change in the life of the client will be more lasting? When should something like dictatorial methods be substituted for the permissiveness, if ever? The answer to each of these questions would seem again to depend upon the good judgment and foresight of the therapist, as we are about to show. It seems that no sweeping rule can be found to cover all cases. We have to assume, for the sake of clarity, that the "prohibition" in the case produced an effect which could not have been produced if it had been made sooner; and we assume also that the change here reported was a more conforming type of behavior, actually was a permanent one and beneficial to all concerned, even the therapist. Both of these assumptions lack any kind of rigorous scientific proof, as so often happens where human behavior is concerned; nor can the truth of the assumptions be ascertained from the data presented in the case.

If, however, the experience of therapists has shown that an interference in behavior at too early a date will not be as effective as this one was, then the therapist must have had some rather clear signs of a movement or change in the patient, before he could take the risk of being other than "permissive" in his treatment procedures. Thus, since we must assume with some kind of evidence that the dictatorial treatment in the early sessions is not very effective of changes, we may perhaps also assume that the patient was so mentally disturbed, in the estimation of the therapist, that she could not take on herself the full responsibility for the social consequences of her acts. Thus the burden on the shoulders of the therapist is indeed a heavy one.

In all such cases the "personality" and "attitudes" of the therapist seem to be the deciding factors, as to what form of treatment will best obtain the desired results for all concerned. Thus we are finally led to the conclusion that whatever course of action is pursued by the therapist—whether he steps in early and advises a more conforming type of behavior, or whether he waits longer, in the hope of even greater success—depends ultimately upon the judgment and prudence of the therapist.

There is another possibility, namely that the therapist never steps in and assumes an authoritarian role. In this case his very permissiveness becomes equivalent to his decision to "let the patient set his own course of action." It is obvious, then, that the behavior of the therapist can and often does have grave consequences for the total outcome, both as regards the best interests of the individual, and as regards the group. Thus he will be in need of a code of ethics to guide his decisions, but the manner in which this code is interpreted and put into practice will always be a function of the life experience, the frame of reference, and the values of the therapist. There does not seem to be any other alternative.

Do therapists generally, and theorists on morals and values always, take these things into consideration when they write their directives? The case, as viewed by the present critic, is crucial for pointing up these vital issues in the whole question of social values, and gives us more insight into the manner in which values influence the lives and behavior of individuals and groups.

In the case reported, it also becomes clear that persons giving treatment feel a keen sense of responsibility, and realize that they have certain obligations to their clients to seek their best total good. If they do not live up to these obligations, the patient may suffer and be harmed because of the action of the therapist. In this case it is not as clear as it would be in the case of permitting a person to threaten suicide, just how the client, by being permitted unsocial acts, is also injuring him or herself. Yet in both cases the reasoning is basically the same. In both cases the professional person who wants to help others knows that he has responsibilities toward the people whom he serves. These obligations extend so far, it would seem, that they have a duty to prevent the client, as far as it is in their power as treatment persons, from injuring himself *and* others. The thoughtful reader will see numerous implications contained in these straight-forward speculations. One of them might be that a therapist who proposes a code whereby he merely sees to it that, as a consequence of his treatment, his client does not *do harm to others,* is taking a one-sided and narrow view. The code must take into account the extent to which a treatment will deter the client from *injuring himself.* Of course all this presupposes that there are some valid norms for deciding when a person injures himself and others. Space will not permit further pursuit of this interesting question, and how it is related to the anti-social behavior known as sex deviation, and to the other touchy problems of "individual-versus-group" goods.

J. W. KLAPMAN . . .

An amazing case, and if we interpret correctly, one demonstrating the extremes to which parental influence can go. It is not at all rare that an individual will take violent exception to a parent's dictation, but still be so profoundly influenced by it as to develop very deep guilt feelings over rebellion, but superficially be entirely compliant. In this case this conflict apparently led to neurotic acting out. For, on the one hand, she secretly rebels; on the other hand she is a passive, very compliant child. Her rebellion results in acting out secretly, which if her mother knew about it, would certainly curl her hair. She can do that because it is more or less unknown to her mother, but at the same time the conflict situation is actually a stalemate and impasse, leaving her drained of any surplus will and energy. From this she longed, in the final depths of her being, to be rescued. (It is remarkable that a subject under such conditions could still carry on with an exacting artistic pursuit. However, most likely it would finally tell in the creativeness required in the pursuit of her artistic endeavors.) This stalemated conflict without therapist's mediation might well have ended in a schizophrenic withdrawal. As it was there resulted a helpless state resembling that of a hypnotic subject. In the passive attitude of the first part of the treatment the therapist was just another parent-surrogate, demanding the same kind of unconditional fealty and dependence that her mother did.

A most surprising thing in therapy, which we see in increasing number of reports, are situations where, in a genuinely critical climax when the "chips are really down," only a direct, forceful, authoritarian intervention will safely negotiate the crisis with a resulting favorable denouement. While I don't endorse a consistently dictatorial, authoritarian approach throughout the course of therapy, it must be remarked that the awesome injunction against authoritarianism, inherited from psychoanalysis, is a kind of sacred cow amounting to a therapeutic obsession and phobia.

One is also struck, in this case, with another order of dynamics which is not strictly of the psychoanalytic genre. As already stated, there is some resemblance in the girl's attitude and behavior to that of an hypnotic subject. What was the effect of the therapist's standing up on his hind legs and giving a direct order? In this action, as a parental figure, he gave the subject absolution from the previous parental commands. She was now freed of her thralldom to her mother's behests, free to be herself, and to exercise her own will and judgment.

FREDERICK C. THORNE . . .

We often see patients who seem to be cooperating with and gaining insights from psychotherapy but who never translate such progress concretely into action. In such impasses, it may be indicated to confront the client forcibly with the inconsistencies of her professed intentions and her actions in order to precipitate a conflict which we hope will be resolved in a desirable way. Such action was taken in this case when the therapist became impatient and directively ordered the patient to desist. Such directive therapy does not result in client resistiveness as inevitably as nondirective theory would postulate.

If a good rapport has been established which will survive transient disagreements between client and therapist, the therapist may persist actively in gently but firmly insisting that the client accept a suggested line of conduct. We have often put it up to the client as follows: "You will eventually have to change your conduct along these lines anyway. I have plenty of patience to go along with you until you find it out for yourself. Why don't you try it and see how it works? You can always experiment a bit to see what works best." Unless the therapist takes decisive action in such impasses, the client usually will lose respect and confidence in the therapist, particularly when the client knows what she should do and tests the therapist to see how long he will let her get away with not doing it. Nondirective handling of impasses such as this will usually result in a gradual breaking off of the therapeutic relation.

On a Saturday
Afternoon

3

History

Joan is a nineteen-year-old college freshman. She was first seen while she was attending junior college. The school psychologist had diagnosed her as a paranoid schizophrenic on the basis of a Rorschach test and had referred her for psychotherapy to a counseling center which uses a client-centered approach.

The therapist to whom Joan was assigned (the present author), noted no psychotic symptoms until the sixth interview when she had a hallucination and expressed some bizarre ideas. After this interview, the therapist asked for a consultation with a psychiatrist which was followed by a joint interview with the patient and continuing consultation during the course of treatment.

The critical incident described occurred in the fourteenth interview. Joan had been seen initially for eight interviews, followed by a month and a half of summer vacation, and then five more interviews before she left town to go to a state university. She had been at the university for one week when she called the therapist and said she wanted to come back during the weekend for an appointment. One was set for five o'clock on Saturday.

Incident

Joan arrived almost on time, breaking a precedent of coming consistently 20 to 30 minutes late. She said she was quite disturbed and had tried to reach me twice during the afternoon.

I asked her how much time she would like. (Our previous interviews had all been for whatever was left of 50 minutes after her late arrival.) I opened the possibility of a longer interview in reaction to her apparent degree of disturbance and the inaccessibility of the clinic to her new residence at the university. She asked, "What do you mean?" I said, "I wonder if you would like more than an hour today?" She said, "Yeah, I would." I asked her, "Well, how much time would you like?" She did not try to answer the question so I said, "Suppose we continue until we both get hungry and it's time to go home for supper."

She began then talking about her experience at the university. She described the loneliness that she felt—the isolation. Nobody really loved her. She just felt all alone in the world. Life was so depressing that she couldn't work up interest in anything. She didn't have the push to do anything. If she had the push, she thinks she would commit suicide. If the future were merely an extension of the present, then it would not be worth living for. She was expressing a deep despair when she began to pull herself together again. There would be some hope if she could change herself. She began to feel that maybe she did have the possibility for changing.

During a pause in this working through of feeling, I wondered about the time. Taking out my watch, I discovered that it was six-thirty and that we had been together for an hour and a half. I put my watch on the desk and asked her, "How much more time do you want?" She didn't answer. The watch sounded loud ticking away, so I put it back in my pocket. We went on until about seven, when I began to feel weak and wasn't following her very well. I said this to her and she looked up at me like a scared rabbit. She smiled in a forced way and began putting on her coat as if preparing to leave. I said, "You looked frightened when I suggested it might be time to stop." She nodded. I said, "Almost as if you thought I were rejecting you then." She said, "Yes, that's what it looked like to me." Then she pulled her coat together over her chest. Her hands clenched strongly on the coat and she started to stare at the wall. Her eyes got red but no tears came. She began to tremble. I did not understand what was happening and said. "It seems as if the feelings you have now are making you afraid." She just nodded without looking at me. Her trembling and staring went on for about eight minutes. Then she stood up in front of me. I asked her if she wanted to go home. She looked at me, smiled again in a mechanical fashion, and shook her head "no." Then she began wringing her hands, staring at the wall, and shaking all over. From time to time her body would lean toward me and then lean away. My heart was beating like a trip hammer. I didn't understand what was happening to her. I was afraid that she might be going into a psychotic break. After about ten minutes of throbbing silence, I said, "It's hard for me to understand what you are feeling." Then she said that she was looking at the lambs on the wall, the faces of the lambs. (There was a flower print on the wall.) "They have two eyes. One is a mean eye and the other is a kind eye. I see the faces of my mother and my grandmother. They are telling me to control myself and I hate them."

I told her I was puzzled. Then I said, "I wonder if you are saying —in part you like yourself, in part you don't like yourself." She said, "No. It's other people's reactions to me. They partly like me and partly don't like me." She said that one of the eyes was covered over with wool. I said, "I wonder if you are saying that if people really knew you—could see the real you—that they would not like you." She said, "Yes."

In between these times when we talked together, she was still standing, trembling, wringing her hands, and staring at the wall. Then she began to tell me, in a very circuitous way, about her relationship with her father. She started out by saying that when she was thirteen years old, she had seen the divorce papers of her parents. In those papers it said that her father had not wanted her before she was born. Then she went on to describe her father's attitude toward her and after many hints told me about having incestuous relations with her father. She described this as the experience which made her dirty, no good, horrible.

She had been standing and shaking for half an hour, but having brought out this report of incest, she sat down and relaxed. She looked at me while she talked, really seeing me for the first time since she had stood up and described how this experience had affected every part of her life. She had never told this to anyone before. She felt she could not tell her mother or her grandmother. Even with her father, she pretends that it never happened, and he never mentions it. She no longer has sex relations with him, but when she visits him (her parents are separated) she takes along a friend to protect herself.

When it was about eight o'clock, I found I was again beginning to get hungry. I said, "Well, I'm beginning to get weak again." She said, "You know, I've got a headache and I'm hungry. I'm just all worn out and I really haven't much more to say today. But I couldn't tell you. I couldn't suggest that we stop." It developed that she was afraid that would be rejecting me.

Discussion

What part did the handling of time play in this interview? Did the indecisiveness of the therapist lead to a seductive interplay which aroused transference reactions, helping to precipitate the temporary psychotic break? If so, how should this be evaluated therapeutically? Would a firm initial definition of limits by the therapist have cut off the possibility of the intensive catharsis which occurred during the last hour?

The therapist interpreted the client's hallucinatory thoughts in terms of her attitudes toward herself and her relationships with other people. What would have been the effect of merely reflecting the ideas which she was verbalizing? What would have been the effect of interpreting her behavior in terms of a transference neurosis?

C. Knight Aldrich . . .

The diagnosis of paranoid schizophrenia implies the likelihood of behavior which is dangerous to the reputations or even the lives of the patient and others, behavior which often requires commitment. Although the psychiatrist usually welcomes the collaboration of the responsible psychologist in the treatment of paranoid schizophrenics, he believes it is essential that a psychiatrist actively participates in the collaboration in order to provide the patient with appropriate medical and legal safeguards.[1]

Even when the psychologist in independent practice makes a conscientious effort to refer patients with recognized psychotic, organic, or psychosomatic conditions to a psychiatrist, his lack of a medical background handicaps him severely in narrowing the range of his diagnostic tools. Physicians, including psychiatrists, make their share of diagnostic

[1] *Psychology and Its Relations with Other Professions* (American Psychological Association, 1954), Principle 5.44.

errors, but their patients have had the benefit of a comprehensive diagnostic approach. A Rorschach diagnosis is never enough.

From the discussion it appears that the therapist realizes to some degree the serious implications of his seductiveness and his failure to protect the patient, and correctly questions the appropriateness of "merely reflecting" or of "interpreting her behavior in terms of a transference neurosis." Most significant in that which he does not see (except in terms of rejection) is the patient's fear of her own and the therapist's hostility.

The question is asked in the discussion: Would a firm initial definition of limits by the therapist have cut off the possibility of the intensive catharsis which occurred during the last hour? My reaction to this question is: I would hope so. Catharsis is not the only goal in psychotherapy, and part of the skill of the experienced therapist lies in knowing when to discourage as well as when to encourage catharsis. One of the advantages of setting time limits in treatment hours is to give the patient the opportunity to pace himself.

RUDOLF DREIKURS . . .

This is another example of the difficulty in evaluating an approach based on a different methodology than that used by the reviewer. The therapist obviously felt obliged to give up his usual procedure, and entered into a much more active and interpretative interaction with the patient. It is difficult to understand what else he could have done—his general orientation notwithstanding. But one could have approached the situation differently from the beginning. The fact that the patient came on time almost for the first time and was obviously quite disturbed and eager to talk—having tried twice to reach the therapist before—would indicate that she had something urgent to discuss. Consequently, one could have started by probing what was on her mind, and gently coaxing her if she hesitated to reveal it. In this way, one would not have waited for the terrific pressure at the conclusion of the interview which forced the therapist to give her so much more of his time and drove the patient close to a psychotic break before she could reveal what apparently was on her mind all the time, namely, her relationships with her father.

Another hint which she gave at the beginning of the interview which one could have followed up immediately, was the description of her apparent depression, which led her even to consider suicide. Depression is usually an expression of anger. Therefore, one could have probed to determine at whom she was angry—and probably would have found the father who was on her mind at that time.

In this light, it seems that this highly charged emotional climax could have been avoided if the therapist would have tried to understand why she was so upset and why she was so urgent in seeking this particular appointment. Without exploring this area, it was natural that the therapist did not see what was happening. It seems that a rigid procedure as to the therapeutic technique may often invite such a predicament, which is less likely to occur when the therapist is willing to sense an undercurrent and tries to explore deliberately and systematically what is going on in the patient's mind.

None of that is brought forth by the therapist in his exploration of the incident. Actually, it was not he who was "handling the time." His only alternative was to terminate the interview on time regardless of the patient's condition, or to permit her more time. He invited her to take more time, but it was she who determined by her excitement how much time he had to give her. In other words, his only reaction to the impression that there was something very much wrong with the patient, was his offer of more time. But since nothing happened during the interview to stimulate the patient to present her problem, it was only the attempt of the therapist to terminate the interview after an hour and a half which pressured her to open up. And it was she, then, who played the time element by staring and not saying anything. One can, therefore, say that the time element was *not* utilized well on the part of the therapist. He merely yielded to the patient's request for more time. How the therapist could consider his indecisiveness as "seductive interplay" is not quite clear to this reviewer. One can hardly understand his sudden reference to "aroused transference reactions" and "the intensive catharsis" which occurred—in his opinion—in the last hour. His report gives no indication of either transference or catharsis. In the described procedure it just took so long until the patient could speak about what she apparently came to talk about in the beginning. It took the detour of a struggle, of pressure of time, of a dramatic climax, of high-pitched emotions in which the patient succeeded in frightening the therapist almost as much as she was frightened. It is hard to see where transference reactions and catharsis came into play. But it seems obvious that the therapist began to make headway when he— perhaps against his indoctrination—attempted to give an interpretation about the patient disliking herself. Then the crucial problem of what she was really like came into the open.

JEROME D. FRANK . . .

It seems to me that the therapist missed the point in his description of this incident. This is an adolescent schizophrenic girl who is probably full of sexual phantasies and very apt to distort the therapist's remarks,

expecially if they are ambiguous, to accord with these. She has been consistently coming late to the therapist's office, suggesting conflict about him.
On this occasion in contrast to her previous behavior she comes on time,
and immediately indicates that she had tried to reach him twice during
the afternoon, indicating a temporary resolution of the conflict in the direction of accepting her dependency on him. The meeting is at 5 o'clock
on a Saturday when presumably other people will not be in the building.
Under these circumstances the therapist's opening question as to how
much time she would like is probably perceived by her as a command that
she stay until he lets her go. Her answering question "What do you mean?"
indicates some uneasiness. She doesn't know how to take it, and twice
she cannot tell him how much time she would like. Finally, at the end
of the interview she says "I couldn't suggest that we stop." Furthermore,
it is likely that the patient interpreted the therapist's questions as indicating that he wished to hold her for sexual purposes. His suggestion that
"We continue until we both get hungry and it's time to go home for supper" could easily have such a connotation to a patient like this under the
circumstances. She talks about loneliness and feeling unloved, which would
confirm this interpretation.

Her behavior when, at seven o'clock, the therapist suddenly indicates
that he is not listening to her, is consistent with this view. The degree of
her upset at his "rejection" leads to the surmise that she was having amor-
ous phantasies about him, perhaps stimulated by her misinterpretation
of his initial offer. In any case, her following behavior is a dramatic por-
trayal of ambivalent feelings—leaning towards him and away from him,
speaking of the two eyes, one mean and one kind, and then rejecting the
therapist's interpretation about referring this to herself and pointing out
that it refers to other people's reactions to her, "They partly like me and
partly don't like me." This is probably how she must have interpreted
the therapist's behavior. In this connection, the therapist's interpretation
of one eye being covered with wool, is, I suspect, a response to his own
anxiety, and her ready assent is probably a manifestation of hers. In context a more likely meaning of this symbolic remark is that the therapist
is trying to pull the wool over her eyes.

The following material about incestuous relations with her father
in this context is probably in part her way of expressing her conflict over
sex relations with the therapist—something desirable and yet something
which would cause her to feel even more dirty and horrible. In view of
the fact that the patient is psychotic, one would have to keep in mind
the possibility that much of this is phantasy.

Had I stumbled into such a predicament, as any therapist can, and
had I been able to perceive it at the time as well as I can in retrospect,
I would have handled it by firmly and clearly asserting the realities of the

situation, especially with respect to the meaning of my initial offer of a longer interview.

This incident is an excellent example of what can happen when a therapist fails to perceive a schizophrenic's "paratactic distortions" of his remarks.

VIKTOR E. FRANKL . . .

It seems questionable whether or not we are dealing here with a frank psychosis. What may be the reason for so believing? The interpretations of the Rorschach? I would never make a diagnosis of psychosis on the basis of a mere test. Bizarre ideas? They would then have to be bizarre in a specifically schizophrenic sense and even then it could be a schizoid personality. Hallucinations? What kind? Acoustical ones—hearing voices? If not that, they need not be specifically schizophrenic. We learn in this case that the apparition was not a real hallucination but more or less of an illusion or an illusory distortion of visual impressions (the wallpaper).

Even the described acute condition happening during the consultation at the office I would never describe as psychotic. It was more like a crisis within which the patient realized in an intense manner the failure of her emotional and existential claims. I define emotional claims as the satisfaction of the need for love and for being loved, and I define existential claims as *the satisfaction of what we call will-to-meaning in logotherapy*, that is the thoroughly primary (and therefore not at all in the sense of so-called "*secondary* rationalization"!) desire of everybody to give his life a concrete and personal meaning; in other words, to invest as many values as possible into one's existence in the course of one's lifetime.

The patient had not felt life worth living. This was made intensively evident in the description. In logotherapy this condition has been called "*existential frustration*"—*the unfulfillment of the will-to-meaning*—but also "existential vacuum." Existence then remains empty because life seems to lack content. It is clear this kind of condition is eminently dangerous as far as suicide is concerned, and this is illustrated in the present case. The emotional emptiness is shown in the words in which she describes her abysmal loneliness, "All alone in the world." The reasons are obvious. She felt herself "not wanted" or wanted via incest, in a way which did not fulfill her social norms.

According to logotherapy, one of the most essential tasks of psychotherapy is to get a person to his will-to-meaning. We have had the frequent experience of Nietzsche's statement: "Whoever has a *why* to live for will be able to endure any *how*." This is the best motto for psychotherapy: visualizing a meaning of life enables a person, like nothing else can, to sustain life even under the most distressing circumstances.

In this particular case, a lucidation—an attempt to make transparent the patient's present situation—to show that there is a meaning, at least in the future, waiting for her, to be fulfilled by her and by her alone—this was what alone could satisfy the patient. Not any meaning can do; it has to be "the" meaning, one exclusive for the patient.

Analysis of existence—logotherapy—is required in such cases to prevent suicide attempts. In psychotherapy it is not only essential to understand and forgive everything, but it also appears decisive to me that the patient be directed toward the concrete meaning of his personal existence—that the patient be reoriented with regard to his personal world of meaning and value. A psychotherapy that merely restricts itself to interpretations of the patient's reactions ("the therapist interpreted the client's hallucinatory thoughts"), or "merely reflects ideas," or solely deals with transformations of psychic energy or libidinous forces—a therapy of this type misinterprets the essence of human beings—who are *primarily* concerned with meaning and value! This kind of psychotherapy adheres to a *monado-logistic* concept of man, as I call it—as if a human being could be equated to a monad, as the great philosopher Leibniz has labeled something like spiritual atoms. That is to say, beings without communication to the world outside, or as Leibniz said, "without windows to the world." *This monado-logistic image of man, I believe, is one of the inherent dangers of one-sided, exclusively psychodynamically- and psychogenetically-oriented psychotherapy.*

Something may be said concerning the diagnosis of suicide since it is important to recognize the danger of imminent suicide and to differentiate between dissimulation and true suicidal intentions. For this purpose a method, proved successful by myself and my colleagues, which I developed during many years as chief of a "suicide ward" in one of the largest European mental hospitals, may be explained. I ask the patient two questions. The first: "Do you still want to commit suicide?" The patient trying to dissimulate still existing suicide-ideas, as well as one who really has no such intention will, of course, answer "No" to this question. But then, as brutal as it may sound, I ask the patient a second question: "Why don't you want to kill yourself any longer?"

Again and again the patients who have really given up such ideas give immediately a variety of reasons for giving up suicide. For example: he has to consider his family; or he has to fulfill a job; or for reasons of religion; and so forth. On the other hand, the patient who tries to dissimulate instantly becomes hesitant in a typical manner as soon as he is asked this "Why" question. He shows restlessness, cannot give any concrete answers, usually explaining, "You can believe me that I no longer have any such intentions." He may add then: "Now you can discharge me from the hospital."

Reorientation of a patient towards meaning and value is the only way to overcome emotional difficulties, all the more as these difficulties often invade nothing but an *existential vacuum*. Complexes, per se, emotional conflicts, and psychological traumata are barely pathogenic. That this is even true in comparatively severe traumata as in this case of incest, I saw in another case of an 18 year old female who came to me because of frigidity. She told me she had been sexually abused by her father at the age of eleven. I was not impressed by this explanation and continued to ask questions with the result that I learned that the patient for many years had been reading vulgar psychoanalytic literature. From these readings she had become convinced that something would occur in later years in the form of a severe neurosis because of her incest experience. In other words, she became convinced she had to become a sexual neurotic. In any case she achieved an "anticipatory anxiety" which interfered with her capacity for orgasm during intercourse; she was not devoting herself to her partner because she was too concerned with observing herself.

A thorough talk about this anticipatory anxiety mechanism and the resulting compulsion to self-observation or *"hyperreflection"* as we call it in logotherapy, finally resulted in *"de-reflection."* Just as an orientation to the meaning of one's life enables him to overcome existential difficulties, so also a loving dedication for the partner lets him overcome emotional difficulties.

Finally, coming to the question of how this patient's critical break-down—emotional and existential—occurred, it seems it happened as soon as the treating psychologist made it clear his time was limited. I believe the patient was in a situation in which she had to give an account of her life. And the failure of it might have been expressed by what is called a "statement suicide." It was because of this "statement-mood" that she wished to consult the psychotherapist this very day. In making this final statement she wanted to confide herself to him. Then she realized that this desire might not be fulfilled because of the external reason of lack of time. This intensified the crisis to such a degree that the patient felt, "Now, I do not care at all." Luckily, this deepening of her crisis led her to talk as she never had before. In other words, as happens often, an acute intensification of a chronic crisis may immediately lead to a reversal of the crisis trend into the first phase of cure.

As far as the psychotherapist is concerned, he acted properly—what happened could not have been anticipated at the beginning of the consultation period. The only mistake he could possibly have committed was to have had no time even under the changed conditions. But, fortunately, he did not make this error. He thereby acted according to a statement applicable to psychotherapists in moments as important as described in this case. The statement is taken from a common caution of Tyrolean mountain guides: "Take your time."

FAY KARPF . . .

It is unfortunate that the *History* in this reported critical incident does not state whether the psychiatrist did or did not confirm, on the basis of his clinical evaluation of the patient, the psychologist's diagnosis of paranoid schizophrenia made on the basis of the Rorschach test. Accordingly, it is difficult to estimate how seriously disturbed the patient or client was. But inasmuch as Joan did apparently, according to the report, manifest hallucinative behavior and bizarre ideas, so that the therapist felt the need of arranging for a joint interview and continuing consultation with a psychiatrist, one might assume that the patient presented at least mild psychotic symptoms.

One wonders, therefore, why the patient was not turned over for psychiatric treatment rather than continued in psychotherapy. One also wonders why she was permitted to leave for a month and a half of summer vacation after only eight interviews without arranging for continued therapy, and why, furthermore, no arrangements were made for additional treatment when she left to go to another university after only five more interviews. In view of this seemingly questionable handling of the case, the critical incident described cannot exactly be regarded as a bolt out of the blue.

There are other questions regarding the early handling of the case:

What were the recommendations for treatment by the psychiatrist and to what extent were they followed and realized?

What was the theoretical orientation of the consulting psychiatrist? Was there a conflict between his view and the client-centered therapy approach?

Why was Joan's consistent late-coming not handled at the outset and more definite treatment limits established for her? The time factor is important in all therapy and in this case seems to have been disregarded altogether. Even if the therapist wished to modify his usual procedure in this case because of the supposedly disturbed condition of the patient, some professional structuring of the situation could have been established, since the patient was apparently responsible enough to be able to continue with her university work.

At the time of the critical incident, for example, Joan is asked whether or not she would like a longer interview period. She replies in the affirmative but fails to answer the question, "Well, how much time would you like?" The therapist thereupon says, "Suppose we continue until we both get hungry and it's time to go home for supper." We are of course told that the client said she was "quite disturbed" and the therapist reacted "to her apparent degree of disturbance and the inaccessibility of the clinic to her new residence at the university." However, the therapist not only failed to maintain professional limits, but he practically turned the therapeutic situation into a sort of informal social contact without any assumed responsibility for termination or goal to be achieved. The informality of the situation may well have been a contributing factor in precipitating the critical incident. As the client herself said toward the end of the interview, she had no more to say, "But I couldn't tell you. I couldn't suggest that we stop."

Throughout the interview the therapist was indecisive: about time, about his watch, about termination, about the patient's disturbed state. All of this placed too heavy a burden on the client for management of herself in the confused therapeutic situation.

Twice the therapist told the patient that he was getting weak from hunger: the first time when the patient was not ready to terminate the interview, so she disregarded his statement and the psychotic episode followed—perhaps as a device to hold the attention of the therapist and to prevent termination of the interview; the second time when she was more ready to end, so she admitted that she too was hungry, had a headache, was "just all worn out," and didn't have much more to say that day. However, she took occasion to rebuke the therapist at this point by making the statement that she couldn't tell him this or suggest that they stop. The therapist states that "it developed that she was afraid that that would be rejecting me." But, more likely, she was really telling him that he was not in control of the situation. For we practically have a reversal of patient-therapist roles at this point, and all one can say is that, since the therapist failed to take firm hold of the reins, the horse wandered off according to her own inscrutable inclinations.

The therapist had admitted to the patient that he was puzzled by her behavior and did not understand what was happening to her. That failed to give her the emotional support and confidence in the therapist which she needed at this critical point. Although she superficially accepted the suggested interpretations in terms of self and relationships, she proceeded to bring forth material which was probably more in line with her need and understanding of the moment—and perhaps also with her reading or indoctrination.

Another possibility is, of course, that it was precisely the informal, drawn out, wholly unstructured and indecisive procedure which enabled the patient to bring forth the searching material of the critical incident, whether actual or fancied. One is at a decided disadvantage here in not having more information about the actualities of the patient's life and also about the nature of her preceding relationship to the therapist.

It is commendable that the therapist himself raises questions about the possibility that the indecisiveness of his procedure may have helped to precipitate the patient's psychotic episode. This is the result of the sort of retrospective insight which self-critical therapists frequently develop and is the process by which progress in the field of therapy is made. In the view of this commentator, the theoretical interpretation of what transpired, about which the therapist also raises questions, is probably less important than the points raised regarding the management of the therapeutic situation and the patient-therapist relationship. While the interpretation used was suggestive and may have led the patient on, it was well directed to the realistic implications of what was transpiring and was, on the whole, readily accepted by the patient.

O. Hobart Mowrer . . .

If by "schizophrenia" one means a split or divided personality, then Joan's case is a classic one. The lamb's two eyes, the one "mean" and the other "kind," represent her two selves, the two contending psychic systems within the one body. And much of the dramatic quality of the incident here reported stems from the fact that it involves a struggle between these two selves for control of behavior in the interview situation. The conduct of the therapist is considerate, generous, kindly, and might bring forth either of the competing trends: seduction or confession.

The pressure toward confession is unmistakable, since it results in manifest action. The seduction trend is more inferential. Joan begins the interview by describing her loneliness and the fact that no one loves her. Suppose that, at this juncture, the therapist had made some physical advance toward her: the ensuing events might have been very different. After all, this would not have been the first time that Joan had seduced an authority figure; and the gains from the original conquest of her father must have been substantial. Imagine the power and control it gave her over her father: she had only to whisper a few simple words to destroy him any time she chose. But the present father figure is stronger and supports the competing drive toward confession.

The immediate gains from the confession are apparent: "she sat down and relaxed." She was no longer hallucinated and could again face the therapist. This was undoubtedly a momentous step for Joan; but it was a beginning rather than an end. She cannot consolidate her confession by extending it to the more significant "others" in her life without damaging her father. Conceivably she might be able to bring him, too, to a confession of his role in the incestuous relationship; but this would, in any case, involve time and complications. Furthermore, even if the affair were fully ventilated, it is still a question as to how far confession alone would carry Joan toward a restoration of self-respect and inner peace. In general, psychotherapists have not as yet given much attention to programs of positive action which might counter-balance misdeeds. Confession may be a powerful safeguard against their repetition, but the acknowledgment of evil is only a prologue to virtue. After this heroic start, one can only hope that Joan and her therapist were able to move forward together as constructively as they have begun.

Although Freud himself took a somewhat more temperate position, many of his followers have adopted the working assumption that the only kind of guilt that makes human beings ill is *false* guilt, that is, guilt and self-recrimination caused by an excessively severe superego. And the therapeutic emphasis was, accordingly, upon trying to get the patient to be more accepting of himself, as he is, rather than upon helping him change and become more truly acceptable. Evidence seems to be steadily mounting that the misdeeds of neurotic and psychotic persons are, alas, not imaginary, but real and that we are going to have to rethink our position in these matters.

At times Freud himself seems to be on the verge of suggesting a different way of interpreting psychopathology. For example, in the *New Introductory Lectures on Psychoanalysis*,[2] we find him saying:

> They [the insane] have turned away from external reality, but for that very reason they know more of internal psychic reality and can tell us much that would otherwise be inaccessible to us. One group of them suffer what we call delusions of observation. They complain to us that they suffer continually, and in their most intimate actions, from the observation of unknown powers or persons, and they have hallucinations in which they hear these persons announcing the results of their observations: "now he is going to say this, now he is dressing himself to go out," and so on. Such observation is not the same thing as persecution, but it is not far removed from it. It implies that these persons distrust the patient, and expect to catch him doing something that is forbidden and for which he will be punished. How would it be if these mad people were right, if we all of us had an observing function in our egos threatening us with punishment which, in their case, had merely become sharply separated from the ego and had been mistakenly projected into external reality?

The only issue here is whether the superego is usually valid or spurious. Sometimes, to be sure, the things of which disturbed persons accuse themselves are either trivial or untrue. Joan's self-accusation was by no means trivial, and it seems not to have occurred to her therapist to question its veracity. But can one generalize? Are there *always* such good grounds for

[2] Sigmund Freud, *New Introductory Lectures on Psychoanalysis* (New York: W. W. Norton, 1933), p. 85.

the fulminations of conscience? Compulsive scrupulosity seems, upon careful inquiry, to be regularly motivated by deeper, unacknowledged guilt;[3] and where self-accusations are manifestly false, they often turn out to be false in content only and to represent disguised or "displaced" versions of real transgressions.

In dealing with a divided, parted personality, it often seems helpful for a therapist to recognize that there are two (or more) "you's." This is well illustrated when the therapist in the present case says: ". . . in part you like yourself, in part you don't like yourself." He might equally have said, "You feel that a part of you is good, a part bad." Also, in respect to technique and attitude, it is noteworthy that the therapist is willing to give of himself. He is willing to give his time, to miss a meal, and, in the end, to suffer with the patient in her attempt to be whole. The extent to which this kind of involvement and sacrifice are a necessary aspect of the therapeutic act is something that deserves more attention than we have previously given to it.

RUTH MUNROE . . .

The therapist's handling of this situation seems very good. Presumably he (she?) gave the patient more reassurance than he reports and arranged for further contact—even the next day (Sunday) if she wanted it.

Slavish adherence to the rules of any therapy is poor policy in a crisis, especially with potential psychotics. Probably the more direct humanity of the therapist was as important here as his acute interpretation in saving the girl from a serious psychotic break. "Reality" for such patients does not go by the clock so much as by the quality of the interpersonal relationship.

Probably the stress of her first week at the university was the precipitating cause of the acute disturbance. It would be helpful to know which aspects of the new adaptation were most difficult. Also one would like to know what led up to the earlier psychotic break during the sixth interview. One cannot hope to "cure" such patients in brief psychotherapy, but perhaps one may hope to reinforce ego defenses in depth through the discovery and handling *with* the patient of areas of special vulnerability.

Disclosure of the incestuous relationship was certainly very important, but we are left to guess at its role in the dynamic structure of the patient's pathology. It cannot have been the sole determinant.

I like this therapist's handling of the acute situation better than the intimations he gives of an earlier client-centered approach. This approach

[3] J. W. Stafford, "Psychology and Moral Problems," *Homiletic and Pastoral Review,* II (1950), pp. 118–24.

has not seemed to me suitable for border-line psychotics. They can remain indifferent, but easily project their own attitudes. The therapist becomes "seductive" and/or "rejecting" out of all proportion to his actual behavior. I think he *must* be fairly active.

In cases of borderline paranoid schizophrenia—perhaps in this case *before* (not during) the acute episode reported—"intellectualizing" techniques seem appropriate. The therapist must be careful (1) to give as little handle as possible for paranoid elaboration, and (2) to check actively on any paranoid intimations whatsoever. The *spirit* should not be one of cross examination but of simple inquiry. "Can you tell me more exactly what you thought I said?" Then—"I must have been unclear . . ." with the request for *immediate repetition by the patient* of a new explanation. One may remark that this is the kind of comment patients often misunderstand, and so forth. The therapist should try to save the patient's face in such situations (reinforce and correct confidence in his ego judgments)—up to the point at which he feels it safe to make the paranoid trend itself a focus of interpretation. For this purpose I think that new material should be used. In fact the *patient's* introduction of past instances at this time are best met with the statement: "Maybe you're right. Those were early days." Relapses are likely, so one must avoid allowing the patient to develop the formulation: "You think I'm paranoid so you don't believe anything I say." Even if the trend is in fact rather generalized, the patient sees it better and with less totalistic ego resistance if it is brought out in limited situations. "You seem sometimes to turn what I say against yourself." "You seem to think 'whosit' doesn't like you [or is against you—however the patient has phrased it]. Any others who don't? Can we see what kinds of people you think don't like you? Maybe you're right, but maybe you're especially sensitive in some ways—and after all, we can't expect everybody to like us."

This relatively direct approach to the paranoid trend should be incidental to more general use of the "intellectualizing" technique. This case would probably have less spontaneous interest in other people's problems and theoretical concepts than the case in Chapter 23, but surely some of her remarks about her own feelings could be used to concretize the point that other people have such feelings too, that they often start in difficult situations in childhood, that children often feel unwanted, no good (whatever words the patient has used) because . . . continuing with *generalizations* reasonably close to the probable constellation of the patient's past. Such procedure *might* have elicited information about the traumatic incestuous experience earlier under conditions of greater ego control.

The main point, however, is building up a better perspective toward "reality," past and present, through transference to and participation in the therapeutic ego. Reflecting the patient's ideas, placing reality limits only on the immediate therapeutic situation, leaves the borderline psychotic patient with too little general ego support against impulses which are all too ready to come to the surface and take over. The potent tools of the client-centered approach should be used with special care to keep vividly emerging insights closely related to reality judgments and social adaptation. The inadequate ego structure of these patients seems to require a measure of *education*, not by lecture, but by direct connecting up of impulse and judgment through the solid reality of the therapist.

E. H. PORTER . . .

Every so often it is fun to conjecture about what factor or factors "precipitated" a particular bit of behavior, and I'm not above having a bit of fun.

The way I would see this situation is that Joan is under sufficient stress that she nearly arrives on time. This would, in, of, and by itself, appear to be a step in the direction of accepting responsibility for herself and accepting the therapeutic hour as an opportunity to be used rather than a situation to be fought and avoided.

At this point she is offered more time. This is the first occasion such an offer has been made. Where, before, the therapist has acted out the implication, "The 50 minutes I set aside is yours, use it as you will, but that is all the time I can give," now he makes an offer that has no clear time limit. "What can be in his mind? It's after 5:00 o'clock now. And on a Saturday. Will he act the same way too? God! How depressed can a person feel?"

But nothing irregular happens. There may be hope here. "Why is he asking me about the time? Just what does he want? Now he's suggesting it's time to stop talking—and start what? He sees how frightened I am. Even though I agree with what he says, my fear is not of his rejecting me; my fear is that if I simply just walk out, it might alienate him, and I don't dare stay and be 'dirty, no good, and horrible' again."

This mixture of unthought feelings are well calculated to find such symbolic expression as a lamb with one baleful eye and the other with "the wool pulled over it," and the faces saying, "Keep your mouth shut!"

So much for the fun on conjecturing as to whether or not the therapist's behavior was seductive. One can make a good case for it.

To me, the significant aspect of this case is that the therapist has, from the first, set a climate in which he has acted out, again and again, a respect for the client. He had demonstrated, repeatedly, an effort to understand rather than an effort to moralize or control. He has apparently felt sufficient self-confidence in his modus operandi to be able to part from a strict adherence to it. I feel strongly that it was the impact of the previous hours that made it possible for this young woman to stay in the "field" of facing her feelings rather than breaking off contact with the therapist. This event was therapeutic, but so were the thirteen previous hours. We would be mistaken if we presumed that this meeting was the one in which the therapy occurred. We might be quite correct, however, in saying that this was the meeting in which a lot of growth was demonstrated.

I should stop at this point, but I can't help wondering what the therapist learned from this dramatic hour. What perceptual-emotional reorganizations did he or she undergo? At least one, I think. To explore in this area we must now forget what the therapist says about the client and look at how he says what he has to say.

Let us look at the Discussion section. The therapist asks "Did the *indecisiveness* [italics mine] of the therapist lead . . ." The therapist could not have been more decisive in acting out his willingness to give completely of his time. He can be using the term *indecision* here only in the sense of *inconsistency with prescribed behavior*. This is Fact One. The therapist has conceptualized his behavior as inconsistent with what others (presumably the others here are Carl Rogers) say you should do. (But if I know Carl Rogers, he is not about to say what anyone should do—except to be as aware as one can about what one does, evaluate the effects of what one does as deeply as one can, and seek to follow only what one can learn for oneself.)

Next we see that the therapist asks, "Would a *firm, initial definition of the limits* [italics mine] by the therapist have cut off the possibility of the *intensive catharsis* which occurred during the last hour?" It is only in retrospect that the therapist can conceive of a *firm, initial definition of the limits*. If he or she had not felt at the moment like giving as much time as was wanted, but had "proceeded as usual" or had deliberately chosen to maintain the previously established limits, I feel most certain that the therapist would not have felt it at all necessary to initiate the interview with a *definition of the limits* in *firm* terms. The therapist's expression here suggests to me that he is conceptually setting aside the possibility that proceeding as usual could have resulted in anything else but a failure for the *intensive catharsis* to have appeared. His very use of the term *intensive catharsis* further suggests that he feels that a catharsis is a therapeutic achievement, that somehow it is a step in therapy, it is a thing to produce, it does good. (I, on the other hand, would conceptualize such a catharsis as evidence that the hours proceeding this one had created a climate which had literally taught the client a sufficient degree of security and freedom— that letting go was possible. The therapy, or perceptual reorganization, was *before* this point, not *at* this point.) This is Fact Two: the therapist

connects an apparently beneficial outcome with a deviation from prescription.

I think the therapist achieved a certain degree of independence from a
presumed prescribed therapeutic procedure as a result of this incident.
To my way of thinking, this is good. Maybe the therapist has learned to
act a little less like he thinks Rogers acts and more like he thinks he ought
to act for himself. (For those who conceptualize client-centered therapy
as a parcel of techniques, a prescribed way of acting, this I hope, will come
as a shock, a revelation, and a breath of fresh air!)

At this point, I'm quite sure I should stop. (If this doesn't appear in
print, I shall understand the editors' admonition to be brief.) However,
this seems like such an opportune time to talk about the difference between an interpretation and a reflection. The difference is not in what
the therapist says. The difference is in the therapist's *purpose* when he
says it.

When the therapist utters some words which are a construing of what
the client or patient has expressed and it is the therapist's purpose to be
asking of the client or patient whether or not the construction put on the
client's expression was the meaning intended—that's a reflection.

When the therapist utters some words which are a construing of what
the client or patient has expressed and it is the therapist's purpose to be
informing the patient what meaning his expression holds regardless of his,
the patient's, intended meaning—that's an interpretation.

Quarrel with me, if you will, on these uses of the terms (reflection,
interpretation) but don't quarrel with the distinction I try to make in
using them.

I get the impression that this therapist—when he relates what he said
to the patient—was trying to catch her meaning, but later—when he labels
the type of thing he said, that is, "The therapist *interpreted* [italics mine]
the client's . . ."—he is evidencing his freedom from the client-centered
"prescription." My conviction is increased as he goes on to say, "What
would have been the effect of *merely* [italics mine] reflecting the ideas
she was verbalizing." Obviously, in the eyes of the therapist "reflecting"
would have been only a *mere* response, hardly adequate to the occasion.

Just as clients and patients are, therapists are buffeted about by what
their experiences with others teach them about the true nature of reality.

I would ask one question here. How do we, on whom others count so
heavily, keep from fooling ourselves?

CARL ROGERS . . .

By and large, I like the way in which the therapist handled this deeply
moving and dramatic incident in the therapy of this young woman. I

think I know the reason why I respond favorably to it. It is because the therapist seems to have respect for his own feelings throughout the course of the incident. I am pleasantly surprised that he was able to maintain this respect for his own feelings even though he was having consultation with a psychiatrist throughout this period. It has been my experience that unless the supervisor handles the relationship with the therapist very therapeutically, supervision can lead to the counselor trying to behave in the way that he believes someone else wants him to behave. He becomes more supportive if the supervisor feels this should be done, or he becomes more interpretative or more acceptant or whatever. This, in my experience, is fatal to successful therapy. It is only if the therapist is transparently true to his own feelings in himself and about himself that the really critical points in therapy can be successfully lived through.

I would like to say a further word of explanation as to what I mean when I state that the therapist seemed to respect his own feelings. It appears evident that he felt genuinely willing to give the extra appointment and genuinely willing for it to be longer than usual. He seems, however, to have accepted his own feeling of puzzlement when Joan was unable to set any limit. He felt free to say that he was hungry at 7 o'clock and yet was also free to react in terms of his feeling of concern (which proved to be stronger than his hunger) when he observed her psychotic reactions to this suggested termination. Yet even after this experience he was willing again at 8 o'clock to express his pervasive feeling that he was again hungry and tired. I believe that it is basically because of this willingness on his own part to be genuine that the experience was therapeutic.

I react quite unfavorably, however, to the therapist's discussion of this incident. (At least, I assume the discussion was written by the therapist. If not, I'll have to change these comments slightly.) In the incident itself he reacted in terms of his feelings and did well. Afterward his raising of intellectual questions shows how far afield one can go from the real issues of therapy. In commenting on the questions which he raises, I would say that his indecisiveness in regard to the ending of the interview would have been a very unfortunate thing if it were a pose or a façade, but it is quite satisfactory as it occurs since it represented his own genuine feeling of uncertainty. I would also say that a strong initial definition of time limits would have been satisfactory if he had felt that he needed that degree of security, but I regard it as fortunate here that he could comfortably offer an extended time when he saw that the client was unusually disturbed.

As to his responses, he raises the question, "What would have been the effect of merely reflecting the ideas which she was verbalizing?" If this is supposed to raise a question about the client-centered point of view, then I would protest most vigorously. An empathic response is most certainly *not* the reflecting of the *ideas* which she was expressing. That seems to me like a perversion of the whole concept of client-centered therapy. Empathic acceptance is the endeavor to feel truly, in oneself, what is going on in the client and to respond in ways that will show that you are sensing in yourself what is going on in the other person. In this incident it most obviously was not words or ideas which were going on in her, but deep, overpowering, disorganizing feelings. As I see the therapist's responses, he made one honest attempt to understand what was occurring in her, but was evidently somewhat mistaken. Personally, I would not call this an interpretation because its intent seems to me to be clearly empathic. Perhaps this is only quibbling. In any event, her freedom to contradict him indicates to me that the relationship was fundamentally good. His second attempt to understand her was more perceptive and evidently helpful to her. With the wisdom of hindsight, one could suggest that the first response to her shaking and obvious disturbance and her statement regarding the mean and kind eyes which were staring at her might have been, "I guess this is an awful struggle in you—whether to control yourself as they want or to let go." This, too, may be erroneous in its understanding. At moments like this, one has to use all the radar sensitivity with which one's organism is equipped in order to sense from her words, her movements, her eyes, whatever it is that is so deeply disturbing her. I do not believe that accuracy of understanding in such complex moments can always be achieved. I believe the main element at a point like this is the therapist's *desire* to understand deeply, and it seems to me that this therapist shows such a desire.

I believe that this incident throws light on what therapy is—namely, living with a person on a real basis in an understanding relationship through the most awful moments of fear or disorganization or anger or whatever. For me it also throws light on the meaning of psychosis—that when the experiences which crowd in upon one are too devastating to the concept one has of oneself, then complete disorganization can occur unless there is a real relational contact with another person which involves full acceptance of oneself even in the worst moments of confusion. Thus, psychotic behavior can occur in a therapeutic relationship, but it does not persist unless this feeling of acceptance disappears.

On quite a different line of thought, one might raise the question "Suppose the therapist had had only 50 minutes that day and another client coming in at the end of that time?" In this case I believe that Joan would not have found it possible to reveal the experience that had been so troubling to her, but I believe it would have come out later. She might have needed another emergency appointment for this to occur. What I am trying to say here is that even in crucial moments, the therapist must accept himself; and if he has another client waiting for him, I doubt very much that he can give himself fully and acceptingly in a situation such as this. Consequently, he had better accept his own limitations and bring the interview to a close when his time is up. If, however, he is comfortable about extending it, then therapeutic results can occur.

WILLIAM SNYDER . . .

The most important aspects of this case are the questions of (1) whether a psychotic patient should be treated in an out-patient clinic specializing in client-centered methods, (2) whether the duration of the critical interview should have been so unstructured as to run on for three hours, and (3) whether interpretations made to the client should have been pitched "deeper" or less deep than those that were made.

On the first question, it is probable that the therapist was fairly well protected legally, since he was obtaining psychiatric consultation. From an ethical standpoint, however, the primary question was whether or not he was sufficiently well-trained to deal with this difficult a case. While it may be only the product of his systematic bias that causes him to appear quite unsophisticated and inexperienced (he was actually frightened by the client's hallucinatory episode), it is my opinion that he really was attempting to work with a case that was much too difficult for his level of experience. In this sense, legal protection does not eliminate the moral responsibility which this therapist had, to see that this highly disturbed client received more experienced help than he was able to provide. From a theoretical point of view, I would question whether a clinic which uses a client-centered approach exclusively is prepared to accept psychotic clients. There has not been sufficient evidence that the method is effective with these cases.

The three-hour interview I found most distressing to read about. There would seem to be very good reasons why time limits are necessary in therapy. Without accepting all of Rank's theoretical defense for his stand, his point has repeatedly been demonstrated. An unstructured duration to the interview is usually a highly threatening experience to the client, and to the therapist. This therapist became weak several times, excessively hungry, quite frightened, and, had things been less exciting, he probably would have become horribly bored in addition! No person can tolerate the necessity to give an unlimited amount of himself to others. Neither the body nor the spirit possess unlimited reserves. It is true that in emergencies, individuals in healing professions and life-sustaining occupations must anticipate extra demands upon their efforts. Generally, in the mental health area, however, such emergencies are handled within the confines of the institution, where an individual staff member can be relieved by another.

It is probable that the therapist's encouraging of an unlimited interview was, as he later suspected, a seductive action on his part. He mentions in his discussion the subject of transference, but he does not bring up counter-transference. This would have been most appropriate. It is obvious that there was a great deal. Mere devotion to duty is hardly a sufficient explanation for what took place.

As a graduate student, this critic, conducting therapy with his third client, allowed a session to run over to two hours, and in fact until the room grew quite dark. The client poured out his soul in describing a highly disturbed marriage situation. But he never returned for another interview. The therapist was told by his supervisor, a distinguished client-centered therapist, that it was not wise therapeutically to permit sessions to run on without a definite limit, and that it was not wise to conduct therapy in the dark!

Regarding the third question, whether interpretation should have been made on a "depth" level, it would be a matter of systematic bias as to how one would answer. One cannot take a position without first identifying his theoretic orientation. Most analysts would certainly favor the recognition of a transference and countertransference, but many would probably not have chosen to make an abrupt interpretation of this dynamic at this rather disturbed moment in therapy. Most client-centered therapists would have done exactly what this therapist did. Some rather extreme nondirectivists would have merely reflected the ideas the client was verbalizing. I would take the position that a gentle interpretation of the transference situation was probably called for at this point. The client's revealing of the incestuous behavior would seem to be justification. Interpreting transference at this point should hardly come as a traumatic or shocking revelation if it is judiciously handled. On the other hand *I* would not have been treating this obviously psychotic girl, because of my personal preference not to work with psychotics in therapy. A neurotic would have been less likely to explode in a dangerous way following such a revelation. Here is where the element of diagnostic and prognostic understanding of a case seems quite important. It does not seem reasonable for therapists to work with cases intensively unless they have a very clear understanding of the dynamics involved. It also seems most important that they have a sound theoretical structure upon which to base their therapeutic work. If the theory can be based on facts rather than wishes, it is more likely to prove tenable and durable as a long-term guide.

Frederick C. Thorne . . .

This incident describes a genuine emergency situation in psychotherapy where a patient is experiencing an acute upsurge or crisis in her conflicts which demands the most careful therapeutic handling. In this critical interview the therapist (who is presumably a clinical psychologist because he mentions referral to a psychiatrist) quickly became aware that the patient was acutely disturbed even to the point of a psychotic break with reality, and the therapist reports his own feelings of inadequacy and lack of understanding of the complex problem the client was faced with. In this situation the clinical psychologist could either terminate the interview as gently as possible and arrange for an immediate interview with a psychiatrist (which would have been inconvenient because of the lateness of the hour but which might have been the safest procedure in protecting the interests of all concerned) or he could strike while the iron was hot and give the client as much time as needed to ventilate her feelings and conflicts. The therapist apparently stumbled into the second alternative and was fortunate to have the emergency handling terminate in a favorable result.

In evaluating the dynamics of what occurred in this interview, it is apparent that the patient had been experiencing increasing anguish over her conflicts and had worked herself up to a point of unburdening herself. Given a sympathetic listener, it is probable that she would have ventilated her entire story with only a minimum of directive prompting or probing. In our opinion, it would have been safer not to have made the interpretations given by the therapist particularly since the therapist was not yet in any position to predict whether the catharsis would eventuate favorably or be followed by a complete psychotic break. However, once the patient got started in verbalizing her conflicts, the therapist did well to allow her to ventilate completely by disregarding such arbitrary limits as a 50 minute limit on the interview or the immediacy of the dinner hour.

Carl Whitaker . . .

Not interrupting the recurrent tardiness in the treatment of a patient is a technical error. This might have been accomplished either by administrative pressure or by cancelling a subsequent appointment after warning her. If this kind of structuring is not done, the patient dares not relax his restrictions on himself and regress to the necessary core phase lest the rest of the structuring be dumped in his lap. Although the therapist may have been justified in using the rest of the therapeutic hour to develop some symbolic relationship, it should have been apparent in a few interviews that the transference was not strong enough to alter her avoidance pattern.

To offer more than a single hour because of anxiety, and by even leaving the decision to terminate the interview up to the patient, the therapist was being "seductive" and breaking his own integrity on the patient's anxiety. Within the incident, the therapist's decision to use his own symptom formation; that is, hunger, as a basis for terminating the hour is good tech-nique.

The patient first expressed the pain of separation from the therapist and then her hope of change. In effect she said, "Do *you* think I can get along without you?" answering her own question by expressing the amount of improvement that had taken place in her living since leaving the therapist.

The therapist unconsciously defined the end of the hour by taking out his watch, but was unable to tolerate the patient's leave-taking, as shown by his perception of the ticking of the watch symbolizing the therapist's sense of aloneness. We owe the therapist sincere congratulations on being able to admit this weakness to the patient. Such honesty is extremely important even though it frightens the patient; it warns the patient that she must accept some responsibility for herself and some responsibility for the thera-pist also. In the therapist's notation that his heart was beating like a trip hammer he was expressing the fear that he himself was going into a panic state. The patient in her hallucination is obviously referring to the therapist who has two sides to himself; a mean side—that is, a mean eye, and a kind eye, or if you will a controlling father imago and a warm mother imago.

In his description of the closeness between them the therapist has not described the patient touching him during the period of what we would call the core phase of the therapy. Was not the patient at this point test-ing the incest feelings of the therapist? Did not the therapist's avoidance of the patient precipitate the subsequent increased effort at seduction by the patient as revealed in her story of her father's seducing her and her note that she was dirty? In this the patient was saying that the therapist need not be afraid of using her sexually; in fact, such incest with the therapist would relieve the patient of feeling so horrible and so lonely. The therapist could also be secure that the secret would be well kept; the patient would not even tell her mother or her grandmother. The final notation in this report indicates clearly that the incident was therapeutic for the therapist. The patient was engineering the whole situation on an unconscious level lest the therapist feel rejected. This was done in the same manner that an adolescent tolerates the immaturity of the parent who is crying at the time of the adolescent's leave-taking for college.

This is not the most effective professional therapeutic functioning, but a firm definition of time initially might have avoided the gains as well as the dangers of deeper involvement, and interpreting and reflecting ideas or other verbal efforts on the part of the therapist would only be a smoke screen in the face of the nonverbal give and take going on in this relation-ship. A relationship of this depth need not be evaluated point by point in terms of technical competence, because the process that is taking place is much more than technical.

A therapeutic relationship at this depth is generated and structured by the maturity of the therapist as a person and is brought into action by the pathological needs of the patient. Only the maturity of the therapist can tolerate the stress of this type situation. Techniques melt like butter. It might have been helpful if the therapist had been comfortable in offering to hold the patient and rock away the trembling.

One question remains: will the therapist be like so many others, treating one schizophrenic and then never trying it again?

"Hold Me!
Hold Me!"

4

History

When this patient entered psychotherapy, she was overwhelmed with anxiety about the disintegration which she was experiencing subjectively and which was markedly observable in facial tremors, shaking, and a cowering demeanor. Instead of presenting defenses to be interpreted or dealt with, she seemed almost completely undefended and vulnerable. In the first hour, content poured out of her revealing the severely traumatic nature of her early life and premarital years. It was only after several interviews that she was able to slow herself down to a normal speaking rate.

Her childhood had combined the deprivations of lower-class poverty with the suffering induced by a brutal, alcoholic, and generally irresponsible father and a negligent and narcissistically manipulative mother. The sordid history provided little to account for the straightforward honesty, self-awareness, and capacity for relatedness which made this woman readily reachable therapeutically. Her capacity for relatedness seemed to derive largely from her childhood closeness to her mother, of whom she had maintained a fantastically idealized picture. In view of this basic defense, the trauma of rejection was intensified when her mother turned her out of the home without a cent to shift for herself at the age of fifteen. She managed to find domestic work, and sought love from a variety of men, who subjected her to devaluating experiences. After rejecting sexual activity for some months, she found herself pregnant with the conception shrouded in amnesia. With an older sister, she left her home state and delivered the baby. She had planned to give it away but could not. She found work and eventually married a man of fair emotional stability, building a stable life for the first time.

The precipitating factors, which occurred more than a year before she entered therapy, were the severe illness of her younger son and the leg injury of her older son, then seven or eight. At that time, she apparently had a psychotic episode, involving the delusion that people were trying to kill her. There was spontaneous remission, followed by development of the anxiety state which brought her to therapy. There has been much somatic preoccupation.

There have been two outstanding crises so far during the therapy. The first, which cannot be recalled in detail, occurred after a year of working through content and reintegrating defenses. Out of what seemed like an impending psychotic break emerged a lost memory or screen memory that, before the death of a younger sister when the patient was four or five, the patient had considered stabbing her in the back with her mother's scissors. Subsequently, there was a complete recovery from a peculiarly nagging back pain she had had for years. However, also subsequently, there was development of arthritis in another back area, a trend toward rejection of dependence on the therapist, and an unrealistic turning to God.

The second crisis occurred after another year of work mainly on her relationship with her mother.

Incident

After a period of unusual well-being, the patient telephoned, badly disturbed because medical tests had indicated possible uterin carcinoma. She expressed fear of complete breakdown; but, in light of recent outstanding gains, I felt able to reassure her. Her therapy hour was due next day, and the medical diagnosis the following day. I gave the support that *together* we would wait for the test results and *together* we would face whatever came.

When she arrived for therapy, I was shocked by her appearance. There were no external anxiety symptoms, but there was the pallor of death, and her face and eyes were those of a person making the last futile, wild struggle for life. Her body seemed frail and limp with defeat. Instead of going to my chair, I touched her head in a gesture of sympathy, whereupon she put her head against my stomach and clung to me, releasing the sobs that had not been able to come. When she spoke, it was of her fear and of this final, terrible defeat after the long, uphill struggle. I spoke to her of faith and courage, of the fact that she might not have cancer, and of the fact that medical science was often able to deal successfully with cancer.

As I sat down, she moved to a position where she could clasp my hands and look directly into my eyes. As I saw the depth of her terror, I felt something that I had felt in my psychotic patients in a mental hospital. "Oh, Dr. —————, I'm so scared," she said; and then, as I spoke to her, she became very calm and began repeating my words in a trance-like voice, "Yes, I *can* have faith," she said, and I realized that for her the only reality was in my voice and in our hands, and in our eyes. As I felt the completeness of her psychological surrender, I realized with a sudden, internal jolt that she had entered a psychotic state. For just a second of time I felt fear and self-doubt, and then I thought, "Of course I can meet it—I can't let B. down." Her eyes were still fixed on mine in that unwavering stare, and the upsurge of strength I experienced went out to her, and then she relaxed and her eyelids flickered; and, as I watched her move and speak, I saw that she was not psychotic, and I felt that I had held her from the abyss of internal isolation on the edge of which she had wavered.

She moved back to her chair, stretched out in it, and spoke of the peace she now felt. I, too, felt a deep sense of peace and unity. She said that, for the first time, she was relaxed. Then, searching the limits of the safety she had found, she asked whether faith in God could keep her from having cancer. Feeling that she needed realistic authority, I told her I believed that God works through natural law; that, if she had cancer, He would not change that; but that He would be with her through the ordeal, if it came to that.

She said the conflicts over her mother now seemed so faraway and unimportant. We talked of various reality considerations; and then, as the hour drew to a close, she again expressed her fear and moved where I could hold her hands. This time the regression was much less severe, and she verbalized our relationship, "I am a little child, and you are my mother." She said also, "I get completely drained, and I come to you to replenish my supply of strength."

The next day, when we had received the negative test results, she spoke of having gained from the experience. She said, "I will never forget how I drew strength from you." She said also, "For the first time I really saw love and kindness in the world, and the old bitterness just seemed to melt away."

Discussion

The critical incident illustrates what I consider a definitive aspect of psychotherapy: the psychological union which provides soil for the growth of the patient's self. This therapeutic relatedness varies in depth according to the needs and capacities of the patient. In this situation, the patient manifested an unusually deep need and trust in the therapist. The reality factor that the probability of cancer was not high was much less real to the patient than the fear of destruction which had been activated, and it was necessary for the therapist to meet the patient at the level of the patient's feelings. A question may be raised regarding the appropriateness of this degree of physical contact. It seemed necessary, as a part of the bridge.

RUDOLF DREIKURS . . .

There can be no doubt that the handling of the incident provided an important therapeutic gain. The points which the therapist stresses in her discussion is the question of the psychological union fortified by physical contact, and the patient's manifested "unusually deep need and trust in the therapist." These elements, however, have to be understood in the context of the larger issues, namely, the patient's personality and fundamental problems. In regard to the limited issues, I can agree more or less with the therapist; but not so in the evaluation of the patient as a whole.

The union with the patient was emphasized by the therapist when she arranged the interview by telephone, in her statement that "together" they would wait for the test results and together face whatever came. During the interview a strong personal interaction and communication took place, from the clasping of the hands and gazing into the eyes, to the intensity of the voice and the emotional response to each other. It is not always clear as to who influenced whom. At least in the beginning, the patient's fear generated similar reactions in the therapist until the latter, with a deliberate effort, gained her own strength, and then could communicate this sensation to the patient, who began to relax.

This interaction deserves some scrutiny. It is not usual that the patient succeeds in generating in the therapist the same panic and fear from which she is suffering. Most therapists are sufficiently trained not to succumb to such influences, and remain calm regardless of how upset the patient may be. In this regard the therapeutic relationship is fundamentally different from the usual interpersonal relationship in which an excited and upset person generally succeeds in creating the same emotions in his environment. There seems to be one area in which the therapist is often prone to succumb to the patient's frightening influence. This is a moment when a psychotic reaction is considered imminent or present. Despite all educational influences which psychiatrists have exerted in enlightening the public in regard to psychosis, trying to eliminate prejudice and fear, they have often failed to free themselves from emotional reactions which they try to combat in public. Consequently, they often get frightened by a patient who is afraid or in danger of a mental collapse. In this incident the therapist caught herself in time and was then able, by her own emotional calmness, to calm down the patient. Physical contact probably serves two purposes; it fortifies the process of intense communication, particularly facilitating a calming and encouraging influence of the therapist, and it expresses warmth and sympathy and involvement. All these factors are essential in any therapeutic crisis, if not—to a certain extent—for the therapeutic process as such. Encouragement is, in our opinion, an integral part of any successful therapeutic effort, and most needed and important in moments of despair.

While the benefit of the interaction during the incident is obvious, its significance for the total therapeutic process may be uncertain. The crucial question is the significance of the patient's statement that she drew strength from the therapist. She comes to her to replenish her supply of strength which was completely drained. These remarks are innocuous on the surface; but seen within the framework of the total personality, their significance has to be carefully weighed.

Naturally, it is difficult to derive a reliable picture of a patient on the basis of information which has been collected within a different orientation. Much needed information is missing and what is provided appears in a different light from our point of view. The available information of her childhood reflects primarily the judgmental attitudes of the therapist who uses many critical adjectives to describe father and mother. Nothing is said about the patient's interaction with them, as if she were merely a passive recipient. No information is available about her interaction with her siblings, within the total family constellation. It is, therefore, not surprising that the therapist herself does not comprehend the formative years and openly admits her lack of understanding by stating that the "sordid history provided little to account for the straightforward honesty, self-awareness, and capacity for relatedness" of the patient. Although a year had been spent "working through content and reintegrating defenses," we have no evidence for any perception of the patient's personality and main problems. From a few items it seems that this patient is operating on the basis of high ideals and a deep sense of her own responsibility, depending entirely on her own strength, trusting neither life nor fate nor people. She idealized her mother whom the therapist describes as "negligent and narcissistically manipulative." We can see how good the patient tries to be, probably better than the people who take advantage of her. In this sense, we can see why she managed to get abused by men. She is probably an easy victim for anyone who treats her badly, because then she can feel morally superior. Indications are that she is suffering from a martyr complex, provoking and seeking abuse and defeat. The only early recollection indicates how she had to fight against asserting herself, otherwise she may become a murderess, as bad or worse as the people who abuse her. She has to be good and take care of others. (This, by the way, is a frequent personality pattern of people suffering from arthritis; and we find indications for such condition here, too.)

The "incident" is related by the therapist as having significance during an exploration of the patient's relationship to her mother. Its conclusions are described as establishing the patient as a child and the therapist as a mother, a better mother than her real one. From our point of view, the significance of the incident appears in an entirely different light. It is related to the problem of death. People who put all their faith in their own strength, who have to control because they cannot rely on any beneficial influence outside of themselves, are usually deathly afraid of death. They can escape from and conquer all other forces; but they cannot escape from succumbing eventually to this force. Death, being killed, having to die, is the main source of their panic. Nowhere do we find in this report any realization of this obvious dynamic element. The therapist realizes the patient's feeling of defeat, her expression "of this final, terrible defeat"—but she does not recognize its significance, as she failed to understand the patient's attempt to make peace with God, with fate, by considering such effort first "an unrealistic turning to God" and then, discussing faith in God in a sophisticated way, distinguishing between natural law and the unrealistic authority of God, considerations completely foreign to the concern of the patient, who is trying to make peace with fate, be it naturalistic or supernatural.

Now we can see the potential danger of the patient's reactions to the therapist, by assuming that she can draw strength from her when her own strength is drained. Naturally, such second-hand strength would serve her well; it does not in any way correct her mistaken assumption that she needs strength, or she is lost. She merely puts the therapist in her service as a new source of the strength which she needs to fight life singlehandedly. She apparently has not gained insight from this incident, that there are other things to rely on besides the assumption of one's own controlling strength. But without such insight and reorientation the patient cannot expect to make a better adjustment to life. For this reason, the therapeutic effect of this incident is subject to reasonable doubt. The therapist gave her strength, but no insight or need reorientation.

J. W. KLAPMAN . . .

Whether it is due to keen native intelligence, constitutional or hereditary origin, or to repeated emotional traumata, some individuals seem to possess a razor-edge sensibility. Because of it, every slightest nuance of the emotions is explored and sounded out, the sharp prick of every spicule experienced. This patient seems to have either possessed or achieved such a keen sensibility. So poignantly does she feel the emotional deprivation of a defaulting mother that she had to create a mythical parent and to invest her with all the desirable qualities.

Reacting so intensely she probably balanced precariously on the very thin edge of reality. In such acute conflictual storms, the line between reality and nonreality becomes very indistinct at times, and thus the transient outbreaks of psychosis. But it must also be noted that it is that excrutiating sensibility, often masochistically determined but so poignant that every variation of emotions is painfully felt, which is the very means of escape from unreality, and morbidity as well, and which makes psychotherapy effective. The relatively insensitive individual who is precipitated into a psychosis is proportionately lacking in this aid to the integrative process and would be correspondingly resistive to the therapeutic process. This is true despite the fact that the therapy of this patient took a considerable amount of time to achieve the results noted.

When the patient is presented with the near-ultimate threat of extinction via cancer, in the storm thus precipitated all reference points and anchorages seem to be swept away. At this critical moment the touch of the therapist becomes an earnest of the tangible reality she has lost contact with. It is perhaps a meeting of minds and feelings which informs the patient of another's sympathy, of another's ability to explore the same reaches of feeling; of having safely negotiated the uncharted distances. That intimates that the suggested reference points and anchorages are trustworthy.

Perhaps, after all, there is more balm in the "laying on the hands" than our objective bias allows us to admit.

Ruth Munroe . . .

I would agree entirely with this therapist's position that such a patient in a realistic crisis (which must have seemed to put the seal of finality on a life of cruel disappointments and defeats) needed as direct a "psychological union" with a strong, loving person as possible. As for the physical contact —it is natural even in a normal crisis situation "too deep for words." It is very useful, perhaps necessary, in reaching some psychotics. While observing at a school for schizophrenic children, I was fascinated by the effectiveness of an affectionate arm around the shoulders, a brief, cheerful hug, a restraining hand accompanied by a knowing smile in bringing out a more socialized response or in forestalling an explosion.

Although firmly against the Reichian approach in general, I must confess to an unholy interest in the possibilities of a direct attack on the "body armor" for stubborn cases of *obsessive-compulsive neurosis,* and to the wish that they could be explored in a different theoretical framework. Our fears of uncontrollable transference and counter-transference reactions to physical contact are doubtless justified, but perhaps it will eventually become a feasible adjunct to therapy in some situations for some patients.

In this situation the therapist was able to bring the patient back to the reality problem through tactful interpretation of her faith in God. Apparently, the connection with the loving mother was made spontaneously, and remained as the kind of profound emotional re-education Ferenczi came to consider so important. A personality so severely damaged cannot become "mature" overnight, but a very significant shift in basic orientation may have occurred. "The old bitterness just seemed to melt away."

The awkward therapeutic problem with such vivid reaction to the therapist as "mother" is the tendency of the patient as "child" to demand constantly renewed proof of love in an increasingly concrete manner. The therapist in this instance was "fortunate" in having a crisis in which her human help could not avail, so the transference reaction was essentially emotional. No pattern of practical help or sympathy with the patient in interpersonal struggles was involved. Such situations are rare and unpredictable. Whereas it is to be hoped that most therapists would show a similar directness in similar situations (see Chapter 3), it is clearly not a technique for everyday use. In my opinion a bit of humanity rarely harms and often helps the therapeutic relationship, but its general structure should be kept firm. After any major deviation from the rule of friendly professional objectivity, the therapist must take careful stock of the effect on the transference and either try to lead it back gently to the general rule or consider very seriously (consultation may help) the special requirements of continuing the deviation.[1]

Because I see my personal contribution to this book as discussion of "intellectualizing" techniques, I mention again the appeal to the patient's reason in the therapist's comment that God works through natural law. Utter faith in the supporting figure is here qualified in a manner the patient's *ego* can accept. The "unrealistic" turning to God is not repudiated, but used to give further reinforcement to the ego in its struggle to handle an unbearable threat. In reasonably qualifying God's help, the therapist qualifies her own magic as just "being with her during the ordeal." Incidental to the main dynamics of the session and quite possibly foreign to the therapist's way of thinking, this "intellectualization" probably played an important role for the patient in recovering and maintaining control.

DAVID RIESMAN . . .

I am not a clinician and have had no experience as a therapist—save in the occasional role of a teacher to whom a student in despair may turn and where I have sometimes tried to administer first aid before turning the student over to a more experienced helper. In this incident, as in a number of others, I am struck as I have often been by the kind of quiet courage which therapists take for granted in facing, alone and with no equipment and protection other than their own selves, the most mysterious, the most obdurate, the most agonized, and often the most opaque patients and clients. Their situation resembles that of an anthropologist who goes to a distant tribe whose language he does not know, whose reasons for laughing and crying he can only guess, and who may for all he knows believe in the witch or sorcerer or have no adequate interpretation of such disinterestedness as his. (See for a most moving and sensitive report on these confrontations *Return to Laughter,* a book whose author protects her tribe and perhaps herself by the pseudonym of Elinore Smith Bowen.)

So in this incident the therapist is dealing with a patient from a "tribe" radically different from her own. In her articulateness and determination the patient has inched closer to this world (conceivably, through some of the men who have exploited her but who may have come from strata to which she would not otherwise have had access). When I read the therapist's reference to "an unrealistic turning to God" it struck me that she (the therapist) was perhaps too cavalierly rejecting a resource on which the patient's mother may have fallen back and which, in the few alternatives open to the patient, may have represented a kind of "native's

[1] See K. R. Eissler, "The Effect of the Structure of the Ego on Psychoanalytic Technique," *J. Amer. Psychoanal. Ass.,* I (1953), pp. 104–43.

return." Thus, I was all the more struck that the therapist during the critical incident did not reject the patient's theistic vocabulary, but reinterpreted it in a way which gave the patient both realism and strength. The feeling gained in the incident—that she had, almost as it were by main force, held the patient from going over the abyss—makes good sense to me. In the kind of support she then provided—courageously in view of her own verbal training—support which was at once moral and physical, this must have meant an immense amount particularly to a person of lower class origin, a woman for whom abstract concepts are perhaps an even later form of communication than they are for most of us. That the patient had earlier kept her illegitimate child at a time when it would have been more "rational" for her to surrender it would seem another indication that she had, in the face of the malice and negligence of her upbringing, a deep need for relatedness (in Erich Fromm's sense). Is it possible also that in that moment when she made contact with the therapist (the "moment of truth" as the bull fighters say) she realized she would let the therapist down if she did not pull herself together? For her own part it must have seemed as if life wasn't worth living if she was to have cancer after all she had struggled through, like being bombed out for the second time. And possibly, not being quite Job, she felt that God had let her down—but then she saw that the therapist also needed her.

CARL ROGERS . . .

In my judgment, what a therapist has to offer is what he deeply and truly feels in himself. This is the integration which exists in him at the moment and this is what he can provide in the relationship. I further have found that the therapist has the most to offer when what he transparently feels is a warmth and concern for his client, a willingness to accept the otherness of this person no matter how bizarre or deviant the feelings and behavior may be. It seems to me that this therapist had such feelings as far as one can tell from the description, and consequently was able to offer the client a relationship in which these feelings were very much evident. It sounds to me as though the therapist was quite comfortable in touching the client, letting the client sob against her, not because these are good or bad techniques, but because the therapist was operating genuinely at the time and basing her behavior on what existed in her. I have assumed from some phrases in the description that this is a female therapist, but it would make no difference to me whether the therapist was male or female. A male therapist might be somewhat more unlikely to feel entirely comfortable in touching and holding a female client, but the criterion would remain the same. If it seemed a natural and entirely comfortable reaction, it would, in my judgment, be therapeutic.

As to the client being in a psychotic state for a few moments, I regard this as perfectly possible, but I wonder about the order of events. I would suspect that there is a slight inversion in the account as to how this occurred. I would regard it as likely that when the therapist saw the depth of her client's fear, that then the therapist began to experience some fear and self-doubt, some tendency to see the client as an object rather than relating to her as a person. At that moment a psychosis becomes real in the client, for in that moment the only real human relationship is broken and the isolation is both terrible and disorganizing. But when the therapist's courage returns (and I am sure that all of us have at times lost that courage, at least briefly), then it is quite true that the psychosis is no longer present because the client is again in a real, human relationship.

Since these ideas about psychosis may seem unusual, I would like to comment a bit further. I feel there is little doubt but that heredity, constitutional makeup, and chemical factors all have a part in the predisposition to psychosis. I feel, however, that psychologically a psychosis occurs when human relationships break down. It is as though the client were saying "When there is no one who dares to accept me in my awful separateness, then I am no longer a self and disorganization must take over." It is my conviction, however, that the reverse is also true. In the reverse situation it is as though the client were saying "As long as there is one person who can feel, deeply and viscerally, that he can accept me as a person, and I can realize and experience his attitude, then I possess a self and I cannot go over the brink."

In my judgment, nothing was added by the therapist when she expressed things which she could not know. The contrast, to me, seems sharp. When she placed her hand upon the client's head, she was expressing her own feelings which she knew at first hand in a very primary and incontrovertible way. There could not be the same reality in the therapist when she says, for example, that God will be with the client. This is something which she could not know in the same primary way. In my estimation, it would have had more meaning had the therapist gone with the client in her questioning, empathically accompanying her in her uncertainty as to whether God could or would keep her from having cancer. To live with a person in such uncertainty, sharing with him the weight of his own unsureness and doubt, is to me far more therapeutic than to be reassuring. I see the therapist's handling of this particular aspect of the incident as being a measure of the limitation of the therapist's confidence in and respect for the client. Evidently, she could not quite trust the client to be a separate and autonomous person and felt she must give her at least this much external support and reassurance. I regard this as a relatively minor criticism, however. The main test of the therapist was in living with this woman, intimately and understandingly, in her desperateness and psychotic terror. This test the therapist met very well indeed.

FREDERICK C. THORNE . . .

We question whether this was a critical incident in the sense interpreted by its author who emphasizes "the psychological union which provides soil for the growth of the patient's self," presumably by drawing strength from the therapist. In our opinion, the behavior of the patient was indulged in completely for her own purposes and as an expression of her compulsive need to be supported. This patient had always been over-expressive emotionally and totally "undefended and vulnerable," and this behavior may be interpreted as defense by an open admission of weakness, that is, throwing herself on the mercy of others to gain sympathy and support. In moments of increased anxiety or panic (as when cancer was suspected) she would melodramatically act out her need for dependency and protection.

In our opinion, the therapist should limit such physical contacts as the holding of hands or allowing the client to cry on his bosom. This may be accomplished by soothing words and gently leading the client to her chair, thereby encouraging the client to contain herself. Needs for dependency and help may be reflected nondirectively. Such a person should be helped to help himself. To allow the patient to achieve support by physical intimacy, no matter how limited the degree, would appear to weaken the client's attempts to unify himself independently by assuring him that his dependent needs will be taken care of. To allow it to happen once or twice, as in this case, is probably not crucial, but recurring episodes should not be tolerated.

Socratic Therapy

5

History

The patient was a 27-year-old male college student who suffered from a moderate to severe case of mixed psychoneurosis. There were a great many varied symptoms. Among them predominated ruminations, scrupulosity, perfectionism, and depressive spells.

Incident

The patient came very often to the interviews in a condition that for my own illustration I had called the "blues streak." It has been my contention that the manipulation of the mood during interviews is an integral part of the therapy. I have been able to develop a series of devices in such a way that it is uncommon for my patients to leave the sessions of psychotherapy in an angry anxious, or depressed mood. Actually—and without forcing the reality of their situation—they often leave the interview in an optimistic and hopeful mood. In the session I am about to refer to I had occasion to discover another device for the modification of depressive moods. During the interview the patient was expressing something akin to the following:

P—I do not see how you can help me, I do not see how anyone could help me. I am afraid this is the way I am and will not be able to change. I shall always allow myself to be led and ordered and then I will punish myself for allowing

76

it. I am always afraid of failure and I do not like myself when I try to be nice. . . .
[Here the therapist interrupted.]
T—Is that the way you always see yourself?
P—What do you mean?
T—I mean this: you are telling me the way you see yourself now, at this moment, but, is that the way you see yourself all the time? Are not there other times that you feel different?
P—Of course there are times I feel different but that does not help me now.
T—Then tell me, what is the difference between such times and now?
P—Well, I don't know, I just feel different.
T—Then it is only a way of feeling that makes the difference. Do you know how people call these ways of feeling which so much change their outlook?
P—I do not know what you want me to say.
T—Well, what do you think of the word "mood"? What does it mean?
P—Well, it means something like what you were talking about, a way of feeling.
T—Now then, if you were in a different mood, would you say the same things about yourself that you are saying now?
[Here the patient seemed to see the entire situation in one sweep. When he spoke I noticed a change to a better mood.]
P—You mean that I feel about myself the way I do because I am in a low mood and that I am not the way I say I am.
T—You *can not be* that way since you just told me that at other times you consider yourself in quite a different light.
P—I can see what you mean, but tell me more.
[Here I broke out with an extemporaneous speech to tie up the suddenly realized knowledge with certain facts of the general psychology of emotions. I spoke clearly and confidently and concluded as follows:]
T—So we know that under certain moods and emotional conditions our thinking is led to exaggerations. In depressive moods, for instance, reality is completely biased and the individual portrays himself far lower than he actually is. You see, you *are not* the way you just told me now, it is only because you are in such a mood that the exaggeration appears.
P—Then I do not need to worry about the way I see myself now since this is just the result of a mood?
T—*Right!* And therefore you must never take such thinking seriously at such times. It is unrealistic.

After these remarks the patient was transformed and for the rest of the hour the "blues streak" was gone and was substituted by an intense and enthusiastic interexchange of suggestions on how to avert future depressive spells. Interestingly enough he became fascinated by the possibility of applying such insight in helping other people beside himself. In this hour the following plan was arrived at cooperatively and followed: (1) Whenever the patient felt blue he would sit down and write his thoughts about himself. (2) He would also sit down and write about himself when feeling particularly good.

In this way we accumulated a great deal of direct, individualized evidence regarding the unreality of the self image during blue spells, and this very direct evidence was most convincing to the patient. He and I were even able, in later interviews, to discover other characteristics of the way he thought while in blue spells which were absent when he felt well. Thus while in a blue spell he felt: (1) more self-conscious, (2) far more aware of his defects, physical or otherwise, and (3) an increase in logical ability—a true speeding up of the ability for induction and deduction, which reminded me of the uncanny ability displayed by the obsessive-compulsive in his ruminations, and by the paranoid in his delusions.

It is fair to note that out of this incident alone and its sequel the blue spells diminished in frequency, intensity, and duration, and the patient faced them with an increased confidence.

Discussion

With this incident I want to exemplify the use of the Socratic method in psychotherapy, and the importance of dealing with the "ongoing" situation as much, or more than, with the historical factors, such as childhood experiences.

The Socratic method is usually described as an inductive approach to generalization by means of a dialogue. The dialogue which led to a more adequate definition of the "blues streak" and its consequences is the example in this case. One difference, however, is that in the Socratic method, Socrates spoke approximately 95 per cent of the time. The other member of the pair usually limited himself to agree with or to state the conclusions to which the thinking of Socrates led. In the incident described one can see a greater cooperation on the part of the patient. Here too, however, the therapist, making use of his greater experience or knowledge, leads the patient by questions to the therapeutic insights. In my experience the patient often cooperates even more, and often it is he who gives the striking answers or observations on the problems set. In this case the patient's later ability to discover by himself some of the characteristics of his thinking while in blue spells is a good example. I should add that the use of this modified Socratic procedure has often made my patients capable of applying the same procedure to the problems of life after the cessation of the psychotherapy.

The value of dealing with the "ongoing" situation cannot be over-emphasized. Although I, too, dedicate many of the beginning sessions of psychotherapy to elucidate the childhood experiences and the interaction of the patient with his parents and other members of his household in the successive stages of his development, I have found myself dedicating an ever increasing portion of the sessions to the problems that the patient faces in his everyday life—his actions and his reactions to himself and to others. The incident here discussed shows that simply elaborating the way the patient felt at this particular interview led to his overcoming a mood and to the development of a device and a plan of action which later proved of value in his case. Dealing with the problems of the patient as they come favors the development of such devices. Finally one can not close his eyes to the valid and realistic ego boosting which is the natural result of discovery and which is favored by the cooperative development of insights which can be put immediately to work upon the immediate problems of the patient.

ALBERT ELLIS . . .

Of all the critical incidents in this volume, this incident is the one which I have personally been most gratified to read: doubtlessly because it outlines a method of handling therapeutic situations which is closest to that which I myself have used for years. My own method, which I generally call rational psychotherapy, but which at more than one public meeting I have likened to the Socratic dialogue, was independently arrived at in spite of, and certainly not because of, my psychological and psychotherapeutic training, which originally was of a fairly orthodox psychoanalytic stamp. I am always gratified to discover that other psychotherapists, who also were raised in one or another of the orthodox schools, have independently discovered that these orthodoxies simply do not work too well, and that some highly unpublicized procedures, such as this Socratic method, are considerably more effective.

What, essentially, must be done in psychotherapy is to change the patient's attitudes, especially his attitudes toward himself and others. This can be done by a variety of ways, including even highly nondirective techniques. But one of the main, and curiously enough often neglected, methods of changing an individual's irrational and illogical attitudes is convincingly to *show* him how he is starting with wrong premises and/or making mistaken conclusions from them. This is what the Socratic method, when effectively used, does beautifully.

In this case, for example, the therapist, after listening to the patient's false generalizations—which amount to the fact that just because he has acted a certain way in the past he must continue to act that way in the future—convincingly demonstrates to the patient that "you *can not be* that way since you just told me that at other times you consider yourself in quite a different light." In other words, the therapist shows the patient how illogical, starting from the patient's *own* premises, his thinking is. This *direct* manner of demonstrating the patient's illogical *retention* of his symptoms is radically different from the usual interpretative technique of merely showing him how he originally *acquired* these symptoms; and it is usually much more effective in getting him to *change* his behavior.

As the therapist in this instance also accurately points out, although the history of how the patient got the way he did has some importance, the problem of his current everyday life—or why he *remains* the way he once got—is in many respects even more important. It is this aspect of psychotherapy which is much too often seriously neglected. My own feeling is that once therapists start consistently concentrating on the irrational thinking of the patient in the here and the now, and why and how he unconsciously keeps thinking in ways that are harming when he erroneously believes that he is thereby helping himself, most of the problems of psychotherapy will begin to be quite soluble. The Socratic or rational method of psychotherapy briefly and admirably outlined in this case has, I am convinced, a most important future.

O. HOBART MOWRER . . .

One of the encouraging things about the field of psychotherapy at the present time is the extent to which new, highly unorthodox methods are being tried out. The present incident is a particularly refreshing and suggestive example.

Recently the present writer came upon an aphorism to this effect: "It is easier to *act* your way into a new way of thinking than to *think* your way into a new way of acting." Perhaps this might be rephrased for the present discussion as follows: "It is easier to act your way into a new way of *feeling* than to feel your way into a new way of acting." Here the therapist is, in effect, refusing to take the client's mood very seriously and is clearly proposing that he look to his actions rather than to his feelings.

All of this is, of course, contrary to the view, expressed to the writer some years ago by an analytic friend, that "While insight is not necessarily a guarantee of readjustment, readjustment never occurs without it." Here the emphasis is quite explicitly upon thinking and, at least implicitly, upon feeling. Behavior is clearly seen as consequential rather than, in any sense, causal. Although Freud was never a stimulus-response psychologist in any formal sense of that term, yet the kind of thinking just cited involves something of the same view of causality: behavior is, so to say, an end result. But we are now thinking increasingly about the *feedback* from behavior. Thorndike, of course, sensitized us to one kind of feedback, or effect, as he called it; and we are now also becoming aware of the great importance of the more immediate stimulus consequences of action, as opposed to the more or less remote consequences which we call rewards and punishments. Although this kind of thinking has not as yet been worked out so that it readily articulates with the approach to the problem of moods exemplified in the present case report, nevertheless it gives to such an approach at least a readier plausibility and comprehensibility.

It is undoubtedly true that, in one sense, feelings do control behavior; but it is equally true that, in another sense, behavior controls feelings. It is probably too much of an oversimplification to assume that, for example, merely *acting* happy *makes* one happy; but it can hardly be denied that acting in certain ways brings gratifying reactions from others, and that acting in other ways has the reverse effect. Certainly in our generation there has been a too primal emphasis upon how we *feel*, rather than upon how we *do*.[1] In one of his books, Henry Link[2] tells of a bust of Socrates at Princeton University with the familiar "Know thyself" under it which had, however, been scratched out and replaced by "Behave yourself." And, as a further illustration of the way earlier generations viewed such matters, Harry Emerson Fosdick, in his recently published autobiography,[3] relates the following incident. When Fosdick was a boy, his father, on starting to work one morning, called back to his mother and said: "Oh, by the way, tell Harry to mow the lawn this afternoon if he feels like it—and that he'd better feel like it." While this do-or-die attitude sometimes had its unhappy consequences or "side effects," the present-day over-evaluation of *feeling* has probably been far more unfortunate.

At least one young psychiatrist whose work on the rehabilitation of deteriorated schizophrenics is rapidly coming into prominence[4] takes the view that this most dreaded of personality disorders is simply the terminal state of progressive abandonment of responsibility. Of course, sometimes it is not easy to tell the difference between our real responsibilities and our false unessential ambitions and desires.

Finally, we note with interest in the present report the therapist's growing conviction about the importance of the "on-going situation" as opposed to the common emphasis upon the individual's past. One of the appeals, no

[1] J. A. Gingerelli, "Psychoanalysis: Dogma or Discipline?" *Saturday Review*, March 23 (1957), pp. 9–11.

[2] Henry Link, *The Return to Religion* (New York: The Macmillan Co., Inc., 1936).

[3] Harry E. Fosdick, *The Living of These Days* (New York: Harper & Bros., Inc., 1956).

[4] J. M. Sher, "Schizophrenia and Task Orientation: An Experimental Study of a Structured Ward Setting," *AMA Arch. Neurol. Psychiat.* (1957).

doubt, of the latter approach is that it relieves the patient of "responsibility" for his predicament—but, alas, also relieves him of *hope*, hope for self-directed change and improvement. If parents, religion, society, or the like is to "blame" for one's personal difficulties, then, by the same token, the only cure is some form of "treatment," again by an outside agency. Although we have as yet only a meager theoretical understanding in such matters, there is something which one intuitively senses as invigorating and healthy about the general approach and philosophic outlook presented in this report. Of course, individuals do indeed sometimes reach a point at which we rightly say that they are not responsible for their actions; but it now looks as if there is a large twilight zone of sickness in which individuals are still "responsible" but do not act *responsibly*. Brute, empirical fact seems to be reasserting itself in this connection and to be giving us a somewhat more sympathetic and respectful view of many of the values and precepts of our forebearers which we so largely dismissed in the second and third decades of this century.

RUTH MUNROE . . .

The "Socratic method" employed successfully in this interview is an example of what I have called "intellectualizing" techniques. I would agree with the importance of the "valid and realistic ego boosting" involved in the patient's self discovery, but would be inclined to stress further the aspect of *cooperative* development—that is, the transfenerce.

It would seem to me, however, that this particular form of "intellectualization" should be used very *selectively*. In the present instance the "blues streak" and self-disparagement are parts of a complex dynamic picture. Probably they serve as a sort of neurotic solution for his problems, perhaps as a weapon against the therapist. With a different psychological constellation behind the depression (that is, psychosis or acute mood disturbance), sustained pressure toward logical thought could become very burdensome. The demand for continued thinking may seem to the patient just too much, leading to very concrete and devastating recognition of his own inadequacy, and/or hostility toward a therapist who knows it all and asks such a lot. I am sure this therapist would agree that the technique should be used only in sensitive response to active interest.

Exception might be made, perhaps, for sparing use as a kind of deliberate pressure with some kinds of intellectualizers, somewhat like this one, literally forcing them to painful insights. But then one must stand by with reassurance for the wounded ego, as well as sympathy and support, that is, "How fine that you were able to see this. . . . This will really help the therapy. . . . I think you're probably right about this trend, but after

all it's generally human. . . . Let's see how you've been handling it. . . ."
—with a leading Socratic dialogue about the patient's *assets*, not as cover-ups but as involving *real* good feeling, intelligence, and so forth. The re-assurance is especially important if the patient has reached deeper levels of insight than the one reported here.

Socrates was more interested in his ideas than in his interlocutors. They must often have felt trapped and resentful, unconvinced by the logic which seemed to come from their own mouths. The therapist must be extremely careful to avoid this impression. Many patients would rather be told some-thing straight than feel that they are being led by the nose into insights prefigured in the therapist's mind. It must often be difficult for the patient to preserve a genuine sense of spontaneity through a long series of system-atic questions. (Note that even this patient remarks: "I don't know what you want me to say.") Unless he achieves a very vivid feeling of *discovery* such as comes rarely in prolonged therapy—an informative speech may further induce a mood of intellectual learning or critical debate foreign to the therapeutic process. It may work against true insight.

Although this therapist is clearly able to use a modified Socratic method flexibly and creatively, imitators might easily become rather too Socratic. The pointed question is one of our most effective means of interpretation. In general, however, I feel that the prolonged series should be avoided. One can usually accomplish the same results with a less systematic logical approach, phrasing a few simple questions in such a manner as to start the patient "thinking," but in close relationship to his immediate feelings. One may often fruitfully share one's special knowledge and experience with the patient, but usually more by intimation than by a didactic speech. I some-times use or pick up from the patient some big psychological word and ask him what it means. Sometimes this is enough, sometimes one must ask further, "How does this apply to you?" The patient's definition often gives the clue to a clinical definition *appropriate at the moment*, which the thera-pist may adopt with some distortion of scientific usage—not so far off, however, that the patient could sniff out a rat in later reading.

The point is to enlist the patient's ego on the side of the angels. For most patients this is accomplished more effectively, I think, by a broad sharing of a benign, understanding approach *with* the therapist, utilizing the transference, than by guided logic and scientific instruction more defi-nite than any of us can fully justify in our slippery field.

E. H. Porter . . .

This case is presented in order "to exemplify the use of the Socratic method in psychotherapy and the importance of dealing with the 'ongoing' situation as much or more than with the historical factors, such as childhood experiences."

For some years I have proposed that perceptual reorganizations take place only when apparently unrelated elements can be brought into juxtaposition. Certainly the therapeutic hour with its opportunity for the consideration of apparently unrelated elements is a setting more likely to promote perceptual reorganization than is an everyday life situation in which contrasts are not so immediately experienced.

Is it not widely agreed that emotional-perceptual reorganizations are much more likely to occur when the emotional elements are present? The therapist is stating here that when a patient talks about how he *felt* some time in the past, little is to be accomplished by dealing with such ghosts. The client-centered therapist would hasten to agree. However, he would probably not need to be urged to point out that the feelings with which *he* deals in such an instance are the feelings the client has *now* about the feelings he had earlier, so that the client-centered therapist is always dealing (or trying to) with the "ongoing situation."

I am tempted, at this point, to reconstruct the patient's flow of words in a manner typical of that found in client-centered therapy as an illustration of how the same emotional-perceptual reorganization could have occurred in the absence of a Socratic approach. I choose deliberately to desist, however, since it would be artificial at best, and because we have numerous examples of phonographically recorded and transcribed client-centered interviews which illustrate the process in fact.

Let us turn to this therapist's rather amazing statement (amazing in that he writes as if he felt himself to be the director of the therapeutic process): "Finally one cannot close his eyes to the valid and realistic ego boosting which is the natural result of discovery. . . ." The client-centered therapist would agree most strongly with this assertion. It is awfully puzzling to the client-centered therapist why other therapists, once they have hit upon this concept, do not try to order their therapeutic behavior more completely around efforts to promote *discovery* by patients and to abandon efforts to *teach*.

DAVID RIESMAN . . .

Rogerian and other therapies which accept the patient and favor non-directive interviewing rather than the kind of challenging Socratic interviewing here employed seem to me especially useful when one is dealing with patients who have been exposed to arbitrary power and for whom a permissive or accepting situation is a radical novelty. But many of the college-educated have been brought up permissively both at home and at schools and find little that is liberating in a therapist who accepts them.

Occasionally such a patient and therapist between them manage to build up a legend concerning the patient's life and the people or circumstances that have harmed the patient—a legend comforting to the patient in the short run but not particularly productive for him (this is especially likely since many therapists have very limited knowledge of the social and cultural backgrounds of their patients and hence can the more readily fall in with their patient's interpretations of "reality"). Indulgence has a quite different meaning with many college students than with patients who come from the radically deprived backgrounds of, for example, those in Chapters 1 and 4.

As just indicated, the modified Socratic method employed here which challenges the patient's own intelligence and own will power seems particularly appropriate in cases where patients "let themselves" run on in a depressed mood. As Allen Wheelis remarks,[5] a long psychoanalytic tradition rejects a concept such as will power as a Victorian spook to be kept in the attic along with those old-fashioned psychiatrists who tell young men, "Just buck up, young fellow, and square your shoulders!" But to come through the patient's mood indigo in the unthreatening way that was here employed is not simply a demand for moral athleticism but rather a demand that the patient take an active part in his own analysis. This is shown by the therapist's requirement that the patient keep a journal or diary in which, rather than simply "accepting" his own moods, he must face the burden of recording and analyzing them with the aim not simply of reportage but of gaining control.

Very likely, in many of these incidents the therapists report misgivings about use of their own powers beyond the usual norms of passivity not only because of ingrained tradition but also because such use of power is easy to exploit and abuse (and possibly some therapists still fear their own tendencies toward omnipotence). Yet the dialectical method used here is a protection against both the patient's dependency and the therapist's aggrandisement and thus, wherever it can be used, seems to safeguard both sides.

FREDERICK C. THORNE . . .

The therapist reports that many of his patients enter interviews in an anxious depressed mood and leave feeling more optimistic and cheerful, and he interprets this change somewhat hopefully to his therapeutic manipulation of devices for modifying depressive moods. Actually, almost all patients feel better at the end of interviews, presumably as a result of

[5] Allen Wheelis, "Will and Psychoanalysis," *J. Amer. Psychoanal. Ass.*, IV (1956), pp. 285–303.

catharsis and therapeutic attention, and it is uncritical to explain such effects as due to any active intervention in the absence of more valid proof. It is obvious that the dynamics of this incident are operating on symptomatic levels to train the client to be more accepting, insightful, and stoic concerning his symptoms, and questionably involve any intervention with etiologic depth factors.

It is important diagnostically to determine how frequently any client may need to ventilate or "blow off" painful feelings which tend to accumulate under increasing pressure until the client feels that he may "blow my stack" or do something impulsive. Clients may need to ventilate the same feelings over scores of interviews, and the therapist should encourage them to come sufficiently often so that undue pressure does not build up. Some clients feel guilty and embarrassed over spending so much time and money just saying the same thing over and over, and may actually terminate therapy prematurely because they do not see what good it is doing, and because they feel they should be able to do it alone at home. With such clients we insist that they come regularly whether they think it is doing any good or not, as long as any pressure symptoms continue to exist.

With many clients, the important thing is to be "doing something about the problem" and some relief is gained symptomatically simply by doing something (we often wonder if it matters what). Some kind of therapeutic activity tends to carry the client along through difficult moods until constructive forces in the personality become dominant again. The fact that the client in this case was able to obtain some benefit from "thought-control" techniques probably indicates that his condition was not too severe, and that he had sufficient control to cooperate and benefit from relatively superficial manipulations. The difficulty with such forms of therapy is that they may be ineffectual with more seriously disturbed clients who cannot control their feelings and thoughts enough to be able to direct them into more positive channels.

We agree with this therapist that it is very valuable to thoroughly acquaint each client with the nature of feelings and emotions and their effects upon other mental processes. We often instruct the client to try to identify states of anxiety, hostility, excitement, or depression, and then to study their effects upon thinking. It may be particularly important to warn the client not to make any vital decisions, such as changing jobs, getting a divorce, or undertaking a business transaction, while in such a mental state. We know of several instances where such warnings prevented unwise impulsive actions. However, the therapist has some responsibility to diagnose whether or not the client is dangerously impulsive and, if so, whether or not he can actually be expected to control himself. It is not unusual for a deceptively mild depressive to attempt suicide, and many cases will give no warning. This means that all depressives should be watched closely for signs of dangerous impulsiveness.

One important effect of desensitizing methods is that the client learns to live with and even accept, disturbing feelings which formerly made him anxious and panicky. We interpret to clients that all people have quotas of anxiety, frustration, agression, and ambivalence which are just as normal as night or day. We reassure them that such states do not mean that they are going to lose their mind, faint while in public, or make some spectacle of themselves. The client is helped to understand that such feelings compose the ordinary vicissitudes of life, and must be accepted as one would accept one's own shadow. We explain that to be anguished is the worst part of being neurotic.

"I Love You,

Doctor"

6

History

The patient was a very beautiful widow, 21 years of age, who had had a bad time during her first marriage, largely because she had weakly kowtowed to a dominating, rather psychopathic husband, and who was being privately seen because she did not want to make the same mistake in a second marriage. She was seen for five sessions of active psychoanalytically oriented psychotherapy and was reacting quite well as far as recognizing her problems and trying to do something about them was concerned. She began dating again, which she had previously been afraid to do; and she began to stand up against the continual nagging of her parents, with whom she was living, and to set about getting a job and moving into an apartment of her own.

Incident

During the sixth session the patient said that she had conferred with the physician who referred her for therapy and had agreed with him that she just had to be perfectly honest and tell me that she was "terribly attracted" to me; that she was sure that she would be just as attracted had she met me socially rather than in therapy; and that she kept having constant thoughts about "going out" with me. She had asked this physician about me, had learned that I was not presently married, and would very much like to have an affair with me for the purpose of seeing how well we got along together, with marriage as the possible ultimate goal.

I quickly pointed out to this patient the transference elements—particularly the fact that I, like her first husband, was considerably older than she, and that, like her father (who was a professor of philosophy), I was a professional person and an authority figure. She said that she had already considered these transference possibilities, but that she had distinctly rejected them. She was certain that she just wanted me as a man, and that if she had met me outside of therapy she would have been equally attracted to me. The tone of my voice, she said, when she first called to make an appointment with me, had distinctly appealed to her; and I just had those attributes which she had always gone for in men.

I saw that there was no persuading this patient that her attraction to me was largely or solely the result of classic transference feelings; so I graciously accepted her sentiments, and spent most of the rest of the session explaining to her that, although therapists might often be equally attracted to their patients as the patients might be to the therapists, the therapeutic relationship was such that it made all social-sex relations between patient and therapist utterly impossible; and that, alas, was all there was to it. Normally, I said, such feeling as she had for me would go away, especially as she became interested in other males; but if she felt too uncomfortable in the relationship, and felt that she could not tell me intimate things about herself because of her attraction to me, then we would just have to terminate the therapy and I would be glad to refer her to a colleague. She said that she thought she would not be able to continue on this basis, since her attraction to me was so intense as to make things too painful for her; but that she would think the matter over more carefully and tell me at the next session what her decision would be.

At the following session, she told me that she had considered everything carefully and that she had decided to terminate therapy with me. I agreed that that might well be the best decision, and gave her the names of two colleagues whom she might see. Then, being convinced that her attachment to me actually was mainly on a reality basis and not the result of classic transference, I asked her how old she thought I was. She said that, judging by my appearance and the dates on my diplomas, she was sure I was thirty-five. I replied that I was flattered by her views, but that actually I was forty-one, and that she had partly been misled by the fact that my bachelor's diploma, which was not displayed in my waiting room, had been obtained many years before my graduate school diplomas, which were displayed.

As soon as she heard that I was rather older than she had thought, she honestly exclaimed that she thought that I was definitely too old for her: since her first husband had been thirty-five, and even he had seemed a little too old at times, and didn't want to go out as much as she did and "have a good time" in the way she wanted. I then took the opportunity to say, very briefly, that I doubtlessly would be much worse than he was in this respect, since I was quite dedicated to my work and did not enjoy dancing, beach-going, and many other activities which other people like herself did. With every word I said her attitude toward me visibly changed, and it could be seen that in her estimation my value as a possible sex companion and marriage partner was rapidly going down. Just before the session ended she said: "You know, in the light of this information I've just learned about you, I feel that I really could never get along with you as well as I thought on a social level. And I'm wondering whether it might not be possible to go on with you in therapy after all. Yes, I think it might."

I told her to think the matter over again, and that I would be glad to continue to see her if she desired. She left; and later that day she called to say that she had decided that she would continue in therapy with me. Thereafter, I saw her for another year, until she became considerably better adjusted and made what seems to be a good marriage; and during the course of our subsequent sessions we never had any difficulty whatever over her feelings toward me.

Discussion

Much of what is cavalierly called "transference" by many therapists, and dogmatically interpreted to their patients as such, seems actually to be the patient's becoming attached to the therapist on a fairly clearcut reality basis. The therapist is, after all, usually quite intelligent; a sympathetic listener; fairly cultured; of good socio-economic standing; and seemingly of a suitable age to many of his female patients. If they met him socially, many of them probably would be quite attracted to him, since he fills the stereotype of what many well-educated and middle-class young women are looking for in a husband or lover. This is not to gainsay the fact that in *many* instances patients fall in love with their therapists because the latter unconsciously represent father-figures, authority-symbols, and so forth. But in many other cases they may fall in love with him because he is a man—and, very possibly, one of the most attractive men, in many ways, that they have ever been able to meet often and on intensive terms. In these cases, I find it best to acknowledge the patient's attachment on a reality level and to try to use it constructively in the therapy or else to continue the therapeutic relationship in spite of the difficulties this attachment begets. This does not always work, and frequently the therapy has to terminate. But to insist that classic transference exists where it patently does not leads to other difficulties, including the avoidance of some of the patient's basic desires and the forcing on her of a false interpretation. Probably no perfect answer to this often-occurring therapeutic problem exists. But at least let us recognize that it *is* a problem!

C. KNIGHT ALDRICH . . .

This one is a problem, all right; in fact, it brings up a lot of problems. One of them certainly is the loose way professional people use the term "transference." Another is the assumption that a patient's emotional reaction must be determined either by reality factors *or* by transference factors, whereas in this, as in most cases, both factors play a part. The same rationale applies to the therapist's reactions; both reality and countertransference make their contributions.

Much of the writer's discussion, therefore, implies a dichotomy which does not exist. For example, the therapist's attempt to reduce this patient's relationship to him to "a fairly cleancut reality basis" can hardly explain the appeal of his voice when she called to make the first appointment. I would suspect in such a case—and of course would need confirmation—that seduction was her usual approach to men, and that it concealed hostility rather than affection.

I further believe that the therapist's initial response of counterseductiveness almost frightened her out of therapy, but that his reversal in the next interview reassured her. So let us look at the therapist. When the patient makes her proposition, the therapist retreats behind her alleged transference, stating in effect that the seduction (attack?) is not aimed at him. She brushes this off, whereupon he retreats again, with alleged grace, to an overlong ("most of the rest of the session") avowal of his professional reasons for not responding to her overtures. At the same time he reveals, or perhaps I should say suggests, the possibility of his personal interest ("therapists might often be equally attracted" but the professional relationship, "*alas,* was all there was to it"). "Alas" may have been said facetiously, but this was no time for facetiousness. In the old joke about this situation, you remember, the patient says: "O.K., I fire you as my therapist; let's go to bed."

So if seduction equals hostility, counterseduction equals counterhostility, and the patient is too scared to stay in treatment. But when he tells her he's 41, not 35, and likes his work better than dancing, all her attraction for him vanishes. Why so? He is still a cultured, intelligent, good listener with the same attributes, tone of voice, and socio-economic position, and not enough extra years to account for quite so rapid a reversal in her feelings. I think that balancing her fear of his (hostile?) sexual interest is such a strong need for help from him that she accepts his age and his devotion to work at face value, and represses her seductiveness (with or without hostility) so successfully that it is never heard from again (". . . during the course of our subsequent sessions we never had any difficulty whatever over her feelings towards me"). This may have been to her advantage, depending on the goals of therapy. Be that as it may, I do believe that in this incident there appears transference and countertransference as well as reality and counterreality.

RUDOLF DREIKURS . . .

The therapist's evaluation of the situation is correct. The attraction of the patient was not necessarily based on transference but probably quite real. The reasons which are given for such attractions can well be accepted. There are a few other factors which may be added. First of all, the therapist behaves usually differently in his consultation room than he would outside as a fellow human being. The patient may be inclined to assume falsely that he would show the same friendly and warm understanding in a man-woman relationship that he shows in his office. Furthermore, for many patients the relationship to the therapist is the best they ever had, or perhaps the first good human relationship in their life. Consequently, if patient and therapist are of the opposite sex, his or her relationship to the therapist is often a much more friendly and understanding heterosexual relationship than he ever experienced. For this reason, falling in love may often be well understood on the basis of the common search for a compatible mate.

However, there is one factor which usually prevents such occurrences, and which indicates a neurotic attitude, if the patient permits herself to fall for such a temptation. As a rule, the patient is aware of the hopelessness of such an attachment. Only a pessimistic attitude toward eventual happiness in marriage would lead the patient to disregard the red light for such a venture and be rather attracted by something that is impossible. These are the patients who usually make a wrong choice, as if to prove the correctness of their underlying pessimism. One wonders whether or not being attracted to the therapist in such an overwhelming way is not indicative in this incident of the patient's intention to fall for the wrong man. This possibility is not explored by the therapist, at least not reported during this episode.

But such exploration seems to be warranted.

Another frequent occurrence is the patient's desire to deprive the therapist of his specific role and function by making an ordinary man out of him. We find such tendencies among patients who try to control the situation, to put others in their services, and to resist influence and control by others. We know too little about this patient to justify any such assumption.

JEROME D. FRANK . . .

Practically all sufferers from neurotic and psychotic illness are demoralized. This demoralization is perhaps the main factor impeding their improvement in treatment, because it detracts from their ability to unlearn old patterns of behavior and feeling and learn better ones. It has many sources, but an important one is the patient's loss of confidence in his ability to perceive himself and other persons correctly. His distorted interpersonal perceptions and responses are usually important sources of his maladaptive behavior. The resulting experiences of failure and frustration lead to progressive loss of morale, against which he tries to protect himself by further misperceptions of others, resulting in a vicious circle.

In the treatment situation the patient's perceptions of the therapist are partly veridical and partly distorted by the patient's motivations and needs. One of the best ways of helping a patient to gain self-confidence is to help him sort out those aspects of his perceptions of the therapist which are, in fact, correct from those which are distorted, and to acknowledge when the patient has perceived the therapist correctly. In this example the therapist, by accepting without false modesty or false pride the fact that the patient might find him attractive, enabled them both to identify a misperception of his age, which again had a reasonable basis, namely the dates on the diplomas. When this misperception was corrected, the infatuation based on it also died down, and the relationship was able to progress. At the same time, the patient's confidence in her ability to perceive others correctly was enhanced, and she was enabled to continue a relationship which was genuinely helpful to her.

The basis of all successful therapeutic relationships is the patient's faith, or at least hope, that the therapist can help him. The patient's favorable expectancies are based partly on the therapist's social role—that is, the cues which indicate to the patient that he is a trained psychotherapist—and partly on distorted perceptions of him based on transference, but also on his real personal attributes. Sometimes it happens that a patient's attraction for or dislike of a therapist is so well based on his correct perception of the therapist that it cannot be resolved. In such a case it is better to recommend a change of therapist than to go on trying to convince the patient of something that he knows is not true, namely that his feelings are based on transference. This attitude on the therapist's part only serves to heighten further the patient's distrust of his own perception and therefore his demoralization. Labelling as transference all of patients' positive or negative feelings for the therapist is the easiest way for the therapist to protect himself. One sign of a therapist's self-confidence and maturity is his ability to acknowledge when the patients' perceptions of him are correct and to accept friendly or hostile feelings based on correct preceptions as genuine.

Iago Galdston . . .

This critical incident touches upon a rather important and not uncommon problem in psychotherapy, and the discussion of the incident contributed by its reporter is all to the good. It is a laudable shaft thrust at and through a classical sham and humbug. Analysts like to pose in the guise of psychic castrates, or as the victims of a "syringomyelia of the libido," that is, immune and unresponsive to their patient's erotic evocations and provocations.

However, this case history and the incident reported do not appear to support the analyst's assumption that this was an instance of "attachment on a clearcut reality basis." I rather think that it was a pseudo-attachment, and part of the fundamental neurotic pattern of this "very beautiful widow of 21."

It is difficult to reconcile the statement that she had had a bad time during her first marriage "because she had weakly kowtowed to her dominating husband" with her aggressive "forward behavior" evinced in soliciting the therapist after the sixth session. She rather presents the picture of a calculating and domineering personality.

Thus, she is not averse to discussing with "the physician who referred her" her enchantment with the psychotherapist, nor does she hesitate to suggest "a sampling affair," hedged in, however, with the *caveat* of "marriage as a possible ultimate goal." This was most likely to sop to her shadowy superego. This then is an instance of manipulative evocation with a herding toward marriage—altogether a far cry from the behavior of a weakly kowtowing female. It rather spells an attempt to take possession of the therapist—lock, stock, barrel, and wedding ring.

Equally significant is the facile way in which the young lady was dissuaded. The six-year error in her estimate of the therapist's age, and the proverbial fifty minutes of the therapist's hour, were sufficient to dissipate her attractions to the therapist, her desires for "an affair," and the dreams of marriage with the therapist.

All this does not vitiate, but rather affirms, the therapist's conclusions that where a patient's attachment derives from reality, and may be, as at times it is, further reinforced by the therapist's counterattachment, it is good "to try to use it [the attachment] constructively in the therapy" and to continue the therapeutic relationship in spite of the difficulties this attachment may beget.

O. HOBART MOWRER . . .

It is fortunate that this incident has been reported and is included in this series, for it typifies an experience that occurs over and over again in the psychotherapeutic situation. Some therapists insist that it never happens to *them* and that when it happens to others it is because they have in some way provoked or invited it. Yet the phenomenon is so very common and, despite its frequency of occurrence, often so surprising that it can hardly be a product solely of the therapist's own wishes.

The therapist in the present incident alludes to one type of explanation that has been advanced in this connection and deals at greater length with another. By "classical transference feelings" he presumably means an inverted Oedipus or Electra complex in which the individual is fatally attracted to the parent of the opposite sex. But, circumstances being what they were in the present case, the therapist is prompted to question this view and to stress instead the less intricate notion that there is, after all, a good deal of sheer realism in the attraction that women have for men in the therapeutic situation. In the present case, perhaps; but generally speaking this hypothesis does not seem adequate. Woman patients often make sexual overtures to their therapists when the latter are twice their age, known to be happily married, and are in no way available or appropriate as sex partners, either in or out of marriage.

In connection with the comments already made regarding the case in

Chapter 3, it has been pointed out that much can be said for the concept of seduction of authority. When a father and his daughter, or a minister and a woman member of his congregation, or a man and a woman employee are sexually intimate, it is often assumed that the man has been the aggressor, the seducer; but we cannot overlook the secondary, nonsexual gains which are involved for the woman in nearly all such cases. Where the man stands in moral and/or practical authority over her, she can, at one stroke, nullify that authority by getting him to transgress the limits of sexual propriety. And in the therapeutic relationship, where the patient is often making a last-ditch stand against the claims of her own conscience and community and where the therapist is so quickly identified as a representative of the latter, what deadlier way to best conscience and community than to show the corruptibility of their agent? In the present case, it is not without significance that, as a result of standing his ground, the therapist was able to convince the patient that he was indeed a therapist and not a potential lover; and with this unmistakable redefinition of the situation, or on *his* terms, she decided that she was not interested in him sexually and could now enter into therapy with him. If he had accepted her proposals (she need not have lived up to them, his mere acquiescence would have been sufficient), she would not have had either to leave "therapy" or go through with it: "therapy" would have been thus thoroughly discredited, demolished, as far as she was concerned.

Yet interpretations based upon the seduction-of-authority notion often seem incomplete, somehow wide of the mark. In what sense can it be that they are misdirected? Although the consequences of sexual intimacy would be thoroughly destructive, it is often difficult to discover conscious hostility in the patient's overtures. And she may seem genuinely surprised and hurt that the therapist should have perceived hostility in the situation. Perhaps we are dealing here more often with a kind of primitive naiveté than with real viciousness. It is now apparently well established that in ancient and prehistoric societies it was common practice to resort to sexual orgies when the group was dismayed and anxious. For example, in their book, *Moses and the Ten Commandments*,[1] Ilton and Roberts vividly portray the intoxication and licentiousness to which the Children of Israel resorted when they became convinced that Moses had perished on Mount Sinai and that they, too, could not survive in the desert without their inspired leader. The old men, in the aftermath of gluttony and abandon, wallowed on the ground and virgins, no longer virgins, smiled vacantly; but, say the writers, "the people no longer felt alone and afraid."

So can it be, then, that for some women at least (and the same holds for some men patients with women therapists), their sexual advances are

[1] P. Ilton, and M. Roberts, *Moses and the Ten Commandments* (New York: The Dell Publishing Company, 1956).

less a means of attacking or discrediting the therapist than of binding anxiety, of making life again interesting, at least briefly, and of giving it meaning of the only kind that easily lies within their power? It is *their* way—primitive, short-sighted, and self-defeating though it be—of relating to others and of vividly experiencing themselves. And just as societies, if they were to survive, had to develop resources other than the orgy as a means of dealing with fear and uncertainty, so also must the individual be helped to find other ways of relating to and of more vividly experiencing himself and others.

Accepting the lead of psychoanalysis, many psychotherapists are careful not to impose their own values upon their patients. Yet, as recent studies show,[2] this cannot be entirely avoided in practice; and it may be that we will soon recognize, even in theory, its desirability and necessity. The two imponderable questions that will then arise are: *What* values can we most legitimately offer to others in exchange for their old ones? And, *how* can we make these alternative values acceptable and attractive to them?

DAVID RIESMAN . . .

I think a good deal of evidence has been accumulated concerning the relation of professional people with their clients and especially of doctors with their patients to support the therapist's interpretation here. For many women, a visit to a doctor is a form of social and intellectual mobility. Where outside a consulting room would they have access (as the therapist says) to a man who is cultured and superior but also will listen? The "helping" professions and of course especially medicine are increasingly attractive to men as careers and the men in these professions appeal to women on the level of soap-opera and glamour and on the more realistic level referred to by the therapist here.

Moreover, I agree with him that the concept of transference is one behind which the therapist often succeeds in escaping from (or even denigrating) his own feelings and his own involvements. The temptation to regard all feelings for the therapist as transference of authority-tenderness feelings having their origins in the family romance may be one bulwark for the preoccupation with childhood as topics for analysis. By regarding attitudes between therapist and patient as valid for the existing situation, and by dealing with them in that context, the patient is not encouraged to retreat to childhood but has to face the fact of renunciation vis-à-vis the therapist as a living and desirable person. Whatever sadness and tragedy this may involve for the person—and also conceivably in one

[2] Werner Wolff, *Psychology and Religion* (New York: M.D. Publications, Inc., 1955). See also O. S. Walters, "Varieties of Spiritual Malpractice," *The Pastor* (June, 1948), pp. 14–15.

or another case for the therapist—becomes a part of the reality on which, as the analysis proceeds, the patient is increasingly able to stand. In contrast with this, discussions of transference might further obfuscate the patient and alienate her still more from her own feelings.

CLARA THOMPSON . . .

The problem of a patient's "falling in love" with the therapist occurs more often between a female patient and male therapist than between a male patient and female therapist. This is, I believe, to a great extent culturally determined. The woman is generally brought up to think of a man as her protector and one on whom she can lean, and she expects this also of a therapist. Conventionally, the ideal husband is a little older than his wife, but he may be very much older and still not attract comment. On the other hand, the idea of a man being dependent on a woman is generally viewed with distaste, although it may often be a fact, and when a woman is noticeably older than her husband, this invariably attracts comment. Therefore, a male patient is more likely to fight against any erotic interest he may have in his woman therapist, who is experienced by him as older and wiser than he, whatever may be her chronological age. Thus, I think the point is well taken that, in this case, there may have been a reality factor in the patient's reaction to her therapist, and that persisting in belaboring the transference aspect without considering the real aspect might lead the patient to feel the therapist was afraid of coping with the real crisis.

But why was this woman so "terribly attracted"? On the practical side, she was looking for a husband. Therefore, any eligible man who came within her ken was undoubtedly sized up and considered. She was afraid of making the same mistake as in her first marriage. She would doubtless think (not necessarily correctly), "Who could be a safer bet than a psychotherapist?"

However, it is my experience that any reaction to the therapist, as a real person in his own right, is usually in response to some, at least, slight reaction on his part. In reporting this case, the therapist does not state how he felt about her. His behavior was absolutely correct, but we are not told what went on in his own emotional reaction, and there may have been fantasies, in spite of himself. Patients are very sensitive to what goes on emotionally in the very close therapeutic relationship which is established in treatment. Something made this patient feel that this was a real situation in which there was some response from the therapist, unless she was more of a nymphomaniac than is described. I do not say this in any way to discredit the therapist. Such things happen because we are human, and it is especially likely to happen if the therapist's own emotional outlets are unsatisfactory at the time. I think great credit is due him for openly dealing with the reality situation. She finally decided that he was not the man for her and grasped at the explanation that it was because he was six years older than she thought. I doubt if this fact brought about the favorable resolution. Even by her own calculations, he was already too old for her at 35. What I suspect happened was that she was, at first, hurt to find she had been mistaken about his willingness to participate and felt she could not go on because of her hurt pride. The therapist must have handled the situation very well. His honesty in rejecting her advances, without becoming defensive or in any way belittling her, must have impressed her with his genuine desire to help. Too often, the therapist, made uncomfortable in such a situation, grasps at the transference idea as a defense against his own anxiety. He says, "You do not love me, but your father," and draws a long breath of relief that he safely got out of that situation. This therapist did no such thing. He accepted her attitude as something understandable in its own right. It must have been a relief to her to find that she could be close to a man whom she could not seduce, and yet who did not reject her. The analysis of many attractive women has come to grief on just this situation, where the therapist, possibly guilty because of his own thoughts, did not dare deal with the direct situation, but insisted on talking only of transference. At the same time, under his professional mask, he continued to enjoy the sight and presence of the patient. I do not imply, nor do I think the therapist implied, that there was no transference factor in this situation. Even falling in love in everyday life usually has some transference element determining the choice. In this case, until the reality situation was dealt with, there would have been no possibility of a meaningful understanding of transference elements.

"Don't Help
Jim Read"

7

History

The client was a woman, 46 years old, a widow with three children. She described her problem as follows: "My second son, Jim, is 12 years old and he is only in the fifth grade. He reads at the second grade level. The school wants to demote him to a lower grade. He tries hard to learn to read and I help him. Last summer I sent him to a reading expert. It cost a lot of money and did not help at all. Every day I go over his work with him, show him flash cards or letters, and drill him. We spend at least one hour a day on reading. I buy him comic books, newspapers, and whatever he wants in the way of reading. He has been tested for intelligence, and every time he is rated as above average or superior. And yet, he reads poorly. The whole family is upset about Jim, and he too is rather nervous and cannot really enjoy life because of the reading."

I questioned the client about the problem, and found out that she was a person with very high standards of morals and performance, and that she had very high expectations for her children. The other two were doing very well and were no cause for trouble. There appeared to be no great difficulties or frictions in the family. Jim's behavior was good in the family, in the school and in the community. In short, on the basis of the interview with the mother, no evident reason for Jim's retardation in reading was evident.

Jim was interviewed, separately, and he supported the mother. He was cooperative, stated he really wanted to learn to read, but somehow or other he just couldn't *get* the material. He had no complaints about the school. As far as could be told, his reading was not related to any personal problems.

It was the mother's opinion, based on considerable reading of the literature on remedial reading, that what Jim really needed was an expert, who used a different kind of system from any attempted thus far.

Incident

The incident really occurred within the therapist, who, as he listened carefully to the mother and to Jim, began to realize that the family revolved about Jim and his reading, and that through a combination of the mother's values and Jim's unconscious desires for her attention, this relatively minor problem had assumed proportions not warranted. In short, he came to the conclusion that it was possible that Jim was "using" his nonreading for his own purposes, but not consciously. It also appeared possible that the mother, with her high standards of perfection, and her need to feel wanted might in reality be contributing to Jim's nonreading by her excessive attention and interest in Jim's school work.

For various reasons, the first interview with me was to be the only one, and consequently, the therapist felt that he was in a very peculiar position. If he did not give the mother what she wanted—in reality, encouragement to go on in the way she had been—she would be dissatisfied, and would just go on somewhere else. If he explained his hypothesis of what was causing Jim not to read, he was certain that it would be rejected. What appeared necessary to test the validity of the therapist's hypothesis was some approach that would get the mother to do what the therapist felt would result in an improvement of the child's reading without, however, letting her know at the time what the rationale was; in short, how to get the mother to stop giving him help, which was hindering him.

The interviewer sent Jim out of the room and explained as follows to the mother.

"I believe that something can be done for Jim, but it will require your absolute cooperation, and I am certain that it will be very difficult for you to do."

"I promise faithfully to do whatever you tell me to."

"Even if it may result in lowering Jim's reading ability?"

"How can that be?"

"It is an experimental procedure, but I must know certain diagnostic information, what happens to his reading when he gets no help. The experiment will take about eight weeks."

"What am I to do?"

"I will give him a diagnostic reading test, and then for eight weeks you are to give him no help whatsoever. He must not know why you will not help him. You must tell your other two children not to help him. If the school calls, you tell them that you have been given instructions not to help him. You tell him that reading is his problem. What I want to find out is how much more poorly he will do when he gets no help whatever at home. But most important, you must not let him know why you are taking this attitude. I know it is very difficult for you to do, but it is essential for Jim's welfare that he believe that you and his brothers just don't want to help him any more."

"But I don't understand. . . ."

"It would take too long at this time to go into details. But do you think you can do it? Absolutely no more help any more for eight weeks. Do not tell him why. Do not tell him that it is for eight weeks. Let him think that his reading is his problem and that you are no longer interested in it. Under no circumstances help him. Then after eight weeks I will test him, will see what his weaknesses are, and then we will be able to do a real psychological job."

The mother was asked to repeat the instructions, and when it was evident that she knew what she was to do, she was asked to telephone the therapist once a week to report on how she was following instructions.

Faithfully, the mother called once a week, and was given further encouragement by the therapist to continue in terms of the strict regimen. She reported that Jim seemed upset by the new procedures, and begged and pleaded for help, but that, even though her heart was breaking at his pleas, she did not help him. By the end of the second week, he was no longer asking for help. About the sixth week she reported that his grade on the report card, which had always been "unsatisfactory," was now "fair."

Jim and his mother came in on the eighth week and the therapist talked to the mother while Jim was put to working on a reading test.

The therapist confessed his duplicity and told the mother that he believed that she was holding her son back through helping him, and that Jim's motivations were to continue to get her attention, which he could do by not reading, and that the past eight weeks had been a test of this hypothesis. The therapist confessed that he believed that she would not believe him if he had told her earlier what the reason was for Jim's poor reading and that if he had explained it to her she would probably not have followed the instructions. The mother felt, however, that the reasoning was logical, and did accept the possibility of Jim's not reading in order to get attention. She stated that the new procedure was a great comfort for her, since she had been quite upset by Jim's constant demands, and that now she had more time for herself and was more at ease. As a matter of fact, she stated, she really did not care so much if Jim learned to read or not. It was more important that he grow up to be a good person, and so forth.

The therapist pointed out that for the first time in years Jim improved in reading, and right then and there called the teacher at her home and discussed Jim's progress, with the mother listening in. The teacher stated that she was amazed at Jim's development, and that she felt that Jim was rapidly coming close to normal.

Jim brought in his test, which was analyzed rapidly in terms of his previous effort of eight weeks before and, as might have been expected, he had shot up from about second grade to fifth grade—within eight weeks! The therapist explained to him that he had been not learning because he wanted his mother's attention, but that now he would be on his own.

Discussion

As I see it, there are a number of issues here which I would like to obtain opinions about.

The first refers to the adequacy of the formulation of the hypothesis: namely, that Jim was using his mother by refusing to learn to read. I think that the results clearly point out that this hypothesis is correct. But could other hypotheses be established?

The second issue refers to the mother. Was she while appearing to want to help Jim actually operating in ways that she unconsciously felt would retard him? Did she want to keep him as her baby?

The more important issue refers to the duplicity of the therapist. Did I, in operating in this way, violate any ethics? Was the end justified by the means? Did my "confession" to the mother compensate for my own conscious knowledge that I had no confidence in her and that she would not follow my real reasons? Was the fact that Jim did improve as a result of the mother following my instructions sufficient justification for my means of operating?

As I see it, I was torn between my desire to help this family, knowing that the mother could not come frequently to get full insight prior to changing her methods, and the desire to explain what was going on. I decided to "trick" the mother into doing what I thought she should do, even hinting that the procedure might make Jim into more of a baby. So, by putting before her the prospect that Jim might not be freed of parental help, I felt that she would comply, which she did.

In a way I see a similarity to a dentist saying, "This won't hurt" when he knows it will; or a doctor saying, "This will help" when he gives a placebo, when he knows that the suggestion of the medicine will do the trick. Are therapists justified in similar manipulations of patients or of having secret understandings when they give counsel?

C. KNIGHT ALDRICH . . .

Taking the writer's questions in order: First, I suspect that the failure to learn to read (I would not assume that it was "refusal" but an unconsciously determined reading block) was *prolonged*, but not *caused*, by the *secondary* gains which resulted from the mother's attention to the problem. I doubt that the *primary* motivation for the reading block was to gain the mother's attention, although treatment directed at the secondary gains was undoubtedly effective.

Second, I would suspect that Jim's mother wanted at the onset of the symptom to maintain Jim as her little boy, possibly to satisfy dependent needs of her own. It would be helpful to know more about the relationship of mother and son to Jim's father, and particularly to know when the father died, the circumstances of his death, and the history of the mother's grief. Further history might also indicate the extent to which Jim's dependency needs entered into the problem. Moreover, since learning blocks frequently are associated with inability to express hostile feelings, I would like to know more of the home atmosphere and attitudes toward expression of aggression, and the relationship to his father's death of Jim's early struggles with aggressive feelings. We already know of the mother's "high expectations" of her children, which probably encouraged them to express their oppositional behavior on an intellectual battleground.

As far as the therapist's "duplicity" is concerned, I am not convinced it was necessary. What made the therapist so certain that his hypothesis would be rejected, even in one interview? I suspect that she was closer to "insight" than he believes. But granted that he felt it was necessary, he seems to have used suggestion successfully. The question is, why did he make such an issue of it? Was the confession necessary for the patient's benefit, or was it necessary to relieve the therapist's guilt, as indicated by his asking, "Did my confession compensate for *my own conscious knowledge* that I had no confidence. . . ."? I think he is feeling guilty about his *knowledge*, which after all doesn't in itself hurt the patient. His confusion is evident in his equation of the placebo and the dentist's promise that "This won't hurt." The placebo works through deception, I suppose, and has its serious limitations as a treatment device, but it is not a betrayal of the trust of the patient in the same way as is the dentist's promise. If your own therapeutic morality excludes any deception, you may well be *ashamed* of using a placebo, but you shouldn't feel *guilty*, or called upon to confess to your patient. If you tell him something won't hurt when you know it will, you certainly should feel guilty because you have betrayed his confidence in you.

ROBERT BLAKE . . .

This case invites a distinction between therapy as ordinarily conceived and what might be described as "psychodynamic engineering."

This critical incident constitutes a rather clear example of psychodynamic engineering: the rearrangement of situational and personal forces for the purpose of inducing alterations in the client's behavior. The rearrangement which takes place is dictated by the therapist's understanding of social dynamics and psychodynamics without the development of insight. There is little basis for designating these procedures as constituting therapy since psychodynamic engineering happens *without* any manifest structural change in the client, without expansion of his understanding or insight, without a "working through" process, and without the acquisition of skills for improved personal problem-solving, all of which are hallmarks of one or another version of therapy as systematically conceived. The positive outcome is by the manipulation from the outside forces, either in the situation, in the person, or both.

In the present study, both the mother and Jim were undergoing psychodynamic engineering rather than therapy. In Jim's case his relationship with his mother was varied over the eight-week period. Through instructions by the therapist was created the necessity for a new adjustment which demanded no insight on Jim's part into his desire for his mother's attention. Similarly, the changed behavior of the mother was through instruction rather than understanding. Although results involved the same kind of improvement in Jim's reading ability through the use of engineering procedures as would have been expected from therapeutic procedure, it can be anticipated that long-term consequences of the two approaches may be quite different. Jim's desire for attention may be manifested in another form, for the basic problem of a disturbed relationship between mother and son has not changed through the therapist's manipulation of the forces in this specific situation.

Grant for a moment the distinction drawn here between psychodynamic engineering and therapy. With the distinction in mind, the question asked regarding duplicity is placed in a new light. To the degree that psychodynamic engineering is legitimate, then no problem of duplicity is involved. Rather, new problems regarding ethical standards for such engineering are required.

As a first approximation to a code of ethics for psychodynamic engineering it can be argued that the client has a right to knowledge that *therapy* in the ordinary sense is *not* being administered. He has a right also to the awareness that forces to which he is not attentive but to which he may be responsive are significant in his situation and that a regimen is being recommended which is not intended for his understanding but from which positive outcomes are anticipated. Beyond these matters considerations that normally apply in the conduct of therapy also hold for psychodynamics.

VINCENT HERR . . .

In this case we have the ethical question which might be stated: May the therapist employ falsehoods in the treatment of a case so that by this means a good result may be attained? The old accusations made against certain moralists come to mind here—but I think history has shown conclusively that most professional persons do not admit the theory of evil means for good ends; and the code of ethics of most professions prescribes that no intrinsically evil act may be performed from which it is foreseen that the only direct consequence is of its very nature intrinsically evil.

Apparently the therapist in the case is asking the question: Was the lie or prevarication used as a means for a cure? From reading the case it would appear that the only person who could answer that question would be the therapist. This reader is of the opinion, just judging from reported data, that the therapist did not certainly use "duplicity," although the withholding of information is sometimes considered a kind of prevarication or tampering with the truth. What probably happened in the case was that the therapist really believed that the overprotection of the mother had caused the difficulties for her child. This was a statement of the truth as it existed for the therapist. Such overprotection and pampering had caused the child to use the device of "attention" seeking, which performance quite effectively prevented the help with the reading from producing any result. The therapist might also have been said to have acted on an hypothesis: if the pampering caused the poor reading, then removal of pampering should improve reading. He then proceded to test this hypothesis with the usual means. It was really no untruth to instruct the mother to tell the boy that reading was *his* problem, without telling her why. Included in this partial truth is the somewhat latent assumption that the mother could suspect the other aspect of the truth, namely that her interference was doing harm rather than good.

This writer has been unable to find in any reputable code of ethics the statement that any person, professional or otherwise, is bound to tell all that is in his mind regarding the motivation for his acts, to do anything that might perhaps lead the person who is acting to keep going deeper into his motives until he discovered their most ultimate unconscious sources. In this case the therapist is trying to diagnose the inner motivations of his own client, the mother of the child. He is bound to have even more uncertainty in trying to assess these motives correctly. Thus the mere fact that he judged for the moment and hypothetically that she was harming her child by too much attention could hardly be a sufficient reason for his telling her the reason for his decision. Moreover, the therapist also failed to know in advance whether or not the mother would even accept the instructions were he to make no mention of his own hypothesis; and consequently the "means" he proposed to use were only "hypothetical" means. The statement in the author's comment: "I had no confidence in her and believed that she would not follow my instructions if I explained why . . . !" gives the clue to the solution of the case. If he judged the mother would not follow instructions if he explained why, he also seems to have judged implicitly that she *might* not even follow them if he did *not* explain his reasons. Again it is a risk the therapist took.

Of course this reminds us of all the other incidents where doctors and dentists tell partial truths, or use suggestion to accomplish results. This writer thinks that every professional person ought to see clearly in his mind the difference between actually telling a falsehood and withholding knowledge that the other person has no legitimate right to possess. After all a "lie" is a telling of an "untruth" whereas "withholding" information is not such a positive act of falsification. The present writer cannot help wondering what would have happened in the case had the mother actually not followed the instructions to the letter. In that case the boy would probably have developed *other* problems and symptoms traceable perhaps to the fact that his own mother *apparently* did not want to help him. In such a case there would have been even greater risk taken by the therapist, but again it is obvious that no one except the therapist in question could possibly know the extent of the risk involved. Any slip on the part of the mother, whereby she would have become abrupt in her manner or have brutally rejected the child's appeals for help, might have made the case turn in quite a different direction. Perhaps it was the anxiety that this might be the end result which really disturbed the therapist, more so than the fear that he had told a lie.

ERNEST HILGARD . . .

The problems of reading difficulty and their remediation have resisted clear solution, despite the thousands of articles that have been written on the subject. Hence every case of successful therapy is worth examining for the light it may throw upon a still-unsolved problem.

There are really a number of hypotheses about reading difficulties, each of which has a certain plausibility. Because they are not mutually exclusive, perhaps more careful diagnosis would help us to find acceptable answers. Let us remind ourselves of a few of these:

1. *The special defect theory.* The child is too young, too immature; he suffers sensory or motor deficiency, is left-handed, or lacks the necessary intellectual level. The remedy is to correct the defect or to give up.

2. *The bad-teaching theory.* Reading is a set of habits that have to be learned. If teaching is stupid (by the whole-word method, by the phonetic method, or whatever the proponent dislikes) then that accounts for the problem. The remedy lies in better teaching.

3. *The psychodynamic theory.* Reading is a social learning task that is part of accepting one's role in a culture. It is therefore an area in which to be belittled for failure or to triumph over adults through defiance. It is authoritarian, for words are what they are, even when the various spellings do not make sense. Hence a resentment of authority may make it hard to accept the authoritativeness of the written word. Furthermore, words are symbolic and fantasy-provoking. Some children's fantasies may get in the way of orderly reading.

The laboratory psychologist finds it easier to go after the first two of these possible sources of difficulty, while the clinician gets into the third, but often with so many complexities it is hard to come out with a generalization useful for a new situation. The present incident certainly falls within this third category, for the boy was bright enough, he did not require different instructional methods, yet he was unable to read because of things going on between him and his mother. The raw fact is that Jim learned to read better when his mother did not try to help him than when she did. This is what we have to try to explain.

The lines of the explanation are clear enough. The mother has very high standards, she works hard to bring Jim up to them; he has somehow failed and has made life miserable for himself and for his family. The anxiety that his mother arouses must in his case conflict with reading (rather than raise the drive to learn, as it might in accordance with the Spence-Farber principle). This might fit those cases in which anxiety reduces discrimination. Another possibility is that the motivation system has collapsed because of failure; when level of aspiration get too far ahead of performance, effort often becomes unrealistic. Still another possibility is that something more complex is happening: perhaps that this is a way in which Jim gets some kind of control over his mother, or works out some kind of problem of sibling rivalry. Unfortunately we do not have quite enough to go on.

One unsolved question, for example, is why this mother's standards and behavior have not done the same things to the two other children in the family. Can it be that this son has some special meaning to her? Was her place in her sibling relationship such that she competed with a brother for whom Jim now stands? We do not have enough information to search further. There must be some reason, however, for the problem focussing on Jim; it may have been his father rather than his mother who was really responsible.

The mother carries the burden, because when she quit putting pressure on Jim he got along all right. A surprising feature of this case is that she was able to do this, that she was able to keep her agreement with the counselor. This bears upon the problem raised by the therapist concerning "tricking" the mother into appropriate action. My guess (and it can be only a guess) is that her ability to cooperate on this basis must have been due to her readiness to cooperate on another basis. Maybe some event that forced her close supervision of Jim was now in the past; maybe something in her own life had cleared up. It is idle to speculate without more data, yet one is led to speculate because she did so well in carrying out the therapist's wishes.

In the interaction between the psychology of learning and clinical psychology there is a two-way process. The psychology of learning has more to say about ordinary reading handicaps and methods of teaching reading than about the subtle processes going on between a child and his mother when he is in this kind of a bind. It is important for the psychologist of learning to recognize that there do exist such obstacles to learning in which the learner, consciously wishing to learn, and suffering because he does not learn, is nevertheless inhibited from learning because of a social interaction that has roots far removed from the reading situation. A complete psychology of learning will have to recognize this psychodynamic context for learning or it will fail to help those who must guide learning.

J. McV. Hunt . . .

This is an interesting incident of the manipulation of social motives and the social stimuli producing them. Jim's reactions to his mother's withdrawal of her help implies that the therapist's hypothesis concerning him and his motivation was correct. The very fact that the mother was able to follow the therapist's direction, and that she reports that she was relieved by not having to give so much help to him indicates that she was not motivated to keep him as her baby. I suspect, therefore, that the duplicity of the therapist was unnecessary, and I question whether it was wise, even though I would be highly reluctant to argue that it was unethical. It was probably unwise because, if the mother had been motivated to keep Jim as her baby, she probably could not have followed the instructions for all the mystery that surrounded their presentation. Moreover, the news that the boy's reading had improved from unsatisfactory to fair, the improvement in the boy's reading-test performance, and the therapist's confession would probably have conspired to create an incident and a bad relationship which would have made it difficult to carry on therapy had the mother really been motivated to keep Jim as her baby. The fact that she accepted the "trick" of getting her to do what the therapist thought she should do implies, I believe, that she would have accepted the same explanation at the time the instructions to withdraw her help were given. It would probably have been wise not to imply at this point that she needed to help Jim because she was motivated to keep him as her baby, but, at least initially, to pay the mother the compliment that she was faced with a reality problem, and show her that the eight weeks could be used as an experiment just as, in fact, it was. My own therapeutic experience leaves me with the impression that it is best always to start with candor tempered with giving the client the benefit of the motivational doubts (in this instance, giving the mother the benefit of being motivated by the reality of her son's deficiencies coupled with her own high standards for his performance, rather than by any pathological need to keep him her baby) until the client's behavior clearly implies motives which stand in the way of achieving professed goals.

FAY KARPF . . .

The therapist in this critical incident states, in reference to the mother of the boy, that insofar as she herself was concerned "for various reasons, the first interview with me was to be the only one, and consequently the therapist felt that he was in a very peculiar position." But the mother did return for another interview when requested, she reported regularly, and carried out instructions faithfully. Perhaps the therapist accepted too readily the view that he could have only one interview with the mother. For this was obviously a situation in which preparation was necessary on the part of mother and child before deciding on such a drastic procedure as the therapist undertook and which left him with justifiable ethical misgivings.

The experience could have been quite traumatic for the child, and despite the seemingly good results that were obtained, perhaps it actually was. For an exceptionally dependent child to be told suddenly and without any explanation that his mother and his brother "just don't want to help him any more" and, whereas the family revolved about him and his reading before, to be led to think without any preparation "that his reading is his problem and that you [his mother] are no longer interested in it," would seem to be not only drastic, but also hazardous handling. As a matter of fact, the mother reported that "Jim seemed upset by the new procedures, and begged and pleaded for help, but that, even though her heart was breaking at his pleas, she did not help him." One might reasonably ask: At what cost in terms of family relationships was the success in this critical incident secured?

As for the mother herself, if the therapist's views about her perfectionistic standards "and her need to feel wanted" were valid, if she was in reality holding her son back through helping him because she wanted to keep him tied to her as a baby, then it would seem that she herself was in urgent need of therapy, perhaps more so than Jim. It is not unusual for parents to seek help for children when they are themselves the major problem. Furthermore, if the above was well founded in fact and feeling, the mother could have obstructed therapy in a hundred different ways by shifting to some other area of Jim's possible dependency. For even considering Jim's improvement, he probably still found it difficult to hold his own against his brothers, both of whom "were doing very well, and were no cause for trouble," and, therefore, he might still be motivated by a compensating desire for his mother's atention. It all comes down again to the view that this was a situation in which simultaneous or at least preparatory therapy with mother and child was indicated, even in the face of noted obstacles and with the possible loss of some time for Jim. This situation was in no sense an emergency, notwithstanding the statement that the family was "upset about Jim, and he too was rather nervous." In the latter case, there would of course have been no need for what the therapist terms his "duplicity" (which, by the way, is a rather harsh term for the therapist to apply to his procedure).

But assuming with the therapist that the above, more leisurely procedure was impossible, was there then a violation of ethics? Evidently the therapist was concerned and felt a little guilty about his procedure. But it seems to this commentator that we are dealing here with a question of judgment and viewpoint rather than with an outright question of ethics. "Was the end justified by the means?" "Was the fact that Jim did improve . . . sufficient justification for my means of operating?" If you believe in authoritarian types of therapy, you might consider the procedure justified, assuming that the judgment of the therapist as to conditions was good. If you do not believe in authoritarian types of therapy, you probably would not approve of the procedure.

When a person comes for therapy, does he surrender his right of self-determination and self-responsibility, even his right to make mistakes from which the therapist could protect him? And when another person is involved, in this case a 12-year-old child, does the therapist have the right to assume responsibility and impose his judgment on the situation without the consent of the parent or even an attempt at securing consent by persuasion or other means? The therapist states: "I decided to 'trick' the mother into doing what I thought she should do." That practically puts the therapist in the role of a dictator who "always know best," which is not a fitting role for him, especially in a democratic society. This latter point has many-sided implications for the socio-cultural interpretation of pyschotherapy, an important aspect of the subject which is just beginning to attract merited attention.

It does not seem that the suggested comparisons to dentist and physician hold. Everybody knows that when the dentist says, "This won't hurt," he is just trying to calm the patient. As for the physician's use of a placebo, he usually does not feel the need of disillusioning the patient through a confession. The situation in psychotherapy is different, since it often deals with one's basic rights and responsibilities as a person, as a family member, and as a citizen. What, in fact, was the reaction of the mother to the therapist's admitted manipulation of her relationship to her son? And with what conception of psychotherapy and psychotherapists was she left? If she ever had occasion to turn to psychotherapy again, would she be able to trust her psychotherapist sufficiently to establish a good psychotherapeutic relationship, or would she expect another attempt at trickery?

The fact that the therapist was able to maintain a positive relationship with the mother is a tribute to his evident sincerity, which he was somehow able to communicate in spite of his insecurity about his procedure. This and the successful outcome of the experiment must have moderated any resentment the mother might otherwise have felt. Her continuing positive relationship to the therapist is evidenced by the readiness with which she accepted his explanation as to why he felt the need of proceeding as he did when he finally made his confession to her.

DAVID RIESMAN . . .

The ethical dilemma here is indeed a real one that is faced in another way by a physician who is called in by parents, who are, let us say, Christian Scientists, whose child has appendicitis and needs to be operated on. If the physician is to save the child, he knows he must trick or even coerce the parents. The problem arises because of the question as to who is the real client here—the mother who is paying the bill, or the child himself? To save Jim, the therapist had to use on the mother the very vices which had previously imprisoned Jim. He no doubt knew enough about the family's cultural values to see how well defended the mother's position was against the frontal assault, and yet by the same token how vulnerable to him when he posed as the all-seeing "expert." But I think he is saved and without excessive casuistry even with reference to her, for in the end he liberates her as well as Jim from such dependence on experts. In this respect the incident resembles the famous Solomon Asch experiment in which subjects are duped by stooges not to "see" what their eyes tell them about the length of lines. Once they are told of the deception which has been practiced on them the effect is often dramatically therapeutic, for they realize either that they were right in standing against the majority or, if they gave way, that they had better look into the cause of such weakness. Other mothers inclined to over-protection might find an experience such as the one recorded here therapeutic for them.

BESS SONDEL . . .

Let us put the therapist's thinking into systemic language[1]—the language of form, the language of pattern.[2]

[1] See Charles Morris, *Signs, Language and Behavior* (Englewood Cliffs, N.J.: Prentice-Hall, Inc., 1946).
[2] See Bess Sondel, *The Humanity of Words, A Primer of Semantics* (New York: World Book Company, 1958).

The therapist analyzed the problematical situation as follows:

The mother's behavior is the *cause* of this boy's trouble (undesirable *effect*).

From this causal pattern, the therapist moved to a means-end pattern: Remove the cause (*means*); alter the effect favorably (*end*).

In presenting this means-end plan to the mother, the therapist communicated two things:

(a) The *means* are absolute: "It will require your absolute cooperation." Here is incitive language with a view to "control."

(b) The *end* is uncertain: "Even if it may result in lowering Jim's reading ability. . . ."

It should be noted, also, that the *operations* to be instituted by the therapist give a promise of control: "I promise faithfully to do whatever you tell me." The therapist's signs have been adequate (again, to use Morris's term); they have had the desired effect on the recipient.

The therapist made a diagnosis. He interpreted symptoms as a sign of an unfavorable relationship between mother and son. He set up a means-end hypothesis in an effort to affect the *causal* factor. The therapist was, in other words, manipulating what he considered to be a determinating factor but keeping the patient as an observable and relatively nonvariable element. The therapist questions the legitimacy of this procedure. If he is concerned with his reasoning, I should ask, *Why?* In order to change a problematical situation, it seems necessary to manipulate causal factors (directly or indirectly) which give rise to the (undesirable) effect. Every means-end hypothesis that involves human beings is uncertain. The therapist made this clear to the mother. He "used" the mother to affect the patient, without her knowing it. Could he have done otherwise under the circumstances without "spoiling" the experiment?

The therapist asks two questions; one which relates to his reasoning, and the other which relates to "ethics."

Could other hypotheses have been established? he asks. If he means by this, *Could other hypotheses have been entertained; analyzed and evaluated?* the answer is, of course, *Yes.* Every diagnosis is differential. If he means by this, *Could other hypotheses have been proved?* he is posing a question that befuddles the issue. The results of his experiment do not, as he suggests, "clearly point out that this hypothesis is correct." As Dewey so clearly indicates in his *Logic: The Theory of Inquiry,* we can never be certain whether or not other factors (unknown or even unknowable) have affected the result.

Does the end justify the means? he asks. Here, I believe the language of the therapist reveals the way he talks to himself—the way he thinks. Here we seem to have—even on the printed page!—nonverbal communication that reveals the value system of the communicator. "Duplicity," "trick," "confession" are terms that are flavorsome of an inner conflict that is detrimental to the therapeutic process. When a medical man gives a placebo, he is not concerned with his own guilt. No thought of duplicity enters his mind. His whole self—ideas filtered by values—is patient-directed and not complicated by inner-directedness. This inner-directedness cannot, in my opinion, be explained away by the therapist through symbols of "high ideals" or "ethical standards." A therapist who is whole-heartedly patient-directed is not troubled by such inner conflicts.

Does the end justify the means? This is an age-old philosophical question and a footless one, it seems to me, unless it is attached to a specific goal that calls for specific operational means. To speak of means and ends as if isolated—on the abstract level—is to invade a universe of discourse suitable to ghosts.

There is much to be gained by manipulation of determinative aspects of a situation-as-a-whole. The mother and son were, in this case, aspects of a situation-as-a-whole in which no sharp division could be drawn between the two. The therapist is obliged to analyze and use the relevant aspects of the field. Indirection is a subtle and powerful means of effecting desired change. In this case, the therapist seems to have moved forward intuitively and with apparent success. It is my opinion that he should proceed in like operational manner but (1) with a clear awareness of the nature of the relationships involved (as understandable and communicable by systemic language), and (2) with a clear awareness of the usefulness of behavior patterns in his strategy for transformation.

All Alone
by the Telephone

8

History

Patient was a girl, 19 years of age, brought from a foreign country by one of her relatives after having been sick for about three years. Withdrawn, nonresponsive, negativistic, almost catatonic. A psychiatrist whom the family consulted diagnosed the patient as schizophrenic and advised commitment to an institution. Friends of the family insisted on an attempt being made with Adlerian analysis.

She was a good-looking patient, delicate, somehow languishing, unwilling to communicate, and obviously in utter anxiety. The relative who had brought the patient from her native country to the first psychiatrist and then to the psychiatrist who was to undertake the therapy had left town again, leaving the patient to her own devices in a rented room where the patient spent whole days without eating, cleaning herself, or dressing; without speaking the language of the country too well; and without knowing a soul apart from the psychiatrist, the family friend, and the therapist. She was unwilling to give her address, but agreed to come every day at a certain time for an hour's interview.

Slowly she revealed her family situation. The father had died, two older brothers were ruling the household consisting of her mother and herself. They also had taken over the father's store and held the purse-strings. One brother especially was brutal, had beaten the patient many times, and had become very angry when three years ago she had gone into a deep depression and could not help in the store as the brothers requested. At that time, she seems to have had hallucinations, which, however, were not apparent at the time of therapy.

She had always wanted to have an education which was refused because "no girl needed to know anything." Freedom of movement and of choice had been denied to her by her family, and she had waxed more rebellious but had lacked the courage for open attack. She became more and more withdrawn; could not get up many days, certainly could not work; lost weight, sleep, and appetite; and offered more and more the picture of a catatonic psychosis.

Basically a person of dogged determination she eventually frightened her family enough so that they were willing to send her away with the one relative, a sister-in-law with whom she had been on good terms. She had been certain that once away from home she would be going to school and get the education that her brothers had begrudged her.

For weeks after her arrival she still was completely despondent, sleepless, talking very little and almost in a mumble. In the street she walked with head bent down; if someone walked on the same curb in the other direction, she crossed the road so as not to have to meet. But she came regularly to her sessions until the incident occurred.

Incident

The day before the patient had talked a great deal about suicide, as she thought that she was worthless, could never get out of her difficulties, blaming her relatives for her plight and, of course, the therapist for not pulling her out of her troubles without bothering her with her having to cooperate in this work. At the end of the session she was given another appointment for the next day, for 1 P.M.

The patient didn't come, didn't call; she still had refused to give her address. The problem was either to give way to one's fear that she might have carried her revenge ideas to the point of attempting suicide and, by trying to interfere, to be drawn into her net of domination; or to wait it out in the hope that one's own outlook on her problem was correct and that she was using this as a means to make the therapist subservient, as she had done with her family.

The decision was made in favor of waiting. At 9 P.M. the patient called and said that she had had a toothache and that, therefore, she did not keep her appointment. She was told that it was a good idea not to run about with a toothache and that she should come back next day.

She came and not a word was said about the whole incident, although the patient apparently wanted to be asked about it. It was considered more fruitful for the continuation of the therapy to accept her fictitious toothache as fact.

From this time on, the patient became more communicative, livelier, as if the realization that no reproach was uttered for not having called on time gave her the impression that, on the part of the therapist, friendly feelings and respect for her decision would make it worth her while to open up more.

Unfortunately, her family decided to take her back home, and six weeks after the first interview her brother appeared and without any consultation with the therapist took the patient away.

Discussion

The short time of therapy was, of course, not nearly enough even to get into some of the more important factors of the patient's illness. But it was considered a much better procedure to use a few points of clarification and interpretation while establishing a relationship of confidence on the part of the patient. It could be shown to her that her desire for education as a means of outdoing her brothers, under whose domination she was suffering, being a girl and, therefore, no good, and her method of sabotaging this very education were one expression of her enormous ambitiousness. About three months after her return home patient wrote a letter ending with the following words: "I have never hated anyone as much as I hate you. Because I know now that I only have one way before me: to get well."

Three years later patient returned for a visit, and only then was the conversation turned to the suicide threat. It was interesting that the patient said, first, that she did not remember that incident at all; then, that she did not do it to try to frighten the therapist; and lastly, that the therapist's action had given her the feeling that here she was understood.

RUDOLPH DREIKURS . . .

It takes the courage of an Adlerian to accept a patient such as this one for psychotherapy. However, this reviewer would not have undertaken this task and assumed the responsibility for such a sick girl left alone in the city, without at least having her address. This would be a minimum contribution on the part of the patient. If she was unwilling, I would express my understanding for her distrust, which was part of her condition, but would have worked out this problem with her, making her realize the therapist's responsibility.

Such undue "permissiveness" is the less indicated since it is obvious that the patient, in a passive way, was concerned with power, defeating the aggressive power of her relatives. It was this obvious yielding to the patient's direction which explained the dramatic effect of the "incident."

One can agree with the therapist that it was handled very adequately and that her (I assume it is a she) response to the patient's exceedingly provocative behavior—which was obviously designed to frighten the therapist—was a crucial moment in their relationship. However, the good effect has not been completely explained. The patient said that she felt "understood." It seems, however, that there must be more to it. The therapist showed not only "friendly feelings and respect" by not reproaching her; she did much more than that, she became for the first time a *match* for the patient. Ignoring the threat and the danger of the situation, she was no longer intimidated by the patient.

There is another important factor involved. Doing the opposite of what the patient expects is very often exceedingly effective, particularly in moments when the patient has the therapist on the run or cornered. The element of surprise deprives the patient of his mostly unconscious scheming procedure. For this reason, actions which produce shock effect are usually helpful in a deteriorating relationship. (In a good relationship, they may have the opposite effect.)

VINCENT HERR . . .

In this incident the therapist has taken a calculated risk as to the seriousness of the client's desire to do damage to herself. Persons who have been in similar situations know what a disturbing experience this can be for the counselor or therapist. The writer has known young therapists who have stayed awake nights worrying about such a risk, and has also witnessed a case in which the therapist made a "false decision" about the seriousness of the client's wish, and as a consequence became so threatened in the role of therapist that she had to take treatment herself. All this shows the gravity of the consequences following upon what seems like a small decision, namely whether to get perturbed with the client or to act as if the client really did not intend to carry out a threat of suicide.

The incident also shows up very clearly the serious consequences in the life of any man which follow upon a loss of life goals and of the meaning and value of life. It would be a real contribution to the science of therapy if more research could be done and published telling us just how a person does become endowed with a conviction of his own worth, and a determination to pursue worthwhile goals when perhaps *no one else in the world* seems to see any good whatever in such a person.

This writer believes the therapist acted with some sort of intuition so that there was very nearly a state of certainty that the client could be helped out of the difficult dilemma in which she found herself. On the other hand it might well have happened that the very action of the therapist in "waiting" it out changed a previous determination on the part of the client. In other words, his treatment method removed some of the hostility that was directed inward on the part of the patient. At any rate the risk seems to have been well taken, and the "understanding" and/or "appreciation" that the therapist showed actually resulted in a favorable outcome for the patient—for which, of course, she would be eternally grateful.

The incident also shows the sufferings and inferiority feelings that women are likely to feel when they are dominated by males from earliest infancy. This attitude on the part of the older brothers, together with the general unhappy state of the client's childhood, no doubt did a great deal to foster the feeling of worthlessness, and to induce the withdrawing tendencies so clearly portrayed in this short statement about the case. It would appear that this again might be traced to culturally determined patterns whereby the roles of the two sexes, are opposed to each other in regard to prominence and life occupations. If women are inferior to men, it is certainly not in basic worth and mental ability. In fact, the realization of a God-given equality in the essentials of a human being, as shared differently by male and female, would go a long way toward dissipating these so-called "inferiority" feelings which women so often have. If the patient in the case had not responded so fiercely to the environmental forces which made her feel inferior to men, and had at the same time realized within her heart of hearts that there should not be this discrimination, there would have been less conflict and therefore perhaps less danger of developing self-destructive tendencies.

One last comment seems in order. Even though the patient had been diagnosed as schizophrenic, the therapist did not thereby consider that a suicide was inevitable. The present writer has saved several similar persons, but only with some trepidation on his part—which, of course, could never be made known to the patient. We see then that the therapist who handled this case had to maintain a delicate balance of appreciation and under- standing of the patient's real needs, together with the feeling of confidence that there would be a favorable outcome. This combination of feelings will certainly produce a healthy effect upon a suicidal patient, and there seems to be no other course for the therapist to follow in certain cases of this sort. It is, nevertheless, a risk in every case, and prudence plus experience can be the only determiners of the therapist's choice.

The ethics involved in permitting a patient to make such a threat with- out protesting and laying down the law, as it were, have been discussed at great length by moralists and ethicians, usually to no avail. That is, they never come up with any answers which really tell us what to do in similar circumstances. Of course, any therapist who was absolutely certain that the patient would walk out and immediately carry out the act of threatened suicide would not allow him to walk out. It has always seemed to the present writer that all the disputes of the moralists could be avoided if we were to remember one simple rule: whenever a patient gives any hope of improvement in his feelings and attitudes, as a result of an interview or a series of sessions with a therapist, then the therapist is certainly not jeopard- izing anybody's life or otherwise committing evil by "permitting" the client to continue to solve his own problems with growing insights and support from without. The most astounding and totally undesirable results of "not permitting" or of "scolding" the patient when he threatens suicide are written over the pages of history. So too are the good results of having a trusted person really understand another and help him with true kindness to bear up under the distressing situations of life.

This writer had just a hint, arising from the final paragraph of the re- ported incident, that the patient was not yet wholly cured. Cause for think- ing this might well arise from the fact that the patient had completely erased her threatened suicide from her memory, and acted as if it never had happened. Coupled with this doubt of a permanent cure is the thought that also there had been real progress over the three years, since the patient after analysis did see clearly the reality of the fact that "she had not made the threat of suicide in order to frighten the therapist."

FAY KARPF . . .

This is both a very interesting and very challenging case and incident: first, because despite an unfavorable diagnosis, the therapist recognized the health possibility of the patient; second, because a strong therapeutic relationship was evidently early established and took firm root in the dynamics of the patient, even though the therapy continued for only six weeks; third, because of the therapist's handling of the critical incident, which highlights an important ethical and professional problem.

It would have been most helpful to get the therapist's view regarding the original psychiatric diagnosis and the basis for his disregard of the advised institutional commitment, in view of the patient's long period of illness and her serious symptoms. But in the absence of any comment on this diagnosis and recommendation, either in confirmation or correction of them, it must be assumed that the therapist disagreed with the diagnosis and the suggested plan of treatment. Furthermore, after only a brief period of therapy, the therapist was sufficiently confident that his "own outlook on her problem was correct" to chance a possible suicidal attempt without interference. What could have been the basis of this risky display of confidence? The therapist's faith in the fundamental soundness of the patient supported by the "relationship of confidence" which he sought to foster? Even assuming a strong therapeutic relationship, indirectly evidenced by the patient's later comments and her subsequent behavior, the question still arises: Was the therapist justified in taking such a risk? In a good working patient-therapist relationship should it not be possible to react as a human being in an emergency without being threatened by what the therapist terms the patient's "net of domination"?

The problem, according to the therapist, was: ". . . either to give way to one's fear that she might have carried her revenge ideas to the point of attempting suicide and, by trying to interfere, being drawn into her net of domination; or to wait it out in the hope that one's own outlook on her problem was correct and that she was using this tactic as a means to make the therapist subservient, as she had done with her family." The decision, he states, was made in favor of waiting. The wisdom of this decision can well be argued. Most therapists would probably feel that the temporary professional hazard, even if it did exist, was by far the lesser risk, and furthermore one that could be counterbalanced in the course of later therapy and hence would prefer to err, if at all, in the latter direction. However, the outcome of the therapist's procedure was apparently favorable and evidently made a deep impression on the patient. Perhaps it indicates the correctness of his appraisal of the total situation.

The next day, according to the therapist, not a word was said about the whole incident, and he accepted the patient's fictitious and insignificant excuse as fact. "It was considered more fruitful for the continuation of the therapy to accept her fictitious toothache as a fact." One wonders about this statement and why the therapist considered it necessary to accept the fictitious excuse as a fact without exploration at the time of the incident or later until the expiration of the six weeks period of therapy.

Similarly, the justification of some of the suggested interpretations may be argued but they were accepted by the patient without protest and seemingly set her on the path of a more constructive use of her personal resources, to the extent that she was able to admit the emotional character of her illness and to realize that the therapist understood her pattern of behavior.

Nothing is said about the possibility that a change of circumstances may have been a factor in the therapy, such as the understanding support of the girl's American relative. But in any event and despite challenging areas of possible difference of viewpoint and interpretation, the case as a whole would seem to represent a triumph of brief therapy. The fact that the patient wrote to the therapist after three months and visited him again after three years is evidence of the continuing significance of the therapy in the life of this desperately frustrated girl.

J. W. KLAPMAN . . .

The therapist has certainly penetrated this patient's deeper dynamics and handled the patient with great finesse. As he describes her, she was apparently an individual with a will and ambition and would make very little compromise with her life situation. In some instances, not rarely encountered, this kind of absolutely uncompromising will is related to even more unrealistic ends, with what might be called utterly "nebulous goals," and very frequently with tragic results.

Not being able in any other way to gain any retribution against her relative or to achieve, in her case, a more practical goal (an education) she resorted to the more extreme device of wreaking vengeance on herself by starvation, withdrawal, and flight into schizophrenia.

And still, throughout such a drastic resort to schizophrenia, there is the longing for that angelic and ethereal being who can and will penetrate the strategem, fulfill her wishes, and rescue her from that estate.

The fallacy of resorting to schizophrenic withdrawal to gain any end, either consciously or unconsciously, very much lies in the fact that schizophrenia, however begun, is often a one-way street and a dangerous strategem. Then, perhaps, the resort to schizophrenia was more hostile retribution than any genuine motivation for an education. For, when the opportunity to go to school did present itself at her sister-in-laws', there was still no pursuit of an education. Unwittingly, she was in the process of cutting off her own nose to spite her face.

But that psychotherapist fellow—there was something interesting there. He actually seemed to have a line on her—and was not displeased, nor did he censure. He seemed "to dig" the patient. Nevertheless, he put little stock in, nor did he buy any of, that process of "nose-cutting" to spite her face. That's why she said she hated him.

The residual healthy part of her personality insisted that the psychotherapist was right, and he said "get well." Therefore, the patient commented: "Because I know now that I only have one way before me: to get well."

Maybe the psychotherapist was not wholly the ethereal, angelic creature she originally looked for, but he was the next best thing to it.

No wonder she came back three years later, in part, to express her gratitude.

E. H. PORTER . . .

One thing which strikes me as being of interest here is the difference between how the *therapist* experiences his handling of the situation and his view of how the *patient* experiences his handling of the situation.

Even to old hands at the game, and this therapist is no beginner, waiting out a suicide threat is no picnic. I would guess that were this therapist to go back over his recording of the hour the day before the incident, that he would find himself reacting at a little higher pitch than ordinarily. The possibility is always present that a patient may make a mistake and his threat will get carried out—a possibility with consequences no one enjoys facing.

How does this therapist experience his handling of the situation? Although it arouses anxiety, the therapist takes a calculated risk. He acts with deliberation. He elects to use a technique of nonintervention. He experiences his handling of the situation as a matter of suitable technique.

How does the therapist view the patient's experience of being handled in this way? He states, "From this time on, the patient became more communicative, livelier, as if the realization that no *reproach* [italics mine] was uttered for not having called on time gave her the impression that, on the part of the therapist, *friendly feelings and respect for her decision* [italics mine] would make it worth her while to open up more." In the paragraph immediately preceding, the therapist has said, "She came and not a word was said about the whole incident, although the patient apparently wanted to be asked about it."

We get at one and the same time the notions that the patient is eager to be questioned about the incident, the patient fears reproach, and the patient feels her decision has been respected in a friendly way.

Since the therapist apparently avoided with some deliberation any reproachfulness as well as any leads which might have resulted in the patient's talking about the incident, we have further reason to feel that he was, in his own view, practicing a technique and not acting out of *"respect for her decision"* [italics mine].

Client-centered therapists have for years endeavored to study closely their behavior during therapy and its consistency with their true feelings. It has often driven us wild (one, at least) as we sought to understand how a therapist can feel he is demonstrating an honest respect for a patient's decision, yet openly say that he was manipulating the situation.

As I look at it now, I see this: even though the therapist's motives may have been devoid of any real respect for the patient's right to decide to come to the hour, to stay away from the hour, or to take her own life, nevertheless, the therapist did not intervene in her decision and that, in, of, and by itself, is respectful behavior.

In my view, every patient (and person, too) not only has dependency needs, needs to keep others around for fulfilling neurotic wishes, but independency needs as well. Could it possibly be that "feeding" independency needs, needs for respect from, and nonintervention by others will make those needs grow and become predominant just as the "feeding" of dependency needs appears to make them grow and predominate in behavior?

What was that the patient wrote in her letter? "I have never hated anyone as much as I hate you. Because I know now that I have only one way before me: to get well."

The therapist says, "The short time of therapy was, *of course* [italics mine], not nearly enough even to get into some of the more important factors of the patient's illness. . . ."

I submit that the therapist, despite his bowing to convention as he says *"of course,"* has given this girl a gift that all too few people obtain in a lifetime, the realization that only she can be responsible for herself.

WERNER WOLFF . . .

Provocations of the patient are his tool to test the therapist. They are rooted in those two phenomena which Freud called the cornerstones of psychoanalysis, namely, resistance and transference. Provocations due to resistance challenge the therapist to take initiative; provocations due to transference challenge the therapist's emotional relations. Both forms of provocations serve the patient to manipulate and to dominate the therapist and to develop a defense system by drawing the patient-therapist relationship into it. Usually, therapists will be watchful and careful not to respond to the patient's provocations. However, in cases of a patient's existential isolation the therapist may have to prove his "human" value to the patient.

In the present case the patient's basic experience was to be abandoned, disliked, and made to feel worthless. A critical incident had to convey to her that an important person trusted her, believed in her, and understood her.

I remember a similar incident with a former child-patient of mine. This boy, 12 years of age, was generally maladjusted, stole, cheated, was vagrant, aggressive, and nonconforming in school. He was beaten by his parents, who were disinterested in his personal problems. The boy tried to provoke me at first by nonconformity and mischievousness, and later by lies (for instance, telling me that he had excellent marks in school). I adopted the policy of believing everything he said, of entering his "game," and of rewarding his lies. After a month he had a breakdown; crying and weeping he confessed that he had cheated and betrayed me. After this critical incident a general adjustment took place.[1]

It seems that in cases of "isolation" neurosis, a therapist can use several ways to establish transference and to win confidence by displaying trust in the patient, who tests the limits before giving up his defenses and overcoming doubts and fears of disappointment.

[1] Werner Wolff, *Diagrams of the Unconscious* (New York: Grune & Stratton, 1946).

"I'll Kill You
If You Leave Me!"

9

History

A female patient whom I shall call Mrs. Ann Perry came to see me by appointment in December, 1953. She had been referred by a clergyman to whom she had talked about getting a separation or a divorce from her husband.

Mrs. Perry was an attractive well-groomed, dark-haired, weary-looking, 39-year-old woman who spoke in a tired voice bordering on despair. She had been married for 18 years to a man six years her senior who had been married and divorced. Mr. Perry had a daughter from his former marriage whom he never supported, visited, or talked about throughout his marriage to his second wife. Mrs. Perry had never seen either this girl or her husband's former wife. There were three teen-aged children from this union.

Mrs. Perry, who became my patient, had two years of college education and for many years had been steadily employed in a responsible, clerical civil service position. For over 10 years, she had been the main support of the family.

Mr. Perry was a blonde, leathery-faced, wiry, 45-year-old man who gave a first impression of being a silent, outdoor, "he-man" type. He "loved" horses, and when I first interviewed him, he owned six horses. He also liked rodeos and for many years had spent many of his weekends away from his family riding in rodeos or being an observer at them.

I saw the patient five times before the case was closed. She stated that for the past three years her husband had been living in Wyoming where he had expected to make a lot of money raising cattle. He came home for a few months in the winter but spent a good deal of his time with horses and at rodeos. Although she wrote her husband once or twice a week while he was away and encouraged the children to write to him, the husband wrote only two short notes in three years. Apparently he did not dislike the children, but he paid little attention to them and had never been much of a father to them.

During the time he was gone, he was supposed to make a substantial contribution toward the support of his family, but he failed to do so. While he was in Wyoming, the patient was happier and less tense than she had been before, and she realized that she could manage to support herself and her children. When he returned home in September, 1953, she told him she wanted a separation and possibly a divorce. Since the time when she first raised the question of divorce, he had made one or more of the following threats about once or twice a week. If she tried to leave him:

1. He would fix her so that she would never be able to work again and no man would ever want to look at her.
2. He would kill himself.
3. He would kill the patient, the children, and then himself.

On the evening before her first appointment with me, the patient stated that while the children were out for a few hours the husband started drinking whisky. (Although he was not a drinking man, he had been doing a little drinking recently.) After two or three drinks, he started arguing with the patient, pushed her into their bedroom, picked up a loaded deer rifle, and threatened to kill her if she left him. Similar episodes had taken place twice before.

During the past two months, he had been forcing her to have intercourse with him every night. He was quite virile and showed no signs of impotency. Recently she discovered that he had punched small holes in her diaphragm. When she confronted him with this, he readily admitted that he was trying to get her pregnant so that she would be unable to leave him. During her first interview, she stated she was afraid she might be pregnant as her menstrual period was about a week overdue.

Throughout her marriage sexual experiences had never been satisfactory, and since her husband's return she felt a strong revulsion when he touched her. When he wanted to make love to her, all she could think was that he smelled like a horse barn and had not bathed in a week. She had never had intercourse with anyone except her husband.

She found it impossible to be civil to him, not only because of his cold-blooded threats but because of the "filthy habits" he had acquired in Wyoming. For example, besides his failure to bathe, when he urinated, he habitually let some of the urine go on the bathroom floor.

She said she had thought of running away with the children but felt he would follow her and kill them all. When I raised the question of reporting his threatening behavior to the police she stated that he had warned her about that. He told her that she would not be able to prove anything and that the worst that could happen to him would be a jail sentence of 10 to 30 days. He added that when he got out of jail he would fix her so that she would remember it the rest of her life —if she lived. He reiterated that he loved her and could not live without her.

The patient volunteered that she did not think their problem was all his fault, as her husband never seemed to get the breaks in life. Frequently, he had had what sounded to me like grandiose ideas about making big money but had never been successful in any of his business deals. However, she simply could not go on this way and wanted to know if I could help her.

When I asked her what he was like when she married him and why she married him she stated it was a result of a summer romance. She had had a disappointing love affair and was vacationing in the high Sierras when she met Mr. Perry. He was a handsome, outdoor type man and paid a lot of attention to her. She was a virgin until then and had intercourse with him two or three times and felt she should marry him. About two weeks after they were married, she realized it had been a mistake, but she never said anything to him about this until recently.

Incident

I saw the husband twice for full appointments and twice for a shared appointment with his wife. He stated that he loved his wife, had always been faithful to her, and was shocked at her attitude when he returned for good from Wyoming. He insisted that up to this time they had had a happy marriage. He explained her rejection of him by stating that she must be sick—maybe she was having an early menopause. He had built his whole life around her; she was a fine woman; he was sure she had never been unfaithful to him.

Several times in each interview he mentioned that he "never laid a hand on that woman." He seemed to feel that this was evidence of the fact that he had been a good husband. He said he would "do anything" to keep her.

When I asked him if he had any guns, at first he was casual in his reply; for example, he liked guns, had several of them, and used them to go hunting. Later he admitted that he had threatened his wife with a gun once, but that he was only joking. Still later and on further questioning he admitted that he threatened to kill her several times. After this admission, he became defensive and hostile toward me. There was a flicker of hatred in his eyes as he accused me of taking his wife's part. During these sessions the husband confirmed almost everything his wife had told me.

In a joint interview I suggested that before I would go any further into the case, I felt the patient should have a complete physical examination and both agreed to this. I then suggested that he, too, should have a good physical check-up, especially since he had a history of several serious falls from horses, including one in which he had been unconscious for over an hour and might have suffered some cerebral trauma. Furthermore, he had complained that he could not work steadily because his back hurt. Mr. Perry said there was nothing the matter with him—but he was sure the patient was sick.

The patient was examined by a very capable internist and signed a release of medical information slip. The physician sent me his medical report which, among other things, stated that the patient was in good physical condition except for some small inclusion cysts of the cervix. There were no objective findings of early pregnancy. Laboratory studies were within normal limits except for a very mild hypochromic anemia.

After I received this report an appointment was made with both of them. I interviewed the patient alone first, then the husband alone, and then both of them together.

The patient stated that the physician had told her she was in good health except for some minor things which could be taken care of easily. Regarding her husband's behavior she stated that although he had not threatened her with a gun during the past week, he had shown her a newspaper clipping of a man who had killed his mother-in-law, his wife, and children, and told her that if she tried to leave him he would do the same thing.

He had again complained that he could not work steadily as a fence salesman because of his sore back, but the previous weekend he had gone to a rodeo and roped steers. She had come to the conclusion that he did not want to break up the marriage because she was providing him with a "good home and a meal ticket." She added that, in general, he had tried to be more pleasant recently but complained that she gave him the "silent treatment." She volunteered that she did ignore him as much as possible and that she had nothing to say to him.

When I interviewed the husband he became belligerent and overtly hostile toward me. He stated that he was sure there must be something physically or mentally wrong with his wife and that the physician who had examined her was a quack. He projected his troubles on the fact that his wife worked, that his mother-in-law was too religious and took his wife to church practically every night in the week (further discussion revealed that actually the patient went to choir practice one evening per week and to regular services on Sunday morning). I indicated that, although she may have some emotional problems and possibly need help, perhaps he, too, could use some help. Again I tried to encourage him to go to a physician for a physical examination and to consider psychiatric treatment. He rejected this suggestion and accused me of conspiring with his wife to get rid of him.

At this point I was thoroughly convinced that Mr. Perry was a dangerous paranoid individual and that his problems were outside my area of competence. I also felt that his prognosis was poor and that he had a strong need to kill someone.

I saw the patient alone for two more interviews and interpreted these things to her. I told her that under the circumstances I did not feel I could be of any help to her and that she should get legal advice to protect herself from her potentially homicidal and/or suicidal husband.

She told me that since I saw him last he had been following her around the house, had watched her constantly, and was suspicious when she left the house. I told the patient that such behavior further confirmed my impression that he was mentally unbalanced and that she was in great danger.

When I asked how the children were reacting, she stated that they knew there was marital friction but had no knowledge of their father's bizarre and threatening behavior as he was careful not to do anything unusual in their presence. Later on I interviewed the children and was convinced that they knew nothing of their father's threats.

In the last interview, the patient told me that her husband still threatened her, although she felt he was trying not to do so. He had also been expressing some hostility toward me by telling her it was a waste of time and money to see me. He told her all she needed to do was to make up her mind to "fly right and settle down," be a good wife, and live with him

I emphasized that her husband needed psychiatric help and that if he decided to seek such help I would be willing to take her on for some supportive therapy. However, if he did not do this, I advised her to seek legal assistance so that she and the children could be protected. *Case closed.*

Several weeks later, I received a release of information slip from an attorney signed by the patient. Later the attorney telephoned me and said he was planning to take her case, file a petition for divorce, and try to get her legal protection. He asked if I thought the husband was really dangerous. I told him that it was my opinion that he was very dangerous and I believed he was a "potential killer." When he asked me about the possibility of having him committed to a mental hospital, I told him that I had already discussed this with the patient but that she was fearful of filing commitment papers on him. Furthermore, since he did not manifest overt psychotic or bizarre behavior in public and was so well controlled that even his children had no inkling of what he did, it was highly unlikely that he could be committed. I further told him I did not wish to be an alarmist but that I believed that if the patient filed on him and if he, as her attorney, was involved in helping her do this, as soon as Mr. Perry heard about it, he would probably try to kill them both. I then raised the question about reporting the matter to the police, and the attorney said there was nothing the police could do in such a case, unless they had witnesses who would testify that he threatened the patient with a gun. In that case, the most that Mr. Perry would get would be a sentence of about 30 days in jail.

Four months later, I received a telephone call from an individual who said he was from the sheriff's department, asking for information about this family. I told the person on the telephone that I could not release any information but asked for his name and told him I would telephone right back. I called the sheriff's telephone number and got this man on the line, thus assuring myself that it was really the sheriff's department that he represented.

Before answering any questions, I asked if Mr. Perry had killed his wife and himself or just himself. The deputy sheriff said that Mr. Perry had been found in his home with the top of his head literally shot off. He stated that he and another deputy wished to talk to me about the matter, as they understood I had tried to help this family some time ago. He added that both Mrs. Perry and her attorney were in his office and asked me if I wished to speak to them, which I did. When the sheriff's deputy got on the telephone again, I told him I could give them an appointment that evening and that they were to bring a release of information slip which I had asked the patient to sign while talking to her on the telephone.

I then asked the deputy if they were going to hold the patient on a possible murder charge, and he said they planned to do so but hadn't decided definitely yet. I told him that I doubted very much if she could have killed her husband, although I felt she had every reason to want to do so. I also suggested that on the basis of what he and the attorney had told me over the telephone I hoped they would not hold the patient in jail because she had suffered a great deal already. I asked if they were having the crime laboratory work on the case, and he replied in the affirmative, adding that the laboratory reports would not be ready until the next day.

Two deputy sheriffs came to see me that evening, and I gave them a complete run down on the case and also had them read all the notes in my case records. They told me that the patient had given them the following story.

That morning Mr. Perry offered to drive her to work because he needed the car. The children had not yet left for school. Instead of taking her to work, he drove around in the back country for about an hour and then returned home. The husband told her to go into the house because he wanted to talk to her. By this time the children had left for school. He made her go into their bedroom, locked the door, picked up the deer rifle, loaded it, and started threatening her as he had done in the past. She stated that at this point she just didn't care what happened any more and yelled at him to go ahead and kill her and get it over with. As he raised the rifle she turned her face to the wall and stood there with her hands over her ears. A few moments later a shot went off. She didn't know how long she stood there before she turned around and saw the husband's decapitated body on the floor. She did not remember what happened until her neighbors found her screaming in the street.

Before the deputies left they told me that on the basis of their discussion with me and an examination of my case record they, too, felt it was unlikely that the patient had killed the husband.

The following day, I learned that the laboratory reports and a reconstruction of the crime corroborated the patient's story The sheriff's department reconstructed the crime as follows: The victim had shot himself by standing the rifle on the floor, tilting his head to one side, and placing his temple over the muzzle. He reached down and pulled the trigger. The bullet was found lodged in the ceiling and there were powder burns on the fragments of the head where the bullet had penetrated.

Discussion

Whenever a tragedy occurs in a case in which a social worker, psychiatrist, or clinical psychologist had been professionally involved, at least three questions can and should be raised:

1. Did the therapist do anything which might have abetted the tragedy?
2. What did the therapist fail to do which might have averted what followed?
3. What lessons can be derived from such an incident?

It seems to me that in this case, the first two questions can be answered in the negative. Several efforts were made to encourage Mr. Perry to obtain psychiatric assistance. Considering my own safety, which might easily have been endangered by such a patient, I did not feel that I should pursue the matter further than I did. However, both his wife and her attorney were informed without any equivocation about my impressions of Mr. Perry.

It should be borne in mind that persons who are apparently suffering from long standing, chronic, "mildly" paranoid conditions are frequently unable and/or unwilling to seek psychiatric help. Furthermore, if such patients do go to a psychiatrist's office they usually do not remain in treatment very long. If they enter a mental hospital, they invariably agitate successfully for their release.

Regarding the third question, I would like to make the following observations.

One of the important things to be learned in private practice and specifically from this type of case, is knowing when to accept a case and when to close it if it turns out to be outside one's area of competence. In an agency setting, the staffing of problem cases and the opportunity to discuss cases with colleagues act as safeguards if an individual therapist gets into a therapeutic jam or acts with poor judgment regarding a hazardous situation. In private practice, it is essential that one's skills in sizing up situations be sharpened and that one be constantly alert and, when in doubt, cautious.

Although there is an urgent need for both cross-sectional and longitudinal research in the field of mental disorders, priority should be given to research into the etiology and treatment of paranoid conditions including both those which appear to be "with" and those "without" psychosis. Every day newspapers all over the nation carry stories of individuals who commit serious crimes. It is not uncommon to learn that such individuals behaved in a manner indicating that for a long period of time they maintained some degree of emotional homeostasis by utilizing the mechanism of projection. These individuals frequently have had long-standing ideas of persecution, ideas of grandeur, and/or a long history of litigation.

Although it is imperative that civil rights be protected and that due process of law not violated, it is also imperative that for the protection of such individuals and the general public laws dealing with the mentally ill be carefully scrutinized. Members of the legal profession, of the medical profession, and especially of the specialty of psychiatry—as well as those of related professions, such as social work and clinical psychology—should give serious thought to the medieval statutes of many states which deal with "alleged" mental disorders. Furthermore, after careful study and research, appropriate action should be taken to modify such laws when indicated.

In the present case, unless Mr. Perry was willing to seek psychiatric help on an out-patient basis or to apply for voluntary admission to a mental hospital, everyone concerned in the case was powerless to do anything about it.

I have wondered why he did not kill his wife before killing himself. I think he was certainly ambivalent about killing her but not about killing her *per se*. I felt that unless Mr. Perry was forcibly institutionalized, he was going to kill. This is based primarily on clinical judgment which, of course, is mostly subjective. There are several possible reasons or combinations of reasons why he did not murder his wife. The one which I think is most plausible is related to the fact that according to the "western code," one does not shoot somebody in the back. Because of his long association with cowboys and rodeos, I suspect that he was an adherent of "western code" beliefs. Therefore, the fact that the patient turned her back on him may have been responsible for saving her life.

One further observation may be in order—namely, it is incumbent upon anyone engaged in psychotherapy to keep at least brief notes of what takes place in therapy sessions.

Rudolf Dreikurs . . .

The description of this very dramatic and difficult situation indicates an attitude and procedure on the part of the therapist with which this reviewer can only fully agree.

However, there is one element which would deserve serious consideration. The correct diagnosis of the husband's condition apparently prevented any concern with the dynamics of the interaction between him and his wife. The fact that the man was paranoic does not minimize the importance of his interaction with those around him. If his action is seen only as an expression of intrapersonal dynamic processes, then one can be satisfied with describing him as aggressive, hostile, paranoic, and dangerous. However, there seems to be more to the picture. This man apparently acts on the premises of a strong masculine protest. One wonders whether or not the question of his doubt in his own masculinity and his desire to prove that he was a superior man was ever brought out in the few interviews with him. He obviously was a tyrant. He tried to overpower his wife both through his behavior and through his sexual abuses. Naturally, he did not want to lose his victim.

But there is a way to deal more effectively with tyrants. It requires first freedom from fear. This may sound paradoxical and even nonsensical when the danger is as real as in this case. But experience has shown that fear is the more damaging the greater the danger is. It does relatively little harm if it is only imaginary; but in real danger it paralyzes the victim and increases the actual threat.

In a case like this, one could have tried to help Mrs. Perry to overcome her fear of her husband. Her fear would certainly not prevent him from doing harm to her, sooner or later, but might actually provoke it. Somehow her fear seemed to have decreased in the turn of events so that she was capable of asking for a divorce. And it seems that it was this freedom from fear which eventually saved her life.

This is the only point on which one may disagree with the therapist. It is dubious that it was the "western code" which prevented the man from shooting his wife while she had turned away. It was her reconciliation with inevitable fate which really defeated him. "She stated that at this point she just didn't care what happened any more and yelled at him to go ahead and kill her and get it over with." *At this moment he had lost his power over her.* There was no longer any sense to threaten, and he probably never really wanted to kill her anyhow. Therefore, the only way out was to kill himself. If she had fought with him or tried to run away, he might have pulled the trigger just to frighten her more, and might have in his rage even killed her. But she did the opposite, she *asked* him to shoot. And he was much too much boss and man to submit to the demands of a woman!

Men such as Mr. Perry, even at the state of personal disorganization and disfunction, can be dealt with very often if their extreme pride and desire for superiority is recognized and acknowledged without submission to their demands. This, perhaps, may have been attempted here, although one cannot be sure that it would have succeeded.

WLADIMIR ELIASBERG . . .

The problem in this case was not only that of the wife; it was also that of the husband.

The therapist asks three questions: in answer to the first, evidently, the treatment given to the wife did not directly abet the tragedy. The answer to the second question is that the therapist failed to avert what followed. He omitted to diagnose or to have diagnosed by a competent psychiatrist the incipient paranoia of the husband. This therapist, like many others, apparently felt confident to tackle cases for which his experience and training did not prepare him. He assumes that contacts with patients can be established always to such a degree that patients can be given the necessary psychological motivations for change. This confidence might be justified if it were simple to recognize incipient psychoses as such, and to differentiate them from neuroses. This is simply not the case. Psychoses may start with a neurotic prodromal stage. In this case, the constant threats, the attempt of the patient's husband to conceal his intent (in the discussion with the therapist), the attempt to make the possession of the gun appear harmless, and the hostility about which the therapist did not seem to be convinced, all should have aroused suspicion. All these are traits within the compass of paranoia, especially that form which leads to acts of violence. Clinical experience would also have led the therapist to probe for homosexuality, not withstanding the overt heterosexual appetites.

The third question refers to the lesson that comes out of this incident. As far as legislation is concerned, the therapist rightly says at the moment our hands are fettered. Here is, indeed, a theory problem. All three professions involved—medicine, psychology, and law—must cooperate in working out regulations that will protect individuals and society, and that would nevertheless stand scrutiny of the Due Process Clause of the Constitution.

J. McV. Hunt . . .

It is difficult to find fault with the psychotherapist's handling of this case. In my judgment, he is to be commended for having interviewed both the husband, to satisfy himself concerning the reality of Mrs. Perry's concern, and the children, to determine the degree to which the husband's behavior indicated a disturbance in him to persons without specific knowledge of his threats to Mrs. Perry. I say that the psychotherapist is to be commended for these interviews because I am convinced that no clinician can determine the reality of a patient's complaints about another person without dependable knowledge of that other person. The psychotherapist is also to be commended because he took into consideration within his responsibility not only the welfare of his patient but also that of her family. The all-too-widespread contention that a psychotherapist has no responsibility for the family of the patient is unfortunate, and all too often tragic in its consequences.

The author of this critical incident correctly predicted that Mr. Perry was dangerous, but he expected murder as well as suicide. In view of the fact that Mr. Perry's verbal threats to harm or kill his wife coupled with his overt hostility toward the psychotherapist strongly imply motivation to harm Mrs. Perry, it is interesting to speculate about why he killed himself without killing her. Mr. Perry's lack of concern for his children and his wife while away from them tends to imply that his concerns were chiefly narcissistic. His long history of "high-flown" plans coupled with repeated failure must have left him both depressed and hateful. Mrs. Perry's expression of need to leave him provided another, and perhaps a more devastating example of his failure. Moreover, this made of her the most obvious frustrating object, and one may guess that his need to harm her was indeed great. Perhaps, therefore, it may have been her own abject submission to his threat to kill her that at once satisfied his need to harm her and intensified his own self-deprecation. Had Mrs. Perry tried to defend herself or to damage him at this crucial time, it is likely that she would have been killed. After the fact, such speculations are of little value, but if they were clearly formulated before the fact, the presence or absence of the act predicted would help test the validity of the diagnostic formulation.

The tragedy of the Perry case is one of social institutions and status of diagnostic knowledge. Since our laws are so framed that no citizen's liberty can be taken from him until he has committed a criminal act, nothing can be done legally to confine an individual who is merely judged to be dangerous by a professional person, unless he is psychotic. The definition of psychosis, unfortunately, usually requires the presence of behavior which is so deviant as to be incomprehensible to typical persons, and also deviant in the presence of a fairly large number of persons. The fact that Mr. Perry made his threats only to his wife, and never in the presence of their children, meant that it was his word against hers. The fact that he tentatively admitted his threats to Mrs. Perry's psychotherapist was not enough to commit him to a psychiatric institution.

The author of this incident points up the need for a change in the law. But this is no simple solution. A change in the law can hardly be justified until it is possible to say with empirical certainty of a high degree that people who show specified behavioral signs will unlawfully damage the lives or the welfare of others. Until diagnostic statements carry specifiable statistical odds, the reluctance of our society to give any profession or group of professions the power to withdraw an individual's liberty before he has committed an antisocial act is probably justified.

This contains a lesson for psychologists, social workers and psychiatrists in practice, and for all behavior scientists concerned with personality diagnosis. At the present time, diagnostic statements seldom contain the element of prediction. They are cast in a dynamic form in which the statements are limited to what goes on within the diagnosed individual. Until these dynamic diagnostic pictures come to contain statements about overt behavior in specified situations, they are largely untestable and largely useless for the solution of a problem such as that posed by the Perry case. If diagnostic impressions were written to include specific predictions about what overt behavior of the diagnosed individual should show in various classes of situations, the accuracy of these diagnostic impressions might gradually be tested. With testing, they would be modified. Probably they would become more accurate. Ultimately, we may hope the accumulated information would justify society changing the law to limit the freedom of individuals before they have committed "the tragic act."

J. W. Klapman . . .

As far as the handling of the case is concerned, this commentator is of the opinion that it could not be better handled under the circumstances. There was nothing else the therapist could have done. It is only to be noted that society has as yet only crude apparatus for dealing with such individuals as the patient's husband. It locks the door after the cow has been stolen. Probably the ideal thing would have been to have the husband committed to an institution, where, if the proper conditions prevailed, a purchase would have been found on his personality; he would have undergone intensive psychotherapy and perhaps have come out greatly improved. But in this, too, the wife was not altogether mistaken, for in all probability in the institution he would have been given only perfunctory treatment, his delusions against his wife would have found some objective confirmation, with a consequent increase of his homicidal tendencies.

The tragedy in this case is not the suicide alone, but also the tragic waste of human material. Society has no adequate means for safeguarding personality. For the husband impresses me as having had some healthy parts remaining in his personality which under more ideal conditions could have led to a more happy ending. This is suggested by the fact that after visiting the therapist his behavior improved for a short time, indicating some degree of insight. Unfortunately he reverted to his paranoid behavior because the emotional conflict was not sufficiently relieved.

One is also much intrigued by Freud's idea about the relationship of paranoid conditions to unconscious homosexuality. Such an instance I have seen. But just as often or oftener paranoid derangements arise from a different source, and were it appropriate I would here cite a case of a young man with paranoid schizophrenia with strong homicidal impulses which rather closely parallels the case of the above patient's husband (from that patient at first I actually feared an untimely demise). I am currently treating that patient with optimistic prospects. The dynamics in this case, as I have formulated them, do not stem from unconscious homosexuality, but from severe narcissistic blows to the ego.

The husband, we read in the above case history, was a well set-up, impressive representative of masculinity. It may have helped altogether in fixing for him an heroic (grandiose) aim in life. His was a great destiny, which became affectively-fixated in what I have labelled as a "nebulous goal"—some big, striking achievement in life. With that goal he could make very little compromise. But time marches on. Inevitably all his enterprises missed fire (most likely poorly conceived and poorly planned to begin with). All of them began to add up to a suspicion that he was a failure. But that suspicion his ego could not tolerate and there resulted a terrible emotional conflict which he could only partially relieve by projecting the blame elsewhere. He returned home, a partial and involuntary admission of his failure. His wife's threat to leave was almost the climax to the growing awareness of his failures. When he watched her so closely it was in the hope of finding evidence of her infidelity, which would not only palliate his failures, but would also supply him with an objective and justifiable reason for homicide, thus exonerating him from that *coup de grace* to his ego, the narcissistic blow of not being able to hold his wife. That probably also explains his increased sexual demands and his attempt to impregnate his wife—the attempt to ward off the worst blow of all—his wife's rejection of him. He is in terrible emotional conflict.

That final climax, so full of tragedy, is worth commenting on. His paranoid delusions have won out and he feels justified in destroying his wife. Had she in that brief instant titillated his narcissistic traumatic by upbraiding him, stating what a coward and failure he had been, there is relatively little doubt that he would have carried out his original design and ended her life. That he might have crowned his homicide with a suicide would have been little comfort. It does appear, however, that her very despair saved her, for when she remarked she no longer cared what happened to her and asked him to go ahead and shoot, in that brief flash of insight he saw himself. Who can describe the full depths of that agonized moment? He was at that profoundest level of the well of despair, and the only way out seemed to him self-destruction. If he had only had the wisdom to desire help—psychotherapeutic help—what a different sequel there *might* have been to this story.

O. HOBART MOWRER . . .

The seriousness and tragedy of the type of case here discussed was brought home to the present writer by an incident recently reported in our local papers. A middle-aged, divorced jeweler, the night before he was to be remarried, killed his three teen-age daughters and his mother with a hammer while they slept and then shot himself. There had apparently been no intimation of such a plan, nor was there any reported manifestation of psychopathology. Of course, we do not know what may have transpired between this man and his daughters or between him and his mother; but he was outwardly successful, respected, and had no known reason to commit such an act. One can only agree with Mrs. Perry's therapist concerning the ". . . urgent need for both cross-sectional and longitudinal research . . . into the etiology and treatment of paranoid conditions including both those which appear to be 'with' and those 'without' psychosis."

From the standpoint of "management," the case here reported is something of a model; and the very fact that, despite every apparent precaution, tragedy could not be averted accentuates all the more the need for deeper study of such cases and, quite possibly, a reconsideration of social provisions for handling them. For example, one wonders what the implications would be for a situation of this kind if there were more severe penalties for intimidation and threats against another person. Mr. Perry apparently knew that even if convicted under present law for such behavior, the consequences would not be very serious, and there was always open to him a means of putting himself forever beyond the law; it is also possible that the law could be used by the unscrupulous or deranged against the innocent.

Lacking the results of researches that remain to be carried out and having no inspired legal solution to problems of this kind, we are thrown back upon the therapist's own question of how he might have handled the Perry situation with a happier outcome. What follows here in no way carries the intimation that the case *should* have been handled differently. All will agree that, in light of our present knowledge, professional training, and laws, it was handled intelligently, humanely, and altogether sensibly. The only question is whether or not there is any other way in which it *might conceivably* have been handled.

In order to get the facts from Mr. Perry, the therapist evidently bore down on him pretty hard. In the beginning Mr. Perry was casual and at least outwardly friendly; but later, "There was a flicker of hatred in his eyes as he accused me of taking his wife's part." Objectively, justice was clearly on Mrs. Perry's side; but, equally objectively, the therapist did not do much to help Mr. Perry, as *he* perceived his situation. The incident in Chapter 1 dramatically illustrates what can sometimes be accomplished with even the most seemingly hopeless individuals by an unexpected kindness or act of generosity. Certainly it would not have been easy to have befriended Mr. Perry in any very vital or, to him, meaningful way. But we cannot wholly ignore the possibility that in the present instance the therapist was so interested in "calling his 'shots,'" diagnostically and prognostically, that he failed to explore sufficiently what might have been done along these lines. Certainly this was a failure, if failure it was, which can easily be forgiven. The therapist was, after all, in a *very* difficult situation; and if he acted simply as an enlightened human being, which he clearly did, rather than like an angel, most of the rest of us would be proud to have done as well. Yet here, if anywhere, seems to be the one handle of hope whereby the case might have been carried to a less sad conclusion.

Although Mr. Perry had no known history of active misdeed or crime, he had a lifelong record of sins of omission; and it would have been by no means easy to have gotten him to assume, at this late date, the responsibilities which he had manifestly been shirking. Yet men and women of all ages can be, and are, "born again"; and there appears to be no very good way of determining in advance where a campaign of restitution and rehabilitation will or will not succeed. The least we can do is to *try*.

Clara Thompson . . .

This is not a case where the primary concern is in a problem of therapy or technique, but concerns chiefly the problem of management of the person who is not in therapy. Although this woman undoubtedly had some problems of her own, the immediate reality danger superceded them. In fact, she could only have remained in an attitude acceptable to her husband if she had remained sick or become sicker. Even then, it is not certain that the husband's psychotic demands would not have become greater and greater, leading to an eventual blow-up anyway.

The therapist rightly shows that this case points up a serious defect in our legal safeguards. Not only are the wife and children endangered by such an individual as her husband being allowed freedom, but any therapist trying to treat her is also in danger of his life. We have, at present, no adequate way of protecting anyone from the destructive behavior of a paranoid, who, when the occasion demands, can appear deceptively normal. The police can do nothing to protect this woman, even if they were alerted by a psychiatrist to the danger. An overt act must take place, and then it is often too late. Even if the police were empowered to send him to a hospital for observation, not even a hospital full of psychiatrists can keep him incarcerated, because he can still fight his case before a lay jury who cannot possibly know the insidious workings of the paranoid mind. So the patient is released, usually feeling more persecuted than ever, and therefore more dangerous. The answer perhaps lies in closer cooperation of psychiatrists with the legal profession towards modifying existing laws. When adequate understanding of a case requires the opinion of experts, it seems to me criminal to ask a lay jury, or even a judge without psychiatric training, to make the final decision about the freedom of a potential killer. As long as there is no way of keeping him in a safe place, psychiatrists will continue to shy away from the responsibility, and families will continue to be murdered.

Frederick C. Thorne . . .

This case is typical of a very common emergency situation in psychotherapy where great danger to life or property exists from the actions of a person suspected of violent tendencies (particularly when overt threats have been made). In our opinion, such cases should immediately be referred to a psychiatrist (or a physician empowered to institute commitment proceedings) and to legal authorities. Any person who repeatedly makes homicidal threats must be regarded as dangerous and should be institutionalized for observation. A clinical psychologist does not have the authority to deal with the situation effectively, and the case should immediately be referred to the proper legal authority. In this case, the therapist withdrew from the case when he could no longer handle it. Hindsight indicates that more directive action should have been taken to protect all concerned. The fact that Mr. Perry had made threats against anyone who took action against him should not have intimidated the therapist since if Mr. Perry actually was capable of violence, it would have been better for him to have developed such tendencies while under observation in an institution.

Here is a situation in which the therapist cannot be passive or nondirective if the rights of all concerned are to be protected. When confronted with a fulminating paranoid state or frustration-aggression reaction, the first step must be to safeguard potential victims while simultaneously striving to control the patient himself. In our own practice, experience indicates a number of steps which need to be taken.

1. Advise family, friends, authorities, and potential victims that the client is potentially dangerous. This is not done to be alarmist, but simply to acquaint all concerned with the facts of the situation.

2. Secure an agreement among all responsible persons concerning how the patient is to be handled. This is important because it is undesirable to argue out differences of opinions in the presence of the disturbed person.

3. Do not confront the potentially violent person with any ultimatums or coercive actions until all is in readiness to protect all concerned. Experience indicates that patients tend to become violent most commonly when confronted suddenly with force. Everything should be ready to handle any emergency.

4. Make certain that sufficient manpower is available to subdue the dangerous person if he becomes physically violent. Violent patients seldom will resist overwhelming force but will fight desperately if they feel they have a chance to win.

5. Usually a period of observation in a psychiatric hospital is desirable to discover how the dangerous person is going to react when he discovers things may go against him. He should be institutionalized until all aggressive impulses are dissipated.

6. Potential victims should receive continuing protection until the dangerous person is known to be under control. If a divorce or separation is necessary, there should be a court order restraining the dangerous person from molesting or disturbing the objects of his aggressions.

Although aggressive impulses in potential murderers are sometimes "silent" in the sense that no overt acts give warning of dangerous violent states, in a much larger percentage of cases there are many signs and symptoms which indicate the need for psychiatric observation. Too often, even open threats are ignored. The difficulty is that at all times there are a large number of potentially violent persons in any community, many of whom have made repeated threats but have not previously carried them out. Unfortunately, there are not sufficient psychiatric facilities to keep all suspects under continuous observation if, indeed, society was willing to pay the costs. While it is a commonly accepted opinion that psychiatric observation and treatment might prevent many acts of violence, suitable screening methods do not exist now to discriminate potentially dangerous persons. Every psychiatric hospital has discharged patients as cured only to have them go out and soon commit homicide. With many borderline cases in which known aggressive impulses appear to be under control, it is anybody's guess whether or not a situation will arise in which the etiologic equation for a violent outburst will be realized. Conservative handling requires the institution of sufficient directive controls to protect all concerned.

The least any therapist can do, not only to protect society but also his own reputation, is to routinely seek independent consultations in such cases in order to get other opinions concerning the gravity of the situation and what should be done. After a therapist has worked long enough in a community, he usually builds up resources and patterns for handling emergency situations.

Client-Centered

Hypnosis?

10

History

The client was a self-referred prisoner, a white male about 40 years of age serving a sentence for forgery and fraud. He was a second offender, having served a previous sentence for fraud. He was an extremely intelligent person, being a self-educated engineer, and had made a number of minor inventions. The expressed reason for coming for therapeutic assistance was to discover the reasons for his criminal behavior.

Therapy was given according to Rogers' client-centered technique, and from the beginning excellent rapport was established. He gave many indications of improvement in terms of insightful statements, reports of better social adjustment in the institution, and changes in his attitude to people in general, to the law, and toward himself.

Incident

Therapy had progressed for about a year. I saw him once a week for an hour at a time. However, I was requested by my supervisor to discontinue the contact because of the pressure of requests for therapy by other prisoners. I conveyed this message to my client, and he suggested that we go on for ten further sessions, and then end the therapy.

Near the end of the ten sessions, he began to exhibit signs of distress, claiming that although he had benefited he felt absolutely certain that there was something else that *had* to come out. He was certain that there was an explanation for his bizarre criminal behavior and that he felt certain he would someday come out with the answer. However, despite his distress and insistence that there was something that "wanted to come out" he never seemed to be able to produce the material he desired.

On the next to last session, without previous warning, I asked him if he wanted me to hypnotize him since through this method it was possible that this "deep dark" secret might come out. He agreed and I hypnotized him. He went into a deep trance quickly, and I asked him to tell me what it was that was distressing him. With tears running down his face he recounted an incident which he had never referred to before: He had been the cause of the death of a childhood friend. His part in the incident, which had occurred 30 years previously, had never been recounted to anyone. I told him that when he came out of the hypnosis he would have no memory of what he had said, but that he would recall what he had said by our next session. He came out with amnesia and was surprised to find he had been crying.

In the next session he produced an explanation for his previously unexplained criminal behavior relating it to his need for punishment for his "murder" of 30 years before, stating that all of his crimes had occurred immediately after someone else in his environment had died. He believed that he wanted to be punished for his earlier crime. Having said this he began to exculpate himself for his part in the death of his friend, and said that he felt greatly relieved.

The therapy was concluded, but the author saw the subject a number of times subsequently for follow-up purposes. The subject continued to believe that he had the correct explanation for his behavior. He went out and for the past two years through correspondence he continues to state that he feels well and that he is a happy person. He has shown considerable energy and ability and has opened a small business which is succeeding.

Discussion

This case is presented because I felt that my behavior was inconsistent with my theoretical acceptance of the client-centered method, and because I feel the hypnosis, while it may have diagnostic values, should not be used in therapy. However, I used it then with the reasonable expectation that my patient could not produce this incident without help from me, and I believe that I did the right thing. I also believe that if he had not brought this incident to consciousness he would not have benefited from the therapy to the extent that he apparently did.

C. KNIGHT ALDRICH . . .

This case clearly illustrates the importance of establishing a dynamic diagnosis before embarking on treatment. If diagnosis is bypassed, as in this case, much time may be lost and treatment may not be used to best advantage. Fortunately for the patient in this case, the supervisor's request to discontinue the contact precipitated enough "distress" on the part of the patient that the therapist was encouraged to carry out more active diagnostic efforts. Had a dynamic diagnosis been sought for earlier in the course of the contact with the therapist, more time would have been available for a more thorough working through of the patient's guilt, and for a more comprehensive consolidation of therapeutic gains.

Adherence to one therapeutic method without discrimination as to diagnosis is not fair to the patient. The same danger of misplaced efforts would results if penicillin were to be given every patient with a fever without further diagnosis: the recovery of some would be due to the penicillin; the spontaneous recovery of others would be attributed to the penicillin; but the recovery of still others would be delayed or even prevented by failure to institute appropriate alternative measures.

ROBERT BLAKE . . .

According to the circumstances of this situation a repressed event is brought into focus with the aid of hypnosis. It then is worked through. The strategy of therapy, involving a change in the therapist's role through use of hypnosis, rather than the dynamics of change itself seems to constitute the issue of discussion.

From a narrow, school-centered view, the therapist's behavior does constitute a shift from a passive accepting relationship to active, controlling intervention in the mental and emotional life of the patient. In a deeper aspect however this shift in role is not too important. For, given unlimited time, the same material would have been recaptured by client-centered or interpretive methods. In a basic sense, then, the theory is the same: material which has undergone repression needs to be experienced, understood, and related by the patient to other significant events in his life if his behavior is to change.

In emphasizing relational aspects in behavior change I am led to ask another question regarding this case. Would the behavior change have been brought about if the circumstances had included the hypnosis with a post-hypnotic suggestion for recall at a point in time with the therapist absent?

My inclination is to answer, "No," and to maintain that the relationship with a nonpunitive *authority* (the therapist) constitutes the significant factor in the change. Exculpating himself *before the therapist*, in other words, was the source of relief and the factor inducing change, not just exculpating himself. If my premise is correct, then dependency on an authority is placed in a position of prominence through such members as the therapist's *telling* him of the requirement of terminating therapy, the patient's *requesting* ten further sessions, the therapist's *asking* him if he wanted to be hypnotized, and so forth. The authority of the therapist had the effect of *supporting* the patient while he dealt with a repressed event. Dependency, in other words, created the condition of resolution. In my view, the nonpunitive, noninterpretative, dependency-creating character of the authority provided the psychological environment of this resolution.

Granted the above, the need for a dependency relationship for personal problem-solving was not altered in the course of therapy, even though the dynamics of behavior related to the repressed event itself were brought to a level of awareness. Perhaps the dependency relationship didn't need to be resolved for effective social adjustment to take place. Yet the evidence suggests that a specific, significant problem was handled rather than that a structural personality change leading to greater skill in problem-solving was brought about.

Wladimir Eliasberg . . .

In this account the patient, a criminal with a record of repeated identical criminology, fraud, seemed to improve under a strict client-centered Rogers' type therapy. However, when discontinuation of therapy was necessary for extraneous reasons, the patient exhibited signs of distress. He had the feeling "something had to come out." This reviewer, too, had the feeling that a passive therapy would not lead to a cure. The general experience with this type of crime, with stereotyped relapses, is that it occurs frequently in persons who for some reason or other are arrested in their emotional development. In a goodly number of cases observed among children as well as immature adults, those typical conflicts in psychosexual development demonstrated by psychoanalysis play a role.

The therapist according to his own discussion is trained and believes in the Rogers method and feels he should not use other therapeutic devices. Such belief in 100 per cent indication of one psychotherapeutic method compares with the belief of a surgeon who would perform amputations of the left leg exclusively, whatever the nature of the illness. It is just too bad that psychotherapeutic training is still often along such lines. Anyone who wants to get training in clinical psychotherapy should have the opportunity to familiarize himself with all available methods and be given guidance in working out indications for any specific method. The selection of a method must not be left to the chance of the therapist's training. This therapist, a nonbeliever in hypnosis, was successful with the first hypnosis he tried on his patient. If such a success, also concerning the depth of hypnosis, was reached, this could be explained by a readiness of the patient for hypnosis, created throughout the treatment without the awareness of the therapist.

This case is of particular interest to the criminologist in that it may contribute to the hard problem of crime causation. It was assumed by both the offender and the therapist that feelings of guilt and need for punishment played a role. The offender believed he had been the cause of the death of a childhood friend. It was, then, the need for punishment for a murder which, however, obviously had not been perpetrated, that seems to have been the "cause" of the crime. Votaries of the sociological crime theory usually blame depth psychologists and psychoanalysts for the easy assumption of such causal connections as are assumed in this case. Quoting Frank Hartung: "The ludicrous position taken by the psychoanalysts on infant criminality is an example of where the informal definition of crime leads one. In psychoanalysis the newly born infant is said to be criminal because of his antisocial conduct. The infant defecates in public and has no respect for the rights and wishes of others; this is antisocial and, therefore, the infant is criminal. . . . One would like to see the concept of infant sexuality applied to the company which falsifies its records." [1]

Such criticism could be countered if, in carefully studied cases, the understandable inner connection between guilt feelings, need for punishment, and type of crime could be demonstrated. The author published such a case. [2] A soldier murdered another soldier in order to get hanged;

[1] Frank Hartung, "White-Collar Offenses in the Wholesale Meat Industry in Detroit," *Amer. J. Sociol.*, LVI (1950), pp. 25–34.

[2] Wladimir Eliasberg, "He Murdered to Get Hanged: A Pre-Analytical Case History of 1783," *The Psychoanalytical Review*, XXXIX (1952), pp. 164–167.

he did not have the courage to do away with himself "under his own power." In the soldier's case, there is a good "Verstehen" of the mental and emotional state before the crime and the nature of his crime. The case referred to in this incident should have been elaborated in this direction. The mere fact of identical repetition, by its very monotony, is an important indicator of causal determination. Still the question of the understandable connection between guilt feelings and crime remains unanswered.

And not only this; as long as neither the therapist nor the patient gets full insight, the danger of relapse is not removed. This should be stressed, although the therapist states that in the last two years no relapse occurred.

ALBERT ELLIS . . .

I feel that the therapist in this case is to be congratulated upon his discriminating use of hypnosis, even though it was at variance with his theoretical acceptance of Rogerian therapy. I do not agree with him that hypnosis, while it may have diagnostic values, should not be used in therapy. But I do agree with his implication that it should only be employed in special instances.

In my own practice, although I am a member of the Society for Clinical and Experimental Hypnosis, I employ hypnotic methods with only a small proportion of the individuals whom I see for psychotherapy. This is largely because I believe that human beings mainly become disturbed because they have little self-confidence and much unnecessary guilt and self-defeating attitudes; and although hypnosis is a most valuable tool in getting to the source of why many clients are disturbed, it is not too helpful in inducing them to change the attitudes which led to their disturbances. Even when hypnosis works effectively, the client still knows that he was helped because the therapist suggested that he do something, and that he did not particularly do this thing by himself. Hypnosis, especially when it makes use of posthypnotic suggestion for therapeutic purposes, enables the client to get better the "easy" instead of the "hard" way. Consequently, it does little to enhance his confidence in himself, and may even, in some measure, serve to decrease it. This is why hypnotic cures are frequently nonlasting ones.

At the same time, in special instances such as those outlined in this critical incident, hypnosis is not only the method of choice, but sometimes is almost the only method that will work. In such cases, a therapist, of whatever theoretical orientation, should not hesitate to employ hypnotherapy. As the therapist says and implies in this case, it is not that hypnosis produces all the benefit in certain instances; but it does sometimes lead to considerably more benefit than would occur without its use.

VIKTOR FRANKL . . .

As was stated by the writer of another case, I must say in relation to this case, the technique and the theory of any system of psychotherapy must give way when the welfare of the patient is at stake. We have to help in whatever way we are able. Therefore, in principle, there is nothing to be said against the use of hypnosis when it seems, as in this case, to be warranted.

At the same time, we cannot limit the freedom and self-responsibility of the patient. On the contrary (and not only logotherapy accepts this as a primary principle) all psychotherapy is to some extent an education of the patient toward self-reliability and responsibility.

In this particular case, however, we should not forget that only by means of hypnosis was it possible to enable the patient to face the past, to regain his freedom of will, and to accept and regain discretion concerning the past, as well as accepting full responsibility for his actions and ultimately for what had happened in the past.

IAGO GALDSTON . . .

This incident, even as its reporter somewhat abashedly observes in his concluding comments, points up a serious limitation in the client-centered method. Seemingly some cases require a "therapist-centered" treatment. After 60 hours of treatment, and when threatened with the discontinuity of therapy, this patient distressfully insisted that there was something that "wanted to come out" which he could not bring forth *by himself*. Palpably he wanted to be "delivered"—with the therapist to serve as his *accoucheur*. Whether or not the therapist's pointed inquiries would have served as well as the hypnosis did, I cannot guess. I do know that quite frequently the therapist's timely, but pointed questions greatly advance the progress of therapy and are of very positive help to the patient.

I am, however, inclined to believe that the patient's subsequent rapid progress was as much due to the therapist's initiative and "activity" as to the uncovering of the "murder" episode. The transference was seemingly very strong. Was the patient panicked by the threat of breaking off treatment? Did he crave a parting show of love? Given this craved demonstration, *itself irregular*, could he then leave happy?

The "uncovering" by itself would not be likely to provide so much release. What happens to a man is one thing. What he does about it is another. His critical psychodynamic problem was not the "murder," but those antecedent factors which structured his reactional behavior. Possibly these were worked through before the hypnosis episode. The author of this incident hints as much.

E. H. PORTER . . .

With all due respect to a competent therapist doing a competent job, the therapist here is obviously a "book-taught" client-centered therapist—and thus provides an excellent opportunity for making a distinction which is not widely understood. As a matter of fact, this distinction is rather widely misunderstood because of the tendency for people trained in other frames of reference to presume that client-centered therapy can be understood only as a variant frame of reference directly comparable with their own and conducted for the same reasons.

Client-centered therapy can be best understood *not* as a body of techniques through which therapy is given but as a body of men and women who have undertaken to explore the hypothesis that *the client has within himself the capacity for directing his own growth and achieving maximum maturity.*

This body of men and women have evolved, evaluated, and discarded procedures and techniques as time has gone on. Always the criterion of evaluation has been the consistency of the procedure with the central hypothesis. In this critical incident, the therapist thinks of efficacy as the measure of suitability of a technique. The client-centered therapists I have known and worked with over the past 19 years would reject the use of hypnosis on the criterion of its being an interventive technique.

It may be difficult for many readers to understand why these people would reject a useful technique. I guess it's the same kind of a difference that exists between the teacher who has a bag of tricks that helps children to learn to read effectively and the psychologist who conducts experiments to learn about the nature of the learning process. Most of the client-centered therapists I have worked with were not satisfied with acquiring therapeutic techniques simply because they were effective. They wanted to learn about the nature of the therapeutic process.

One fact is painfully obvious: you can't test the truth or falsity of a hypothesis if you constantly violate it. The introduction of a procedure which is inconsistent with the hypothesis does not prove the hypothesis wrong. It just creates one more situation in which the hypothesis is *not* put to the test.

Sometime during the late Spring of 1956, in a conversation with Carl Rogers, we agreed that (so far as we could see at that time) it was not until around 1953 or 1954 that there were enough people (10 to 20) whose skills were sufficiently consistent with the hypothesis that one could say there actually existed such a thing as client-centered therapy which could be tested.

It's a big, wide world, and anyone who wants to say he is client-centered is perfectly welcome to do so. If a man wants to say he's an analyst, peace be with him; I guess I'm not interested in labels these days. But when I talk therapy with another man, I'm first of all interested in whether he is a man with answers to the problems of therapy or whether he has only hypotheses. With the latter man, I am *simpatico*, regardless of his label. I guess I feel that for a good many years to come we must struggle for better conceptions of therapy as well as for better ways of testing our concepts.

I can't help but chuckle to myself as I see in myself the tendency to think, "Why did the therapist have to louse it up with hypnosis when the client is just on the very verge of discovering this for himself?" I recognize that others must be thinking, "Why did he waste a whole year in repeating what the patient said when he could have gotten right down to work?" If a number of people are exposed to the same problems of therapy day after day, yet are unable to achieve smooth and easy intercommunication about what is going on in therapy, I'm inclined to feel that our basic concepts are, as yet, entirely too narrow to be scientifically satisfactory.

Hans Finds
a Father

11

History

A 60-year-old patient, who will be called Hans Kurtz, was admitted to a state hospital as a voluntary patient. He was diagnosed as "psychoneurosis-mixed" and the prognosis was "poor."

The patient was born in Austria of German parents but had lived in the United States for about 35 years except for one year which he spent in Germany in the early thirties. He was "psychoanalyzed" for seven months in Austria by a psychiatrist who wore a Nazi uniform in his office. Mr. Kurtz was formerly in the restaurant business and during World War I felt persecuted because of his Austrian-German background. In recent years he had worked intermittently as a landscape gardener. He came to the hospital because he had been very depressed and had suicidal ideas.

He was first married when he was 23, had three children and a long history of poor marital adjustment culminating in divorce after 25 years of marriage. Whereabouts of his family had been unknown for many years. Two years after his divorce, he remarried. His second wife was 25 years his junior, and she left him eight years after they were married. It was shortly after she left him that hospitalization became necessary.

The patient stated that his father was a tyrannical German. His mother had apparently been very indulgent and seductive. He slept with her until the age of 12. He had had a good education in Europe.

The patient's medical history was essentially negative. He was in good physical condition when he was admitted to the state hospital and laboratory findings were within normal limits.

The patient impressed several staff members as a bright, orally-dependent, hostile, demanding individual who might be perfectly willing to spend the rest of his life being fed and cared for in the hospital. Later the psychologist's report indicated that Mr. Kurtz was a bright individual (full scale I.Q. of 130 on the Bellevue-Wechsler Intelligence Scale) who was hypochrondriacal, somatacized his neurosis and intellectualized superficial insight into his problems. The psychologist further stated:

"Rorschach shows productiveness of the very intelligent (97 responses) with the perfectionalism that he demands of himself and others (people and objects) . . . quite marked depressive elements (relation of achromatic to bright color).

"The strong anxiety which is present in this subject is a favorable prognostic sign for psychotherapy. However, his extreme dependence, his age, the severity of the neurosis, with its long standing nature, are unfavorable prognostic signs for therapy."

Despite his advanced age and poor prognosis, at the urging of the hospital superintendent, I began psychotherapy with him a few months after his admission.

Mr. Kurtz was a handsome, well-built man, above average in height, and had greying blond hair. We related well to each other from the beginning.

The patient was seen for psychotherapy once a week for about four months. Early in treatment he resented the interruptions I had. Although I would not answer the telephone during therapy session, frequently the switchboard operator would page me on the loud public address system. After the first two sessions most of the others were held on a bench on the hospital grounds to avoid interruptions.

During the fourth session the patient intellectualized a great deal as usual, using many psychiatric and psychoanalytic terms. The session came to an impasse with the patient trying to manipulate the situation behind a facade of psychiatric jargon. At that point I said, "Mr. Kurtz, time is getting short and we're not getting anywhere. Frankly I am not particularly interested in your use of psychological terms—I am interested in helping you to help understand yourself, and get well, to get on your own two feet and to get out of the hospital."

The patient flushed, a hurt look came over his face and he said, "Here it is again—no matter where I turn, sooner or later I am not wanted."

"Mr. Kurtz, would you mind repeating what I said?"

"You said you are too busy for me, and you want me to get the hell out of here."

"Mr. Kurtz, you only heard part of what I said so I will repeat it for you." (I did so.)

During the fifth session he blocked, was hostile, complained of being rejected. He also made critical remarks about the "stupidity" of our medical and nursing staffs. Then he grudgingly admitted that he felt superior to Mrs. D. (wife of one of the hospital psychiatrists); that he was smarter than she was, and that he resented being in a menial relationship to her, that is, her gardener. Later during this interview, he volunteered the following: "That's funny, isn't it? There must be something in me that makes me so sensitive so that when people say things I may possibly interpret them in a way that I am rejected and unwanted." Although the patient apparently began to show some positive movement in this session, he tried to prolong it beyond the usual hour but I held him to the time limit.

During the sixth and seventh sessions, the patient continued to display hostility, mostly by projection. For example, he started one session by stating, "Why don't you just hit me and get it over with? You know I deserve a good kick in the tail." Later he stated, "Once I had money and lots of people would lick my boots." During most of this session, he continued to make hostile, critical remarks about me and other people, and self-depreciating comments about himself. He ended the session by saying, "Maybe when I was born, they should have thrown away the baby and kept the afterbirth."

The patient started the eighth session by showing me a letter he had received from the Menninger Clinic in reply to one he had sent them asking about treatment there. As I recall, the letter stated that if he could go to Topeka they would be glad to examine him and if admitted as an in-patient it would cost him about $1500 per month. The patient drew invidious comparisons between the superiority of treatment at Menninger's and the treatment at the hospital. I agreed with him that this was no doubt true. He seemed surprised at my comments. The patient did not have any money or any source of income. He asked if I would try to locate his first wife and see if she would pay for treatment at Menninger's. I raised a question about the unreality of such a plan and about the possibility of this being a manifestation of his dependency needs. His comment was, "You mean I want to go back to mama for help?" I replied, "Maybe."

The patient then became abusive, hostile, and critical toward me, our hospital, the medical staff, and so forth. Then he started on me again: "You and your damned superiority; you sit there and look at me like you think you're God."

I said, "You're mad at me and the rest of the staff here because we haven't been able to get you well. You're wondering if someone else could help you more. Ultimately, if you are going to get better, it is necessary that we talk about *you*—not other people you feel are to blame for your problems."

The patient interrupted me with another diatribe, ending with "I suppose now you're going to tell me that you are going to be my father and that I am going to be the child and I must express all my feelings to you and all that baloney?"

Incident

At this point, I deliberately became aggressive. I began pounding the desk with my first and shouted, "Dammit,—look, why don't you just quit this verbal diarrhea and let's get down to the business of trying to understand yourself, and stop beating on me? Whatever faults I have, and I do have a lot of them, have nothing to do with your problems. I'm a human being too, and today has been a bad day. . . ."

He interrupted: "Okay, okay, so I'm no damned good. Why the hell do you waste your time with me?"

"Number one, because you're a human being and my business is trying to help human beings; two, you're worth helping—you've got brains, imagination, you're not the 'bad' person you think you are, and fundamentally I think you may really want to get well and get out of this place; and three, maybe it will be good for my self-esteem if I succeed in helping you."

The session ended early and my parting comments were, "If you really mean business, I'll see you for your next appointment." His reply was a sarcastic, "Thanks."

The patient was prompt for his next appointment and for the first time was not diffusely hostile and did not try to make a display of his psychiatric knowledge.

During this session and the following ones, we began focusing on discussions of the kind of relationships he had been able to establish with people (including me), and why; I tried to help him gain some security in terms of what his real assets were—so that status, and so forth, became less important and he was less threatened by his reduced position in life. He got to the point where he was able to accept the fact that if circumstances necessitated his work as gardener for a woman he considered intellectually and culturally beneath him, this didn't make him intrinsically less worthwhile. Gradually his ability to accept responsibility for his own problems increased, and he was able to recognize that some unfortunate things that had happened to him were "nobody's fault." With these gains, there was reduction of hostility toward others and less projecting of blame on people around him. Eventually I signed him out of the hospital on "leave of absence" (convalescent status).

For about a year while on leave of absence, he received supportive therapy from one of the psychiatric social workers of the state hospital program who was stationed in the community in which the patient lived. The patient became reconciled with his second wife; he was steadily employed at landscape gardening; and he won recognition in a local photography exhibit (he had begun to learn photography in the hospital's occupational therapy department). Reports from the psychiatric social worker in the field indicated that he continued to make a good adjustment, and he was discharged as "improved."

Discussion

The first question is how much countertransference was operating during the eighth session and perhaps in some earlier sessions, such as the fourth one? As the person directly involved it is difficult if not impossible for me to evaluate this objectively. Although I would like to believe that there wasn't any, I am afraid that is not the case. Granted that I deliberately and with some forethought began to pound the desk, I was also aware that I had been getting progressively more irritated at him, and pounding the desk plus my shouting and general attitude were obviously hostile and retaliatory. By most accepted canons of psychotherapy such behavior on the part of a therapist is considered at best inappropriate and at worst traumatic to a patient.

The next question, then, is why did the patient show rapid improvement after the eighth session, improvement which he was able to maintain?

Of course there could have been a number of unknown variables, in operation simultaneously, that could have contributed to his rapid improvement. However, I would like to speculate regarding possible reasons for the improvement from within the therapy situation:

1. My anger was dramatic enough and unexpected enough to make an impact on the patient—as my previous comments had not—regarding the necessity of his working on *his* problems—not on mine or the medical staff's.

2. "Shock treatment" theory—my "punishing" him had the effect of reducing his guilt feelings since he could consider his "badness" paid for.

3. What took place involved "psychic immunization" or "innoculation" which served as a prophylactic dose protecting the patient against more serious trauma and threats to his ego which would result if he manifested similar behavior outside the therapeutic setting.

4. It was pretty clear to me throughout treatment that the patient realized that although at times I did not like his behavior and his attitude, I did like him as a person. After 15 years of social work experience, I have become increasingly convinced that treatment can rarely be successful unless the therapist has a genuine appreciation of and respect for a patient and that this is communicated to the patient—usually on a nonverbal level. This point ties in with point 3—the patient was able to take the aggressive hostility from me because he really knew I did like him and wanted to help him. Also, he must have realized, as possibly he never did before, that his attitude and behavior "asked for" hostility in return. This kind of awareness and insight would have to precede his awareness that he himself was responsible for some of the difficulties he had gotten into in the past.

RUDOLF DREIKURS . . .

The therapist is quite correct in considering the fourth and eighth sessions as crucial moments in the therapeutic process. However, his interpretation of the obviously beneficial results is subject to question and from our point of view, incorrect. His groping for clarification of the dynamics involved in his successful interaction with the patient is due to the fact that he obviously does not understand the patient. Despite his constant urging the patient to "get down to the business of trying to understand" himself, he never shows any progress in this regard, although the patient provides sufficient indications which would permit an understanding in an orientation different from that of the therapist.

It is necessary to attempt our own interpretation of the patient on the basis of the available information in order to evaluate the significance of the therapist's action, which brought about an improvement in the patient. The patient seems to be a spoiled child who wants his own way and gets involved in a power contest with all who oppose him. The "misunderstanding" during the fourth session is quite characteristic of such people and most openly found in children who try to overpower everybody. They may openly say what the patient implies by his action: "If you don't do what I want, you don't love me." For them, being accepted and having a place is identical with having the right to do as they please. Opposition is identified with rejection. This is the reason why the patient interpreted the therapist's firmness as an expression of rejection, of not being wanted.

Actually, what happened in this interview, and then again in the eighth, was a sudden shift in the therapist's attitude. Trained, apparently, in the prevalent mode of permissiveness, the therapist yielded to the patient's undue demands, to the extent of shifting the sessions to the hospital grounds so that the patient would have no reason to resent the interruptions. Indications are that the patient manipulated the sessions successfully until in the fourth session he exhausted the therapist's patience. For the first time the therapist put him in his place. He probably could have done it as well without getting angry. But many therapists are not trained in that way. They act like people who have to please everybody. They cannot say no, unless they first become really angry. This happened to the therapist in the eighth session.

It was this beginning firmness which apparently impressed the patient and made him more amenable and cooperative, or—as the therapist phrases it—"began to show some positive movements." While he still complained, he began to see his mistaken interpretations of being rejected and unwanted. He still tried to overpower the therapist by attempting to prolong the session; but somehow the therapist caught on and kept him in his place. That is what the patient really had hoped for, to find a match, someone whom he could not outsmart and put in his service. (It can be assumed that a great deal of his symptomatology had the purpose of getting service and having his own way, instead of accepting the demands of the situation and playing his part.) His request that the therapist try to locate his first wife and get her to pay for his treatment is not as unrealistic as the therapist assumes. It is an open demand for service. The patient is less interested in really obtaining the money than in making somebody serve him in the indicated direction, by "locating" and "trying" to get money.

The final clash between patient and therapist was on the most important issue, namely, who is superior to whom. The patient, not getting anywhere with his demands, rebelled openly against the therapist's assumption of a God-like superiority. He was right. From the description of the interviews, the therapist defended himself against the patient's criticism and demands by assuming a kind of benevolent superiority. He did not understand why the patient got angry and assumed that it was because the staff was not able to get him well. But this was not the issue at all. It seems it was the therapist's effort to play the father role, a benign authority figure, to whom the patient could not feel superior as he tried to do to the rest of the world. The therapist apparently did not recognize this rebellion of the patient. And, therefore, he could not help him to see what he was doing or to correct his mistaken goals. But he did the second best.

In becoming angry, in shouting and swearing and in using abusive language, the therapist came down from his high horse and became a fellow human being. He accentuated this process of humanization by referring to his own faults, to his being human too, and by admitting that he too had had a bad day. This changed the relationship radically, and the patient relented.

At this point the therapist made his important new approach. *He expressed his appreciation and sincere interest in the patient.* He acknowledged his brains and imagination and his good intentions in trying to get well. He came down to the level of the patient, as a fellow human being, neither giving in nor catering to him, nor treating him condescendingly with the air of a benign superiority which so often characterizes the attitude of a therapist who is confronted with a cumbersome and provocative patient. From then on he was able to establish sincere cooperation for the common task of therapeutic progress.

The final therapeutic success needed probably a variety of encouraging experiences which restored the patient's faith in himself and in his own abilities. One can assume that his skill in gardening and in photography and the recognition which he received played as important a role as his ability to win back his second wife. All these achievements presuppose a change in his attitude, both in regard to feeling defeated and in trying to establish a fictitious moral or intellectual superiority over others.

It is obvious from this interpretation why the therapist's speculations regarding possible reasons for the improvement cannot be shared by this reviewer. We cannot agree that his shouting and pounding was hostile and retaliatory; nor that it was inappropriate or traumatic to the patient. It was simply human, and as such, effective. And it was not the anger which impressed the patient, nor any punishment which reduced his guilt feelings, nor any involved "psychic immunization," be that whatever the therapist may figure out under point 3. We can agree that the genuine appreciation and respect which he could communicate to the patient, both nonverbally and verbally, was the most important factor. But we also have to add the eventual firmness which the therapist assumed after the initial over-indulgence. It permitted him to treat the patient as an equal, without giving in to his undue demands and without looking down on him from a superior "understanding" position.

Albert Ellis . . .

In this case, as in many similar cases I have seen or heard about, I believe that the therapist's first, and simplest, hypothesis probably best explains the reasons for success. That is to say, the therapist's dramatic anger got through to the patient where more nondirective techniques had been previously ineffective.

It should be remembered, in this connection, that some patients keep talking to themselves about their symptoms for years before they get to see a therapist. In the course of this self-discussion, they usually construct involved theories, often of a paranoid nature, of why (1) they originally became disturbed and (2) they are not getting better. Their endlessly repeated sentences and theories about their illness eventually become gospel to them, and they become certain that they know all about themselves and their symptoms. Moreover, they use their explanations of their disturbances as rationalizations for not getting better. They very typically blame others, including the therapist, and insist that they could easily get better if these others helped them. But, since they are not being adequately helped, they "normally," in their own eyes, remain neurotic or psychotic.

To make an effective inroad into this type of repeated, viciously circular thinking on the part of the patient, it is sometimes necessary to employ some kind of a dramatic shock, physical or verbal; and the therapist's technique, in this particular case, would appear to me to be a kind of verbal dramatic shock.

Another way of putting this is to say that patients like the one in this case are usually utterly convinced that their particular pattern of behavior is being helpful to them, that it has some distinct gains as against alternative types of behavior. If they are thus stubbornly, albeit erroneously, convinced that they are helping themselves, mild-mannered counterpropaganda by the therapist is likely to be quite ineffectual in changing their attitudes. But a dramatic, most definite, I-refuse-any-longer-to-take-any-nonsense approach on the part of the therapist may finally convince the patient that his own self-propagandizations are illogical and worthless, and that he had better listen to the therapist or else. This does not mean that this kind of a technique is necessary or useful in *all* cases; but in some instances, especially some of those involving stubbornly paranoid patients, I am convinced that similar dramatic approaches to the one used in this case are almost the only ways of getting results.

JEROME D. FRANK . . .

This incident illustrates among other things the problem of cultural stereotypes. In thinking of tyrannical German fathers, we are inclined to equate "tyrannical" with "unloving," but it is perfectly possible for such a father to love his children dearly. He expresses his interest and affection, however, in ways which Americans regard as showing hostility.

This German man, thrown on his own emotional resources at the age of 60, dependent and full of anxiety, needed above all to be convinced that the help-giver would be strong enough really to help him. In his mind, undoubtedly, strength in a man is equivalent to aggressiveness, as this was the model to which he had been exposed in his childhood. The therapist's initial politeness was probably perceived by the patient as either weakness or a lack of real interest. When the therapist finally told him off, as, incidentally, the patient had requested that he do earlier when he said, "You know I deserve a good kick in the tail," this conveyed to the patient that the therapist really was a strong person who could help him. I believe this is the essence of what happened in treatment, and that once the patient had accepted the therapist in this way they could have discussed anything with the same good results.

Behavior on the part of the therapist such as occurred in the eighth interview would upset most American patients because it is out of keeping with their perception of a truly strong, help-giving person. In our culture strength implies consideration and self-control; our model for this is perhaps best represented by Sir Galahad. But in the German culture strength is conveyed by aggressiveness. For a patient with this stereotype the proper way to convey one's ability to be helpful is through being aggressive when it is appropriate.

Viktor E. Frankl . . .

A quarter of a century ago, even before I had finished my medical education, I founded the Youth Advisory Centers in Vienna. I was the director of one of these centers, and one day the following incident occured:

Just as I was about to leave the building, in a hurry and somewhat excited, because I was to give a lecture on youth counseling that evening, a young man entered my office. It was past my office hours, and I was offended by the undisciplined behavior of the young man—his rude and inconsiderate disturbing of me. I asked him impatiently what he wanted to see me about, and even before I arranged an appointment for the next consultation I could not keep from making several uninhibited and hostile remarks concerning his incredible egotism towards girls, which I learned from him in his few remarks.

At the next appointment, not only was the young man on time, but he also surprised me by telling me that he felt much better. He was no longer depressed. Apparently, our short talk had been enough; but, what had happened to create this result? At last someone had chanced to give him an honest opinion straight to his face, and this had been just what he needed. Had I not been angry that first meeting, I probably would have been careful not to make any value judgments. Who knows if under other circumstances I would have been able to help him, or at least help him so quickly?

The case under consideration indirectly has deep roots. We must not forget that under all circumstances a patient is entitled to have compassionate treatment. However, there are situations which practically call for expressions of an emotional value judgment on the part of the therapist or even an explicit condemnation of a patient's specific actions.

In Chapter 16, Franz Alexander is cited in a case analogous to mine; in Chapter 15 mention is made of verbal shock-therapy; and in Chapter 12 it is argued that sometimes one must transcend verbal limits. In Chapter 15, it was stressed, and in my opinion justly so, that the anger of the therapist made the patient realize that the therapist, too, is after all a human being, and reacts accordingly.

Thus, the aggressiveness of the therapist serves to indicate his willingness to meet the patient on a man-to-man level, putting himself on the same level as the patient. A manifestation of such encountering on the man-to-man level even if displayed necessarily in a negative manner, as in the case under consideration, was overdue and finally broke through. A positive form of expression was not possible in this case. But, whether positive or negative, or whether it was reward or punishment, it proved to the patient that he was considered seriously, as a person accountable for his action—in other words, as a person who should be ready to take responsibility.

As well as any other person, a patient has the right to be punished as well as rewarded. This is a trend of thought that the late German philosopher, Max Scheler, has emphasized. The criminal has a human right to be punished for his crimes, and not to be pardoned because understanding leads always to forgiveness, or because he is to be not considered responsible since he is not in reality a free agent but rather a psychologically determined entity—a psychic mechanism, a *"Triebapparat."* Such universal forgiveness is in reality a degradation of the patient or of the criminal.

I may refer once again to Chapter 21. In my opinion, ethics and values are to be esteemed more highly than techniques and theoretical points of view. I would go so far as to state that as long as the therapist remains consistently nondirective and is unwilling under any circumstance to change his emotional balance; when he sees himself merely as a technician in relation to his patient, this proves only one thing to me—he looks at the patient as a mechanism—and not as a human being.

He does not see the "homo patient" but the "homme machine." He sees a machine-like being without will, purpose, intuition, or meaning, and not a suffering man.

Iago Galdston . . .

This is an interesting case, descriptive of a rather definitive and not too uncommon type of personality, whose psychiatric difficulties are not easy to label.

Though such individuals are to be found among all nationalities, they are seemingly more common, in my experience at least, among those of Austrian or German derivation. It may be that the dislocation suffered by the Austro-German person appreciably contributes to his personality and hence to his reality difficulties.

Quite commonly these are "superior individuals," as likely to be big of frame and energetic as of high intelligence. Quite like the case described they are prone to be hypochondriacal, to somatize their neuroses, and to exhibit a mercurial—that is mobile, inconstant, and shallow—appreciation of their problems.

These personalities extrapolate their difficulties, projecting them upon their immediates, both in personal life and in business. They are markedly manipulative of their environment.

They are at the same time both demanding and disparaging of their intimate associates. They are markedly narcissistic and self-indulgent. They are prone to obesity and likely to be profligate in their spending. They are bright persons and likeable quite in the way that bright children are likeable. They are assaultative emotionally and verbally to their therapists.

These patients are not suitable for analysis—classical or active. They require guidance, together with a rather pressing uncovering therapy.

In this incident the therapist though entirely correct was seemingly frightened by his own aggressivity, and yet he was not truly aggressive, but rather dealt realistically with a situation that could not be effectively handled save "just in that way." Frieda Fromm-Reichmann dealt with this problem, the limits of permissiveness, most penetratingly.

It would be well for therapists to worry less about "the canons of psychotherapy" and to be less fearful of "traumatizing" the patient, if and when in their judgment such traumatic experience can effect substantive improvement.

J. W. KLAPMAN . . .

There may be more than meets the eyes in this incident. It does appear that, possibly as the result of psychoanalytical training, the therapist here is an impassive, almost inanimate sounding board at the beginning. The therapist asks how much countertransference was involved in the earlier sessions. On this matter there is little objective data to go on, except the reactions of the patient and the patient's earlier history. The reactions of the patient would tend to indicate that he sensed little countertransference on his therapist's part. On his own part there are some indications that the patient was quite willing and ready to accept the therapist. When the explosion came it broke the ice because being the object of anger is better than being ignored altogether or being the object of contempt. There is reason to believe there was more sub-verbal communication here than is apparent—of a negative character.

Whence came the disturbing influence? There is no certainty of it but in the history it is reported, "He was 'psychoanalyzed' for seven months in Austria by a psychiatrist who wore a Nazi uniform in his office."

That together with the patient's "psychologizing" conceivably put the therapist on edge. First, the patient's previous analysis could have stirred up any professional insecurity the therapist might have harbored, suggesting the comparison (usually odious) the patient might make with his previous analyst, and, second, the fact that the previous analyst wore a Nazi uniform in his office may not at all have tended to ingratiate the patient in the therapist's affections. This the patient must have sensed unconsciously. Proof of this may be seen in the passage where the therapist asks the patient to tell him what he, the therapist, has just said. The patient replied: "You said you are too busy for me, and you want me to get the hell out of here." Also a statement about his always having been rejected and unwanted.

Thus the therapist's attitude and demeanor actually provoked certain reactions which might not otherwise have appeared. The patient was actually trying to woo his therapist. The posturing, the psychologizing on the patient's part may be seen as an attempt to win the therapist over to himself. He is disappointed in this and tries the tack of trying to make his therapist jealous, as it were, by showing him correspondence from the Menninger Clinic and inquiring about the therapy there. But jealousy is a two-edged tool; in this case, most probably, it only stiffened the therapist's negative feelings about the patient.

However, as much as we may decry these negative incidents in therapy, it is just a fact that real therapeutic movement occurs through them, just as when a dermatologist, confronted with an indolent ulcer which will not respond to medication, will apply a very irritating medicament to make the ulcer flare up into an acute inflammatory state, which then is amenable to treatment. This should indicate that a natural, almost instinctive reaction of a therapist is often far better designed to achieve the projected aim than a cool, carefully understood, reasoned out approach. For it is very conceivable that an extremely well-polished therapist who saw all these possibilities beforehand and avoided them, would not have aroused all the negative feelings, with the possibility that the treatment and the patient would have wallowed in the doldrums for an unnecessarily protracted period of time.

As it was, the mounting irritation of the therapist finally led to an affective explosion which cut across façades and charades, the superficial gyrations of the patient, and the polite but probably disdainful unconscious attitude of the therapist. And the patient's reaction to this incident is to mobilize his guilt feelings over the posturings and gyrations which he had previously exhibited and which he now sees were useless and unjustified; he had done an injury to the therapist by maligning him in his (patient's) mind.

Now because, as we must assume, some healthy part of the patient's ego (and unconscious, as well) genuinely desires help, conditions are created for a real meeting of minds and feelings, and the healing ministrations can proceed to improvement or recovery.

CARL ROGERS . . .

I find myself wishing to comment on this particular incident because while it is quite different from the way in which I would be likely to handle the situation, it illustrates one of the principles of therapy which I regard as highly important and often overlooked.

The therapist is understandably puzzled because an outburst of anger on his part seems for some reason to have had a better therapeutic impact than the several previous interviews. In his own puzzling about it, the therapist engages in considerable speculation as to countertransference, psychological "shock-treatment," and the like. My own understanding of the incident would run along somewhat different lines.

As I have gained additional years of experience in the conduct of psychotherapy, I have acquired an increasing conviction that there is no substitute for the genuineness and reality of the relationship. If the therapist is to some degree putting on a "front," playing a role, he is not likely to be of maximum aid to his client. In the early interviews with Mr. Kurtz, it seems to me that the therapist was getting increasingly annoyed with Mr. Kurtz's attempts to manipulate the situation, with his "superiority," and with Mr. Kurtz's constant criticism of the therapist, the hospital, and others. This annoyance on the part of the therapist shows up in the fourth session where he asks Mr. Kurtz to repeat what he, the therapist, has said. It also shows up in his statement of resistance to Mr. Kurtz as he "held him to the time limit" even though Mr. Kurtz wished to prolong the hour. This phrase sounds more like an annoyed struggle than like a simple holding to personal limits. During the eighth session, the one in which the incident occurred, the therapist reports that in response to Mr. Kurtz's first expression of abuse and criticism, he handled it rather understandingly, saying, "You're mad at me and the rest of the staff here because we haven't been able to get you well." Probably underneath this, however, was a rising tide of impatience and resentment.

Let us consider the situation as it exists up to this point. Mr. Kurtz has many serious problems within himself, yet he is maintaining a defensive façade which insists that the hospital, the therapist, the medical staff, and many others are the ones responsible for his problems. In other words, he is not an integrated person in this relationship but is unable to express his true attitudes and deeper feelings. At the same time, the therapist is being outwardly understanding and therapeutic but his inner feelings do not match this façade. He is building up an increasing degree of resentment and annoyance. Façade is being met with façade, role with role, "front" with "front." In this kind of situation, it is not likely that much therapy can occur. Movement in therapy seems most likely to take place when at least one of the people is thoroughly integrated in the relationship; that is, he is aware of his inner and deeper feelings and is able to express them when appropriate.

At this point the therapist's real feelings break through and he does a thorough job of expressing his anger toward Mr. Kurtz. Although he says that he somewhat "deliberately" became aggressive, there is nothing in the account of this incident to make it sound as though he was playing a role. One feels that this is the therapist expressing his real feelings. This is particularly true when he even asks for sympathy by saying, "I'm a human being too, and today has been a bad day."

I believe that his willingness to bring his whole self into the situation, both his anger and his caring for the client, has a positive effect on the relationship. Mr. Kurtz now feels that he is in relationship with a real person, and it tends, as it always does in such a case, to bring out the real person of Mr. Kurtz. It is not surprising to me that therapy proceeds on a much better basis from this point onward.

The kind of impasse in which this therapist found himself can be expressed in somewhat over-simplified fashion as follows: Most clients feel that it is quite impossible to bring all of themselves into the relationship because they feel certain that the therapist cannot accept all of themselves. The client is sure that his bad and horrible and bizarre aspects cannot be understood or accepted by the therapist. When the therapist, on his side of the desk, feels that he cannot bring all of himself into the picture because the client cannot accept his annoyance or anger but only his understanding and sympathy and the like, then we have a real impasse in which neither person feels that he can be a full person in the relationship. We cannot expect the client to break this impasse. It is necessary that the therapist do so, and I feel that this is what is occurring here.

I would not wish to be understood as saying that anger and annoyance are always therapeutic. It is, in fact, interesting to speculate on what might have occurred had the therapist, in this case, not felt so threatened or so annoyed. I believe that therapy would have gone ahead equally well had the therapist felt completely accepting of Mr. Kurtz's projections. Suppose that he had experienced Mr. Kurtz's diatribe quite comfortably and had responded along lines such as these. "It seems to you that it is the hospital and the medical staff and myself who are really responsible for your difficulty." Or, "I guess it seems to you that I just revel in being a perfect, superior being who looks down upon you." Or, "I guess you expect that I'm going to just give you a lot of bunk and tell you that what exists here is a father-child relationship." Had the therapist been genuine and comfortable and real in feeling a complete acceptance of these hostile and critical attitudes on the part of Mr. Kurtz, therapy would have moved forward, perhaps would have moved forward even more rapidly than in the case as reported. If, however, we do not possess these attitudes which most optimally facilitate therapy, then it is highly important that we be and express the attitudes which genuinely *do* exist in us in order for the relationship to have a solid reality in which the client can come to live.

This also seems to be a good case in which to comment on an entirely different issue, the historical and diagnostic materials. Here is a man who certainly has had an unusual background history, who shows a number of interesting characteristics on the diagnostic tests which were administered.

Yet what earthly significance do these facts have in relation to his therapy? I would submit that it is only because of tradition that we go through the mumbo-jumbo of psychological diagnosis in a situation of this sort. We have the feeling that because diagnosis plays a sound and important part in dealing with physical illness it must necessarily play exactly the same function in dealing with the learned behaviors which constitute psychological maladjustment. I have in the past challenged this and I would certainly challenge it in this case and in many others. The fact that Mr. Kurtz has an I.Q. of 130 and that he is an orally dependent hypochrondriacal individual has no relevance to the incident which is so important to his therapy. Therapy is a relationship which exists at the moment if it is to be of any significance. A relationship is not built up of bits and pieces of past information; it is built up out of the kind of interaction which takes place in this incident, the client complaining and hating and criticizing and scorning and being in close interaction with a person who, in this case, meets his attitudes first with some degree of understanding and then with an annoyance and anger which is as real as Mr. Kurtz's own. I would hypothesize that to the degree that the therapist is thinking about the diagnostic information during the therapeutic relationship, then to that degree the therapy is poor. I would also suggest that if the 10 or 15 or 30 hours of professional time which goes into making a psychological diagnosis—giving and scoring the tests, holding the case conference, and the like—if those hours were invested in a therapeutic relationship with the individual, many a patient would be walking out of the hospital at about the time that, under present circumstances, his diagnosis is completed.

It seems to me that because so much of our professional history in clinical psychology is tied up with the development of tests (which have many legitimate uses in research) we are fearful of facing the fact that they do not play a useful part in therapy itself. I would maintain, in fact, that their only useful purpose in psychotherapy is that some therapists cannot be comfortable without having some of this official, evaluative knowledge. In such a case, I would by all means advise the therapist to undertake diagnostic studies, because I am completely in favor of comfortable therapists as opposed to uncomfortable. But when we try to rationalize this situation into claiming that diagnosis in psychological situations is a necessary prerequisite to therapy, then we are simply following the lead of a few traditionally-minded psychologists and psychiatrists who are fearful of taking a square look at the facts.

We may, at some time, from studying *therapy*, begin to learn some cues which are relevant to therapy—the indicators of good or poor prognosis in therapy, or even the quality of relationship which will be most helpful. If this day arrives, it will make sense to "diagnose" these elements in the individual before undertaking psychotherapy. But our thinking and our efforts along these lines will not, in my judgment, be helped by continuing our present ritualistic "diagnosis" of each individual.

FREDERICK C. THORNE . . .

This case illustrates some very vexatious problems in psychotherapy with patients who use treatment and even psychiatric hospitalization to serve deep personality needs. Many of these cases became preoccupied with psychoneurotic maladjustments early in life and have run the gamut from psychoanalysis to shock therapies, consulting all sorts of specialists but never finding any help. Some of these people possess excellent personality resources and give the impression that they might have achieved outstanding success in life if they had not become hypochondriacally concerned with themselves. The clinical problem becomes very complex when the client has mental ability equal to or greater than his therapist, and also may have picked up a superior psychiatric knowledge through years of therapy or hospitalization. In such cases, one sometimes wonders who is doing the manipulating as the client knows just what to say to make the therapist happy or defensive, how to banter interminably in psychiatric jargon, and otherwise get the therapist to do just what the client wishes. One of our cases with years of psychiatric experience said of a former therapist: "I used to imagine I was sitting behind Dr. X, pulling the strings and saying just what I knew he wanted me to say." Every psychiatric hospital has a coterie of such patients who enjoy sitting club-like on the lawns, discussing their diagnoses, the shortcoming of the staff, and the daily gossip of ward administration. Such patients may know the inner sides of mental illness better than the psychiatrist does.

When faced with such a client who has made no progress in spite of years of all types of treatment, one is often tempted to use drastic "shock" methods. We have dealt with numerous cases like Hans Kurtz who would exhaust the patience of a saint. Frequently they are very possessive, going out of their way to be friendly to their new therapist. At first, all is like a honeymoon as the therapist begins the relationship with enthusiasm and patience, hoping to succeed where so many other famous clinicians have failed. The client may be quite adept in making us feel that our approach is more promising, and otherwise making a variety of appeals that we take a real interest in him. Nondirective or passive handling of cases of this type may end up with the client completely in charge of the situation and manipulating it for all it is worth by taking up hours of time, requesting more frequent interviews and all kinds of special services, and pouting if they are not given. Such patients are very adept in needling the therapist by making invidious comparisons with former doctors, criticizing therapeutic methods, pointing out that he is no better or even worse under the new treatment, or even openly stating that he doesn't like you personally. Such behavior generates considerable conflict in the therapist and is particularly difficult to take when the client has no money or repeatedly creates unpleasant scenes in the office.

The tendency with such clients is to become more directive as nothing passive works, and usually to end up with some sort of "shock" methods to try to "snap" the patient out of it. We have done the same thing as did the therapist with Hans Kurtz, and sometimes it works. But most often it doesn't, and we lose the patient to some new therapist who repeats the cycle. We have rationalized such active intervention as involving a therapeutic use of conflict in which we deliberately try to initiate sufficient shock in the client to force him to reorganize or reorient himself to his problems. Essentially, we are seeking to transform a basically "ego-positive personality" (who is satisfied with his style of life even if it is maladaptive) into an "ego-negative personality" who becomes so conflictually dissatisfied with himself that he not only wishes to change but is so powerfully motivated as to actually do so.

We have recently treated a 19-year-old catatonic schizophrenic girl who for several months began each interview by stating how badly she felt this week, that she had been much better two weeks ago, and that she wished she could make us aware how exquisite her inner anguish was. On contacting former therapists, we found that she had related to all of them in the same way, apparently using piteous complaints to gain sympathy, to secure attention and compassion, and to gain a hold possessively on the therapist, of whom she was demanding in time and patience. After several months of this type of relationship in which no type of passive handling seemed to improve the situation, we finally made a blunt interpretation to the girl that she was using this mechanism to serve her power needs, and that we would no longer continue such a relationship with her. We insisted that she must relate more positively, stop reciting her old complaints, stop being passively resistive in therapy, and actually try to do healthy things. She protested to this directive initially, saying that I was a "bad" doctor, and often deliberately interjecting psychotic symptoms to see what I would do. This plan was not immediately successful because the girl was too sick to be able to control most of her feelings and thoughts, but gradually she became more positive.

CARL WHITAKER . . .

In answer to the therapist's question, there is a great deal of countertransference involved here and I am thankful for it. Countertransference is only a problem if it is concealed to help maintain the patient's delusion that the therapist is God. Thus the therapist can enjoy the aroma of the delusion while protecting his own homeostasis by not actually believing it. The therapist's honest expression of his irritation, like an honest statement of reasons for doing therapy, did help the patient get courage to lose face and "get honest." In his anger the therapist answered, one or two interviews later, the patient's implicit question, "If you aren't going to kick my tail will you be the one to lick my boots?" The therapist said, "I am me, professional and yet personal, in and of myself." This evidence of his integrity is the foundation on which the patient could base a conviction that he himself could develop some integrity. The patient's improvement followed the therapist's pushing his own countertransference to the point of counter-identification. In this sense the therapist dared to become the patient for the nonce, proving that patient status itself is not a death sentence. One could recover from it and one gained from it. The therapist himself said this.

The patient's improvement was based upon the therapist's mature conviction of the patient's worth as a person. In other words, the therapist was able to identify with the patient, and the patient then also was able to identify. The patient's improvement was also based on the fact that the therapist was not tyrannical like his father, nor was he seductive like his mother; that is, he was worth loving without being "used." Thereby, dependence is safe; regression is available and once it is available the patient takes advantage of it since regression is a basic need. The therapist's discussion with the patient was unnecessary; he had already found the breast and he was feeding and growing on it. I do not agree that the therapist's anger was dramatic, it was just "honest confession." It was neither shock treatment nor punishing, just loving concern. The therapist suggests that he, the therapist, was able to endure the aggressive hostility. This is at best an inept statement. This aggression opened the relationship for available usefulness. The therapist functioned maturely, not immaturely. Any mother who loves her child will be angry if the child endangers himself as this patient did. Social taboos about anger in public are not pertinent when the child needs to be taught the fear of an oncoming automobile.

Such significant incidents as this should not be distorted by any smoke screen discussion of awareness or insight. Love is no respecter of time, place, social systems, or even psychiatric terms.

WERNER WOLFF . . .

This incident presents the problem of the use of countertransference in psychotherapy. Critical incidents in psychotherapy seem frequently to lie at a point where unconscious processes of therapist and patient converge. When an unconscious communication has been established, the patient's defense mechanisms give way and he is able to internalize goals developed during therapy.

In the discussion about possible curative factors the therapist's first idea is the problem of countertransference. We may accept this lead of the therapist's conscious-unconscious motivation, and he himself admits his emotional involvement. Countertransference seems to have developed from the beginning. After describing the patient very positively, the therapist states: "We related well to each other from the beginning." Owing to the countertransference the patient was not only considered as a patient but he mobilized non-neutral attitudes in the therapist, such as the therapist's need for assertion and dominance, as told with reference to the fourth session.

The emotionally dominant attitude of the therapist seems to have facilitated the transference projection of the "tyrannical father." But, on the other hand, the displayed emotional interest produced in the patient the feeling that the father-figure, despite his tyranny, accepted him. The masochist tendencies, "Why don't you just hit me . . . you know I deserve a good kick . . . ," which the patient satisfies by his provocation and hostilities (probably originating in his submissive attitude toward his father and his identification with his mother) are in the critical incident lived out on an unconscious level of transference-countertransference. As G. B. Shaw remarked: "Never hit a child except in anger," the patient felt that the therapist was "engagé," and thus accepted him as a person. In that moment he did not feel rejected but wanted.

This critical incident indicates that countertransference may draw the patient into a dramatization of his projections, which are acted out, relived, and observed. At that moment the patient accepted his "existence"[1] as no longer being a mere function of father, mother, and their substitutes. His mishappenings were "nobody's fault" against which he had to protest. What formerly had been projected was now internalized, and with this general internalization the father, the therapist, and the people around him ceased to be functions of his threatened ego but were perceived as independent figures of reality.

The other problem, namely, of dealing with a patient's defense mechanisms, indicates that defenses should not be treated merely as a general phenomenon of resistance, but that they should be treated with reference to their structure. In the present case we deal with an intellectual form of resistance of a patient who actually uses the tools of the therapist. To counter this resistance, intellectual responses would indeed have been less successful than nonintellectual spontaneous reactions as they appeared in the blow-up of the therapist, who unconsciously acted as the patient demanded.

[1] Werner Wolff, *Values and Personality: an Existential Psychology of Crisis* (New York: Grune & Stratton, 1950).

Rescue at the Cliff-House

12

History

By the time the patient reached the age of 18 she had begun what appeared to be a promising career as an actress. At this time she felt that she "knew where she was going" and all of her behavior was directed toward achieving the goals she had set for herself in her career. Her relations with others were calculated primarily to facilitate the attainment of these goals. At 20 she was unhappily married to a man who could help her professionally by his connections in the motion picture industry but who was detested by her family.

For a period she vigorously resisted any attempt by her family, which was ruled by a sentimental iron-handed patriarch, to destroy the relationship. However, when she was 22, they succeeded in forcing her to obtain a divorce. As a result of this the patient developed severe depressive symptoms for which she was hospitalized and treated with approximately 20 electro-shock treatments.

Throughout the patient's life she sought to win the approval of her parents and to ameliorate the intense feelings of guilt which she felt toward them. Her success in training as an actress seemed to be an appropriate vehicle for the gratification of this need. However, the conflict generated by her marriage and her family's reaction to it was interpreted as a dictate from her parents to abandon this avenue of gratification and led to her feelings of impotence and rage, and behaviorally to an inability to pursue the career for which she had prepared.

Upon her release from the hospital she abandoned all thought of pursuing her career. But her obsessive curiosity about shock treatment, which she associated with sexual intercourse, led her to seek and complete training as a practical nurse, whereupon she secured a position at a small psychiatric sanitarium in the community. Her experience in the shock room at the sanitarium was so disturbing that she was forced to resign.

As a defense against the threat of reactivating the depression the patient went through a hypomanic phase during which time she sought assistance from a vocational guidance center in the community. At the center, it was suggested to her that she seek "emotional counseling." Following this advice she entered into treatment.

In the initial hours she acted out her anxiety about treatment and its implications by coming late to her appointments and by being highly critical of the therapist. Her aggression in the office served merely as an appetizer. The full course of hostility she served at home to her father by monopolizing the bathroom, keeping her room cluttered in a compulsively neat household, falling through the roof of his convertible coupe, and drinking up his favorite brandy. Her reaction to each of these and other episodes was intense fear of her father.

During this period the therapist found himself in the unwilling role of referee. The father frequently called him and raged at his daughter's antics, although he feared he might in his anger do or say something that would interfere with therapy. The therapist discussed his reactions without at the same time becoming identified with him.

By this time the therapist was becoming weary of the intense trial to which he was being put and suggested to the patient that little could be accomplished therapeutically if some semblance of structure could not be maintained in the relationship. The therapist felt that the patient was capable of meeting her responsibilities in treatment to the extent of keeping her appointments on time. Shortly after this limit had been set the incident occurred.

Incident

While the preceding events were taking place the patient was engaged in a relationship with a young man which had its gratification in the intense amount of hostility that was being discharged between them. In the hours which were not devoted to criticizing the therapist she spoke of this relationship in an equally hostile manner, expressing her attraction for the young man and at the same time engaging in almost overt fantasies of castrating him during intercourse.

One Saturday evening he took her to a friend's home and spent the night with her. The following morning she called the therapist, and tearfully explained her predicament. This was the first time she had spent the night away from home while living with her parents. Afraid of her father's reactions she asked the therapist what she should do. Although she was reassured by the therapist's uncritical acceptance of her behavior, their conversation did not help her to decide upon a course of action, except that she would inform her parents of her well-being.

The patient in a panic again called the therapist at 6:30 that evening. She had been abandoned in a house overlooking a cliff without funds or means of transportation. She was disorganized and at times incoherent, and finally asked the therapist to come and get her.

Her request presented a dilemma. Since one of the major foci of treatment at that point was to establish some limits in therapy, complying with her request would contradict this. It also seemed that picking her up might well alter the relationship to such a degree that its therapeutic effectiveness would be destroyed.

On the other hand, leaving her in that situation could possibly create so much anxiety that further hospitalization might be necessary. It was further recognized that this was a reality situation with which the patient in her condition could not cope and that little could be gained by insisting that she contend with the problem alone. These considerations led the therapist to decide to pick her up and take her to her home. In the light of subsequent events this decision is open to question.

When the therapist picked her up he could empathize with some of her feelings at being isolated in this desolate house, the only access to which was a not too sturdy wooden bridge. When he arrived much of her composure had been regained and she greeted him in a defiantly flippant manner. As they drove to her home she described in greater detail the events of the preceding two days. The therapist suggested that she was trying to exasperate him in the same way she had exasperated her father, and in doing this could deny their therapeutic efforts; further, he pointed out that if she wished to dissolve their relationship, she did not have to go to such dramatic lengths. By the time they arrived at her home her flippant manner had dissolved into what seemed to be a serious self-evaluative examination of the incident and her use of the therapist in it.

Upon their arrival her parents were waiting contritely in the living room apparently anticipating instructions or criticism. In the patient's presence the therapist told her parents that the situation had been discussed with her and that he would talk with her further about it at their next appointment. It was his hope to indicate to the patient as he had done previously that her problems would be discussed only with her.

In the following interview the patient resumed her disorganized and almost hysterical denial of guilt feelings about the incident. These feelings were interpreted to her. It was further indicated to her that it was not the therapist's role to be critical or evaluative concerning her behavior and that he recognized her discomfort at this time.

Following the above hour the patient abandoned her hypomanic defenses. Since that time she has kept all of her appointments at the scheduled time, moved from her parents' home, and worked for a brief period of time as a practical nurse. She has developed some insight into her hostile feelings toward her parents and has been able to maintain a relationship with another young man for almost a year. In addition, she seems to be able to experience much of her anxiety without feeling called upon to act it out.

Discussion

While on the surface there are some gains which appear to be related to the therapist's behavior in this incident, he cannot help but wonder if the effects have all been on the positive side. In addition, there has been an intensification of the patient's dependence upon her parents, her boyfriend, and the therapist.

With this increased dependence the patient abandoned the overtly hostile elements in the negative transference to the therapist and assumed a complaining, dependent attitude in her therapeutic work. It is possible that the therapist's intervention in the incident made it more difficult for her to abandon her passive dependent needs. The conflict of these needs with her hostile feelings led to periods of fairly intense but not incapacitating depressions. These have been ameliorated partially by her increasing insight into the effects of repressive mechanisms.

This incident is reported because the writer feels that it highlights the problem that frequently confronts the therapist in developing a relationship with a patient manifesting such massive acting out resistance. However, this does not deny the question which was raised above concerning the possible complications generated by this kind of intervention in subsequent therapeutic work. In an attempt to rationalize this course of action one might speculate that it is necessary at times for the therapist to intervene in a physically demonstrable manner, as a means of communicating to the patient the possibility of establishing a stable, nonpunitive relationship in an otherwise chaotic interpersonal world.

While the therapeutic relationship is ordinarily developed in a purely verbal medium, in some cases communication must be established by a positive act on the part of the therapist. At times verbal techniques seem to be feeble therapeutic tools. Kubie described this feeling when he characterized words as ". . . busily screening and denaturing a full-bodied psychological experience."[1]

NATHAN ACKERMAN . . .

This psychotherapeutic incident, dramatic and provocative as it is, poses a special difficulty for critical discussion for two reasons: first, some aspects of the history, which are crucial to a clinical judgment, are inadequately elaborated; second, the therapist took appropriate action at some points in his dealing with this patient and inappropriate action at others.

Most striking in the whole account is the therapist's dilemma in assessing the true nature of the patient's psychopathology. At some stages he seems to recognize that he is challenged by a trend toward disorganization which approaches psychotic intensity; at other stages, striving to establish control of a chaotic situation, he seems to plead with his patient to contain her conflicts much as a conventional neurotic person ought to do. But human beings, especially sick ones, don't always mold their behavior to suit the convenience of a psychotherapist.

[1] L. S. Kubie, "Modern Concepts of the Organization of the Brain," *Psychoanal. Quart.*, XXII (1953), pp. 21–68.

The story of this psychotherapeutic experience reveals poignantly the quality of the therapist's distress. At times the chaotic instability and the destructive outbursts of the patient are just too much for the therapist. He reacts in an indecisive, contradictory manner. He begs, cajoles, and even scolds the patient as part of his effort to induce her to behave. At one point he threatens to quit. Yet he also states later that a therapist ought not be critical or judgmental toward the conduct of his patient. Here the therapist engages in a denial of his own troubled emotions. Insofar as he is critical of the patient's behavior, he ought freely to admit it. In the ultimate test, however, he did not desert his patient. His decision to stick with her "through thick and thin" is an important influence on the final outcome of the relationship.

While this patient shows some prominent hysterical features, the fundamental pathology is borderline psychotic behavior. The therapist seems not to be entirely clear as to the nature of the condition he is treating. He seems to wish that she would act like a simple neurotic. Surely a sick patient cannot be expected to shape her illness to the therapist's special area of competence, or his subjective need for comfort in the therapeutic process. It is rather the therapist's responsibility to understand and accommodate fully to whatever affliction the patient brings to him. He must receive the patient wherever she is in life.

Another angle of the case which falls into a place of special prominence is the therapist's failure to cope with the troubled relations of this young patient with her family, especially with her father. The therapist tries desperately to confine his therapeutic intervention to the intrapsychic aspect of the patient's disorder, as if this could artificially be divorced from the disturbing interpersonal processes which characterized her present family life. In fact, at no point in the history is the girl's disturbance effectively contained within her personality. Her destructive urges and anxiety continually burst into irrational action. The conflicts she experiences with her father from day to day seem to feed back into her inner emotional life to affect the older patterns of internalized conflict, and vice versa. This is only to be expected. In a situation of this sort it is unreal to dissociate the intrapsychic component of illness from the interpersonal aspect of her illness expressed in her conflict with family.

One may easily conjecture that the girl's conflicts with her father, her husband, and boyfriend and also her conflicts with her male therapist were all of a piece. The patient acts out her hostility to her father with the therapist. She goes one step further, and acts out her hostility to her therapist in a chaotic sexual affair with another man. One might readily speculate that her vindictive, castrative assaults on this man friend provoked him to desert her after an all-night sexual binge. Likely this hostile behavior was an acting out of the urge for vengeance on her father, and a negative transference toward her therapist.

In reaction to this, the therapist was strongly tempted to desert the patient, just as her lover did, with the feeling "it serves you right." Fortunately a "second think" impels him to go to her rescue, reluctantly to be sure, but he did go.

The disorganized behavior of this young lady suggests borderline psychosis. When she confronted major choices in life, her parents made critical blunders. Her father interfered with her training as an actress; he intruded upon and broke up her marriage. Both parents seemed willing for her to shift from theater to a job as practical nurse assisting in the administration of electric shock treatment. She was traumatized in this whole series of calamitous errors of choice. She suffered an invasion of her career as actress, a destruction of her marriage, a push towards "execution" by way of electric shock. Can it be the least surprising that her whole system of defenses against anxiety disintegrated? Can it be any mystery that this young woman became disorganized, depressed, manic, and then indulged in despairing provocations of suicidal nature?

The background of violent conflict with her brutal father raises a question as to the existence of an undercurrent of incestuous attachment between father and daughter, which both conspired to deny. It could well be that the underlying attraction of father and daughter was camouflaged beneath a barrage of mutual cruel aggressiveness.

I wonder as to why the therapist failed to recognize the urgency of the girl's need for protection from her pathologically involved father. The therapist speaks of being forced into the unwilling role of referee. Why was he unwilling? In the case of a chaotically disturbed adolescent the therapist should be ready to intervene, and treat critical family conflict as preparation for treating the internal conflicts of the patient. One cannot delude oneself that it is possible to achieve access to the intrapsychic disorders of a young person, as if those disorders existed in a social vacuum. The therapist neither undertook to confront the issue of the girl's conflicts with her father, nor did he consider the possible wisdom of placing this girl away from her family in a protective situation, such as a girl's boarding home. It is conceivable that were the patient removed from the trauma of daily violent tensions at home, the therapist might have had an easier time of solidifying this girl's commitment to psychotherapy. An appropriate program for understanding and coping with the family conflict is here a first priority. Unless this component of disturbance is confronted first, the therapist has little chance for effective access to the intrapsychic conflicts of a patient, viewed as an individual.

Surely the psychotherapy of an adolescent or young adult still trapped in a pathologically warped pattern of family interaction must be defined differently from the psychotherapy of an independent adult free to choose place of residence, occupation, love relationships, or marriage.

The severe acting out of this patient is dramatic expression of an underlying panic and helplessness. It is a significant omission that so little information is offered concerning the patient's mother. It is as if she simply did not count. Likely she does not appear in this history because she provided the patient no protection from the father's assaultiveness. I might guess that the patient had a need for a therapist to take the place of a good mother, able to offer this girl some refuge from the father's traumatic attacks upon her.

In the record of this incident is reflected not only the therapist's distress and weariness, but also a feeling of impotence and anger stimulated by the impotence. Had he assumed the more appropriate role as mother and had he given this young female patient some security from the distortions and dangers of her family life, he would have no need of anger, nor any futile self-deluded expectation that he could treat this patient as if she had an ordinary garden-variety psychoneurosis.

The therapist's distress, impotence, and angry pleading with the patient is nowhere so clearly revealed as in his dilemma about responding to the patient's request to come to her rescue after a sexual escapade and desertion by her man. Though strongly reluctant to leave his barricaded position as an office psychotherapist, he nevertheless decided finally to move out to rescue the abandoned princess. In other words, his "heart was in the right place." This genuine show of interest "saved the day."

It is reassuring to observe that this therapist reaches out finally to a new piece of learning, that psychotherapy by way of pure "talk," while failing to listen to the emotions of the heart, is no therapy at all. He is correct in recognizing in Kubie's statement a substantial core of truth, that therapy requires "a full-bodied psychological experience" not empty mouthings, stripped of emotion.

J. W. KLAPMAN . . .

Here is the immovable colliding with the irresistible force. The *amour propre* of this patient's life and the greatest good and the greatest value she could conceive of was to be a famous and successful actress. Any other goal paled into insignificance by comparison. It is impossible to exaggerate the strength of this fixation, for she has been willing to sacrifice anything for it —to the point of marrying a man she did not care for, perhaps even despised. And about this and the defiance of her father and family she undoubtedly has a profound sense of guilt. The affective relationships to her family are probably as strong or nearly as strong as her fixation on an acting career, which gratifies the narcissistic element in her make-up. These two opposite forces make for an iron-bound impasse. All of this, accompanied with great guilt and tremendous anxiety and depression, eventuate in a psychotic breakdown.

Under these circumstances, the personality when it sought reorganization, would look for escape routes to get around the impasse. Whatever reorganization, therefore, that occurs after the breakdown is predicated on the possibility that there are avenues of escape from the impasse, or around the impasse, to attain the original ends. Of course, such avenues are no longer pursued as a result of a clear vision and good judgment. They are now dictated by a desperate, compulsive search for a way around the impasse.

But the other escape attempts also fail, with much resulting disappointment.

In all the more substitutive escape attempts she finds nothing to compare with the original fixation, that of being a famous actress, and resents the bitter necessity for any kind of compromise. Thus the hostility to the young man toward whom she feels a genuine attraction. Thus the hostility to the therapist, who, at the very best, can only endorse some substitutive compromise in her way of life, only an ersatz gratification.

Because of this she cannot naturally enjoy or express her natural inclinations, such as her attraction for a young man, but is driven to disrupt, tear these inclinations apart, and destroy their appeal. She has a compulsive need to throw the monkey wrench into any relationship which she might come to enjoy, for such trends would tend to overshadow the original fixation and weaken the latter. She must not permit any compromise with that goal nor dim the effulgence of that bright star.

Here, then, is a victim of a terrible impasse, between two powerful forces. The ego is being ground to bits and is really very sick and almost absolutely helpless. The therapist was right to come and pick the patient up in the house where she had been abandoned. For, in that struggle she is left prostrate and helpless emotionally and the usual precautions with regard to active interference by the therapist can be suspended. In such a grave emergency, some drastic measures are justified.

Possibly a flash of insight about the ultimate dangers she was flaunting occurred to the girl as a result of therapist's calling and rescuing her, for thereafter we see she has adopted a less hostile, less truculent attitude. Even a little insight may have been gained. This may be improvement, but it may also herald the approach of the final complete and more or less permanent breakdown. With that unyielding, uncompromising fixation on her more or less nebulous goal of being a famous actress, her personality is more or less in the condition of "the one-hoss shay." She cannot make a genuine compromise and really value the compromise. That is always stark, absolute capitulation, and to her capitulation means death to the personality; it goes all at once.

Therefore, her new improvement may be looked at askance, and merits close examination. That emerging dependence on parents, new boy friend, and the therapist; what does it betoken? Possibly it means genuine progress, and just as possibly it betokens the final capitulation in the schizophrenic breakdown.

O. HOBART MOWRER . . .

Here again we see the tendency to abrogate established therapeutic concepts and practices: "While the therapeutic relationship is ordinarily developed in a purely verbal medium, in some cases communication must be established by a positive act on the part of the therapist." Here the positive act took the form of the therapist going for the girl when she was in trouble and of respecting her confidences in the presence of her parents. Can it be that we are cautiously moving away from the "imago" of the therapist who sits comfortably in his office and receives fees for listening, impersonally and only by appointment, to what the patient says? Such a procedure is, of course, based upon the premise that the essence of therapy consists of releasing, through expert interpretations, repressed instinctual forces. Can it be that we are discovering that *relatedness* is more important than release and that what Nicholas Hobbs once referred to as "the concrete social act" may, on occasion, be more meaningful in this connection than any amount of interpretation?

In the case of the girl under discussion, there seemed to be so little to release either in the way of hostility or sexuality—so what, in the usual sense, was there to interpret? What she seemed to need, perhaps much more, was intimate experience with someone who, unlike herself, was not "calculating," not "hostile," not inconsiderate, impulsive, and self-willed. When the therapist tells of "becoming weary of the intense trial to which he was being put" and suggesting certain limits, one is reminded of the apocryphal remark of another analyst in a similar situation who, when his patience had finally been exhausted, exclaimed: "Lady, you don't have an inferiority *complex;* you really *are* inferior." By, so to say, returning good for evil, did the therapist in the present situation *show* the patient her inferiority in an unusually compelling and effective manner? She had been critical; the therapist was not. She was unreliable; the therapist was reliable. And so the contrast goes. The time may be approaching when we will need a whole new theoretical structure in which to deal with such manifest realities.

Considering how insular and limited the therapeutic relationship was in this case, it was surprisingly powerful. Granted that the transformation of the patient's character was not complete, one wonders what it *might* have been if two other conditions could have been met: (1) if the girl could, in some way, have become a member of a natural "therapeutic community" where the forces of therapy would have been augmented and (2) if she could have had access to a body of literature which would have given her a clearer understanding of the rationale and implications of this kind of therapy, so that she could work at it herself and perhaps even begin to practice it with others. Alcoholics Anonymous provides a possibly instructive object lesson here.

DAVID RIESMAN . . .

In this as in so many of these incidents, therapists are understandably troubled when they violate the norms of passivity—much as anthropologists and sociologists often worry when they become "emotionally involved" with the human object they study. The therapist starting on his own outside an institutional context is in a terribly vulnerable position both personally and professionally, but beyond these realistic dangers lies the fear of going outside the bounds of the dogmas which have been set up for the metaphysical protection of those who explore new and "occult" areas. What I find missing in the therapist's discussion here is any imaginative account of the alternative courses of action. Suppose he had sent a taxi for the patient? Would she have interpreted that as a rejection in her hour of need and particularly of no help in dealing with the family to whom she dreaded to return? Suppose he had done nothing? He might have then "interpreted" her behavior all he liked without her understanding his apparent desertion as a human being. It would seem as if the assumption underlying the write-up—and a good many of the other write-ups too—is that there is one possible course of action which is not a choice of evils but a clear and unequivocal course. But, of course, we all know that in human events we seldom have such luck and that the missteps which later make either course of action hazardous and inept are usually beyond our control whether in public or in private affairs. Though we all know this intellectually, some feeling on the therapist's part seems to persist that history is wholly reversible and that therefore alternatives will be open to him—if he can only find them and is deft and gifted enough—which will bring only good and positive consequences.

As a matter of choosing one of severally almost equally unpalatable alternatives, a particular therapist may "use up" his power to help the patient and may have to find another therapist to take over from there. Thus one can imagine situations where a therapist, to have any access to the patient, would have to be extremely permissive and accepting while after the patient had been somewhat thawed out, a more dialectical interchange would be requisite—and then, conceivably, the therapist's adeptness would lie in his ability to change roles and present the patient with other facets of himself. However, this will not always be possible, not only because of inevitable limits to the therapist's own flexibility, but also because the patient's "set" may be such as to prevent him from noticing that the leopard has in fact changed his spots.

WILLIAM SNYDER . . .

This client appears to be characterized by neurotic immaturity reactions in her behavior toward all authority figures, and particularly toward men. She exhibits controlling tantrum-like behavior whenever she is thwarted in any way. This has apparently been successful in gaining for her retreat on the part of her over-dominating father. When she undertakes her "big effort" in the form of the sexual escapade in the abandoned house, she actually proves this point; her father and mother respond to the situation contritely.

It appears to me that the therapist's acquiescence to the client's demands that he come and rescue her from her abandoned cliffside hideaway is a very poor handling of the situation. The therapist has just completed structuring the therapy along lines of her being required to comply more adequately with the normal demands of a therapeutic relationship, when the client goes to great extremes to violate this structuring, making excessive, compromising, and even improper demands upon him. That he complied was an admission of defeat on his part, a demonstration of his willingness to be completely controlled by the client, and it permitted a reenactment of the client's typical abreactive behavior in the form of the client's struggle with the father for dominance. Her masculine protest is one of her outstanding symptoms, and the therapist, instead of helping her to find a way of accepting her feminine role, acquiesces to letting her assume the masculine one. It is doubtful whether this is therapeutic for this client.

The therapist is correct in seeing this client's problems as a strong conflict between her needs for passivity and for aggression. It is also apparent that for her sex is a form of aggression; thus she equates shock therapy with sex. Her desire to work in a situation where she assists in administering the shock reveals her desire to dominate sexually, but it is countered by her fears of such behavior, and she is forced to retreat from the situation. Her conflict of sex roles is a classic indication of her Oedipal problems.

After the incident where the therapist "rescues" the client, she becomes much more passive in her behavior toward him, and toward other persons in her life situation. The therapist seemed to be somewhat distressed by the intensification of the client's dependence upon her parents, the boy friend, and himself. And yet this does not seem to be an undesirable development in the case of a client who has been severely acting out her aggressive needs. It would appear to be in the direction of a more healthy adjustment. It is possible, therefore, that the therapist's behavior had a somewhat beneficial effect upon the client's adjustment, despite what seems like a methodologically poor procedure.

I would differ with the therapist regarding the need to intervene in a physically demonstrable manner. While recognizing that some writers like Braatoy[2] make a strong case for this point of view, it seems to me that it should be used very rarely indeed. At such times a gentle pat on the hand or the shoulder might be considerably therapeutic. Perhaps with a psychotic other behaviors would be required. Perhaps a highly excited child should be gently restrained. But for the therapist to comply with demands which symbolize submission, or nurturing physical care, seems hard to defend in any theory of therapy thus far developed.

FREDERICK C. THORNE . . .

Every therapist is confronted by emergency situations wherein the acting-out behaviors of the client create reality situations which must be dealt with effectively in order to rescue the client from potentially dangerous complications. Ideally, the therapist should clearly differentiate between therapeutic and administrative roles, and may delegate administrative actions to others. However, local situations may require the therapist to assume both roles. In the present situation of the patient abandoned at the cliff house, a therapist who was a psychiatrist might have more latitude than one who was a clinical psychologist because of the greater authority and responsibility granted by medical licensure. In either case, the therapist should not go to the cliff house alone but should be accompanied by a nurse or friend in order to protect all concerned. Ideally, a physician might be delegated to bring her home after the family had been forewarned not to create any further disturbance but to allow the therapist to deal with the incident. It is idle to speculate what might have happened had things been done differently. In our own experience, we have known of clinical psychologists who limited their own usefulness and greatly exceeded their professional responsibilities by allowing themselves to become administratively involved and emotionally entangled in attempting to act out too many different roles in solving reality situations contrived by patients.

Emergency situations such as this make it desirable to establish procedures and facilities for handling them most expeditiously. Generally, it is desirable to establish close working relations with other specialists who can be depended upon to cooperate without completely taking over. This

2 Trygve Braatoy, *Fundamentals of Psychoanalytic Technique* (New York: John Wiley & Sons, 1954).

may require considerable experimentation and wise selection to discover someone who is congenial to work with, and not too alarmist. It requires expert judgment to determine when a genuine emergency exists and how to handle it most expeditiously without too much excitement.

Every therapist accumulates a number of anxious hysterical patients who show genius in getting themselves worked up at odd hours and places. What should we do when we get a phone call from a distraught patient saying that we must come and do something because he can't stand it any longer? Most of the time it is sufficient to handle the problem nondirectively, allowing the patient to ventilate until his feelings are expressed, until he spontaneously says that he feels better now and won't need to see us immediately. More actively, one can reassure the patient over the phone and give instructions what to do to try to get over the emergency. But what about the case which actually sounds desperate and seems to be genuinely in need of emergency help? Unless the therapist is in a position to assume complete responsibility for whatever may happen, then it is wise to call the proper specialist in consultation.

We agree in this case that the therapist probably had to do something, but we think it might have been safer to mobilize a few more resources in the form of consultants or chaperons. One never knows what may develop in such a situation, and it is necessary to improvise until the situation can be diagnosed. It is always wise to keep in mind that such a call may be an attempt at sexual seduction, particularly if the therapist is young and personable. As the law now stands, only a physician or a law enforcement officer has any legal authority or responsibility for taking any coercive action to bring such a distraught person under control if he is unable to cooperate voluntarily. It is always desirable to secure family cooperation to avoid any misunderstandings or criticisms later either in the event that the therapist fails to take protective action and something serious occurs, or if the therapist takes some action which does not work out well. Clinical psychologists are at a considerable disadvantage in handling emergency situations, and this is why ethical practice requires them to work with a legally recognized medical consultant.

WERNER WOLFF . . .

This incident poses the problem of the orbit of psychotherapy. The question arises whether psychotherapy may be extended beyond the confines of the therapist's office (or hospital) and, furthermore, whether the verbal medium may be supported by action on the part of the therapist.

Action of the psychotherapist beyond the office may easily be interpreted by the patient as a gesture of friendship rather than of a professional nature, and this may interfere with the transference. Although most therapists advise against social relations with their patients,[3] certain psychotherapists will actively interfere in the personal life of their patients.

Freud recommended as a basic condition of psychotherapy the relative independence of the patient, so that the therapy could function outside environmental pressures. One of the therapeutic goals was the establishment of independence within the patient himself, his freedom from the compelling forces of Id and Superego, the ability to make free choices, the development of his individuality directed by reason. This goal included the solving of parental, interpersonal, and therapeutic dependence.

Experience, however, has shown that a rigid insistence upon a therapeutically neutral atmosphere may be as dangerous as to demand the patient's independence at any costs. In certain cases therapeutic neutrality may support the patient's experience of rejection and existential isolation, thus contributing to the patient's development of an armour, of defense systems, and of resistances. A rigid insistence upon the patient's independence may promote regressions and even psychotic reactions.

In the present case where the patient's individuality and spontaneity (who "knew where she was going") were coerced by a "sentimental iron-handed patriarch" and by the suppressive therapy of shocks, the situation of the incident had been prepared so that the separation from home and her being "abandoned in a house overlooking a cliff without funds or means of transportation" produced a crisis. The natural (abandoned, cliff), symbolizing her internal situation, drove her into a panic.

According to my own observations, psychotic states may be provoked when a predisposing internal reality finds its correspondence in a sudden external reality, causing what I call a "stereoscopic experience,"[4] that is, the same situation viewed from slightly different angles gives the situation a new depth, making it threateningly real. Phases of stereoscopic experience demand emergency reactions from within or from without, producing a "critical incident."

When the therapist decided to act beyond the confines of office therapy, at that moment the transference received depth, the former tyrannical interference of the father now was replaced by a helpful interference of the therapist, thus changing an imposed dependence to a desired one. The resistance by which the patient exasperated the therapist as she had exasperated her father now changed since after experiencing *active* help the patient was able to drop her defenses and resistances and to accept interpersonal relations as well as personal reliability. The positive turn of the critical incident appeared through the humanization of the therapist who,

---

[3] Werner Wolff, *Contemporary Psychotherapists Examine Themselves* (Springfield, Ill.: Charles C. Thomas, 1956), pp. 197 ff.

[4] Werner Wolff, *The Threshold of the Abnormal* (New York: Hermitage House, 1950), p. 442.

I believe, should be able to give up general principles of behavior in a crisis situation that might endanger the patient's life.

Dramatization and symbolization have been found to function as self-healing processes within a homeostatic psychic goal. (Psychodrama, occupational therapy, fantasy mobilization, and dreams are stimulators in this respect.) In certain cases the therapist may function as a dramatization and symbolization of the patient's projections, thus initiating a homeostatic process.

Science and

the Soothsayer

13

History

A woman of about 35, of foreign extraction but native born, came to me for help with a very troublesome obsession. There was "running through her head" the obsessive thought, "I don't love my husband." She also related that sometimes when she saw her husband or her children she was seized with the terrible compulsion to grab a kitchen knife and run it through them. When she came for psychiatric advice, she had just separated from her husband.

On the second interview, while I was still engaged in obtaining an anamnesis, she reported she felt much better.

On the third interview, she came accompanied by her husband and her four-year-old son. She was in excellent spirits and reported a reconciliation. The obsessions and compulsions had gone, thanks to my treatment! When the interview was concluded, and I walked with her to the reception room, her husband enthusiastically shook my hand, remarking on the wonderful things that doctors and psychiatrists can accomplish.

She never returned for any subsequent interviews, and I was left wondering "about the wonderful things psychiatrists accomplish." It seemed evident that I had done something "wonderful" and had alleviated her obsessive-compulsive psychoneurosis; but what was it?

I studied my careful anamnestic notes to try to find the answer.

Incident

According to my notes, the patient's mother had been a very superstitious woman who never undertook anything of importance without first consulting a fortune-teller. Although my patient had denied being superstitious, she, too, had consulted a fortune-teller just before marrying, allegedly one of the few times she had followed her mother's example. Among the many things the fortune-teller had told her was a statement to the effect that she would remain married to her husband five and one-half years.

I searched my notes for dates, and sure enough, the onset of her obsessive-compulsive reactions coincided exactly with the end of the five and one-half-year period, some two and one-half months before she came to see me. This explained the cause of the condition, but what explained its remission? As far as I could tell it was simply my statement, in reply to her question on the subject, that I had no belief in fortune-tellers.

Discussion

The great importance of minute cues is here well demonstrated. Psychologically we dealt here with an intellectually quite primitive individual. The role and high degree of suggestibility is well demonstrated.

Now it can only be hoped that the writer himself is not suffering from an exaggerated credulity in the following hypothetical reconstruction: The fortune-teller's prognostications acted as a post-hypnotic command. When the time arrived, the command began to exert its full effect. But she did not want to separate from her husband, and when she resisted the suggestion, she developed the obsessive-compulsive symptoms.

My role in the entire affair became clear according to the foregoing hypothesis. Unwittingly, I had given her absolution from the post-hypnotic command. With my "magical powers" I had uncast the spell over her. The fact that neither I nor my patient had any idea at the time what we were doing was, after all, only a minor matter.

NATHAN ACKERMAN . . .

This experience of miraculous dissolution of a neurotic symptom in the opening phase of the patient-doctor relationship is exciting but by no means unique. It is certainly not as novel an event as the therapist seems to imply. It is by no means rare that hysterical symptoms, obsessive thoughts, and compulsive acts, suddenly disappear as the expression of some favorable turn in transference. But such disappearance of organized psychoneurotic symptoms need not always be the product of favorable transference. It may occur as a result of the patient's entry into a new human relationship, a new friendship, which of itself holds no explicit therapeutic purpose. Unconsciously, however, the patient seeks in the friendship relief of emotional distress, a "love cure." Through the newfound intimacy, even though unadmitted, the patient wins acceptance, support, affirmation of a favored self-image, and a buttressing of crucial defenses against anxiety, which either dispel or submerge the acute symptom.

While giving full recognition to this phenomenon, it is nevertheless of more than passing interest that tormenting symptoms may come and go in this manner, influenced by an unintended transference stimulus or by a chance friendship. A fortunate turn of this sort should not be belittled, since from the point of view of the patient, this is a sheer delight, manna from heaven. For the moment the patient is relieved of acute distress. It may even lead to a euphoric reaction. The patient has no way of knowing that the symptom may recur, that other symptoms may intervene, and that there is no guarantee of permanence of cure.

Nonetheless, as therapists, we are dedicated to the effort to relieve emotional suffering in our patients. If a patient is relieved of a plaguing symptom, whatever the means, we should thank our lucky stars. We must be relieved, too, even though we recognize this fortunate turn may be a temporary one.

Under such circumstances, it is the therapist's responsibility, while welcoming the subsidence of the symptom, to stir curiosity in the patient's mind as to how it all happened, in order to open the way to further useful psychotherapeutic work. In this case the patient offered a hint as to what was happening in the second interview. The patient reported that she was feeling better. The therapist, being absorbed in the preliminary task of history taking, was not alerted to this clue. He might then and there have evinced interest as to how and why she was already feeling better. This might have aroused a more vital emotional interchange and energized a quicker crystallization of significant transference processes. This is necessary preparation for a sustained therapeutic experience, so as to move toward a more dependable quality of cure.

Another relevant aspect of this problem is reflected in the therapist's clinical judgment concerning the patient's abrupt separation from her husband. The separation was apparently precipitated by the patient's critical emotional upheaval, as if she feared she might really pick up a kitchen knife and run it through her husband and children. The patient plunged into a panicky flight from her husband as if she might really live out her irrational obsessive thought. But this is an obsessional neurosis, not a psychosis; there is, therefore, virtually no danger of the patient acting out the obsessive murder. The very structure of an obsessive symptom provides reasonable assurance that the patient will not live out the murderous thought. Why, then, should this woman leave her family?

Had the therapist picked up the clue in the second interview, and activated the patient's curiosity as to how she felt better and crystallized the transference process, he would then have been in a better position to challenge the unreasonableness of the patient's panicky flight from her family. This seems especially significant since the description of the emotional climate of the family relations reflects a basic bond of love, rather than hate. It is entirely possible that in an essentially good marital relationship, a woman with obsessional traits may find somewhere in that relationship a threatening stimulus which evokes the phantasy content of an original ambivalent conflict with her mother. Such a stimulus may easily serve to precipitate the symptom. Where the present marital relationship and family is basically good, a therapist has sound reason to dissuade a patient from any unreal flight from her family.

It seems plain in this therapeutic incident that the prime defense involved in the disappearance of the murder obsession is magic doings and undoings. This must somehow be implicated in the patient's unconscious phantasy of still being psychically under the control of her hostile mother. The murder obsession is a fragment out of a buried ambivalent conflict with her mother. In the patient's phantasy, the fortune teller takes the place of mother, who tempts the patient with diabolic thoughts. The therapist substitutes symbolically for the patient's father who enables her magically to undo the mother's power over her mind.

I do not myself go for the therapist's explanation of a hypnotic influence. It is a bit too cute; in one sense, it seems naive, and in another it is too fancy and sophisticated. From the therapist's account, I cannot be clear as to when the therapist made the statement that he had no belief in fortune tellers. Was it in the first or second interview? It might have made some difference in the therapist's handling of the emotional interchange with his patient, if he had made this denial of faith in fortune tellers in the first interview rather than in the second. In any case, if one understands the basic dynamic structure of the obsessional character, there is no need to drag in the hypothesis of hypnotic influence. An investigation of the relevant transference processes would provide a clear answer.

It is somewhat regrettable that the therapist did not succeed in laying a firm foundation for continued treatment. This teaches us once again the lesson that the taking of history, and psychotherapy, go hand in hand. It is not good practice for a clinician to become so wrapped up in the mechanical task of obtaining personal history as to be unaware of the emotional interchange that is going on all the while between the patient and himself. The therapeutic influence begins the very moment the patient lays eyes on the therapist. Contact with the patient cannot be arbitrarily divided into a first phase of history-taking and a later phase of concentration on the specifics of transference emotion. The potentials of transference structuring of the processes of communication need to be understood and exploited from the beginning. If one bears this in mind, there is less risk of overlooking early significant clues. One need not then miss the opportunity for cultivating the matrix for a sustained therapeutic relationship in which a more dependable kind of cure is possible.

ROBERT BLAKE . . .

Here is a description of "unwitting" manipulation which had positive effects on adjustment. It does not constitute therapeutic change in any rigorous sense. Why? The patient was as susceptible to the influences which led to her presenting difficulties at the termination of "treatment" as she had been before she came for "help." The change induced was not associated with improved skill in personal problem-solving. Neither was it accompanied by increased insight into the nature of her own situation, involving "acceptance of commands from authorities," two hallmarks of therapy. It *was* associated with her reaction to the "authority" of the therapist. Had he done willfully and with insight what he did "unwittingly," this would constitute a good example of the distinction between therapy and psychodynamic engineering drawn in connection with the reading case in Chapter 7.

Her reactions to both the fortune-teller and the therapist are evidence of focal significance of dependency on authority in social adjustment, and her husband's positive reaction to the therapist is similar. Dependency needs constitute the stuff out of which "prestige" is created. Those who will exercise authority and satisfy such needs stand in a position to exert significant influences on others who look toward them for direction or help.

But why? The answer in psychoanalytic writing is clear. The significant role of authority in family organization and in child growth and development is also clear in sociological writings. Yet, as the case study is written, the subtlety with which "authority" operates to influence behavior is such that the therapist in this situation only perceived the power of his own "authority" after treatment had been terminated! Indeed, the therapist is careful to report that the proceedings between himself and the patient were fact-gathering interviews.

A basis is provided by this case for distinguishing two approaches: psychodynamic engineering, although unwitting in this case, and therapy. From my standpoint, *change* was induced, but "therapy" was not involved since afterward the patient is no more insightful or skillful in problem-solving than before seeing the therapist. Rather a psychodynamic aspect was manipulated to the positive advantage of the client. Had the therapist planned it that way, the outcome would have been the same. However, the patient is rendered no less susceptible to the exertion of influence by authority.

ALBERT ELLIS . . .

Assuming that the therapist in this case is correct, as he well may be, and that his remark about the fortune teller actually enabled this woman to get over her obsessive-compulsive behavior, the therapist's hypothesis about post-hypnotic suggestion may or may not be valid. Certainly, it is one possibility. It would seem to me, however, that it only partially accounts for this and similar psychotherapeutic "cures," since it leaves unexplained the nature and effectiveness of post-hypnosis itself.

A simpler, and at the same time more comprehensive, explanation of the phenomenon in question might be hypothesized along the following lines. If we ask what is the basic origin of any neurotic symptom, the answer would appear to be: some kind of illogical, inappropriate, or irrational perception or thought. For if any human being were *completely* logical and rational, he could hardly keep perpetuating any childish or "neurotic" behavior. All adult behavior, including all so-called "emotional behavior," is accompanied by some kind of (conscious or unconscious) ideation; without this ideation, the behavior would not exist. Thus, if an individual were not telling himself something like, "this is fearful," or, "this is something that I should be afraid of," he would never experience fear; and if he were not telling himself something like, "I must kill my wife and children with a kitchen knife," he would never feel compelled to carry out this thought into action.

If, as is here hypothesized, adult human beings invariably accompany their overt behavior with underlying ideas (or internalized sentences); and if illogical and irrational ideas (or self-repeated sentences) lead to childish or neurotic behavior; then, basically, neurosis originates in (1) inappropriate suggestions which are first made to human beings from some outside sources and (2) in their autosuggestively then repeating, or reinfecting themselves, with these suggestions, over and over again, ad nauseam. Or, otherwise stated, the fundamental cause of human emotional disturbance is the original indoctrination and subsequent self-reinfection of the disturbed persons with what are essentially illogical, silly, or superstitious notions or sentences.

If this hypothesis is true, then it is easy to see how the patient in this case could have been originally indoctrinated with the superstition that fortune-tellers give correct information; and how, continually reinfecting herself with this erroneous belief, she could have become fearful of her marriage ending, in one way or another, and if necessary by her own violent attacks on her husband and children, after five and a half years. Then, coming into contact with a respected therapist, she could have been effectively depropagandized of her original superstitious belief, and accepted as gospel his simple countersuggestion that fortune-telling is worthless.

In general, I feel that virtually all disturbed behavior in adults is caused by some original illogical, irrational, or superstitious suggestions from external sources; that this suggestion is then internalized, continually acted upon, and "reconfirmed" over and over again, until it leads to "emotional" or other overt acts; and that it and the disturbed behavior to which it leads can only be overcome by effective countersuggestion of one kind or another. Usually, it takes a competent therapist many sessions, with the use of several different countersuggestive techniques (such as acceptance, permissiveness, analysis of transference relations, frank suggestion and advice, and so forth) to undermine the original and long-standing pernicious suggestive influences. But occasionally, as in the case reported here, his countersuggestion can become instantaneously effective, especially when his general demeanor arouses confidence in the patient and when she, as in this case, has a strong incentive to listen to his countersuggestive influences.

IAGO GALDSTON . . .

To my mind this "incident" points up two significant considerations. The first is the need for the therapist to calibrate his communication patterns, media, and range with those of his patient. The second is the potent factor of suggestion, ever present in all communication. In this "incident" both these considerations are set forth in stark pattern. The patient was "intellectually quite primitive." The therapist dealt with her primitively. He communicated with her on her own level and in her own vernacular. He was the soothsayer, the fortune teller, the shaman who cast out the evil spell another had set upon her. I doubt that the woman's obsession is indeed comparable to a posthypnotic command. It was rather an affirmation which operated as an enduring suggestion.

It is reported by Jones that when Freud was still under the influence of Fliess' "numerology," he anticipated an early death because it was forecast in certain of his vital dates. Not only the "intellectually quite primitive" are subject to suggestion. Every man is. We differ only in susceptibility, and most of us are more susceptible than we are prone to admit even to ourselves.

Suggestion enters into every therapeutic contact. When conscionable and deliberate, it is useful and salutary. Strive to disbar it, and it will smuggle itself in, all your efforts despite, and not always to the benefit of the therapeutic enterprise.

As to calibration of communication, it is not always downgrade. It is as requisite when dealing with the intellectually overinvested as with the intellectually primitive. It is only a bit more demanding.

ERNEST HILGARD . . .

The correction of a superstitious belief evoked by a fortune-teller through the countermagic of a therapist sounds plausible enough, but calls for some discussion not only of this case but of magical beliefs in general.

Superstitious (magical) thinking is far more widespread than we usually suppose. According to a careful estimate, there are 24,000 "water witches" in the United States compared with a little over half that number of psychologists. Although there is not a shred of evidence that a forked stick bends in the presence of water, this does not, in an age of science, seem to make much difference to the belief in the efficacy of such devices.

It is supposed that magical beliefs begin in childhood, where the distinction between wish and reality, between fantasy and perception, is still blurred. A little egocentricity is enough to engender feelings of omnipotence because there is no effective counterargument. The same thing continues, however, in some fraction of adult fantasy, some of which is expressed in beliefs such as those studied in the book *When Prophesy Fails*.[1]

What happens when a false belief is magically inculcated? There may develop a "saga" that will help the belief to perpetuate itself. That is, as in the case of systematized delusions, events will be interpreted as pointing toward the expected fulfillment. It is not unlikely that for this patient her fear that her marriage would terminate at the end of a few

[1] L. Festinger, H. W. Rieken, and S. Schecter, *When Prophesy Fails* (Minneapolis: University of Minnesota Press, 1956).

years made her interpret any disagreement with her husband as a fore-boding of worse to come. While she did not talk about this openly, it was near the surface and expressed itself in the hostile fantasies.

It is not necessary to think of the fulfillment of the fortune-teller's prophesy as a post-hypnotic suggestion; it is rather a controlling belief that operated all the while, but with a target date. It is rather surprising that the denial of belief in the fortune-teller could reverse the result of so much build-up, except that the frightening nature of the fantasies could mean a readiness to give up the false belief provided something could be found to substitute for it.

To reinterpret these events according to learning theory is really no easier than to explain them in any other way. Many kinds of propositions are relevant, but few if any of them could stand up as firmly applicable. Here are a few to try out:

1. Prestige suggestion serves as a powerful secondary reinforcer for ideas.
2. The interpretation of events is molded by strongly held beliefs.
3. When channels of free expression are blocked, alternative channels of expression are chosen, including fantasy.
4. Strongly held beliefs are subject to change under certain conditions:
   a. If the belief is causing pain or discomfort, it is more likely to be changed than if it brings gratification.
   b. The competing belief must promise more in the way of secondary reinforcement, and less in the way of pain or discomfort, than the belief it replaces.
   c. The agent or agency through which the belief is changed must be of equal or greater potency than that upon which the original belief depended. (Unless the psychologist has as much prestige as the fortune teller, it is unlikely that the psychologist will prevail.)

An interesting issue here has to do with the psychotherapist's use of his prestige to counter other sources of prestige that have influenced belief. Obviously he will sometimes prove to be effective in influencing a patient by impressing his opinion, but this has the dangers inherent in any other form of authoritarianism. If the therapist uses "magical" power to overcome ideas that are themselves of "magical" origin, the result is likely to be a kind of truce in which the balance of influence may again shift to the other side; that is, beliefs taken on faith are likely to be shattered by other acts of faith. While we need to avoid glibness in making any pronouncements about psychotherapy, it would appear better to have the belief modified through the more realistic processes of gathering evidence and making a judgment on the basis of the weight of evidence. But sometimes this process may not be feasible, and prompt results may be obtained by more direct attack on the beliefs. Once the dislodged belief leads to more realistic action, the sustaining effect of the real world may make the new belief prevail on rational grounds even though it was at first accepted on irrational authoritarian grounds.

WILLIAM SNYDER . . .

This short excerpt of an fantastically short case happens also to be a classic example of the compulsive-obsessive psychoneurosis. The woman's remarkable cure of the compulsion to stab her husband and children after only three therapy interviews is typical of many highly suggestible compulsives. It is the magical "cure" of the hysteric, and its counterpart is evident in the thousands of crutches tacked to the walls of shrines throughout the world! Some of these people "recover" as a result of faith cures, some following hypnosis, and others subsequent to the various and sundry types of psychotherapy which abound. Some just get well by their own power of autosuggestion. They are a form of simple resistance cure; certainly neither this cure nor those so similar to it should be dignified by the name of psychotherapy.

The principle surprise to this reader was that the therapist could be so unfamiliar with the process; this would suggest a very limited training. His rather labored explanation or theory, constructed *a posteriori*, is credible but hardly necessary. To describe the woman as superstitious is accurate but almost tautological. That she is "intellectually quite primitive" is utterly true. That is about all the explanation that should be required. Her behavior manifests the magical thinking of primitives and small children. The explanation of the eradication by the therapist of a five-year-old post-hypnotic suggestion made by a fortune-teller is hardly consistent with the best scientific findings on hypnosis. It is certainly an unnecessarily cumbersome description of a rather simple event. It *explains* nothing.

A better handling of this case, it seems to me, would have been for the therapist to tell the patient in the third interview that she was indeed not the slightest bit improved, but only hoping to escape the painful task ahead in undertaking genuine therapy. After all, why did this woman have her murderous obsessions? It is unbelievable that people carry about such urges only because bidden to do so by a fortune-teller, a witch, or even by an imaginary voice! The therapist in this case seems almost as gullible as his client. I am not sure a drastic psychic shock approach would have persuaded the client to get down to business; most likely not, if our experience is any measure of prediction. But at least it would have been more likely to produce an effect, than was the supine acceptance of the client's erroneous attesting to a faith-cure. Actually she most certainly was not cured; she likely found a new obsession a week later.

Christmas
with Mother

14

History

While teaching at a private university, one of my students, a very handsome statuesque young woman from the woman's college came to see me. We had just been discussing the psychoneuroses in the course in general psychology. This girl slipped into my office just a little before noon when no one else was around. I had noticed her several times and wondered about her. She had a pretty face and a figure good enough for the movies, but she wore in her gestures "don't you touch me" signs: rigid and forbidding.

Incident

She sat slowly down in the chair beside my desk and asked in a voice barely audible whether she was normal. I wanted to know why she was asking. Her reply propped me up quickly. All last summer, she said, she had been obsessed with a picture of herself cutting her mother's throat. She would be washing dishes, for instance, see the butcher knife and feel herself reaching for it and imagine cutting her mother's throat. Her mother would call her and at being called, she would imagine getting the butcher knife and going through the act. I tried to suggest that she should go to the lady psychiatrist at her school, but she refused adamantly. I was doing a good deal of psychotherapy then, and because it was just before Christmas when this girl was going home, I decided to give her the help she was apparently asking me for.

First, I suggested that she must hate her mother pretty strongly to want to cut her throat. In typically ambivalent fashion, she protested that she did not hate her mother at all, that she and her mother had never even quarrelled. I had to listen for nearly 30 minutes to a review of all the fine things her mother had done for her. Her father had left her mother before she was born, and the mother had had to work as a school teacher to rear her. The mother had made her pretty dresses, given her an education, and sacrificed in a thousand ways.

I could see that I was getting nowhere on this track, and I suspected that all this description of maternal sacrifice was partly a recital of things her mother had been telling her over and over. Considering the notion they had never quarrelled, I reckoned I would have to pierce this defense in some other way, so I said:

"But it is you who have the images of cutting your mother's throat. This is a mighty hateful and aggressive thing. You must be a terribly ungrateful girl to hate your mother so when she has done so much for you."

Then I got a new tirade, now in a hotly resentful voice. Did I know that she, a college senior, had never had a date in her life? Did I know that she might have had a chance to go with a boy to the high-school junior-senior banquet, but her mother had seen the boy she hoped to go with in a grocery store and told him to let her daughter alone? All her life she had had to hear what terrible people men were. It all seemed to have started, according to her retrospective account, when this girl was involved in some mild sex play as a five-year-old.

She must have talked for twenty minutes, railing continually at her mother as if in justification of her felt hostility. Then suddenly she seemed to "come to" and realize what she was saying. When she did she began to cry miserably. She had not known that she felt this way. She regarded herself as a terrible girl. At this point I assured her that she was not terrible, but that she and her mother had never been honest with each other, that she had never faced the hostility she felt toward her mother. She guessed this was true.

She planned at the time to go home for Christmas and say nothing to her mother, but just continue to be the same apparently sweet repressed girl she had always been. I requested her to be sure to see me at least once after the holidays. I was fairly confident that the hostile obsession would be gone, but I was afraid mother might be in for a stormy vacation with her daughter. I expected what had happened in these two hours of talk to release the inhibition of hostility and leave this girl overtly the hostile girl toward her mother that she always had been internally.

This expectation was confirmed. The girl's interview, after Christmas, was one long tale of arguments. This girl no longer had an obsession to cut her mother's throat, but she had cut her mother's spirit with the knife of language repeatedly.

Then came an unexpected turn of events. The student's mother wanted the Dean of my student's college to know what terrible things can happen to girls who take psychology. She wanted that psychologist fired who had turned her daughter against her. This was not too hard to straighten out, but it shows that dynamite can explode in unexpected directions in consequence of emotional changes obtained very quickly. All this happened in one interview of about two hours of therapeutic talk with this girl.

Discussion

Emotional habits are considered hard to change. One usually hears about how long it takes. This is what makes such help so expensive. Sometimes, however, a significant change can be obtained quickly in psychotherapy, but some unforeseen consequences may also occur.

One might ask what were the considerations that I took into account while the client was defending her mother, when I came to a decision that it would be safe to attempt to pierce her defense with the charge that she was being ungrateful to a mother who had done so much in her behalf.

I put a great deal of importance upon the fact that this girl had a waking fantasy of cutting her mother's throat. This implied, in psychoanalytic language, that the repression of the hostility was not very deep. It implied that the amount of anxiety aroused by hostile impulses towards the mother were not so tremendous that the charge of being ungrateful would serve to throw her into a severe depression. I was thinking in terms of my own behavior theory of repression that it is a response of inhibiting one of one's own responses which tends to produce cues which have been conditioned to strong anxiety responses. The escape from these strong anxiety responses is to stop the response that produced the cue, just as an escape from an external cue which arouses anxiety is to run away from that cue.

ALBERT ELLIS . . .

This case represents to me another solid proof of the folly of completely passive, nondirective methods of psychotherapy when more active confrontation seems to be called for. Nor do I believe that this is an exceptional instance of the successful use of a goading or provocative approach. On the contrary, I find that in a great many instances where clients at first resist admitting certain facts and feelings which can be obviously deduced from their behavior, a forceful insistence by the therapist, or a dramatic accusation as employed in this critical incident, is most effective in breaking down their "resistances."

It has always been surprising to me how seriously therapists tend to take so-called resistance and how easily they are intimidated by it. Much of what is called the client's "resistance," especially as this term is used in the psychoanalytic literature, is, I am convinced, largely the result of the client's quite healthy reactions to the therapist's poor technique. The client comes to therapy asking for help; the therapist, because of his own prejudices, maintains a passive attitude and refuses to give any substantial help; so the client, quite naturally I believe, "resists" the therapist and often ends up by quitting therapy.

At the same time, considerable genuine resistance must also be expected in therapy, since the client has normally been disturbed for a considerable period before coming for aid and cannot be expected to change his behavior simply because the therapist explains why he has been acting in a given manner or asks him to act differently. Particularly in cases like the one under discussion, where the client has "repressed" or is loathe to admit certain underlying feelings of hostility, we must expect resistance to insight and action to occur.

All right, then; so the client often resists. School children as well as college students also resist learning new things, changing their behavior. But is this any reason why teachers should stop trying to get them to learn and to change? The therapist's job, more often than not, is to accept resistance for what it is worth—namely, highly expectable disinclination to give up a well-trodden road for a relatively unexplored one—and to keep hacking away at it, often by a sheer process of attrition, until it is overcome. To be bulldozed by it, and cravenly retreat in the face of its "hopelessness," is certainly to take a nontherapeutic, and often an anti-therapeutic, attitude.

In the case in question, the therapist fortunately takes the client's resistance with a bucket of salt and (1) tries an unsuccessful frontal attack on it then (2) tries a very successful flank attack. My own feeling is that if the flank attack had not worked, the best procedure probably would have been to return to the frontal attack, and to keep at it until the client's resistance had been beaten down. In my own cases, no matter how stiff the client's resistance originally was, I have rarely seen a case where I could not, by one method of attack or another, eventually overcome it. Naturally, this procedure of attacking clients' resistances has its own dangers, especially that of the client leaving therapy. I find in actual practice, however, that very few of them do leave for this reason, and that still fewer experience the pernicious effects, such as psychotic breaks, which the literature so cavalierly assumes that they may experience under these circumstances.

What is commonly forgotten in this connection is that the therapist is, almost by definition, supposed to be emotionally stronger and healthier than the client. If this is true, and if in addition the therapist is adequately trained, there should be relatively few instances where, in the long run, his strength and knowledge cannot overcome the client's neurotic (or even psychotic) resistances. If the therapist is unduly intimidated by these resistances, then it would be my feeling that he is not sufficiently stable and healthy to do effective psychotherapy and that he had better stick to some nontherapeutic speciality.

JEROME D. FRANK . . .

Two of the factors which impede rapid change of attitudes in patients are lack of sufficient emotional involvement in treatment and lack of self-confidence. Emotional involvement supplies the motive power for change of attitude, and self-confidence gives the patient courage to look at his feelings squarely and to attempt new ways of dealing with them.

In this incident both factors were favorable for rapid change. The girl was in severe and acute emotional distress so that the motivation for change was high. The therapist was able to strengthen the patient's self-confidence in two days. Part of her demoralization sprang from the fear that her phantasy of cutting her mother's throat with a butcher knife was "abnormal," that is, that she was crazy. The therapist, by giving her a plausible and rational explanation for this thought, markedly alleviated this fear. He further bolstered her self-confidence by his acceptance of her hostile feelings which were strongly laden with guilt.

The actual means by which the therapist accomplished the latter is also of interest. The patient could not directly accept the thought that she hated her mother; but when the therapist put himself in the mother's role and threw up to the patient the same accusation of ingratitude that the mother must often have made, the patient was able to ventilate her feelings about the mother in the guise of defending herself against the therapist's accusation. In this way her initial guilt was circumvented long enough for the angry feelings to come out.

Parenthetically, I have noted that medical students who come to see me because the psychiatric course has aroused fears that they may have a psychiatric disorder, have a good prognosis. This, I think, is partly because their reaction to the course shows that they are suggestible, that is, readily accessible to interpersonal influences, and partly because their coming to the psychiatrist indicates a readiness to accept the type of help he can offer and an expectancy of relief from it.

A final factor which accounts, I think, for the rapidity of change was that the patient was able almost immediately to test out her new way of behaving and find out that it worked; in terms of learning theory, it became reinforced. Even though the scenes with the mother must have been very painful for both, I doubt if they were as painful to the patient as her previously bottled-up emotion.

I must confess to some sympathy for the mother. She undoubtedly had not been aware of her daughter's hostile feelings and had, in fact, made many sacrifices for her, so that the shock must have been all the greater for her.

I wonder what the psychologist "straightened out" with respect to the mother's complaint to the Dean. Does he mean that he straightened out his position with the Dean or that he was able to help the mother to see what was happening? In this connection it would be interesting to know whether this episode was followed by an improved relationship between mother and daughter. To what extent was the daughter able to get past her hateful feelings to a genuine appreciation of what the mother actually had done for her, and was the mother able to understand the extent to which she had inhibited her daughter? Also, was the change in attitude towards her mother accompanied by any lessening of her inhibitions with respect to men?

ERNEST HILGARD . . .

The girl who both loved and hated her mother, but was mixed up about it, represents what is perhaps the most familiar type of conflict, namely that in which there are both approach and avoidance tendencies or what we usually call ambivalent attitudes. Such conflicts can be simulated in the psychological laboratory in experiments with animals, and have led to interpretations based on behavior theory whether of the Lewin type (as by Barker) or of the Hull type (as by Neal Miller). The usual demands of the social environment, reinforced by all manner of secondary reinforcers, as well as by anxiety-reduction, tend to favor the overt expression of the more accepting and pleasanter attitudes. What becomes of the other side of the coin furnishes special problems for theory. If the negative attitudes are not expressed, are they lost (through some sort of forgetting through disuse), or are they merely inhibited (perhaps by some sort of conditioned inhibition that is subject to disinhibition) so that they exist but are "repressed"?

The case material suggests one kind of answer: the "repressed" behavior has expressed itself in fantasy, so it has not been lost; the later outpouring shows that resentment of the mother is pretty near the surface. If one were to stick with a learning interpretation, he would have to distinguish between the reinforcement of the overt statements, and some kind of subtle reinforcement of privately-held but covertly expressed statements. Thus overt actions are punished, but fantasy is not. Fantasy, which serves some kind of gratification and reduces anger, is thereby reinforced, without facing the rebuff of overt social action. This may in some way keep alive the source of the anger also, even though it does not come to full verbal expression under usual circumstances.

Had there been a more self-punishing conscience, it is probable that the fantasy of cutting the mother's throat would have been deflected to some less forbidding action, such as perhaps the fantasy of hurting an animal. The fact that the mother appeared directly in the fantasy suggests that the inhibition against the expression of hostility toward the mother was not very strong. The therapist sensed this and was guided by it in trying to release statements of anger against the mother.

An interesting feature of the therapist's performance was his shift from the position that the fantasy indicated hatred of the mother to the position that the patient was hateful for having hostile thoughts about a mother who was good to her. This shift in tactic had the desired results, that is, release of statements of anger against the mother, but this calls, too, for explanation. Learning theory tends to be weak in discussing the organization of motives that are built around the self, the self-image, or self-perception. The need to appear as a "good girl" was very strong. This was her self-perception while she was saying proper things about her mother. When, however, she was accused of being hateful because of her fantasies, she faced a change in her self-perception which called for restitution, or, in Festinger's expression, she had to reduce the "dissonance" between her self-image and the statement about her by the therapist.[1]

[1] Leon Festinger, *A Theory of Cognitive Dissonance* (Evanston, Ill.: Row Peterson & Company, 1957).

The best way out was to show that she was all right and her mother all wrong. That she proceeded to do. It is almost a reversal of figure-ground relations: first, I am good because I say nice things about mother; second, I am not bad for saying unkind things about a mother who deserves them. In both cases, she maintains a favorable self-image. This is undoubtedly important, but learning theorists, as such, have had little to say about this kind of motive.

A further problem arises concerning the therapeutic value of the release of anger. The author of the incident has his own answer. He says that the anxiety responses of the girl were conditioned to the very act of inhibiting anger; that is, when the girl inhibited expressions of anger to her mother she aroused in herself the disturbing fantasies as conditional responses. When she no longer inhibited anger, the inhibition that triggered fantasy was gone, and the fantasies were then gone, too.

There are always a few steps missing in all of these interpretations, and we have to be very careful about offering plausible interpretations. A positive effect of permitting the expression of anger was to put the young woman on the road to problem-solving behavior, a point that would perhaps be made by Mowrer. She could not talk in the presence of her mother about her need to have dates with boys if she were to grow up normally, that boys, with all their faults, are part of the world, that mother had to lay off her or she wouldn't grow up. Once problem-solving behavior occurs, some of the deflected behavior may disappear because it no longer serves any purpose.

The problem of fantasy-production is a very important one that has not been well-integrated into contemporary psychology, despite the use of projective tests and the awareness of psychoanalytic interpretations. It is often forgotten that Freud made the production of fantasies a very primitive process (wish-fulfilling under the pleasure principle) and in regressed states we tend to find hallucinations (for example, in schizophrenia; in restricted environments). Perhaps the use of fantasy, especially spontaneous and uncontrolled, as in this case, always indicates some loss of normal interaction with the physical and social environment, so that it may be thought of as a sign of regression as well as of repression. But all this is too speculative to derive from this case!

FAY KARPF . . .

In order to be able to interpret this critical incident, it would be necessary to know why the student "refused adamantly" the suggestion of her instructor "that she should go to the lady psychiatrist at her school." It may have been for one of any number of important reasons which could affect subsequent therapy. Was it because she did not like the psychiatrist for some valid or questionable reason, or because she had disqualifying information about the psychiatrist, or perhaps because she had already seen this psychiatrist (in which case the instructor should certainly have consulted her before undertaking treatment himself)? Or was it that the instructor was a flirtatious challenge the student was going to "make" (in which case her dramatic formulation of her problem may have been connected with her choice of the instructor as therapist), or was it, finally, that she was just more comfortable with an instructor, like her mother, despite her expressed hostility, or for any number of other significant therapy-related reasons?

The purpose of these questions is to indicate that unless the instructor knew a great deal more about the student than appears from his account of the critical incident, he might have been getting into a serious situation without the preliminary exploration that every cautious therapist routinely undertakes. Further, with regard to the student herself, we should know something more than the few appreciative remarks the instructor makes about her physical appearance and his impressionistic judgment that "she wore in her gestures 'don't you touch me' signs: rigid and forbidding." What kind of person was she? What was her level of performance as a student? How did she get along with other students and other instructors? What were her extracurricular activities, her basic interests and aspirations? Who were her close associates? And so on. As for wondering whether or not she was normal, what imaginative student at the time of his first acquaintance with the psychoneuroses doesn't wonder whether or not he or she is altogether normal? The alert instructor must be prepared to appraise the situation with therapeutic responsibility.

In the absence of all this information, one can only say that the instructor was taking on a very risky professional responsibility unilaterally, and he may have been just fortunate that the "unforeseen consequences" were not more serious than they actually were, for dynamite can indeed "explode in unexpected directions in consequence of emotional changes obtained very quickly" if you have not taken measures to wall off the explosion properly.

And what was accomplished in the single two-hour interview of release therapy? Was the mother perhaps justified in complaining about the therapeutic result, especially since the instructor's procedure was, according to him, based on his thinking "in terms of my own behavior theory of repression," which seems a rather flimsy basis for treatment of an obsessive hostility. For the girl was left with an overtly hostile attitude toward her mother without any attempt having been made to give her real insight into her reaction to her mother's behavior or to develop a more constructive outlook toward their continued relationship on a more wholesome basis. The girl already felt guilty because of what transpired in the interview, and for her to continue to depend on her mother while moved by such overt hostility toward her, could only result in an accumulating burden of guilt which, in the long run, might be as destructive as the original difficulty. And yet the instructor was planning to see the girl only once more to get a report of what occurred during the Christmas vacation visit with the mother. He could instead have taken the opportunity at least to attempt to build up a sound basis of relationship between mother and daughter. It is often possible to do much for another family member (or even a whole family unit) through planned constructive therapy with a single patient member. But this is a rather controversial point and hence requires further comment.

Quite apart from specific details, then, this critical incident highlights an important problem about which there have been differences of viewpoint and position since the early period of the modern psychotherapeutic movement, to which the controversial literature of the period, especially following the break between Freud and Jung, amply testifies. This is the difficult and controversial problem of goals in therapy, which remains vague and ill-defined and often completely unformulated. It would be a significant clarifying step ahead if this troublesome problem could be more definitely and systematically considered in the light of the major theoretical positions current in the field today.

RUTH MUNROE . . .

The therapeutic contact in this case was not limited to the two-hour session. It clearly included the course in psychology. Quick cures usually depend heavily on a transference relationship to what we personify for the patient. It is unlikely that this girl had confided her symptom to anyone else. Her confession reflects her strong trust in the lecturer's benign authority, perhaps in contrast to fear of the "abnormality" she may have considered already confirmed by "going to the psychiatrist." The stage is set for an intense emotional reaction. Although she was doubtless aware previously of specific resentments toward the mother, the violence of her outpouring in response to his "attack" on her ingratitude must have been really shocking to her. It was, however, easily accepted by her chosen authority and explained in an ego-syntonic manner. Whether or not he referred to the course materials, whether or not she understood them, the therapist gave her the absolution of Science and at least the *feeling* that she could understand the problem. This transference to the therapeutic ego seems to me quite as important as catharsis and release from repression.

While generally sympathetic to this therapist's handling of this case, I wonder if he could not have accomplished the same result without the overt "attack" of the words precipitating the girl's outpouring of resentment. In my experience any sharp *exaggeration* of the patient's conscious attitude, any *implication* that one is taking sides against her, is enough shock to provoke the mood-reversal. If the therapeutic shock does not come off (that is, if the patient *was* depressive or detached) or results in low moods later, the patient too easily remembers overtly hostile phrases (for example, your image "is a mighty hateful and aggressive thing") without the attitude and resolution vivid at the time. The *shock effect* is a necessary phase of the therapy, the importance of which should be fully recognized. Unless the patient is really committed to continued therapy, however, I think that one should be very careful to utter no rememberable hostile phrases, and that one should offer vivid positive verbal tags, such as "Everybody has hostile feelings. You and your mother haven't faced them honestly."

I speak from experience with patients who come back to me after referral, notably college students. A frequent pattern is an initial lift, followed by a refusal to return to the therapist, "justified" by hair-raising quotes. My stock rejoinder is: "What do you think he really meant? Why don't you ask him?" One tries not to modify or soften the essential interpretation, but to reinforce the *benign* intent of the therapist. He can't treat a patient who isn't there.

I wonder also whether or not the mother-daughter relationship might not have been handled more constructively, and whether or not therapy could not have been continued beyond subsidence of the obsession. The neurotic symptom is usually part of a neurotic character trend. A college senior who has never had a date, who has been indoctrinated with hatred of men and guilt about sex, is likely to have problems beyond repressed hostility to the mother. Her own attitudes toward men would probably need ventilation and reorientation if she is to avoid some continuance of the mother's neurosis despite the current rebellion.

"Cutting the mother's spirit with the knife of language" does not seem an altogether healthy substitute for a literal knife. This poor mother deserves sympathy in her own right, but is probably not amenable to such "therapy" as a college can offer. (Some parents *are* helped by friendly discussion of a daughter's problems. Often they are much more understanding than one expects from the account given by a rebellious child. At times, however, tough talk by the Dean is the only recourse. I have known deans to say: "Dating is part of the normal student life at this college. If you do not wish your daughter to share in this life, we must ask you to withdraw her.")

Toward the end of the two-hour session with this student I would have asked *why* her mother should be so unreasonable about dates—shifting focus by leading questions to some sort of sympathetic understanding of the *mother's* problems, even remarking that she really had been pretty heroic. "You are right to rebel, you *must* rebel for the sake of your own life, but you have also been right in loving and respecting your mother. Now *you* are the stronger person. Probably you will still have to fight to prove your strength to yourself—you haven't known about it very long. Do you think you are strong enough to be gentle? To give in on trifles without feeling that you are giving in the way you used to? Remember it's only for a week or two. Don't expect too much of yourself or of her." (Of course, not given as a continuous homily.)

This technique does not eliminate vacation quarrels, but it helps keep them below the boiling point. Even more important, it recognizes the ambivalence always present in the newly rebellious patient and is pointed toward a more mature resolution. If the therapist supports only the rebellion, he may find himself repudiated by the daughter as well as the mother. Indeed, the rebellion itself may be short-lived, giving way to renewed submission and/or more stubborn neurosis. It is not expected that the patient will fully assimilate understanding of the tangled relationship in one dramatic session, and there must, of course, be clear support of the rebellion.

In practice I have never found *this* support inadequate. The problem is rather shame at failure to avoid quarrels. This I have tried to handle by reassurance, plus effort toward clarification of what behavior was essentially childish rebellion and what was necessary for true independence. One is quietly repetitious about how people are not always rational. One listens to a few self-justifying recriminations and asks, "Why was this so important?" Often this question leads to deep material which one may use or hold back, depending on the design of the therapeutic relationship. In the designedly superficial college set-up, I have usually held back to the level of ego understanding, slightly deepened by joint recognition of outworn childhood patterns; release with sympathy for failure, but a clear statement of a new generosity as an ideal.

The student living currently in a difficult home, or the very sick patient, cannot be handled in this way. The demands on a new ego orientation are too great.

This therapist handled his patient well, but in my opinion did not sufficiently consider her background and future. Symptom-cure is only the beginning of psychotherapy.

FREDERICK C. THORNE . . .

It is fortunate that the client happened to react so well to such brief directive handling (therapeutic?) under conditions which might just as well have had more explosively dangerous results. It is generally contraindicated to open up potentially sensitive areas just before an enforced intermission in therapy such as a Christmas holiday vacation where the client goes directly back into the situation provoking her difficulties without adequate preparation. Ideally, the therapist should remain in close enough contact with the situation to deal constructively with complications as they arise. In this case, the explosion between the girl and her mother could probably have been avoided by sufficiently bleeding off the girl's hostilities so that she had no great need to revenge herself on the mother directly. In our opinion, the mother had a legitimate complaint against such abrupt case handling which might have had very dangerous results. While it is true that desirable therapeutic outcomes frequently result from superficial case handling, it should not be overlooked that less traumatic outcomes probably could have been achieved with more sensitive handling. In particular, the therapist's judgmental evaluations as expressed in the following: "But it is you who have the images of cutting your mother's throat. This is a mighty hateful and aggressive thing. You must be a terribly ungrateful girl to hate your mother so much when she has done so much for you?" may be regarded as examples of what *not* to do in directive psychotherapy. Such comments are superfluous because the client's anxieties are already so intense as to reflect intense inner conflict, and she does not need to be told that something is the matter.

Clinical situations where a client is dangerously near an explosive outburst toward some source of frustration, such as a wife or parent or employer, require careful handling if the interpersonal situation is not to deteriorate badly. Ideally, it is probably desirable to avoid overt personal conflict or scenes in which the distraught client "tells someone off." Such confrontations, although they may give the client immediate satisfaction and ventilation of his conflicts, may have dire long term consequences as when a parent is irretrievably hurt, a wife estranged, or an employer outraged. While the other parties *may* be entirely to blame, and the client entirely justified in his resentments, it is more desirable psychologically to solve the issues in ways which do not strain interpersonal relations so badly.

In such cases (for example one in which a child is about to blow up in resentment against a parent) we have developed the practice of keeping the two people apart until both can handle themselves constructively. This may be accomplished if both parties have sufficient resources and control by establishing a state of psychological isolation or quarantine in which the conflictual areas are tabooed as subjects for conversation. Generally, we ask the client if he feels able to handle himself, and if not we advise that he not go home until he can control himself. Or, if he does try going home, we advise him to leave immediately the moment that things get out of control. Rarely, where extreme tension or incompatibility exists, we advise the client to stay completely away from the persons who frustrate him, at least until such time as he becomes healthy enough to react constructively.

Actually, it may take intensive counseling among all parties concerned to interpret what is happening to all concerned. There are cases, for example, where a child must live with a hated parent, as when the child comes home in a state of breakdown and with nowhere else to go. The parent may be counseled to accept whatever the child says, making no attempt to justify past behaviors and permitting the child to express great ambivalence and hostility. Many parents have sufficient resources and control to patiently work out a new relationship once the therapist has structured desired outcomes sufficiently. Again, however, we must emphasize that such a therapeutic objective may involve a good deal of work and should probably not be attempted unless conditions seem optimum. Rarely, the antagonistic persons may have to be separated completely, even for life, if the unhealthy chain of interpersonal feelings is to be broken up.

WERNER WOLFF . . .

This incident invites a discussion on the role of fantasies in psychotherapy. Fantasies form part of the psychic reality, just as experiences do, and according to psychoanalysis they follow the pleasure principle (the guiding principle of the unconscious). Inasmuch as fantasies are an expression of the principle of wish-fulfillment, they are produced in opposition to the reality principle (created by the physical and social environment). Fantasies are interrelated by perception and behavior in that perception of the fusion of external and internal reality produces fantasy, and fantasy (conscious and unconscious) influences behavior. In psychotherapy a patient is made aware of the interplay of perception, fantasy, and behavior.

The varieties of behavior may be distinguished according to ten categories as: (1) cultural expression; (2) communication; (3) subjective habit; (4) mask; (5) defense; (6) release; (7) compensation; (8) conversion of experiences; (9) symbolization; and (10) part of an integrated personality pattern.

The *fantasy* in the present case, of cutting the mother's throat, appears to be opposite to the patient's apparent *perception* of her mother: ". . . all the fine things her mother had done for her . . . she and her mother had never even quarrelled." The fantasy of violence is also opposite to the patient's apparent *behavior:* " 'don't you touch me' signs: rigid and forbidding." The clear opposition suggests a basic ego-superego conflict. According to the case history, the ego conflict consists in social-sexual impulses, but "all her life she had had to hear what terrible people men are," thus paralyzing her social adjustment. The superego conflict consists in the patient's double attitude toward her mother as a model of care and as a source of prohibitions.

The therapeutic analysis of attitudes made the patient aware of her antagonistic response in behavior and fantasy. Before the critical incident her behavior was over-correct and her fantasy was violent, while after the incident her behavior became aggressive but her fantasy became tolerant. The therapeutic interview produced what I call an "existential switch," namely, "a sudden change in the structure of the existential target or in the means of approaching it"; the existential target being "an ultimate goal which attracts all of our efforts; which determines, unconsciously, our actions."[2]

Although the present therapeutic approach was successful, I feel that not enough material was discovered to warrant the danger of dealing with this case in advisory fashion, since at first glance it could not be decided whether it was an id-superego conflict or an ego-superego conflict—as it happened to be. Rather, the girl and her mother should have been informed of the need for regular psychotherapy, in which the structure of the fantasy should have been approached slowly and systematically. As the therapist admits, the sudden piercing of defenses may cause a collapse of an internal structure, mobilizing deeper lying disturbances, anxieties, and depressions and possibly even producing psychotic processes. Theoretically, a therapy of fantasies should be preceded by an analysis of the structure of fantasy in terms of behavior and perception in order to decide upon the therapeutic approach to be taken.

[2] Werner Wolff, *Values and Personality: An Existential Psychology of Crisis* (New York: Grune & Stratton, 1950), p. 217.

The Therapist

Was a Demon

15

History

The patient, Homer, was first seen by the writer as a member of a psychiatric team, working in a prison. After the prisoner had been presented, the conclusion of the staff was that he was a neurotic with some psychotic tendencies, but that he might be helped by psychotherapy. No one had the time to work with him except the writer, who was asked whether or not he wanted to take him on. The writer accepted the assignment, although he did not particularly like it for two reasons: first, he had not been favorably impressed by the subject or his history; and second, he felt that successful therapy depended, to a great extent, on the patient's demand for it.

Before seeing the patient, I looked over his history. I found that he was 40 years of age. At the age of 16 he had entered a theological seminary belonging to a small Protestant denomination of which his father, a minister, was a member. He had been ordained at the age of 20 and had been sent as a missionary to Africa. However, in Europe, he changed his mind and returned to the States, where for a number of years he held services as a pastor in a number of small churches. At the age of 24 he had been arrested for forgery, but was not sentenced. At the age of 25 he had committed himself to a mental hospital, but was released after a week with the diagnosis of "psychoneurotic." He married at the age of 28, became a father at the age of 30, and worked from the time of his marriage until his first conviction at a number of jobs: a clerk in an airlines, a high school teacher of English, and finally as a counselor in a correctional camp. At the age of 34 he was convicted of fraud. It seemed that he had represented himself as a clergyman who wanted to erect a Protestant Boys Town, and had collected money for this purpose, but had spent it on his own needs. As far as could be told, he used most of the money for publicity purposes, taking his "victims" out to dinner, making trips in connection with his fund-gathering, and so forth. He protested lack of criminal intention but was nevertheless convicted. He entered prison at the age of 35 and served three years. During his incarceration, he was declared psychotic and was given a series of electric-shock treatments. After the treatments, he was put to work in the psychiatric clinic as an attendant. He left the prison at the age of 38, rejoined his wife and daughter, and went to work in a small Protestant settlement house.

He worked in this settlement house for about a year and then was arrested for violating his parole. The violation was quite similar to the original crime: he had persuaded people to give him sums of money for various charitable works but, instead of using the money for the purposes intended, had actually spent it improving the settlement house where he worked as a clerk. Instead of being reconvicted, he was returned as a parole violator, and it was immediately after entrance that he was brought to the staff meeting where I saw him in the group.

I called Homer in that afternoon, introduced myself, told him that in the opinion of the psychiatric staff he might be helped by psychotherapy and that it had been suggested that I counsel him, but that whether or not he had psychotherapy was up to him. He stated that he was overjoyed to be given therapy, that he had often felt this was what he needed, that he would cooperate fully, and that he was most thankful.

We discussed how often he should be seen and agreed to meet three times a week in my office. I also explained to him that I would use a nondirective method, which meant that he would take the burden of the discussion. I finally explained that I would under no circumstances ever repeat or make any notes about what he said, but that I would give, if required, an over-all evaluation of him with respect to changes. He agreed to everything, and we began.

For about ten sessions he spoke rapidly and I listened with very few comments. The content of his statements was mostly to the effect that he had meant well, but that circumstances in his life had been too difficult to cope with. He showed some resentment toward the clergy in general, feeling that they were too worldly. He had some mild criticism of his parents, but expressed great tenderness and love for his wife and child.

But about the tenth session he came to a halt, informing me that he had told me "everything" and that now I should tell him something: what his errors had been, how he should act in the future, his analysis, and so on. I merely reflected his demands, which at first puzzled him, then angered him. Finally, he demanded to know whether or not he was cured, and how long he should continue with me. I kept reflecting these attitudes, which continued to puzzle him. We continued in this way for about ten more sessions, and his production became less and less. Finally, we had sessions in which he would come in and say, "I guess you are not going to tell me anything." I would respond somewhat as follows: "You expect me to say something, and you believe that I will not tell you what you want to know." He might counter: "Well, I want to know whether I am through or not. I have told you everything. What I'd like to know is whether I should continue any more. I want to know what you think of me. I want to know what I should do. Can't you tell me what is wrong with me, why I did what I did, and how I can avoid any future peculiar behavior?"

Inexorably, I reflected all statements, trying to maintain as even and as unperturbed an attitude as possible, but my replies did not satisfy him at all, and so we went, from session to session, he relapsing into a hurt and puzzled silence, while I would wait patiently for the end of the hour, wondering meanwhile what I ought to do.

By this time I had come to the following conclusions: Homer did not really want psychotherapy. What he really wanted was my approval that he was "cured" and possibly a statement to that effect which might be of help in getting him released. I did not feel that he had been "honest" with me, but rather that he had regarded me as a person whom he could not trust, and who was to be manipulated. In his prison folder I had read a number of letters he had written, which were frankly enthusiastic, expressing gratitude for the help he had gotten from members of the psychiatric staff on his previous stay in this prison. I had read, carefully, the various notes on him and came to the conclusion that he was a scheming, suspicious, hypocritical individual, who was attempting to take advantage of a situation.

My own feelings had two parts: first, I could understand his reluctance to talk about himself in terms of materials that might hurt him, since his main desire was to get out of the prison, and I could understand his lack of confidence in me; second, even though I thought I understood him and his motives, I felt that he really did need psychotherapy, and that my present procedure would eventually terminate without any success. The question was what to do to help this person, and consequently his family, his community, and the state. How could I gain his confidence?

I discussed Homer with the ward psychiatrist who informed me that Homer (1) was serving as a stool pigeon, informing on other inmates and (2) was really a schizophrenic and could not be helped by psychotherapy. He advised me to give up the case as impossible.

Incident

About the twenty-first session, after about seven weeks of "treatment," I finally said to Homer: "You have continually asked me to evaluate you, to give you my opinion. Against my better judgment, I shall do so. But you must promise that as soon as I finish telling you what I think of you, you must leave."

He agreed and I began a five minute summary, that went something as follows:

"I see you as a very, very stupid person, one who is so steeped in deceit and hypocrisy that you cannot accept another person at face value. You have told me a lot of unimportant material, and you think that I am stupid enough to believe you. I really want to help you, but I think all you want to do is to manipulate me and the situation. You are a liar and a dishonest person, because as I see things, you are getting an opportunity that you may never again have in your life—to really get to understand yourself. I resent your bootlicking tendencies, all the sweet words you have said, which I feel certain you do not believe. You have wasted my time and yours, and you think I am foolish enough to fall for your nonsense."

I waved him out of the office when I concluded. I was agitated and angry, and he looked pale and stunned.

The next appointment he did not meet. I went to see him the day after, and he said he would come to the next session, but he did not. I went the day after once again, and this time he came to my office, bringing with him a manuscript which he offered me. It was entitled, "The Demon of ———." I asked him to read it, and he did, and the essay went to the effect that in prisons, physical torture had given way to psychological torture, and that the way it was done was to gain the confidence of a prisoner and then hurt him cruelly. The main devil of the particular institution was the therapist.

After he finished, we looked at each other, and suddenly he stated: "You were right, I did lie to you. I thought it over. Now I want to really get therapy."

I shook my head and ordered him out of the office, saying, "You had your chance; it is too late."

The next day, however, I called for him, and when he came in I told him: "Yesterday, you wanted to continue therapy, and said you wanted to tell the truth, but I sent you away for this reason: I did not want to take advantage of your mood of excitement. If we are to do therapy, you should know what it is all about. I am not particularly interested in learning about you. What I do want, however, is that you should accept me as I state myself to be, and that you do not try to take advantage of me."

We began once again, still using the nondirective method, and this time the story was completely different. For about 20 sessions I listened to a variety of stories: how his parents fought bitterly about money; how the mother had driven one of her sons to suicide; how Homer used to go to the attic of the seminary to pray, but in reality to masturbate; how he sinned in smoking, gambling, and whoring, sins of equal importance; how he did not really love his wife; how he did not believe in God; actually hated Christ; and so forth. And then, during the therapy, slowly, he began to change attitudes towards religion, his parents, his wife, and so forth. He began to manifest signs of maturity, self-acceptance, and humility. We finally, on his request, terminated therapy. He was produced before the psychiatric committee and was considered "much improved."

The writer followed Homer for several years, both in prison and out, the latter through correspondence, and he appeared to have made a good and uneventful adjustment.

Discussion

The incident, of course, was the "verbal shock therapy." As far as I can see, using it did cause a considerable change in the climate of the therapy, with Homer changing from an extremely self-protecting individual, with no confidence in his therapist, to a person who did have confidence.

Why should this have had this effect? From where I stand: he simply did not trust the therapist before, but did afterwards. Why? Before, I had been a kind of official, interested in doing a job, but not interested in Homer. After, because of my anger, I became a person, and one who was interested in him. Refusal to listen to his "confession" when he was in a hysterical mood gave him further confidence that I was not interested in "prying" and "learning about him," but that I was really interested in him as a person.

When I freed myself from artificial restraints and let myself go, and when I manifested an attitude of fairness, this gave Homer confidence in me, and consequently in himself. By unmasking both of us simultaneously, I produced a situation that could develop satisfactorily.

IAGO GALDSTON . . .

The crucial factor in this "critical incident" is palpably the therapist's shift from the patterns of nondirective to pure aggressivity.

Seemingly the patient made no headway as long as he was treated in the "nondirective pattern" but allegedly "did turn the corner" when the therapist stepped out of his role and literally assaulted him.

This critical incident invites a penetrating review of the limitations of nondirective therapy. The limitations are many and stringent. Only that patient can profit by nondirective therapy who is himself therapeutically active and resourceful, and who broadly and deeply scans his past, his present, and his projected goals. Nondirective therapy is applicable only to the case wherein scanning is likely to yield the patient a deeper and more effective insight into the nature, derivation, and resolution of his difficulties.

Cases in which deprivation is an important factor, either in the patient's psychopathy or in his personality defects or deficiencies, are not likely to benefit by nondirective therapy, nor, for that matter, are they benefited by the free association of classical psychoanalysis.

In such cases the transference-countertransference relationship provides the essential *vis* for an effective psychotherapy.

In the development of the countertransference relationship the therapist is often called on to provide, within the therapeutic situation, some ersatz to the experiences and insights which were missed by the patient.

That the therapist in the case under consideration "broke through" was both understandable and desirable, but the countertransference, as acted out, was completely negative; nor was the transference neurosis dealt with.

The patient was in prison, he was labelled a liar and a cheat. What need then for the therapist to underscore the label? It probably would have been more effective if the "breakthrough" had not been on the basis of "Look, you're cheating me, your therapist! You are wasting my time and wearing me out." An evocative, supportive appeal to that portion of the patient's psyche which was still healthy and responsive would have been more promising. The appeal could have been phrased somewhat in this spirit: "Come now, you are in trouble and I am trying to help you. What's the sense of your blocking yourself and me too? Surely you can see that this kind of relationship will get you nowhere. Let us get down to brass tacks. Do give me a chance to help you."

Phrased in this way the issue as set off is clearly "between the patient and himself" and not, as it was framed in the incident, between the patient and his therapist.

One final comment: The therapist himself proved an unsteady agent. One day he spoke with finality: "You had your chance; it is too late." The next day he called the patient back.

J. McV. Hunt . . .

The case of Homer is probably only the threshold incident for the comment forthcoming. In reading this series of critical incidents in therapy, I have been impressed by the number in which the therapist is reporting, somewhat sheepishly, an incident in which he himself has become so emotionally involved that he reacts with some spontaneous hostility toward his client or patient only to find this emotional incident followed by a wholesome change in the relationship, which leads to improvement in the client or patient. Perhaps the change which takes place in psychotherapy must always come in a context of emotional distress on the part of the client. Such a proposition would follow from both the behavior theory of Dollard and Miller[1] and the physiological notions of central firing systems which

---

[1] J. Dollard and N. E. Miller, *Personality and Psychotherapy* (New York: Mc-Graw-Hill Book Co., Inc., 1950). See Part II on Basic Principles.

Hebb has set forth. In the Dollard and Miller theory, change, or learning, appears when a response leads to such levels of distress that the individual is motivated to try another response in his hierarchy. In Hebbian terms, change appears when the situation upsets the cortical pattern subtending a given response pattern and provides the basis for another system of firing to provide another response.[2] Unless the client's own personal distress is enough to motivate a change in him, one of the tasks of the therapist is to disrupt somehow the pattern leading to trouble and to provide another, presumably one calculated to lead to more fortunate consequences. Although Alfred Adler has been quoted to have said: "Never strike a child except in anger," I wonder if this implies that a therapist must become highly involved emotionally in order to achieve this disruption.

Perhaps the frequency with which these instances of spontaneous hostility on the part of the therapist toward his client derives from an unfortunate stereotype which has grown up about psychotherapy. It is commonly believed that therapy is impossible unless the patient is so distressed that he demands it. It is undoubtedly true that under such circumstances the therapist's job is made relatively easy. His task is merely to listen and respond with sympathy and understanding while the patient pours out his genuine distresses. But when persistent defenses get in the way, or the individual himself is ambivalent about changing, the psychotherapist has a more difficult job. His task is to use his relationship with the client to provide the client with a healing emotional experience.

Homer's psychotherapist was trained in the nondirective school, but in my judgment he broke one of the main tenets of Rogers when he entered the therapeutic relationship conceding that the therapy would fail and feeling unfavorably impressed by Homer. On his side, Homer may have been partially honest in his joy about therapy, but he also had a long and well-established pattern of deceit and of using other people for his short-term goals. In a sense, therefore, this therapist and Homer entered the psychotherapeutic relationships without candor on either side. Under such conditions, the nondirective approach became a travesty of what I understand Rogers to mean by this approach.

Although it would probably have been unwise for the therapist to have expressed his own doubts in the first interview or two, it may be surmised that during the ten interviews (in which Homer related how he had tried but that the circumstances of his life had been too difficult to cope with) there must have been instances in which the things he said conflicted, so that the therapist was provided with an opportunity to indicate, in all candor, that he doubted the relevance of what Homer was saying, that he "could understand Homer's reluctance to talk about himself in terms of

2 Donald Hebb, *The Organization of Behavior* (New York: Wiley, 1949). See Chapter 10.

materials that might hurt him inasmuch as his chief desire was to get out of prison," and that he could understand his lack of confidence in the therapist. At this point, he could have uncovered the deceit and even expressed indignation that Homer should, on the one hand, be delighted by the opportunity for therapy, and then use it to relate how a cruel world had put upon him. I wonder if such an experience could not have achieved the therapeutic relationship required to help Homer as well as the truly emotional outburst of the therapist at the twenty-first session. Of course, one will never know in the case of Homer, and moreover, this suggests the need for experiments to test the issue; the frequency of these reports suggests that psychotherapists need to conceive their job as something more than guiding the highly distressed, and that even nondirective therapy should include in its reflections of feeling a reflection of those feelings read between the lines of talk or from the gestures. This need not mean presenting the patient with a doctrinaire interpretation far removed from his own concerns, but it does mean that the therapist should react to what he understands the patient to be expressing before that understanding provokes in him a major emotional explosion.

O. HOBART MOWRER . . .

The device by which therapy was apparently forwarded in this case is certainly most unconventional. It violates various dictates about being non-judgmental, permissive, accepting, uninvolved. Yet it illustrates a perhaps more basic principle—the principle of *concern*. One of the most remarkable experiences a person can have is the discovery that someone else, who is not in any practical or utilitarian way dependent upon him, is nevertheless willing to exert himself and make sacrifices in his behalf. What do we not owe and what are we not ready to give, in return, to such a person? In fact, it makes one wonder about the whole conception of professional therapy on a strictly *quid pro quo*, market-place basis. Is it possible that the best therapists would be, in a sense, "amateurs" who make their living or are at least supported in some other way?

Here were "countertransference" and "acting-out" of a most vigorous and emphatic kind. If the effect was as good as it appears, then where is the evidence on the basis of which we have been so carefully warned about such things? In a recent paper Zilboorg cites two occasions on which a fellow analyst allowed herself to become thoroughly angry with patients, also with an apparently favorable outcome. "This seems to be a terrible thing, particularly from the strictly Freudian point of view. It seems almost unethical—particularly if not you but somebody else does it. But Edith

Weigert courageously described a couple of cases [where] anger got results."[3]

Of course, the procedure used by the therapist in the present incident was "shocking" in another, more literal sense of the term. Because the therapist had been passive, permissive, and uninvolved up to the point of the "incident," his sudden change of role must have been pretty dramatic, to say the least: "Stupid, steeped in deceit and hypocrisy . . . manipulator, liar, dishonest person . . . bootlicking, sweet words, nonsense." Little wonder that the patient "looked pale and stunned" and that the therapist "was agitated and angry."

Was there something strategically significant about this sudden turnabout? Let us assume that nothing particularly important would have happened if the therapist had continued in his originally permissive role or, equally, that nothing of therapeutic value would have occurred if the therapist had started "picking on" the patient at the outset. What *was* there about the procedure actually followed that was so effective? Could it be this? By being consistently "nice" to the patient for a long period of time, the therapist gave the patient his chance to be nice in return: he manifestly wasn't—and thus incontrovertably proved what a real "stinker" he was.

Says the therapist in conclusion: "By unmasking both of us simultaneously, I produced a situation that could develop satisfactorily." But suppose that he had freed himself "from artificial restraints" earlier. Would the effect have been the same? Perhaps not. Do we have here, once again, an intimation that the therapist must in some sense suffer and sacrifice in order to achieve the moral advantage that somehow seems uniquely powerful, therapeutically?

David Riesman . . .

I am not the only reader of Carl Rogers' *Counseling and Psychotherapy* to have the suspicion that the college student who the therapist thought was improving may primarily have been staying long enough to build up a record for use with his draft board. For the verbal college-trained person, clever in deceit, nondirective therapy may present a new kind of "feminine" passivity to be victimized (even though he may also hate or despair of himself for doing so). In the hands of a saint (and I think of Rogers as something of a secular saint), this method of nonviolence may nevertheless get through to many otherwise case-hardened folk (although for this particular patient as a disillusioned theologue, even saintliness had prob-

[3] G. Zilboorg, "Rediscovery of the Patient: An Historical Note," *Progress in Psychotherapy*, F. Fromm-Reichmann and J. L. Moreno (eds.) (New York: Grune & Stratton, 1956), p. 109.

ably lost its charms). It is the intelligence and pertinacity of the therapist's shock response here which would seem to me no less important than its humanity.

CARL ROGERS . . .

There are two statements in the description of this critical incident that have a good deal of meaning to me. One is the statement that the counselor kept "trying to maintain as even and unperturbed an attitude as possible." The other is the statement "by unmasking both of us simultaneously I produced a situation that could develop satisfactorily." I would like to comment on the meaning that these two statements have for me and their relevance to the incident under discussion.

I have lived through and learned from therapeutic experiences basically very similar to the one described. The client is too defensive to be truthful. The counselor may first accept his statements in a genuine manner but may then begin to doubt the truth of them and be unable to really accept them. At this crucial point, the counselor often makes the operational decision that what he should do is to maintain a façade and put up a pretense of acceptance, even though he does not feel it. Once this vicious circle is started it may continue for some time with all of the elements of a tragic farce. Each party to the relationship now consists primarily of an unhappy role of pretense and façade, but neither member knows how to get out of the dilemma. Consequently, untrue statements are met by dishonest responses, and therapy goes out the window.

As I would handle such a situation now, it would never reach the point at which this incident occurred. In listening to my own feelings as well as to those of the client, the point would have come where I would have said something like the following: "I can hear you telling me that your situation is generally satisfactory and that you understand all your past difficulties, and I am willing for that to be the way you see it. In my own feelings, however, I find that I am simply not believing these statements." In my experience the acceptance of the client's own point of view as being his own and the presentation of my feelings as they exist in me would lead to the same kind of constructive change as occurred in the case of Homer. It would occur with less tension and melodrama but with, I believe, equal gain.

But where the situation has reached the complete impasse described, then the counselor's open expression of his own feeling of disbelief along with his feeling of wanting to be of help is better than a continuance of the façade. In other words, I feel that the counselor in Homer's case was doing something much more constructive when he confronted the client with his own feelings and views than he was during the preceding interview.

Personally, I regard only one aspect of the counselor's behavior as unfortunate. I feel that the impact would have been wholly constructive if it had not included the name-calling. Much of what the counselor said to Homer is his own feeling as it exists in him. This is the vital and useful part. This is the part which the counselor knows with assurance. He is simply expressing the feelings which factually exist in him at the present moment. The counselor does not have the same kind of direct knowledge of the objective truth about the other individual. To term him stupid, a liar, dishonest, and so forth, is simply to invite defensiveness on the part of the client, and it is this defensiveness which emerged in his document describing the therapist as a demon. In my judgment it also accounts for his unwillingness to keep the two following appointments. All of this defensiveness, I believe, could have been avoided had the counselor expressed to Homer only those elements of himself of which he had direct and immediate knowledge; namely, his own feelings.

For myself, the dramatic elements of dismissing the client from the office on two occasions and in general building up a certain attitude of mystery and suspense would have been unnecessary. Perhaps, however, they were necessary for this counselor, and I have no great quarrel with that fact. Each of us has his own style of doing things.

I do not feel that it was the "verbal shock therapy" aspect of this incident which was effective, nor do I think there is any therapeutic magic in calling a client names. On the other hand, after the counselor's blow up, he was free to be and to express his own feelings and so there came about an existential encounter between two real persons. This is perhaps closer to the heart of psychotherapy.

WILLIAM SNYDER . . .

It is first necessary to understand some of Homer's dynamics, in order to evaluate properly the psychotherapy. There seems little support for the diagnosis of schizophrenia made in this case; it probably only indicates the frequency with which that diagnosis tends to be made, at present, whenever a case is rather puzzling. Upon reading the case notes one is tempted to suspect first that Homer is a psychopath. But such a diagnosis is not well supported by the fact that he was able to stay in therapy for a rather extended period (and, of course, by the later outcome of the case). It seems more likely that Homer presents a true immaturity reaction, and that his "delinquencies" are really manifestations of a neurotic passive-aggressive tendency. A subtle aspect of this condition is the intrapunitive and masochistic element. Homer's misadventures are poorly perpetrated, and suggest that he is punishment-prone. His dependency needs are strongly evident, and his request to be told what is wrong with him, endlessly repeated, is clear evidence of his underlying sense of guilt and desire for punishment and expiation. This is probably not at all inconsistent with his religious upbringing and is also revealed in his vocational uncertainty, especially in his tendency to pursue temporarily service professions with close personal contacts, which he is later unable to maintain for any extended periods.

When the therapist admits that he believes that Homer did not really want therapy, he is probably correct. What then did he want? It seems evident that he was seeking punishment; it might be surmised that in childhood love and affection were experienced subsequent only to incidents of punishment and atonement. Certainly this might be a common experience in the religious milieu which characterized his background. Many writers have attested the sense of fulfillment which follows confession, punishment, and expiation. Homer was not particularly scheming and suspicious, and certainly not hypocritical, as postulated by the therapist. His behavior, if understood in the light of the dynamics indicated above, seems entirely reasonable.

What then is the significance of the critical incident of psychic shock therapy, with its seemingly magical outcome? It is obvious that the therapist, unconsciously, finally acquiesced to the client's demands for punishment. More likely, the client really goaded the therapist to the point where he administered the punishment with a sense of righteous indignation; he admits "I was agitated and angry." And the client, after showing a proper amount of righteous anger himself, confessed his wickedness, took his punishment with a sense of satisfaction, and pleaded for forgiveness. The therapist, with almost dramatic qualities, after pouting a bit, forgave the client, and allowed him to confess all his past wickedness. This permitted the establishment of the relationship which the client needed, that is, a guilt-expiating dependency on a strong but loving authority figure. As long as the client could "fool" the father-figure, there was no therapy relationship; when the therapist revealed his awareness of Homer's "badness," but also his acceptance of him, Homer could make effective use of the situation.

The therapist is correct in feeling that when he freed himself of his artificial restraints on his "natural" inclination to let the client know he saw through his deceit, progress began. He had at this point dropped his own pretenses of being a loving person who would not admit that the client was right in considering himself bad. Therapy cannot be very effective when the therapist is forcing himself to maintain a role inharmonious with his real feelings. But it is probably more important that the therapist was at this point also unconsciously orienting his therapy along the lines of the client's needs, rather than toward some arbitrary direction of what he or the psychiatrist felt the client's needs ought to be. It may be, also, that the unconscious masochism of the client was at this point countered by a certain amount of unconscious sadism on the part of the therapist. He seems to show quite a bit of satisfaction in his recounting of his punative behavior, and talks about "freeing himself" of artificial restraints, and "letting himself go." He found satisfaction in being the fair, but punishing, and loving father. Herein lay a true transference and countertransference situation. Both client and therapist were acting out their needs in therapy, and because of the rather fortunate juxtaposition of complimentary needs, the situation worked out advantageously for the client. There is no reason to believe that this would necessarily be true for a client with a different set of dynamics. It is unfortunate, in a way, that this happy outcome of therapy was gratuitous; had it been planned and understood by the therapist, it could have been accomplished more economically, and perhaps more effectively. A near-failure, saved only by an accidental case of righteous indignation, is not really desirable; successful therapy should be able to be planned, and to be deliberately contrived.

FREDERICK C. THORNE . . .

This case illustrates a dilemma encountered by nondirective therapists with patients who waste a great many sessions talking about nonsignificant things and never face up to their problems. Usually, as in this case, rapport gradually peters out unless the therapist utilizes more directive methods to get the client to face his problems. We do not agree with the therapists' preliminary interpretations that Homer did not really want psychotherapy; was not honest, only wanted approval and help in securing his discharge; was scheming, hypocritical, and attempting to take advantage of the situation. While these evaluations have some surface validity, they may also be interpreted as reflecting his character neurosis which could not be penetrated, unassisted, by nondirective handling. While the therapist's verbal shock therapy in the twenty-first session was somewhat amateurish, it nevertheless engendered a conflict in the patient which resulted in further catharsis and abreaction which was handled nondirectively and eventually has a favorable outcome. Here we have a critical experiment in which a single directive action transformed the course of therapy. A more experienced therapist, however, probably could have achieved the same result long before the twenty-first session by confronting the client with the basic issues after the first two or three interviews failed to result in any progress with nondirective methods.

In our own practice, we attempt to administer "verbal shock therapy" in an impersonal objective manner which does not run such a great risk of antagonizing the client permanently. We have never used such terms as: "I see you as a very, very stupid person, one who is so steeped in deceit and hypocrisy that you cannot accept another person at face value. . . . You think I am stupid enough to believe. . . . You are a liar. . . . You have wasted my time and yours, and you think I am foolish enough to fall for your nonsense." If we wished to communicate the same idea (as we often have), we might say "Let's see now, this is the twenty-first interview we have had, isn't it? I wonder if we are getting anywhere. What do *you* feel about it? I suppose that it's not words that count but actions. It doesn't do much good to say how much you want to improve, it's your actions which indicate how you really feel and how much you have gotten out of it. . . . I am willing to go along with you but you've got to do the work. . . . Thus far it seems to me that maybe you have been using these interviews to see what it could get you rather than really doing much yourself. How do you feel about it?"

There are many little ways short of a direct confrontation whereby the therapist can indicate to the client that he knows what is going on. For example, when dealing with patent falsehood, we come right out and ask the client which of two stories is true. If he persists in deceit, we introduce further contradictory information until the truth comes out. We also take the client up on any insincerities or inconsistencies which may develop, refusing to be "used" by the client to gain his own ends but always attempting to cooperate with anything which seems legitimate. After the client discovers that the therapist is scrupulously fair and does not use anything against him, it usually is possible for the client to accept any criticism or derogatory information with which the therapist may see fit to confront him. For example, with a client who is being treated for lying or stealing, we never hesitate to bring up instances of subsequent conduct disorder which may have been reported by outside sources. Instead of implying that the client is "stupid" for repeatedly trying to conceal misbehavior, we usually interpret such conduct to the client as maturational behavior by saying that everyone does impulsive things when young and immature and that such occurrences won't recur when the client "smartens up."

Psychotherapy is the hardest kind of work, and both client and therapist must expect that nothing worthwhile can be learned instantly. To control emotions and motivations is the hardest task in life and requires years of patient practice. We interpret this fact to the client by the analogy of the Notre Dame football coach taking a green high-school kid and patiently hammering him into a skilled quarterback.

"Go

Plumb to Hell"

16

History

The patient was a young man in his late twenties. He came into my ken because he was eager to marry one of my patients. However, he was entangled in a very complicated marital situation and had a bad antecedent history. He had been married and divorced. His marriage was contracted on a neurotic basis and was pathological throughout its rather short duration. He was sexually promiscuous and incestuous. He was an aggressive, belligerent, conceited, arrogant and generally destructive young man. It appeared desirable to recommend that he should undergo an analysis. A therapist was recommended to him. This widely experienced and able psychiatrist sized him up quite correctly and in effect refused to take him on. Given a bad prognosis and asked to pay an impossible fee, the young man returned to me pleading that I should treat him. This I refused to do for a variety of reasons, but notably because I felt it would jeopardize my work with the young woman in whom he was interested.

Some seven months later, however, I felt warranted in taking him on and did so. Initially, when he was under a great deal of pressure, he cooperated very well. This is neatly reflected in one of his dreams:

I was walking along a beach where many people were fishing without much luck. I encountered an old man who was in the act of uncovering a hole in the sand. I stopped to watch him. To my surprise, the hole was an opening to a large cavern underneath the beach. As I looked, the old man began to pull all kinds of fish out of the hole. Then I saw that actually the hole was swarming with all kinds of fish; huge lobsters, trout, tuna, and even a couple of sea lions. These fish seemed to practically climb on his hook.

I walked on a short distance to where X (the young woman in whom he was interested) was waiting, and told her about this amazing discovery I had made; while everyone else failed to catch a thing, here was this old man who just hauled them out.

However, as he was relieved of pressure, he reverted to his former patterns. The change is pointedly reflected in the following dream:

X and I were sitting together in a class, where a number of other students were present. The professor began to speak, and I could immediately see he was a fraud. He was struggling to keep his lecture going and was talking nonsense. Some big boys in the rear began making noise, and finally turned on a portable radio.

I thought the professor was stupid, but still felt the boys' behavior was inexcusable. I got up, went to the rear, and took it upon myself to assume an authoritative position (I was a boy myself) and to ask who turned on the radio. They wouldn't answer, but I could see who did it. I put a headlock on the boy and dragged him to the floor. He did not resist, I took the radio and put it on a table at the front of the room. The boy I had thrown down walked sullenly out. Another larger boy got up to come to the front. I anticipated trouble and knew he could whip me. In an attempt to avoid this fight, I walked slowly, trying to appear casual, to my seat. To my relief, the boy just walked out of the room. The professor went stumbling on with his lecture.

Incident

He persisted in his aggressive and offensive negativism for several months. Finally at the end of one session I made clear to him the impossible position in which he placed both himself and me, and ended my exposition with a firm recommendation that if he so chose, he could *"go plumb to hell."* This was intended to first indicate the natural consequences of his attitude and behavior, and secondly, my sentiments about him.

On the following night he dreamt four dreams as follows:

1. I was visiting Professor Y in the psychology laboratories. In connection with some experiment, a student was printing some bills which closely resembled money. I showed them to Professor Y saying, "wouldn't it be nice if he could use these instead of what they represent. That would be a very productive experiment!" I was thinking how I would like to be able to "make" money so easily.

Professor Y said he had to pay a call to some friends of his in order to give them his donation to the community chest and asked me if I wouldn't care to come along with him. I was delighted, feeling flattered that he had asked me. We drove over in my car to the home of some friends of ours. Professor Y went in, while I waited outside. Some of the children of the house asked if they could use my car for a minute, and although I did not like it, I felt I couldn't refuse. They took it, and I waited near the house. When Professor Y came and we were ready to leave, the children returned with the car, only to my great dismay and anger, they had practically ruined it. There were many tears in the top and a smashed fender.

I told the lady of the house I was awfully sorry, but I would have to collect from her for this damage. She seemed to regard this as fair, but I could tell that it would be difficult to actually collect enough to cover the damage. I began figuring, and saw that I would have to have a new top, since my present one was ruined. This was somewhat embarrassing, since I would be getting a better top than I had and would be charging them for it. I was also embarrassed because the amount I was totaling up was almost equal to what Prof. Y had given them for Community Chest. The dream faded in a feeling of embarrassment.

2. Walking along Z Avenue, near the two main movie theatres, I realized that I was dying and *going to hell*. I found the aspect of anything at all after death to be quite pleasant and was not at all afraid of going to hell. I was especially happy that I apparently was retaining my bodily shape and a certain amount of free will after death.

As I began to descend down into the lower regions, which looked like many floors of underground building, I came among many other dead people. All of these, however, appeared to be very depressed and very passive. They filed along in moaning masses, all very sad and hopeless. As I joined their lines, since we were apparently filing into the large cafeteria for a meal, I couldn't help pitying them, and at the same time feeling a certain contempt for their passive acceptance of this miserable state. I asked them why they didn't try to get out of this, and all said that "He," the great power, was omnipotent, and it was useless to oppose. I gathered that they were referring to the Devil. I argued that as long as we were able to move about, and think, there was still hope. They were unconvinced and regarded me as foolish. One of the young women in particular attracted my attention. She was very pretty and I found out she had died leaving two children. I tried to cheer her up and even flirted with her, but she was so depressed she couldn't respond.

After the meal was over, we all began to file back up. I thought this was my chance, and when we got near the surface I boldly walked up out onto the sidewalk. I was with the living people again, and felt proud of my accomplishment. Some of the dead from below could see me, and they shook their heads and made dire predictions about the fate which was in store for me. Suddenly, there was a great rumble of thunder and a terrifically bright beacon shown above us all. This seemed to be the pointing power of the Devil. The light groped around some, and then came to bear directly upon me. I knew this was to be a "showdown," and still determined to fight to the last. I looked up and yelled at the light to do his damndest. All the people about, both alive and dead, wailed in fear and pity for me. I felt impervious, and shook my fists at the light when suddenly I felt myself being lifted up into the air. I had no control and screamed in despair. I awakened, hearing a low moan from myself.

3. X (the young woman with whom he was in love) and I had bought a new car, a beauty. It was a Lincoln convertible, but for some reason we had loaned it to some people and were still using my old Plymouth.

Later, we drove by where the people were and saw that they wished to leave the car with us. I went over to look the car over. To my surprise and dismay, there was a large dent in one front fender. Next, I stepped inside and started it up. The motor idled too fast and sounded rough. I thought they must have treated it very badly, and in order to find out, I asked one of them if they had been able to get any speed out of her. He said, "Oh yes, we did 90 without any trouble." This confirmed my fears. I was raging mad and began to yell at them, asking what the hell was the idea of treating a new car this way? The dream faded with my frustration at finding the car in such bad shape and yet being unable to do much about it.

4. It was a usual weekend day here in our apartment. I was conscious of the material I was preparing for tomorrow's classes. Then I went to bed.

When I began to awaken, I had the feeling that something was out of order. I looked around and found myself in a strange place. It appeared to be sort of a large shed, and the bed I was sleeping in was more of a firm, hospital-type cot. As I began to move I was conscious of being weak and of some discomfort in my abdomen. I rested for awhile, awake, thinking how terrible it was that apparently I would not be able to take care of my classes.

Later, some people came in to see me. My parents were among them. I asked them how the devil did I come to be here and what about my classes today. My mother explained to me that it was now three weeks since I had gone to sleep that night, and that I had had an appendicitis operation. I looked down at my belly; sure enough, there was a new ugly scar in addition to my old one. The scar was not completely healed and gave me that half-tickling, half-burning sensation my other one used to as I moved. The people said I could get a job here if I wished while I got back in shape. There was a contractor doing some building nearby so I went over and signed on. I was quite well satisfied with this arrangement. Dream faded as I began to work.

After having "gone to hell" he was a cooperative and responsive patient. He settled the affairs of his previous marriage and married my patient who in the interim had completed her therapy. His second marriage is successful and effective and he himself has done much better socially and professionally.

Sending him to hell palpably had a beneficial "purging" effect upon him.

Discussion

How the psychiatrist should deal with the aggressively negative, obstreperous, and otherwise nasty patient, who, after a prolonged period of therapeutic permissiveness, support, and indulgence, moves not one whit toward insight and cooperation, is a problem little dealt with in psychiatric and psychoanalytic literature. Franz Alexander, in one of his works, somewhat timidly and apologetically reports an instance when he became fed up with just such a patient and proceeded to tell him off. To his surprise the patient improved from that point on. I recall also an occasion when one of the ultra-orthodox Viennese analytical brethren addressed a group of American confreres on the hazards of negative countertransference. He urged his listeners to be just as chary of rejection of the patient as of too ready identification with him. At the end of his presentation, one of the senior American analysts spoke up in the following vein—"Yes, I agree with the Herr Professor, there are some dangers in a negative countertransference and one must guard against it. But, would the Professor be kind enough to say just what he does do when he comes up against a first-class 'stinker'?" The Professor had nothing constructive to say on that score.

NATHAN ACKERMAN . . .

A useful comment on this particular incident might appropriately begin with the final question placed before us by the therapist: how should we feel and act in the psychotherapeutic role with a patient who is a "first-class stinker." The patient in question, a young man, is conspicuously destructive in his human relations. When a person points his destructiveness outward against other persons, he does so in order to relieve himself of unbearable internal tensions. In effect, he imposes on other persons the emotional cost, the penalty for his own failings. "Psychopathic" acting out of destructive motivation is a component of emotional reactivity which may appear in a range of psychopathological conditions: neurosis, character disorder, psychopathic personality, psychosis, and even in organically induced mental states. By itself, acting-out is not diagnostically differential. In the final analysis, it is the role of this destructive pattern in the total economy of personality which reveals its true dynamic significance and the likely prognosis. The science of psychopathology has not yet clearly demarcated the type of destructive acting out which is expressed in the neurotic character from similar behavior asosciated with a true psychopathic personality.

In this critical incident we are confronted by a neurotic character who has been viciously destructive in his human relations. It is this nastiness which leads to the colloquial label, a "first-class stinker." In their everyday work therapists encounter both nice people and nasty people. In every known category of psychopathology there are sick people who may be either nice or nasty. We naturally like the nice ones better. We have more hope for those human beings who, although sick, are nevertheless decent human beings. They preserve good values, despite their illness. The emotional problem of the psychotherapist is how to feel and what to do with a "nasty" neurotic, a kind of person whose values clash severely with our own, and who persists cruelly in making other people pay for his own inner conflicts and distortion. This is the nature of the challenge which confronts us in this particular critical incident.

Of dramatic significance is the paradox that effective progress begins only when the therapist tells this "first-class stinker" to "go plumb to hell." In this way the therapist informs the patient, in unvarnished language, that his viciousness is unacceptable. Is this an appropriate tactic and has it the effect of a potent therapeutic interpretation? This is a value judgment which calls for critical assessment.

The whole tradition of permissiveness and nonjudgmental tolerance in the profession of psychotherapy places inhibiting obstacles in the path of any therapist who is tempted to tell a nasty, destructive patient "where to get off." Nevertheless, in this case it is exactly at this point that therapy begins. The therapist expresses an emphatic and total rejection of the patient's antisocial behavior and the patient earnestly goes to work on himself. Before that he merely toyed with therapy. The challenge here is to try to understand how this happens.

Some aspects of the psychotherapeutic ethos with regard to permissiveness and nonjudgmental support of a patient are misunderstood. If a therapist undertakes to treat a patient he can respect the patient for his own basic worth as a human being, but he is not called upon to be fond of the sick, distorted, injurious aspects of the patient's personality. He is not in any way obligated to accept and love all parts of the patient. He can accept the patient as a person while totally rejecting the twisted, destructive parts of his interpersonal adaptation. What is involved here is some misconception of the appropriate value orientation for the role of therapist, and an unclear definition of those basic conditions which are essential to effective progress in any form of psychotherapy. For one human being professionally trained to help another one in distress, it is *sine qua non* that control of destructive interpersonal behavior be established. In the final analysis each time a patient injures another persons he is also injuring himself. This is somewhere along the path of murder and suicide.

A therapist cannot fulfill his role in a useful manner until he has stopped murder and suicide. Therefore, no patient can be permitted to override the rights of any other person, whether a family member, another patient, or the therapist. This is the responsibility that any human being must assume if he is to be a part of society. A basic condition of effective pursuit of psychotherapy is proof in the patient of his intention to take sides with the therapist against the sick, destructive part of himself. The shunting of the goal of human relations away from love to purposes of power and destruction is the essence of perversion.

A therapist places himself in an impotent position if he even appears to tolerate such perversion. This is pseudo-permissiveness, not true acceptance of the patient's worth as a human being. In essence, then, as therapist we accept what is human and fundamentally good in any suffering patient. We have no choice but to reject that part of his sick behavior which is perverted and inhuman. With regard to this question, the therapist must take a clear stand.

There are indications in this therapeutic tale of persistent doubt in the therapist as to whether or not he can work with this patient. Here is a young man described as arrogant, belligerent, destructive, promiscuous, and incestuous. At the outset, the therapist rejects this patient outrightly. Inferentially, he judges this patient to be hopeless, but seven months later the therapist decides to try. Why? Unfortunately, we are not informed as to how the therapist changed his mind. This is a significant circumstance which is in no way elucidated.

The sequence of therapeutic events can be understood in stages. In the first stage this destructive patient is still influenced by his experience of initial rejection. Unconvinced as to his acceptability, he makes an effort to be a good boy. He attempts for a period of time to propitiate the therapist as if one wrong move on his part would once again cause him to be ostracized. During this period we have the report of a dream which is presumed to epitomize the dominant emotional attitudes of the patient.

Since no associations are given with the dream, it is necessary to speculate on the meaning of the dream in its bare form. The dream begins with the patient walking along the beach where many people are fishing without much luck. In this dream it would appear that the patient feels alone, that he is in a hungry, needy state. One might say he is fishing for love, and there is some unsatisfied sex striving. This is implied in the description of the old man uncovering a hole in the sand, from which he pulls out all kinds of fish. The old man might be interpreted as representing the therapist; the fish may symbolize multiple penises and multiple sex experiences.

The second part of the dream enables the patient through his phantasy wish to get access to his girl friend. The patient shares with his girl friend the amazing discovery that where everyone else failed, the old man seems to have, so to speak, a boundless good fortune in his sexual potency. The connotation of this dream is that the patient hopes through the omnipotent powers of the therapist to become a potent male and win his girl friend.

In the second stage the patient's need to hurl a defiant, competitive challenge against the therapist is reflected both in his waking behavior and in the sample dream of that period. In the dream the patient launches an attack on the professor or therapist. He competes with the presumed omnipotence of the therapist. He tries to usurp the authority of the therapist. At the same time, there is conflict. There is anxiety about failure. There is guilt and a provocation for discipline. In essence, in this dream the patient neurotically asserts his competitive power drive; he seeks to be the father before he is the son, but fears retaliation.

Then we have the description of the critical incident. This follows a period dominated by the patient's provocative, negativistic behavior. The therapist's apparent tolerance is exhausted and he tells the patient to "go plumb to hell." This is the critical turning point; we then see the effect of this upon the patient's attitudes.

In the third dream it appears that the patient confesses that his way of loving, his manhood, and his power are counterfeit, whereas by contrast the manliness of the professor or therapist is genuine. In this dream the patient's car may be interpreted as the symbol of his masculinity. He is deprived of the car by several children. In essence, he is castrated by the child in himself. This in effect represents unconscious self-punishment. After emasculating himself in this self-punishing move, he demands to be paid off for his injury by the parent figure, the mother. But then the patient experiences a further level of conflict. If the mother accedes and compensates him for his damages, in the end this will penalize the father figure, the professor, and the therapist. The patient reacts with remorse. He does not wish to do this. In effect this is a disguised confession that he has developed a liking for the father person, and this inhibits him from inflicting a penalty.

In the fourth dream he attempts in a futile way to defy the therapist's or God's power to punish him. In a typically adolescent manner he pits his own omnipotent striving against the power of God and loses. This admission that he cannot fight God, that he really is not possessed of omnipotent powers, is in the direction of health.

This trend continues and in the fourth dream the patient seems for the first time to admit that he is a sick person and assumes a genuine responsibility for his involvement in psychotherapy.

In the discussion of the incident the therapist raises the issue of the appropriate attitudes of the therapist toward a nasty, destructive patient. His own story points home the lesson that inappropriate permissiveness toward this kind of perversion in human relations passively accentuates the illness, rather than opening the way to a basic change in the patient's character toward health. As earlier indicated, the prime question is one of finding a suitable ethics for the therapeutic role with destructive persons. To be permissive toward this form of perversion of human relations is not in the interest of either patient or therapist. Effective control of such behavior is a necessary condition to the initiation of therapy. Without this the likelihood of therapeutic progress is virtually nil. Even if a patient of this sort comes to his sessions, he misunderstands and misuses the experience; there is danger that he may exploit the therapeutic relationship as the pawn of his machiavellian machinations. To meet such a threat, the therapist must take a firm, clear position.

If such a therapeutic situation were better understood and the intrinsic value conflicts more clearly defined, it would likely be unnecessary for the therapist to tell any patient to go to hell. It might serve better the interests of both patient and therapist for the therapist to hold no guilt in asserting firmly and in no uncertain terms that such destructiveness is a totally unfair imposition on the lives of other people and will not be tolerated. This is a position of strength and a forthright assertion of a basic value in human relations about which a therapist need have no guilt, whatever. If the therapist shows strength and objectivity, it becomes unnecessary to tell a patient to "go plumb to hell."

ROBERT BLAKE . . .

The critical incident is telling the patient, "Go plumb to hell." After this incident the patient became cooperative and responsive. The therapist's instruction is said to have excited a "purging" effect. Rather than accepting his reactions in the therapy situation, the therapist in effect *rejected* the behavior of the patient, which constitutes a dramatic shift in the role of the therapist. The rejection results in the patient's feeling more compelled to do what apparently is expected of him: to act in a manner consonant with the therapist's conception of how patients should behave. The patient became more cooperative and produced more and possibly even "better" dreams, perhaps even in compliance with his perception that the therapist regarded *dream* material as the *sine qua non* of a cooperative patient. Perhaps the incident had the additional effect, as reported, of providing a dependency relationship under which the client could adjust. A person in a position of authority rejects his past conduct. With the increased pressure to be "good" he is able to *be* "good," with a happy outcome in terms of life adjustments.

If the analysis above is in the right direction, then I would interpret the outcome to be due as much to this engineering aspect as to any significant increase in "insight" or to problem-solving skill. It is as though superego structures have been strengthened by an act of punishment. The consequence is "good" conduct, rather than insight into the reasons for needing to be "bad." Satisfactory change from either direction may be enough of a criterion to justify engineering of this sort, but I feel that greater maturity of adjustment would come from understanding of the need to "be bad" rather than reinforcement of the obligation to "be good."

RUDOLF DREIKURS . . .

This is one of many examples of how a shocking experience, in a deteriorating therapeutic relationship, can have beneficial effects. This incident clearly indicates why. The therapist states that the patient "persisted in his aggressive and offensive negativism for several months." The inability of the therapist to change this situation cannot help but diminish whatever respect the patient may have had for him. One can well assume that the sessions were neither interesting nor impressive. Suddenly, the therapist showed some spunk by telling the patient to go to hell, and that apparently made an impression on him and had some good effect. After that, he became cooperative and responsive.

The examples provided as critical incidents are full of such psychological shock treatments. They are often reported by therapists whose technique is more or less permissive and noninterfering. Many therapists function adequately only under optimal conditions, preferably with the patient on the couch. When action, decision, or definite steps are necessary and indicated, the therapist is often at a loss, psychologically speaking. His psychological indoctrination and training do not provide him with guides for such situations. If he is resourceful, he usually devises a variety of shock treatments. Then he either loses the patient, or gains his attention and perhaps even confidence. At any rate, such an incident permits a reconsideration of the therapeutic relationship and a realignment. With better training in interpersonal relationships and interactions a therapist may not need to resort to such shock treatments.

ALBERT ELLIS . . .

I have had a few experiences with patients which closely parallel that outlined in this critical incident, and I am therefore entirely in favor of telling a patient, under some circumstances, to go plumb to hell or some reasonable equivalent.

In one instance, where I was seeing a schizophrenic girl who had had no less than 16 years of previous therapy with several competent therapists, and who, when I saw her, was still exceptionally disturbed, I took all the patient could give for several months. And she gave plenty! She would call me up literally in the middle of the night; would refuse to leave the therapeutic session when her time had expired; would yell at me in a loud tone of voice, so that any other waiting patients could hear; would phone me while other patients were being seen and would refuse to make the call brief, so that I finally would have to hang up on her; and would do all kinds of other negative, hostile acts. I absorbed all this hostility and obtained a fine degree of rapport with her; but still, from time to time, she would be hostile in an overt manner.

One day, when she was refusing to leave my office when her session had expired, I deliberately raised my voice and said: "Now, look here: I've taken enough of your nonsense as far as not getting out of here on time is concerned. I've spoken to you nicely about this several times before, but apparently it hasn't done any good. Now I'm telling you once and for all: if you don't get out of here *pronto* whenever I signal that the session has come to an end, you can take yourself straight to another therapist. And that goes for those telephone calls and other annoyances of yours, too. If I ever so much as receive one single unnecessary call from you again, especially when I tell you that I am busy and cannot speak to you at the time, that's the end of our relationship. And I mean it! I've taken enough of your nonsense, and it seems to me that I've been pretty nice to you in the meantime. But enough is enough! Either, hereafter, you are going to show some respect for me and my way of working, or you can go to the devil and get another therapist. And, if you want, I'll be glad to recommend you to one right now."

My patient, with a terribly shocked look, immediately became conciliatory and apologetically left. Thereafter, for a period of several months, I had no trouble with her. During this period, she also improved considerably, for the first time in her long history of psychotherapy. She then began to slip slowly back into her previous negative behavior toward me; and, after taking this for a few sessions, I again let her have it, right between the eyes as it were, and again told her that I would refuse to see her again if she did not immediately change her ways. She quickly became much more considerate; I had very little trouble with her thereafter, and she made even more remarkable improvements.

On two other occasions, with male patients, I told each of them, after I had seen them only a few sessions, "Now let's stop this nonsense. You're giving me an obvious pack of lies and evasions, and at that rate we'll get absolutely no place. If you want to go on kidding yourself, and refraining from trying to get better, that's your business. But my business is helping people get better, and I don't intend to waste any time with those who keep giving me a lot of trouble. Now either you quit or stew in your own damned neuroses for the rest of your life. Which shall it be?" In both these instances, my patients made remarkable changes in their attitudes toward me, toward therapy, and toward themselves.

I feel, therefore, that the therapist in this critical incident was wise and courageous, and that a good deal more well-timed and well-aimed harsh language on the part of therapists is often called for in effective psychotherapy. I find the use of well-chosen expletives, especially with certain patients, usually useful in this connection. To paraphrase an old Chinese saying, one good picturesquely chosen word may be worth a thousand mild-mannered ones in getting over to the patient the idea the therapist really means business.

J. W. KLAPMAN . . .

There is really little to add to what the doctor has already remarked about this critical incident. It does appear that there are some primitive, narcissistic egos who delight in perverse behavior toward others which gives them a feeling of omnipotence, and feeds the narcissism.

If, after a more or less lengthy period of enduring the patient's pranks and seeming to be taken in by the patient, the therapist calls the turn, it is like suddenly pulling the rug out from under the patient. To this kind of individual there is no clearer, more definitive way of exploding his self-concept and demonstrating that all the time the therapist had taken the patient's true measure.

Is it that on a deeper level the therapist is seen as a magician whose potency rivals or exceeds that of the patient, and he, the therapist, had better be made a friend rather than a foe?

There was enough of a healthy part in this patient's personality to arrive at some such conclusion, and therapy could proceed to a happy ending. In other individuals this challenge sets off no insight, and the patient proceeds on his downgrade path.

CLARA THOMPSON . . .

I seriously feel that the therapist should not have taken this patient for treatment, if the patient was all the things described in the first paragraph, especially since he was treating the young woman in whom the man was interested. It would be helpful to know why it was suitable seven months later. If the case is that the young woman had ceased to be interested in the man by then, I suppose a courageous therapist might attempt the work, but, since she eventually married him, that does not seem to have been the case. Even if that were the situation, I would expect that such a patient might hope to manipulate the therapist into influencing the woman. If the woman was still in treatment at the time, I would expect even more effort on the part of the patient to influence her therapy. In either case, I believe the therapist would start with a handicap. It is difficult under any circumstances for a therapist to analyze two people closely involved with each other, although some workers report success in so doing, and even recommend it as having advantages. My own experience has been that it is difficult to maintain the necessary loyalty to both people, and this difficulty is greatly increased if no eventual rapprochement between the two is likely. I would think, unless a miracle happened, that this patient was not likely to be a suitable husband until after many years of therapy, if ever. Therefore, I am interested in why the therapist took on this difficult case.

In the first dream presented, I think there is some confirmation of my point of view. The old man, presumably the therapist, had a trick way of getting fish. In other words, if you hang around him, you'll get what you want.

Next, I should like to know what is meant by his being "relieved of pressure." Is this the point at which he got the girl, for instance, and, therefore, need not be on his good behavior anymore?

The question presented for discussion, however, is not whether this was a suitable therapeutic situation in the first place, but whether one should express one's feelings of annoyance and anger to a patient, and why, having done it, there was a beneficial effect on therapy. The beneficial effect on therapy, I believe, was due to clearing up the insincerity in the therapeutic situation. I believe the therapist did not like the patient in the first place. The patient, as described, was not a likeable person. Possibly the therapist believed that, in his role, he had no right to personal feelings about the case, and managed to suppress them for a time. The patient, on his part, had a stake in getting along with the therapist, as I have already discussed. So the two entered into a fake relationship of pseudo cooperation, but the patient couldn't keep it up, and presently reverted to his accustomed defenses. The therapist may have felt hurt that his own efforts at good will were ineffective, and eventually his true feeling for the patient came out. I believe that until this happened, no real therapy was taking place. Only a sincere relationship between therapist and patient can produce lasting results. The therapist's personality is the instrument through which the patient eventually experiences insight. Any falseness on the part of the therapist acts just as much as a defense against the relationship as falseness in the patient does. It would, therefore, have been better if there had been an honest understanding between the two to begin with. The therapist was under no misapprehension about the character of the man. He must have had some understanding from treating the young woman. Moreover, a psychiatrist, in whom he had confidence, had refused to take the patient. It would have been better, I think, to have started the treatment by pointing to the obnoxious qualities of the young man, frankly stating that these would be a great hazard in treatment, and that the therapist was not going to be very patient with them when they appeared. It is, of course, possible that the patient might have refused treatment under these conditions, but, if so, I would think he had not been very strongly motivated for treatment to begin with, but was entering therapy for some other purpose: for example, in the hope of manipulating the therapist into influencing the young woman, or hoping to win her by going through the motions of therapy. If these had been his only motivations, time, money, and energy would have been saved by nipping this ambition at the start.

However, apparently this young man had more sincere motives for therapy, although he may, perhaps, have had the other hopes also. So I think he would have begun therapy in spite of the therapist's doubts, but the situation would have been more sincere from the beginning, and it would have been possible to point out his behavior patterns as they appeared, as something already anticipated and unproductive. The therapist might never have had to "send him to hell" because he would have been less frustrated. On the other hand, the obstructionism may have been so great that not even these initial safeguards would have prevented the feeling of complete frustration which found expression in telling the patient to "go to hell."

In short, I believe the therapist's act was a good therapeutic move under the circumstances; it was good because, for the first time, he was completely sincere with the patient, but it would have been even better if the therapist had been outspoken from the beginning about the problems of therapy.

We are not told how long therapy continued after the crisis. I would expect this to have been the turning point where real therapy began, and that a far from placid course continued for a long time after that event. In the more sincere later dreams, the patient's tendency to project blame shows very clearly. In my experience, the analyst who is tolerant and accepting under all circumstances does not really help the patient because he has assumed a God-like pose which he cannot maintain with complete sincerity.

"Get Well—or Else"

17

History

The patient, a 27-year-old woman, single, nurse in a department of child neurology, had three months of individual therapy, then combined individual with group therapy. She was a person of considerably higher intelligence than her functioning at the beginning of therapy warranted. Her energy was dissipated by anxiety. Her main conflicts stemmed from dependency—loyalty to traditions and religion—on the one hand, and independence, emancipation, and doubt on the other. She had separated from her family, yet she had not succeeded in resolving her dependency. She was consumed by guilt feelings and driven by masochistic needs to provide danger and its punitive consequences.

She came for treatment after the traumatic experience of an impregnation by a married man, an illegal abortion, followed by a rather promiscuous sex life, moderate addiction to barbiturates, and occasional bouts of alcoholic intoxication. All this, of course, endangered her position as a nurse, although her working adjustment was an excellent one. She loved her work and the children in the ward, and could forget and/or hide all her problems during her working hours. Yet, at any moment, even this last basis of her shaky ego integration could be destroyed by her masochistic acting out.

246

Incident A

After a few months of combined treatment a new, male patient was introduced to the group. After a short period of flirtation between this young man and the nurse, she seduced him, which was followed by the usual self-accusation—"I am a bad girl"—and demands on the therapist to scold and punish her, mixed with the anxious expectation to be discharged from treatment as "hopeless."

I felt that this situation could be handled in different ways. I could remain objective, emotionally uninvolved, and could interpret to the patient her masochistic acting out and hysterical demands. Whenever that had been done before, it had only led to further, more punishment provoking actions.

The obvious "oedipal" elements of the last incident could have been pointed out, as the patient verbalized both her triumphant and her panicky feelings about having "taken your patient" from the (woman) therapist. I answered with the joke: "*I* did not want to sleep with him," in this way pointing out the reality of the situation without "deeper" interpretation.

The episode was then discussed with great concern on my part, pointing out her need to dominate and subjugate the man through seduction, culminating in the sex act; her competitiveness with other women by "taking the man away from them"; her disregard of consequences for herself and others, (the male patient had acted according to his neurotic needs, by insulting and humiliating her after intercourse). She understood that she continued her neurotic vicious circle of acting not only in a way which she herself considered wrong and for which she wanted to be punished, but also in a way which was asocial toward a co-patient, since it aggravated his neurotic problems.

Discussion

My emotional involvement gave her the feeling (and rightly so) that I really cared that she, a human being with so much sense of responsibility and love for children, such a worthwhile person with social feeling, could be driven to acts so destructive to herself and others.

All this was discussed in the group, too. The patient "confessed everything" to the group (the confession served her masochistic needs), but as she was liked and respected for her many good qualities, the group members responded spontaneously in a way similar to mine. One man, who made a contemptuous remark, was attacked by the others. All this gave the patient a new sense of belonging, with group values less conflicting and confusing than those taught her by her parents and given up by her with guilt feelings.

Incident B

The second incident seems to have dynamics similar to the first, but it has even more intensive emotional involvement for all people concerned.

In the second year of treatment the patient was again involved in a sado-masochistic relationship, this time with a doctor in her hospital. One evening, when she felt rejected, humiliated by him, she drank enough liquor to behave with another man (who exploited her drunken state) in a way that seriously endangered her reputation in the hospital. She was panic-stricken by the possible consequences of her actions when she related the details of this episode during her session with me. At this point I became quite angry and told her she was in the process of becoming an "alcoholic nymphomaniac." I said I would have to hospitalize her if she was unable to control herself. She had to abstain completely from alcohol and sexual intercourse for three months, otherwise she most certainly would lose her job and "end in the gutter." She cried and asked me not to hospitalize her, and promised to obey these "rules of abstinence."

During all this I felt that this attitude of mine was the one she desperately wanted. I expressed my unhappiness about being put into the position of the threatening authority, but this seemed to be the only way to protect her from further damage and to help her accept the reality experience of "actions have consequences."

In the next group sessions the patient felt better and reported rather realistically what had happened in the hospital and in her individual session. The group members turned against me. How could I have taken such a moralizing, punishing attitude? I explained again my own anxiety about what could happen to a patient who cannot learn to act within socially acceptable limits, and I added that I had had some sleepless hours the previous night, because all this was happening in the second year of therapy. I told the group that I had explored the whole course of treatment in my mind, asking myself whether I "had failed the patient in some way or whether the group had failed her" in her need for friendliness and friendship without domination and exploitation.

Discussion

This incident seemed to help the patient a great deal. From then on she was able to change radically. She developed a certain dignity in all her relationships, like a person with inner worth, and could control her impulsive acting out. She was less competitive towards women and less seductive and demanding towards men. She became warm, friendly, and pleasantly flirtatious, a thoroughly reliable person as she had been previously only in the job situation.

Jerome D. Frank . . .

Patients like this one, whose self-respect is very severely damaged and who have difficulty controlling their own impulses, need to feel, above all, that the therapist has real concern for them based on respect for their potentialities, if not for assets already evident. This concern is best conveyed by a strong attack on the deviant behavior as unworthy of the patient. This type of attack, paradoxically, heightens the patient's self-esteem rather than damages it, because it is obviously based on real concern and respect. The contrary attitude of "permissiveness" or of interpretations of the behavior which are "not emotionally involved" often convey to the patient that the therapist is indifferent or really does not expect much of him, thereby further damaging his self-esteem.

I agree with the therapist that her behavior in the two incidents was felt by the patient to be similar, even though ostensibly different. The first, although couched in terms of interpretation, is loaded with words containing value judgments and thereby was undoubtedly perceived as strong disapproval of the behavior. In the second this disapproval was expressed directly with even more benefit.

The role of the group in the episode is somewhat unclear. I suspect that they mirrored the therapist's attitudes; that is, they attacked the patient's *behavior* as being unworthy of what she could be but did not criticize her as a person. This is suggested by the note that they attacked one man who made a "contemptuous remark." I wonder whether or not the man involved in the seduction played any part in the group episode.

I doubt the wisdom of the therapist's telling the group and the patient of her own unhappiness at having to be in the position of threatening authority, and her self-doubts. In a well-established group like this, the therapist's expression of anxiety probably does no harm and may be helpful in conveying that the therapist feels herself to be a member of the group and not above it or aloof from it; in early groups, however, or in any early therapeutic contacts, this may be risky. Patients come to therapy to straighten out their own problems and do not wish to be burdened, as they see it, with those of the therapist. Also, breast-beating by the therapist is apt to undermine the patient's initial faith in him which is so important for the establishment of a therapeutic relationship. The therapist can reveal his own problems in order to show his common humanity with the patients, but not in such a way that he undermines the patients' confidence in his ability to handle emotional problems. Sometimes, too, hearing how a therapist has solved a problem only discourages certain patients and makes them feel even more inadequate than before.

FAY KARPF . . .

The first critical incident reported in this case, in which the patient boasts about having taken one of the therapist's other patients in group therapy away from her through seduction, and to which the therapist replies with a questionable joke intended to be a reality interpretation, immediately defines a strange therapeutic situation. For the patient was evidently challenging the authority of the therapist in the *therapeutic* situation rather than on the *sexual* basis to which the therapist directed attention and which placed her in competition with her patient.

The more serious discussion of the episode, it seems to this commentator, did not really get down to fundamentals as defined by the therapist herself, perhaps because the therapist's theoretical orientation led away from these considerations. But what about the dependency-independency conflicts mentioned in the *History*? Why did the patient rebel so destructively and so defiantly against her background, against her established loyalties, and against what she still so strongly believed in that "she was consumed by guilt feelings and driven by masochistic needs to provide danger and its punitive consequences"?

One gets the feeling that we really do not know enough about this patient to discuss these matters in their important and meaningful setting. Can it really be that after the episode noted above and the equally destructive past history, she could so readily develop "a new sense of belonging, with group values less conflicting and confusing than those taught her by her parents and given up by her with guilt feelings"? Can such basic conflicts of value and conduct be successfully resolved without going into the

complex socio-cultural aspects of the patient's background and her destructive rebellion against this background, thus enabling the patient to see her
problem in the broader setting in which she must eventually solve it? This
in any event is the trend of the recent socio-cultural approach, and it is the
view of this commentator that it has much to offer in psychotherapy in dealing with such problems.

The second critical incident confirms this commentator's view that what
this patient needed was a more integrative approach directed toward
building up a new positive outlook on life to replace or repair the guiding
values which she had so defiantly discarded, but which still had a sufficient
hold on her to make her feel guilty and worthless. We have here a patient
who is severely conflicted because she evidently cannot control her impulsive nature apart from her youthful loyalties, about which she has become
skeptical but which still determine her estimate of her behavior. Therapy
must obviously direct itself to this central problem, and this requires a more
constructive approach than many therapists are at present prepared to
adopt.

The therapist states that she became "quite angry" with her patient as a
result of the second incident and threatened her with hospitalization. It is
difficult to imagine that the patient actually observed because of this threat
the "rules of abstinence" ordained by the therapist at this point but, as the
therapist says, "this seemed to be the only way to protect her from further
damage and to help her accept the reality experience of 'actions have consequences.'" In any event, it is clear that the patient still had made little
progress toward the positive inner direction and control which she so
much needed.

The therapist herself admits her great anxiety because the later incident
occurred in the second year of therapy, so that she felt the need of review-
ing the whole course of treatment and to question whether she "had
failed the patient in some way or whether the group had failed her in her
need for friendliness and friendship without domination and exploitation."
The implication here is that support and permissiveness were all the patient needed. But it is the view of this commentator that she needed
something in addition, namely, the mobilization of her inner resources
toward the re-establishment of guiding values and controls, so as to break
into the vicious circle of her impulsive acting out and her resulting need
for punishment.

Though very apologetic about being forced into the role of "the
threatening authority," the therapist nevertheless felt that this was what
the patient "desperately wanted." The incident, the therapist states,
"seemed to help the patient a great deal. From then on she was able to
change radically."

Could it have been that the "moralizing, punishing attitude" of the therapist and her angry explosion were just what the patient needed to set her along the path of reconstructing her behavior by reactivating her old controls and mobilizing her still needed, if restrictive, background? For here was her therapist, representing the very core of her new life, giving expression to the same reactions, caught up in the same moral indignation, which the patient had previously associated only with her old discarded life. Here was the experience she needed to establish the linkage between her past and present; the old and the new were at last merging and opening the possibility of reunifying her world for her. In this reunified world she might perhaps function again as an integrated person, instead of being torn apart by uncontrolled urges and fixed loyalties. Her two years of therapy, her supporting relationships with her therapist and her therapy group, and her emerging insight into still needed anchors and standards, could all come to her aid to help her find her bearings again if only an acceptable reorientation were available to her in line with these developments.

This was the challenging therapeutic task at the moment. And strangely enough, this is what the therapeutic situation as it developed unexpectedly provided, through the therapist's concerned defense of herself in group therapy and the serious discussion by the group of the patient's disturbing behavior. This is one of the great advantages of group therapy: it provides a laboratory for the exchange of attitudes and opinions, a "community" proving-ground for the individual views of the therapist, so that the patient can see himself in relation to the complex of community reaction and thus more realistically find his own way, in terms of readiness and level of insight, toward necessary community living. In this case, the outcome was evidently the more organized and controlled behavior of the patient which the therapist reports.

FREDERICK C. THORNE . . .

It is not unusual to have patients act out while under therapy the essential instabilities and immaturities which characterize their disorder as did this 27-year-old nurse who twice became involved in sex irregularities. We agree with the therapist that such situations can be handled in many ways. Except when such acting out behaviors have a social consequences requiring some directive control, we are inclined to regard them as simply symptomatic and not to place any particular emphasis on them. Certainly we would not take any punitive or disciplinary action beyond pointing out the practical limits of behavior which can be tolerated in the therapeutic situation.

We know of a similar situation in which a patient took advantage of a therapist's friendship to seduce another patient in the therapist's office where he had been allowed to wait. Such behavior had, in fact, occurred repeatedly in the past and on one occasion had led to institutionalization as incorrigible. This patient was rather proud of himself for having used his wits and gotten an unexpected dividend. He stated, probably truthfully, that the strength of the sex urge inhibited all other considerations—nothing else mattered at the time and possible consequences were completely disregarded. We handled this as just another symptomatic episode capable of recurring until such time as the client became mature enough to develop a strong self-concept and to act out in a self-conscious manner.

Diagnostically, it may be important to discriminate the actual causes of such behavior in order to determine the correct therapeutic approach. In making a blind diagnosis of this case simply from the facts given, we might arrive at an entirely different formulation of its underlying dynamics. The fact that she is still single at 27 and has had an illegitimate pregnancy followed by abortion followed by further sex irregularities and additions, suggests that we are dealing with a frustrated person, probably rather unattractive, who has become rather desperate about the chances of marriage. Driven by conflict and unexpressed needs, she shows increased impulsivity and pleasure-seeking which establish a vicious circle of self-defeating behaviors, further frustration, and final demoralization. Whether such behavior is primarily masochistic in the psychoanalytic sense of self-punishment, or whether the masochism is secondarily aroused by guilt feelings over having failed again, requires further study. For example, suppose this patient's seduction of the young male member of the group had successfully led to an happy marriage? Many seductions do eventuate happily, and in that event there is usually little guilt or masochistic acting-out. There is a hen-egg diagnostic problem involved which we are not given enough evidence here to answer. We would at least consider that we are dealing with a demoralization state in which the patient is bogging deeper and deeper in her attempts to solve a very practical life problem.

In our own practice, we usually attempt to handle demoralization problems by a gradual reconditioning program centered about securing a stronger and more healthy self-concept around which the patient is taught to behave more self-consistently. For example, we try to find out what the person really wants to be and what his deepest needs are, and then use these as foundations for demonstrating the inconsistencies of self-defeating behaviors. Most people wish to be strong, healthy, and mature, and these can be used as the basic values for a new self-concept. Much patience may be required to help the client to gradually learn to control less mature impulses.

Although we would prefer not to have to do so, it may be necessary to threaten the client (as did this therapist) concerning the dire consequences of a course of action. We would justify this as heightening the contrast between what the patient professes to want to be and what he actually is, and thereby possibly creating a therapeutic conflict which the patient can only resolve by being self-consistent with his professed ideals. In this case if the patient can be carried over the immediate period of greatest conflict and impulsiveness, can be led to accept the fact that sex is never constructive unless acted out in the right way, and can practice the new program until it begins to pay some dividends—then there will be some hope for eventual complete rehabilitation solely by conditioning methods and without recourse to less parsimonious psychoanalytic approaches which should be reserved for genuine intractable character neuroses of demonstrably unconscious origin.

Carl Whitaker . . .

The change from professional to personal in the quality of the therapeutic relationship clearly makes the difference between a therapeutic impasse and a growthful experience. The oedipal testing of the parent, that is, the therapist, is not merely trying to seduce the parent, but also an effort to prove that the therapist's affect is both personal and mature. The therapist passed the test and proved that she was willing to be personal in the face of the group's opposition and that she had enough belief in the patient's "wellness" to demand both maturity and social conformity from her. Then the patient could re-evaluate all the past of their therapeutic relationship and in this new perspective readjust her own integration and proceed in her own growth.

Werner Wolff . . .

This incident leads to a discussion of whether or not the therapist is entitled to impose conditions concerning the environment and habits of a patient. In my inquiries with psychotherapists,[1] 14 per cent of them stated that principally they would not make any conditions nor give suggestions to the patient; 40 per cent said they would give advice; and 46 per cent would impose conditions if necessary.

It has been observed that conditions have to be imposed upon certain types of patients, namely, alcoholics, delinquents, drug addicts, psychotics, psychopaths, suicidals; and that the imposition of conditions is necessary in all those cases where a patient endangers himself or his environment. Also in the treatment of adolescents and children some therapists make

[1] *Contemporary Psychotherapists Examine Themselves* (Springfield: Thomas, 1956).

conditions. In treatment with conditioned reflex therapy and with hypnosis, conditions are made more frequently than with other forms of psychotherapy.

In a "dependency neurosis" the self may have been threatened to such a degree that the individual in his reaction formation tries to forget himself through alcohol and promiscuity. Under such circumstances it seems indispensable that the patient experience a confrontation with himself. But since these patients tend to escape from themselves, a shock that arrests them and forces them to face their life is necessary.

In a critical incident the therapist will take the opportunity to dramatize the patient's life. The present case exemplifies that a therapist may have to act out a paternal superego role in order to force the patient into a self-confrontation. The patient was shocked into recognition of a desperate situation and faced a boundary situation. Experiencing arrival at the end of the road, the turn was made and values were accepted.

However, although it appears that the therapist's threat produced a positive turn in the therapy, it may be argued whether or not this kind of threat was admissible. In my opinion the therapist may be allowed to make conditions and even to use threats; however, he should not be permitted to abuse his role, assuming power over the patient's existence. In other words, he might have threatened the patient to discontinue therapy or to discharge her from her duties in the hospital, but not to hospitalize her, equivalent to putting her into a straightjacket. Threats on life and freedom, depriving an individual of his existential sovereignty, should not be permitted in education and therapy. They transcend the rights of therapists, teachers, and parents to include the danger of crushing the individuality up to a point where masochist dependency, insanity, or suicide may be the outcome. At this point, occasionally successful measures of psychotherapy collide with principles of values and ethics to which a therapist should be ultimately bound.

It's Difficult
to Treat a Friend

18

History

The patient is a 29-year-old married male with two children and a member of a highly esteemed profession who is also very intelligent and well liked. We had known each other professionally and socially in a relationship which seemed warm but was a little more than just casual. As if by accident when we were alone one day he brought up the question of therapy in general, then expressed his interest in it and that he could consider it only with me as a therapist. I told him I would be willing to undertake a series of exploratory consultations with weekly visits and, because of his economic limitations, a nominal fee. These visits became highly involved with evidence of a passive hostility and resistance characterized by inability to talk or give a history, forgetting and coming late to appointments, forgetting the bills, insistent demands for help and denial and argumentation of any of the history he had given. Unfortunately and unavoidably the relationship seemed, in spite of my intentions and interpretations, to be shaping up into one in which he appeared to be reluctant as far as therapy was concerned and I seemed to be pressuring him to keep in treatment, and any attempt on my part to clarify the issue only reinforced this highly unsatisfactory stalemate.

Other than his behavior, the only information I had about him was that he was nervous, had some problems about sex, was vaguely interested in women other than his wife, and was the product of a disturbed, hostile, dominating, and castrating mother and a withdrawn, submissive, and passively hostile father. Inadvertently, from other sources, I learned that the patient was submissive, had a whispered reputation for being morbidly and vicariously interesting in sex, had engaged in some sort of extramarital relationships, and was noticed to be physically seductive with girls in the early teens; in short he was known to be getting himself in an increasing amount of hot water which could only be disastrous to his career as well as personally.

Incident

Without any clear formulation as to the technic of doing so, I was resolved to push the matter of therapy to some conclusion after about three months of irregular work. During this interview I started off by expressing this thought, and the patient was quite firm in his insistence that therapy be concluded, and that appeared agreeable to both of us.

Just as he was ready to leave, but before the hour was up, I spontaneously reopened the conversation by something like the following: "I don't know whether I should do this, and I would prefer that you not investigate the sources, but I have some information about you which perhaps, because of our relationship, I should tell you about."

Then I proceeded to tell him the things I had heard about him, things which he had not discussed with me, somehow emphasizing— almost cruelly at the time, it seemed to me—that many people knew about his difficulties and symptoms and that it could almost be predicted that some real difficulty would stem from this. Following this confrontation I remained silent, offering nothing to soften the blow and purposely not offering therapy as a solution.

The patient blanched, became visibly disturbed and tremulous, and visibly shaken and deflated. After a while he started speaking about how he felt cornered, should commit suicide, and was in a panic. After continuing in this vein, he then asked what he should do and how could he handle this. I asked if he was sincerely interested in this to the extent of some sacrifice and work on his part, to which he eagerly and genuinely responded that he was at the end of his rope and would do anything. When he committed himself to this, I calmly and realistically brought up the question of therapy and its demands in terms of time, giving information, and finances. Details were left up in the air, but I told him that when he felt able to work them out I would stand by and assure him time for further work of a serious nature.

The patient left town for a few weeks because of a prearranged trip, approached his relatives for financial assistance, and made the necessary arrangements for time off from his work. Shortly after his return from his trip we resumed therapy on a much different basis than previously. It has been over a year since this incident occurred, and while therapy has not been easy or uncomplicated, it has been approached, on a conscious level at least, on a sincere and consistent basis. There is no more evidence of the sexual difficulties he was having previously, and his ability to assert himself, which was nil before, has developed markedly.

Discussion

There is no question that the interview described above constituted a critical turning point of therapy, in a way creating a situation with which therapy should have started off in the first place, by the formulation of a problem, the patient's appeal for help, and a commitment to the realistic demands of treatment. It is not known, but is at least highly doubtful, that the patient would have come to the same conclusion himself, had therapy stopped without the disclosure made to him. In retrospect it would seem that this approach had some validity in this regard. Further study of the patient disclosed a personality which is best described as a sheer exaggeration of Riesman's "other directed" character, someone whose whole orientation in relationships was consciously to direct himself to be completely devoid of any feelings or needs in himself and to live only with an eye toward satisfying or gaining approval from others; in addition, he, by a psychological sleight-of-hand, managed to deny that his peccadillos were observable to anyone else—this being verified by difficulties in other areas. In other words, the confrontation of his difficulties in the interview struck him in his most vulnerable area, his appearance to others, and also made ineffectual the protectiveness of his denial of the effect of his activities on others.

This case also illustrates complications inevitable when one attempts to treat acquaintances, when one attempts to encourage someone entering treatment even though inadvertent, and when business relationships are somewhat less than business-like under these circumstances.

Nathan Ackerman . . .

This particular incident in psychotherapy raises a whole series of problems:

1. The importance of a clear and appropriate emotional preparation of the attitudes of both patient and therapist for the commitment to a responsible treatment relationship.
2. The problem of devising strategy and tactics with a patient who is discovered to be consciously evasive (dishonest).
3. The specific nature of the complication which intrudes upon a treatment relationship where the psychotherapist withholds from his patient a body of personal information concerning the patient which has come to the therapist through extraneous sources.
4. The complication of a therapist's special emotional need to prove his professional competence with a friend in the role of patient.
5. The complication of the issue of dealing with fees in a therapeutic experience with a friend.

In order to clarify these problems, I must first recount the relevant sequence of events in the early phase of the relationship. The question of treatment began with exploratory consultative interviews. So far as the story goes, the patient in the beginning committed himself only to exploratory contact, not to a systematic program of psychotherapy. It is not clear in the text as to when the therapist shifted his orientation from the initial goal of discussing the problem to a goal of intensive and prolonged therapy. Nevertheless the therapist, by his own admission, pushed the patient toward submission to treatment. I do not understand why!

The therapist was aware that the patient was evasive, that he did not reveal relevant background information, and that he was inappropriately motivated to accept his responsibility in therapy.

This being the case, a difficulty arises in the therapist's delay in having a showdown with the patient. The relationship is conducted for some time without the required measure of honesty on the parts of both patient and therapist. An element of polite, conventional insincerity prevailed for a time in the behavior of both persons.

The therapist became increasingly impatient with the patient's resistance and withholding. It seems likely that the therapist had a special investment of personal pride insofar as he wished to avoid a failure in the professional treatment of a friend. The friend offended the therapist's self-esteem by failing to come through with a full emotional commitment. The therapist confessed that he exposed the patient in a somewhat cruel way, finally. This suggests that the therapist's own retaliatory anger crept into the experience; in effect, he punished the patient for his stubbornness. The therapist does not like being defeated or shown up by a patient who has been a personal friend.

When the therapist finally put his cards on the table, disclosing to the patient the personal information he had earlier obtained from other sources, the patient was shocked, injured, and reacted with panic. One may assume from this that one reason which induced the patient finally to enter treatment was sheer fright. The therapist intimidated the patient into submission to his therapeutic powers.

The stumbling block to the establishment of necessary conditions for effective therapeutic progress is not the sheer fact of a previous social bond between patient and therapist. This creates special problems, but they are in no sense insoluble. It is rather that the element of insincerity which is so often a part of casual social friendships has no place in psychotherapy. An indispensable requirement of psychotherapy is honesty and sincerity concerning the emotional commitment of both patient and therapist. In a psychotherapeutic process one cannot ever blame a patient for what is below the level of his consciousness, but one can hold him responsible for withholding any conscious conflicts. It is difficult enough to get access to the deeper layers of emotional distortion, but those experiences which are within the patient's consciousness must be reported honestly.

However, we have here a peculiar wrinkle in that the therapist also experienced some conscious conflict. Just as the patient withheld information, so also did the therapist. The special feature of the availability to the therapist of information from extraneous sources is an understandable reason for the therapist's indecision in sharing this with his patient. But it is not the more excusable, therefore. This leads to the conclusion that the responsibility for the difficult beginning of this therapy is shared jointly by both patient and therapist. One might even wonder if the therapist possibly overidentified with some of the patient's sexual troubles. If so, this might also have been a factor in inhibiting the therapist's urge to frankly talk over with his patient what had been learned from some other persons.

This particular case illustrates a trend which emerges in a number of the reported psychotherapeutic incidents: the psychotherapeutic experience gets off on the wrong foot. It is common knowledge in the profession of psychotherapy that a poor start is an almost certain warrant of failure. Why is it that so many therapists initiate a relationship with a new patient in a fumbling, inappropriate way? Adequate preparation of a new patient for responsible involvement in psychotherapy is crucial to a favorable outcome. Such preparation requires, first, a correct assessment of the patient's psychopathological condition within the context of his life situation, and reaching a mutual understanding with the patient as to their shared view of the illness and the resulting disturbed modes of living; and, second, agreement as to the appropriate goals and procedure of therapy. This is important in providing for the experience a firm foundation of sincerity and mutual responsibility to the task, which strengthens the genuiness of the patient's motivation to get well.

RUDOLF DREIKURS . . .

This is another typical shock procedure, clumsy and brutal besides. It is evident that the relationship was mismanaged from the beginning. The therapist was unable to establish a cooperative relationship based on mutual respect. As usual, he blamed the deteriorating relationship on the patient's "passive hostility" and "resistance." Resistance is the stock in trade to excuse the therapist's inability to win and maintain the patient's cooperation.

It is evident that after three months of work the therapist had only scant information about the patient except what he had heard through gossip. And this gossip he communicated to him. It is hard to believe that a therapist would need such a shock experience to discover that his patient felt cornered, was in a panic, and was considering suicide. If the therapist wanted to inform the patient about his knowledge of his difficulties, he could have done so in a less cruel and brutal fashion. But it is exactly this shock technique which is so often employed by therapists who do not understand their patients, their inner thoughts, and their private logic. One cannot be too happy about the prevailing tendency to need shocks in order to put the relationship with the patient on a sound basis. With better skills, the therapist should have been able to induce the patient to arrange finances and time needed for a workable therapeutic procedure.

One can agree that the patient would not have come to "a commitment of the realistic demands of treatment" by himself, nor could therapy have continued without such commitment. But there is serious doubt that such a harsh and brutal form of "disclosure" was the only way. Particularly since the therapist finally came to the realization—what he should have known early in the treatment—that the patient depended on approval from others.

We cannot share the therapist's hesitation about treating acquaintances. A therapist who considers therapy primarily as a learning procedure and not one of a peculiar emotional relationship, specific only for therapy, can take on the treatment of acquaintances as well as relatives without running necessarily into complications. They are only inevitable when the proper safeguards for a therapeutic relationship, namely, mutual respect, alignment of goals, and earnest work on a common goal, are either neglected or not achieved. But without them any therapy, regardless with whom, has little chance of success.

ALBERT ELLIS . . .

This incident raises two interesting questions: (1) Should a therapist attempt to treat acquaintances? (2) Should a therapist confront a patient with material that he has learned outside the therapeutic relationship? On the first of these questions I am inclined to answer "No" and on the second "Yes."

Treating one's personal acquaintances certainly is not entirely disadvantageous; it has, in fact, several obvious advantages: (1) The therapist knows them better—on the basis of witnessed overt behavior—than he normally would while only seeing them therapeutically. (2) He is presumably very strongly motivated to help them because they are friends of his. (3) It may be easier for him to gain rapport with them, especially at the beginning of the relationship.

Nonetheless, treating acquaintances has distinct hazards, as this present case shows. It can result in evasiveness; severe countertransference problems; embarrassing involvements with third parties whom patient and therapist also know in common; and particularly unfortunate results when the therapy does not go well and the patient wants to quit or see another therapist. Because of these disadvantages, I generally feel that a therapist's seeing his acquaintances is likely to do more harm than good, and I avoid this in my own practice. Nonetheless, especially when there seems to be no alternative because the patient simply will not see any other therapist, I can see where this kind of a relationship might be chanced.

On the question of whether or not it is justifiable for the therapist to confront the patient with material he has gathered from other sources, I take a strong affirmative stand. Assuming that the therapist uses good discretion in this connection—since he certainly could traumatize some patients seriously if he rashly confronts them with externally gathered information—he may be able to help his patients considerably, as in the case under discussion. In marriage counseling cases, I frequently and quite openly confront one partner with information gained from the other partner; and sometimes this is almost the only possible way to break down certain therapeutic resistances.

In one of my regular psychotherapy cases, where the patient was not one of my acquaintances, but where she happened to become involved with some people I knew, and where I accidentally learned from them certain acts which she had refrained from telling me about, I frankly confronted her with her own behavior and achieved a psychotherapeutic break-through that otherwise might have never occurred or might have taken considerably more time to attain. Although this kind of confrontation—like virtually all active psychotherapeutic procedures—has its distinct dangers, I find that, when judiciously employed, it often has most felicitous results.

David Riesman . . .

Here once again we see the therapeutic consequences in a post-Victorian type of compelling an indulged patient to make contact with the disturbing reality. Previously, as the therapist says, the patient had managed to live in an invisible cloak and to conceal from himself the consequences of his acts by assuming that what he did did not matter (as distinguished perhaps from what he said) since he himself did not matter. To suddenly see himself in a sociometric network of those who had his number gave him at least a sense that he was real—and the therapist real too.

In the nineteenth century and thereafter it must have been a tremendous shock for a sensitively raised patient, for example a sheltered but well-educated girl like some of Freud's early patients, to talk turkey about sex with a male physician—the unheard of words themselves could under such circumstances be "real" enough. But what would it avail the therapist in this incident and in many others of this type to talk about screen memories and about sex? The patient has already played that game vicariously and is only too ready to talk about it on his own terms. Thus to provide the same sort of challenge that Freud found requires today, for the emancipated strata, a very different orientation on the part of the therapist. Psychoanalysis and the mental health movement in general has had for so long a time to fight the Philistines—the Philistines who insisted on "hard reality" and "fly right and settle down"—that there may be a certain lag against copying the neuroses of those strata in which Philistinism has in large measures been vanquished.

WILLIAM SNYDER . . .

The most outstanding aspect of this case is that the therapist actually decides to function in two different capacities in this client's life. He first offers to fill the role of therapist, although not at first in a very straight-forward manner, but rather in a situation of accepting initial resistance amounting almost to indifference on the part of the client. At the moment of the critical incident, the therapist decides to fill the role of social mentor, conscience, and to some extent diagnostician of the client's difficulties. He does not tell the client he must undertake therapy, but he informs him, quite abruptly, that he is a very inadequate person, quite unlike his self-ideal, and, by implication, much in need of help. He then re-structures therapy on a working basis, and it apparently is accepted on such an arrangement, and according to the report proves to be fairly effec-tive.

Two questions deserve attention. The first is whether or not the thera-pist was justified in accepting the client, initially, under the conditions of indifference which characterized the client. It is reasonable to say that he should not have done so, had he known that the client was as resistant as he was. Seldom does therapy take place in the event of such strong initial resistance. In most cases resistance is likely to develop, even quite extensively during the course of therapy, and when it does develop in this manner, it can frequently be worked through. But when it is so great initially, it has little chance of success. So the question really is whether the therapist should have been able to recognize initially the extent of the resistance. I believe that he should have. Whenever therapy is casually requested it is practically axiomatic that it is strongly resisted. A further sign of this is the client's indication that he would consider therapy only with the specific therapist who happened to be a personal acquaintance. This is virtually always a sign of strong initial resistance. The really ill person does not refuse help from anyone who might be a competent phy-sician, and even from many persons who are not. The client who indicates that there is only one therapist in the world who will suit him does not really want help much.

In addition the therapist compromised this situation by offering to con-duct the therapy for a nominal fee. He mentions the client's economic limitations, but also identifies him as a member of a highly esteemed pro-fession. Certainly there are several professions whose members are de-cidedly underpaid, particularly ministers and teachers. But it is very doubtful that a professional person would not be in a position to pay a reasonable fee for a necessary service. The therapist undoubtedly cheapened the significance of his service, and certainly failed to evaluate the client's motivation for therapy, when he offered the nominal fee. He must have realized this, for when he set more realistic terms for therapy later, he apparently asked a more reasonable figure.

Furthermore, therapy performed by a friend is like a "favor" which the therapist is somewhat obligated to extend, and not a bona-fide professional relationship. The relationship is more one of co-equals, neither of whom can exercise critical judgment because of the element of friendship. But the therapist who cannot exercise scientific criticalness is likely to be hampered in the conduct of real therapy.

Also this therapist had advance information about the client's generally passive-submissive personality pattern. He knew of a considerable amount of evidence of immaturity of reactions combined with a denial-of-responsibility type of behavior. These, I feel, were evident signs that this client could be expected to "bluff his way through" unless required from the beginning to be honest and straightforward about his inadequacies and his need for help.

The second major question is whether or not the therapist's method of salvaging this case was justifiable. Admitting the initial error in judgment in having accepted the client on his own terms of indifference toward therapy, the therapist probably salvaged the case in the most feasible manner. He really had to assume a nontherapeutic role and face the client with an accurate diagnosis of his adjustment, and then offer to establish therapy on a new set of terms. He could, of course, have merely permitted the case to terminate itself, but this would not have been salvaging it. If the therapist believed it was possible to work out a satisfactory sort of therapy relationship on the new terms, or even if he believed it worth the attempt, he was probably justified. The only possible harm from such an effort would have been if he had shocked the client so badly that he not only fled from further therapy but was also traumatized to such an extent that he would be able to function even less adequately in life, or would more strenuously avoid facing himself realistically at some future date. This would always be a somewhat difficult judgment to arrive at, but the evidence of the client's rather strong dependency needs would cause a therapist to suspect that he would quite likely accept therapy on the new terms rather than withdraw from it, providing he realized that the offer was *bona fide* and really therapeutically motivated.

Bess Sondel . . .

Here is a patient "of a highly esteemed profession who is also intelligent and well liked." But the patient is behaving *unintelligently* with possible disastrous effects—personal and professional.

The therapist gives a history of treating this patient under unsatisfactory circumstances for about three months with unsatisfactory results. Therapy was about to be terminated by mutual consent. But, just as the patient "was ready to leave," the therapist made his pronouncement: I know something about you; I shouldn't tell, but I will.

What was this? Was it revenge? Was it rebellion at defeat? Was it incitive with the objective of continuing therapy? Or was it a long-delayed burst of common sense in the interest of the patient? I do not know. But I agree with the therapist that the incident created "a situation with which therapy should have started off in the first place, by the formulation of a problem...."

More sensible words were never said. The analysis of a problem is the first essential step toward the solution of that problem. What's the trouble? The trouble is usually stated as an undesirable *effect*. Effect of what? When this question is answered by the therapist or the patient or both, remedial measures may be begun.

This patient's problem was one of communication, in my opinion. He erred in two principle ways:

1. He erred in the way he talked to himself.

This patient was unable or unwilling to face himself. Every human being wants and needs the approval of others. This patient was being denied approval. He refused to see himself as others saw him. He protected himself by deluding himself by his own signs. He talked to himself without intelligence.

2. He erred in the way he talked to others.

This patient did not analyze or evaluate the responses of others intelligently. He directed his words and actions outward. But communication is not a linear experience. He failed to look. He failed to listen. If the communicator will perceive in every possible human way, something comes back to him. And this should be received and entertained as new information by which to proceed further in goal-seeking behavior. The communication process is circular. This "intelligent" man did not use input as information by which to make corrective responses, thus to establish more favorable relationships with others.

This patient ignored the fact that every time we open our mouths something besides words comes out. The value system is forever expressed —with or without words. This patient was not, apparently, transmitting anything worthy of respect. And, since he deluded himself with his own signs, he made no effort to use corrective devices by which to establish satisfying relationships with others.

Such things an intelligent person can be told, with almost immediate effect. Let the patient see himself as part of an interactive situation-as-a-whole. By perceiving others—with his head and his heart—he is reinforced.

He becomes a *personality in a field* with some degree of control of himself and of others. The self is not a prisoner in solitary confinement.

It is the responsibility of the therapist (1) to understand the role of communication in human relationships, and (2) to help the patient reach that understanding.

Frederick C. Thorne . . .

The necessity of confronting the client with reality problems which the client would "conveniently" ignore if allowed to do so nondirectively (in actuality permitting him to maintain his neurotic defenses intact), constitutes a therapeutic problem which appears in all depth analysis where evaluation and interpretation goes beyond what the client is willing or able to do by himself. In this case the therapist apologizes for having confronted the client "almost cruelly at the time, it seemed to me" with objective evaluations of his self which were very painful for the client to accept. In our opinion, no such apologies are necessary since all effective depth therapy involves painful probing and manipulation of sensitive areas which the client would prefer to have left alone. The situation is analogous to dentistry in which it is necessary to drill out the painful cavity before permanent reconstruction can occur. "Painless" psychotherapy is at times as much of an impossibility as painless dentistry since it is only by dealing with painful areas that the very essence of the matter can be attacked. If the client protests against painful confrontations with reality, it is our custom to advise him not to put on the shoe unless it fits; but if it does fit, then to take it seriously and do something constructive about it.

Our practice is to confront the client with reality in small doses, gauged carefully to see how much he can stand at any one time, and also being careful not to overwhelm him with massive discouragement. We attempt to balance off unpleasant topics by "sugaring off" the interview with pleasant topics so that the client is left with a predominance of positive feelings to balance off negative feelings. Thus, if some inadequacies of the client have been brought up earlier in the interview, we try to mention some positive characteristics which might be used to compensate for defects, that is, trying to make the client feel that all is not hopeless and that a very positive solution is possible.

Some of our worst clinical mistakes have resulted from failure to secure evidence from independent sources both as to the past history concerning how the client's difficulties have actually manifested themselves and also as to the degree which behavior has changed during therapy. As in this case, a client may choose or be able to reveal only superficial aspects of his problems and motivations. Psychoanalysis and nondirective therapy stand at opposite poles with regard to the question of what to do when resistances are confronted. Psychoanalysis attempts a direct interpretation while nondirectivism chooses to reflect them passively. Perhaps some compromise solution is best in many cases. We have used the approach of asking the client if he ever thought what some behavior pattern might mean in terms of unconscious dynamics. If the client can learn to take a curious attitude toward his behavior instead of a defensive one, it becomes progressively easy to introduce new bits of evidence to be analyzed.

Love Was Enough

19

History[1]

Mr. X, a white male in his early thirties, consulted me because of some difficulty he was having in his work as an accountant. The patient was the eldest of four siblings in a white family of Northern European descent in which the mother was the dominant parent. He may be described as being ambitious with a thin facade of modesty; conscientious, sensitive to slights, intelligent, and well educated. He had married two years before I saw him and had one child. The marriage appeared to be reasonably successful. During the anamnesis he recounted the following situation, the objective portion of which has since been verified.

About nine years before, when he was enmeshed in a complicated life situation, the patient developed an acute paranoid psychosis for which he was hospitalized in a state mental institution for 13 months. Upon admission he was examined by a psychiatrist who noted that he was withdrawn and suspicious, and expressed beliefs that people were making fun of him, that his food was poisoned, and that he was in jail because of a large gang that was persecuting him. After several interviews with the psychiatrist, the patient showed less suspicious-

[1] This case previously was reported at greater length in the *Bulletin of the Menninger Clinic*, XIX (1955), pp. 129–34.

ness and was less reluctant to talk about himself; he then abruptly refused to see his physician and the relationship was terminated.

The patient withdrew completely, responding with only a brief "yes" or "no" to direct questioning by the staff, seemed oblivious to his surroundings, became compliant and apathetic, and made several surreptitious suicidal attempts. His physical condition gradually deteriorated because of inactivity and poor food intake; this and the presence of an intercurrent infection necessitated his being transferred to an eight-bed medical ward about seven months after admission.

During the first month on the medical ward he was bedridden, stuporous, and incontinent. The patient's interpretation of his experiences on the medical ward during this month of severe debilitation is the salient point of this paper. After this period, the patient's physical status improved, and he was transferred to another ward. While there he showed progress in a sort of "total push" program which included recreational and occupational therapies and, in the way of psychotherapy, infrequent talks of a supportive nature with a social worker. Under this regime the patient gradually recovered and was finally discharged from the hospital. Aside from some anxiousness after discharge and the difficulty for which the patient consulted me, nine years later, there have been no recurrences.

Incident

In describing his experiences before improvement took place, the patient related the following: He had believed during his illness that he was the object of attack by an organization which was set up for the purpose of punishing and humiliating him; the head of this organization was a former employer. The organization was acquainted with his past, and he was placed in a novel kind of jail which had been specially designed for the purpose; moving pictures and recordings were made of his activities in the hospital and transmitted later to the public to deter them from committing errors and crimes similar to his. The plot included all those about him—other patients, visitors, members of the hospital staff, and people he had previously known. They were all dedicated and specially trained actors who appeared highly knowledgeable about his past life, extremely competent, brilliantly sophisticated, and superb in their ability to insult and torment him in a sarcastic manner. Mainly they were brisk, deft, and certain in their actions; their voices were harsh and rasping, their coloring vivid, their speech polished. There were a few persons who did not seem to fit this pattern, but their costumes appeared so outlandish, their accents of speech so exaggerated, that he believed they were enacting an intentional caricature to mock him. He was excruciatingly aware of all sensations, an agony from which he could escape only by sleep.

At first he had thought that he might gamble by tentatively accepting his first psychiatrist's disagreement with his delusional beliefs —it was at this time that he became more cooperative—but later he withdrew from the relationship when the psychiatrist appeared to him to be a member of the organization which was persecuting him. Aside from this transient doubt, there was no question in the patient's mind at this period of his illness, concerning the reality of his experiences or his interpretation of them. Outstanding in the patient's mind, and the factor to which he attributes the onset of his recovery, were his experiences on the medical ward when he was acutely and seriously ill. His perception and interpretation of the people and events about him were similar to those mentioned, except that his sensations were dulled, creating the feeling of his being in a relative vacuum. He knew that he was physically weak and sick but thought that this was part of a plan to make him absolutely helpless. He was not sure whether he had served his purpose and they would let him die, or whether they intended to bring him back—if so, he thought that they might make a miscalculation. He felt comforted by the possiblity of his dying as an end to the torment.

The patient recognized among the ward personnel people whom he had seen previously. One of them, Mrs. O, was a large Negro woman in her late thirties. The patient believed that she had been placed on the ward as a representative of the Negro race in order to demonstrate that even she was superior to him and contemptuous of him. She appeared to be quick, sure, highly intelligent, and worldly, with an excellent command of English; her appearance seemed extremely neat, her skin, full, smooth, and light in color. He was aware of only one difference between her behavior and that of the others— and that difference lay only in its consistency. On starting work, Mrs. O would first ask about him by name when reports about patients were exchanged. She usually tended to his immediate needs before engaging in idle conversation, or leaving the ward for meals, or at the end of work. Her remarks to him seemed no different from the others and were limited to "Here is your food, Mr. X," "We are going to bathe you," "I would like to change your bed."

He recalled her attempting to spoon-feed him, but he turned his head aside more as a matter of policy than conviction. As the days passed, he began to feel that her voice sounded less harsh, but there was no change in her appearance. His own behavior was impassive, and he consciously made every effort to avoid showing any responsiveness to his surroundings. It should be remembered that at the time the patient was making these observations and deductions, he was considered by the ward personnel to be stuporous and out of contact. Although his determination of Mrs. O's position in the plot had not changed, the patient had a vague feeling that there was something different about her and that somehow she had a genuine kindly interest in him. He became extremely aware of her actions, and much of his thinking centered on her. He would feel comfortable when she was on the ward, would eagerly await her coming on duty, and was aware of her absence from the ward on her days off. When she was away, he would pray for strength to endure the pain of the situation while she was gone.

Earlier in his illness, in order to escape from thinking about his believed predicament, he thought considerably about such philosophical matters as life, death, love, affection, and religion, in a frantic, mechanical, and detached way, using polysyllabic language. During this period he experienced a resurgence of these thoughts but in a completely different way—they were considered important, enabled him to survive in a harsh, uncompromising, unfair, and disappointing world; specifically, this is what enabled a Negro, Mrs. O, to survive in a difficult white world. It was too bad, he felt, that he finally recognized these ideals, because he was already doomed and beyond redemption.

Mrs. O left the medical ward before Mr. X was transferred, and he did not see her again until just before his discharge from the hospital. During the period of his recovery, he covertly searched out people who were present earlier in his illness in order to compare his impressions and to reconstruct his illness. He considered looking for Mrs. O many times, but each time found convenient excuses, until he met a nurse who had been on the medical ward. He asked a guarded question about Mrs. O, and the nurse replied that Mrs. O had been extremely interested in him and had hoped to see him, but was backward about doing so. Mr. X told of his wish to see her, and a meeting was arranged.

Mrs. O appeared, in contrast to his previous impressions, to be relatively slow, dull, and awkward; her uniform was soiled, she appeared shorter, her skin was darker and wrinkled, and her complexion imperfect; her movements were unsure and her language limited, with an obvious accent. The conversation was simple, clumsy, and conventional. Mrs. O told about her pleasure in hearing of his recovery, wished him luck, and said that she had been very interested in him. Mr. X said, "I felt that something was going on and that you were interested—but why?" She replied, "A few years ago my husband caught tuberculosis and had to go to a hospital. I started to work at a medical hospital but it wasn't enough. So I came here and liked it better. I don't know why I was interested . . . maybe . . . I guess . . . it was because you were sick . . . you were a man . . . you were in trouble . . . I was a woman . . . and there was something I could do."

Discussion

This description of the origin of recovery from a psychosis arising from a meaningful but almost obscure relationship between the patient and a kindly female attendant reveals some possible interpersonal mechanisms connected with recovery. The narration illustrates some things we are inclined to underestimate: A disturbed or withdrawn patient may be acutely aware of his surroundings even if his impressions are distorted. Also, in each such patient there exist at least transient islands of reasonableness and valid experience with responses to the environment which are appropriate, and it is the utilization of these which form the basis of any therapeutic approach. Perhaps this anecdote illustrates concretely the theoretical and practical importance of the more recent research which concerns itself with social interaction and the importance of the environment and the attitudes of those surrounding the patient—the "attitude" or "milieu" therapy of a hospital.

NATHAN ACKERMAN . . .

This is a fascinating story, sensitively told. It is the story of true love of an extraordinary kind, which, in effect, saves the life of a sick, dying

man. In the depth of this patient's psychosis are revealed the subtle
nuances of a torturesome, spiritual struggle. In the end, it is this struggle
which decides recovery or nonrecovery from psychosis; in fact, it makes
the difference between life and death.

At one point this patient is dangerously ill, both mentally and physically.
He is so severely debilitated that death is imminent. At the climactic
point of his illness, the patient is tortured, agonized, without hope, and
praying for relief in death. From the tender, devoted care of a Negro
woman attendant this psychotic man gets a ray of hope, a new faith. He
is inspired to live for her. He survives and makes a remarkable recovery.
This is what we must explain.

In order to do so, we must reconstruct the sequence of events. This
man takes a plunge into an acute paranoid psychosis. He transforms his
perceptual view of the world so that he experiences himself as a haunted,
tortured victim of a world of persecutors. He is utterly alone, without love,
without allies, and completely exposed to assault and humiliation. He is
crushed and feels no chance for life or love. He wants to die, tries to die,
and almost succeeds.

He meets one other person in the world whose behavior challenges
his paranoid misconception of the universe. At first he is convinced that
she, too, is placed there for the explicit purpose of only deepening his
degradation. However, the sincere, warm, and steady way in which she
ministers to his needs challenges his entire paranoid system. Gradually,
he corrects his misconception of her intentions toward him. He discovers
that this woman is true to him, consistent, dependable, and loving as a
good mother. She rescues him from the jaws of death; nurses him back
to health. She gives him a new trust and a reason to live. In the beginning
she is the sole exception to his systematized paranoid image of human
relations. It gradually dawns on his clouded senses that there is in the
world at least one other human being who must herself have been profoundly wounded and humiliated. Since she is a Negro woman, she must
have suffered, and yet despite this she sustained her faith. As a member
of a demeaned minority she must have experienced insults and degradation. Nonetheless, she preserved her self-esteem, her dignity, and her
capacity for loving. There is much in this story that suggests an experience of the nature of a religious conversion. It is through this patient's
identification with the presumed anguish of this Negro woman that he
is led back to an affirmation of the positive value of life.

The torturesome quality of the man's moral struggle, the pathos of his
conversion experience, is echoed in his preoccupation with the fundamental value problems of human existence. In the depths of despair he
scrapes the very bottom of his soul; he strives agonizingly to discover the

true meaning of life. He finds an answer in the simple, dignified faith of a Negro woman.

But love is blind, they say. During the height of his psychosis he does not see her as she really appeared in actuality. He feels more than he sees. He feels her goodness and idealizes it. He makes of her a kind of idyllic mother figure. Through union with her he finds goodness in himself.

Many months later in his recovered state, he compares his two images of this idyllic mother, before and after psychosis. Once again restored to the world of reality, he sees this Negro woman in a very different light. The clash of the two images is painful. Now she is slow, dull, awkward, and has a blemished skin. He is plagued with the need to know from this woman why she nursed him back to life. Could it be that she loves him? Does she find in him something worthy of love? The late reunion between the patient and his adoptive Negro mother is an awkward, labored one. He gets his answer by indirection, and in a veiled allusion. Yes, she loves him; she loves him in place of her sick husband from whom she was forcibly parted. But at this meeting both are constrained, self-conscious, conflicted. Neither can be emotionally free or spontaneous in confessing their empathic love. It is a sad commentary on our culture, on the insincerities of conventional social relations, on the barrier imposed by the color line, that a profoundly meaningful bond of affection cannot be freely admitted. In this long postponed reunion, the love feeling cannot be fully shared and enjoyed. It is cloaked over by a clumsy, self-conscious casualness.

This recapitulation of a case of recovery from an acute psychosis influenced by the devoted ministrations of a Negro woman points significantly to the issues raised by the therapist himself. What is the content of interpersonal experience necessary to recovery? Are there islands of preserved health even in severely psychotic patients? Can we design a milieu therapy which incorporates the crucial elements of emotional nutrition necessary for healing?

This clinical story makes clear first that the care of psychotically ill persons cannot and must not be mechanized. No matter how fine may be the architecture of our new mental hospital buildings, no matter how improved may be the physical care of psychotic patients, none of these attributes can in any way replace the ingredients of warm, kindly interpersonal intimacy which are indispensable to recovery. It is necessary not only to put "brains ahead of bricks," but even more important, "heart ahead of brains." The inclusion of this essential emotional diet is not a question of professional training. It is more a question of finding the right kinds of human beings, human being with heart and a sense of dedication. The loving of a patient and the inspired contagion of hope and faith cannot be prescribed. It must simply be there.

The profound sharing of the true value and worth of every human life must be a silent presence in the milieu of psychotic patients. Is it possible to planfully introduce these ingredients into a hospital ward? The answer is yes. It can also be introduced into institutions for delinquents. It can be created and nursed in the psychological core of family, neighborhood, and community. An intriguing question arises as to the existence of a cultural trend in our society which tends to mechanize human relations, foster denial of emotion, and choke off spontaneity. When this happens the structure of human relations moves toward the sick side. To counteract this, it would be necessary to re-examine the culture pattern to see how it might be possible to enhance those values in human relations, in family and community which are on the side of emotional health.

JEROME D. FRANK . . .

This incident raises the important question of the validity of material produced by patients in therapy. Much of the data on which theories of psychiatric illness and therapy are based consist of patients' memories of past events. Despite the accumulation of much evidence to the contrary, memories still tend to be accepted as close approximations of what occurred. Actually, the patient's memories are apt to be grossly distorted by his motivations at the time he reports them. One such motivation is his need to make sense of his past life and his present symptoms. Furthermore, there is increasing evidence that the patient's productions in a therapeutic situation are influenced to a hitherto unsuspected degree by the expectations of his therapist. The patient's remarks are guided by cues of approval or disapproval emitted by the therapist, even when the former believes himself to be completely nondirective. Neither patient nor the therapist need be aware that this is occurring, but its effects can be profound. A classical example is the way Freud's patients fabricated early experiences which confirmed his theory of the causative role of infantile traumata in neuroses.

Both the desire to make sense out of his illness and the therapist's expectations may have distorted this patient's account of the role of the colored aide in his recovery. He seems to have had an acute schizophrenic episode of a kind which is usually self-limited although it may recur. In the latter connection it would be interesting to know what the patient's current symptoms were. Was he again having a mild paranoid psychosis? Did he come out of it promptly or did he get sicker first? In any case, after a patient has gone through such an experience, he tries hard to find an explanation for it. The human mind abhors a vacuum, and the inexplicable is all the more frightening if it happens to one's self. Patients who have recovered from psychosis can almost always find some experience connected temporally with its onset or its termination, to which they attribute getting sick or getting better. If the colored aide had not been there, this patient would in all likelihood have attributed his recovery to some other incident or person. Patients who have recurrent psychotic depressions, for example, are often able to account for the onset of each depression by referring it to an upsetting experience, even though it seems more than likely that most such depressions are caused by physiological rhythms that we do not yet understand.

It may well be, incidentally, that one of the important functions of interpretation in psychotherapy is to supply the patient with a rationale for his bewildering and upsetting emotional experiences, thereby increasing his self-confidence. Interpretations based on different theoretical frameworks seem to be equally effective. The effectiveness of an interpretation seems to depend, not on its truth, but on whether or not the patient and the therapist believe it to be true, with resultant allaying of the patient's anxiety.

Therefore, it is not surprising that this patient has an explanation for his recovery. The question next becomes, why he picked this particular one. The therapist obviously assumed that he did so because it is the correct explanation, and, for the purpose of this discussion, I shall make the same assumption. However, it is only an assumption. This report is made nine years after the fact, which gives ample time for retrospective falsification. One wonders whether this patient really clung to so many details for so many years or whether he made some of them up.

Also, the fact that this patient offers an interpersonal explanation for his recovery is in keeping with his turning to psychotherapy for help on this occasion. That is, he presumably accepts the notion of an interpersonal basis for his psychosis. I cannot be sure what the orientation of the therapist is, but feel confident that it is one which also lays great weight on interpersonal and psychogenic factors in mental illness. In this connection, I wonder if he has had much experience with psychotics because he seems surprised that "a disturbed or withdrawn patient may be acutely aware of his surroundings." This is commonplace to those who work with psychotics; in fact, some have called the catatonic state one of vigilance rather than stupor because of this fact. In any case, it seems likely that the therapist was oriented towards finding a psychogenic explanation of the patient's recovery and may have unwittingly influenced the latter's report of his memories in accord with this expectation.

Assuming that the patient's account does actually correspond with what transpired, several factors may be thought of as contributing to his recovery. One is that he became physically very ill. It is well known that a life-threat often produces remissions in schizophrenics, and some attribute the beneficial effects of insulin coma therapy to just this fact.

Practically every psychiatrist who has thought about this subject has speculated about it. I know of no evidence which enables a decision between different theories. One can think in terms of the instinct of self-preservation, for example, and hypothesize that a life-endangering experience forces the patient to come back to reality in order to preserve his existence—that is, he has to make some sort of appropriate adaptation to the world again in order to survive. Or perhaps severe physical illness mobilizes the physician's interest and concern, and this is the chief therapeutic factor. Betz and Whitehorn,[2] for example, have been able to distinguish two kinds of psychiatrist, termed "A" and "B" who have consistently good and poor success, respectively, with hospitalized schizophrenics. "A" psychiatrists who offer a relationship characterized by "active personal participation" do not improve their results by using insulin. The patients of "B" psychiatrists, on the other hand, when given insulin show a rise in remission rate equal to that obtained by the "A" physicians.

For this episode, an appropriate hypothesis would be that the patient's illness caused him to regress to an infantile state, in which he again becomes accessible to a primitive mothering type of approach.

Mothering involves physical contact, which may offer the most useful means of communication with a severely disturbed patient. It is an attractive notion that the phylogenetically more recent distance receptors—the eyes and the ears—are more subject to distortion of signals in accordance with the patient's private meanings than are the more primitive receptors of touch, taste, and smell. Some think that a measure of the seriousness of a schizophrenic's disorganization is the depth of the disorganization of his communication system. The patient who has tactile and gustatory hallucinations, for example, is perhaps sicker than one who has only visual and auditory ones. It follows that a patient who is too disorganized to interpret words correctly can still respond appropriately to physical contacts. Conversely, since taste, smell, and touch are most important in the preverbal stage of development, a confused patient may be less likely to symbolically distort stimuli in these modalities than sights and sounds, which are closely linked to words.

The record suggests that the colored aide gave the patient more (or more kindly) physical attention than the other aides. It is noted that she attended to his immediate needs before engaging in idle conversation or leaving the ward for meals or at the end of work; also, that she attempted to spoon-feed him. Through these primitive channels the essential good intentions of the treatment personnel might first be able to penetrate his delusional system. These became the only stimuli that were not acutely painful or anxiety provoking to him, so it is understandable that he would

[2] Barbara J. Betz, and J. C. Whitehorn, "The Relationship of the Therapist to the Outcome of Therapy in Schizophrenia," *Psychiat. Res. Rep.* (1956), No. 5, pp. 89–105.

become very aware of the aide and miss her when she was not on the ward.

At a more symbolic level, he may have been able to accept her good intentions as genuine because he identified her as a member of a persecuted minority such as he also felt himself to be.

With respect to the course of the illness, one might wonder whether he broke off with the psychiatrist at an earlier stage simply because his illness was getting worse or whether the psychiatrist had done something to disrupt the beginnings of a trustful relationship. This is another example of the difficulty in deciding what is cause and what is effect with these patients.

Finally, it is impossible to decide whether the total push program really contributed to his recovery or whether it was just an accompaniment of his spontaneous convalescence. In short, until we know a great deal more about the natural history of these illnesses and the kind of influences, both endogenous and exogenous, that affect their course, any attribution of cause to events in the patient's environment must be very tentative. All we can say is, many kinds of experience and intervention can be therapeutic, not just those of the psychiatrist or psychotherapist. Kindliness and consistent warm interest conveyed by anyone in a simple manner appropriate to a patient's badly confused receptive state may have a significant healing effect.

VINCENT HERR . . .

The patient, in his apathetic withdrawn state, might well have been given up as hopeless, were it not for his infections, which necessitated his being put in the medical ward. We are not told in the case whether or not the infections were self-caused. Probably it is not known and never will be known how much the patient was out of contact when they occurred. There is reason to suspect, from the subsequent history, that the patient may at some future day recall their origin. After all he must have recalled his suicidal attempts, and this writer definitely believes he should be kept on an out-patient basis with some therapist.

The happenings of that first year in the medical ward must have been critical. It is possible that the influence of the Negro female attendant may have turned the tide. It is thinkable at least, that the psychiatrist had prepared the soil, as it were, for the patient's salutary reaction to the Negress. For the patient had "tentatively accepted the psychiatrist's disagreement with his delusional beliefs." Just why the patient relapsed, thinking the psychiatrist was part of the persecuting organization, will be known only when more interviews are had with the recovered patient, if even then. But when one reads this case he cannot help being impressed with the extremely volatile and fluctuating character of this patient's perceptions even at the time of his dismissal from the hospital. There is an obvious contrast between the way Mrs. O struck him on the ward and then upon dismissal. First she seemed contemptuous of him, yet sure, quick, neat, skillful, smooth, and light in color, *first of all attending* to his needs; then upon dismissal, the patient finds her slow, dull, awkward, untidy, skin wrinkled. Yet she seemed to have conveyed to this confused patient something of her own feeling of sympathy and understanding, which power of communication may have been related to her own personal life experiences with her suffering husband.

The case described here gives a marvelous and typical picture of the gradual systematization of delusions of persecution, which could well be included in textbooks. If there should come a day when the science of blood chemistry reveals more of the hidden causes of such delusional formations with their accompanying somatic and sensory disturbances, researchers will be in need of accurately reported case histories.

As for the subtle interpersonal relationship that marked the turning point of recovery, we are still left in the dark concerning its true nature. Was it one of satisfying the need for affection, or attention, or just common ordinary "respect for the person"? The data given do not enable us to decide this question. Ample extraneous evidence points to an obvious universal human need for respect.

It is abundantly clear, however, that attendants, physicians, and external observers generally, can be extremely far from the truth when they report that a particular patient at a particular moment of time is here and now totally out of contact with reality! While there is life in an intact organism there also seems to be some "appropriateness" in its responses to some aspects of the environment.

J. McV. Hunt . . .

This incident is interesting in that it suggests that there are subtle cues of interpersonal communication which have thus far escaped systematic organization in psychological theory. It is quite unnecessary to assume anything especially mysterious about this communication. On the other hand, assuming that what this stuporous patient got from Mrs. O, who served as his nurse, was truly of significance in his change, an assumption which may not be true, the patient's retrospective account of the experience indicates that some of the cues that serve as interpersonal communication are poorly understood.

This case reminds me of an experience I had at Worchester Hospital in the middle thirties. One of the patients assigned to me, as a subject in an experiment, was a stuporous catatonic who had not talked for some six or eight months. At that time I was studying the effects of my taking various roles in my relationships with noncooperative schizophrenics on the co-operativeness of these patients. In about half of the 25 cases I had in the study, I found deliberate changes of my role produced changes in the co-operativeness of the patients. In the other half of this group of 25, nothing I could do influenced their cooperativeness. In each case, my first interview was to make a direct request for the kind of cooperation I wanted. In the case of this stuporous schizophrenic, I told him directly that there were those who believed that he could not cooperate, and that there were those who believed that he could if he would. I told him that I was a member of the latter group, and that he could be of real service to mankind if he would come down to the laboratory and demonstrate that he could do the various tests that I had there. Fifteen minutes of such talk produced not a single flicker of change in this man's expression. He sat rigidly erect in a chair, and I found myself wondering if he were playing God. I knew that he had had the background of a Catholic seminary. My question was how can one communicate with God. I reckoned that if he were playing God, to take a superior role, or to treat him in the diminutive, should be very irritating. When I tried this, the prediction was verified. The trial consisted of walking in, taking the patient by the arm, calling him "Jimmy-my-boy" and saying "You are coming into my laboratory now." He did not come. In fact, the cords stuck out on his neck as he clenched and ground his teeth.

Again the issue arose about how to communicate with God. I thought of adopting the posture of prayer, but I rejected it because it would have reinforced the patient's delusion if this were his delusion. Next it occurred to me to play the role of a person in trouble within his ear-shot. When I did this by sitting down on the window sill near his chair and complaining about the difficulties of trying to do anything at the Worcester State Hospital, and of the difficulties of getting patients to participate in experiments, this patient suddenly whirled around, and in a clear voice, asked: "What's the matter, Dr. Hunt?" It is interesting that, even though he was apparently playing something like the God role, he did not lose my title. Furthermore, the fact that he knew that I was Dr. Hunt clearly implied that he was quite aware of what had been going on about him. Further evidence of this came from the fact that in half an hour of conversation he showed that he knew a great deal of the factual material about the various attendants, professional persons, and patients on the ward. He would not go to the laboratory to do my tests because this would be disloyal to his Alma Mater where he studied psychology. Moreover, he pointed out, since it was his job "to keep order on this ward, a job more difficult than yours, Dr. Hunt," he dared not leave the ward.

In a later series of interviews, I was able to replicate these three responses of this patient. Furthermore, a psychiatric resident, who got interested in the process, also replicated this patient's responses to these three roles I have described. Shortly after the resident's interviews with this patient, the patient appeared in the doorway of his room with a grin on his face and asked me for a cigarette. The period of "stupor" had come to an end.

What I am suggesting in relating this very interesting experience, is that some of the cues of the roles one is playing may take on special meanings to a patient and start a major shift in the direction of his behavior. I had hoped that I might discover some lawfulness in these relationships, but I was unable to do so.

Recently, Fred Fiedler[3] has got what appears to be the beginnings of lawfulness in such behavior in the tendency for therapists of favorable reputation to show higher assumed similarity (a tendency to describe their patients as they describe themselves) with their patients than do therapists with less favorable reputations. In a similar study, Parloff[4] has shown that patients who are described by their therapists as closely approximating the therapist's ideal patient seem to feel they are getting more out of the group experience than do patients who are described by the therapists as unlike the therapist's ideal patient. These investigative hints can be coupled with experiences we have all had in listening to ex-patients describe their therapist. I have known several people in psychotherapy to describe a therapist, whom I regarded as skilled, as a "quack." This same patient would find exceedingly helpful another therapist whom I might regard as much less skilled and, to me, much less personally attractive. I am still intrigued by the idea that there must be some lawfulness in this business of "who attracts whom" in the psychotherapeutic situation. The notion of lawfulness, of course, is merely an assumption. It may be that what strikes the patient is so ideosyncratic as to escape encapsulation in any general proposition. On the other hand, to accept such a negative assumption without a search for lawfulness may well leave a highly important area without investigation.

One cue given in this incident may be worth following up. In Mr. X's retrospective account of his memory of his colored nurse, Mrs. O, he reports that she would ask first about him by name when reports about patients were exchanged, that she attended to his immediate needs before engaging in idle conversation, or leaving the ward for meals, or at the end of work. It may well be that just these cues of personal interest on the part of ward personnel are of major importance in motivating the withdrawn, or in giving an individual the impression that he exists as something of value to someone else. All this suggests that one might set up an experiment in which the various ward personnel would each adopt a patient for such

[3] Fred Fiedler, "Quantitative Studies on the Role of Therapists' Feelings toward their Patients," in *Psychotherapy: Theory and Research*, O. Hobart Mowrer (ed.) (New York: Ronald, 1953), Ch. 12.

[4] M. B. Parloff, "Some Factors Affecting the Quality of Therapeutic Relationships," *J. Abnorm. Soc. Psychol.*, LII (1956), pp. 5–10.

shows of interest to be followed up through a series of weeks. The percentage of remissions under such treatment might then be compared with the percentage of remissions under impersonal treatment. If we are ever to develop a kind of "milieu" therapy for general adoption in hospital situations, it is important that such hints be followed and tested.

BESS SONDEL . . .

This history is interesting communication-wise mainly because it indicates the potency of *nonverbal* communication.

We know very little about nonverbal communication beyond that it happens. Every time we use words, we communicate something far and beyond their literal significance. The uniqueness of an individual derives from the character and organization of his physical structure and from the pattern of his learned experience—from his ideas and ideals. This uniqueness is associated with the *values* of the human being and is expressive of all the years of his biosocial past and living present. The value system is, it seems, so tied up with the language system that it expresses itself—through the voice, the manner, through silence itself—on the nonverbal level every time we use words.

In the case of this patient and the nurse, it seems that the patient identified himself with other "persecuted" individuals and that the nurse identified the patient with her tuberculous husband and, indeed, with all "helpless" men who need the care of a woman. Over and beyond the words said, these two people communicated something deeply within them—something intimately associated with values. Something—somehow—made itself *felt* by the patient which affected his behavior, and possibly his recovery.

Notice that the comments made by the nurse showed no explicit intention of achieving an attitude response:

"Here is your food, Mr. X."
"We are going to bathe you."
"I would like to change your bed."

These statements are primarily in the informative use of language but incitive to the degree in which they invite cooperation. The complete absence of explicitly valuative content (language that is intended to elicit a preferential attitude response[5]) is, I believe, noteworthy here because the nurse's comments did, nevertheless, produce an attitude response. This is indicative, in my opinion, that nonverbal communication did, in this in-

[5] See Charles Morris, *Signs, Language, and Behavior* (Englewood Cliffs, N.J.: Prentice-Hall, Inc., 1946), and Bess Sondel, *The Humanity of Words, A Primer of Semantics* (New York: World Publishing Company, 1958).

stance, supplement verbal communication to an appreciable degree. On the verbal level, the nurse asked for nothing but understanding and cooperation on the physical level. There is no overt solicitation of empathy. But that empathy occurred is apparent. That empathy was more on the unconscious than the conscious level seems to be indicated by the fact that the patient endowed the nurse with attractive physical attributes. Had the response been on the conscious level, the patient would have noted wrinkles, and so forth, which he did, indeed, note in his more adjusted state.

The significant thing to note in this history is the fact that nurse and patient were aspects of a *social field* in which there was no sharp division between the two. Here is a situation-as-a-whole whose complexity goes beyond our ability to analyze it. If, as biologists say, the human being is but one organismic pole in interaction with the environmental pole, and if there is no strict line of demarcation between the two, it follows that the depth value of words penetrates to the deep unconscious. And what happens on the outside of the patient in the social and physical environment is very nearly as important as what happens in his inner self.

This broadens the scope of therapy. It places an added responsibility on the therapist, for *his* values are communicated over and beyond the literal significance of his words. But this provides the therapist also with such means as are discoverable and available for use in the relevant situation-as-a-whole.

CARL WHITAKER . . .

This incident as described may illustrate milieu therapy or illustrate social interaction and its efficacy. To me it illustrates more important aspects of the psycho-dynamic status of the psychotic patient, for example, (1) his perceptions of interpersonal reality are exceptionally acute though described in symbolic terms; (2) the presence of a psychotic and decompensating illness does not preclude a degree of wellness and competence which we often disregard.

The more vital deductions from this incident relate to the psychotherapeutic process. (1) The therapeutic antibiotic is the maturity of the individual with whom the patient is relating. The Negro attendant is pictured by the patient in her true colors when he is psychotic; that is, mature, giving, loving in a manner that set him free. His reality picture of her in later years was painted in the colors of the culture as dull, awkward, and conventional. It seems to me we have an illustration here of the fact that maturity is not a function of intellect, of beauty, or of good English. (2) The countertransference vectors in Mrs. O, identified by her as relating to her dead husband, were effective in helping this patient recover from his psychotic episode. Maybe this case will help us develop a new respect for maturity and deep feelings on the part of the therapist. The definition of when countertransference is damaging and when it is growthful may thereby be easier for us to study and understand. (3) Communication between the psychotic patient and the persons around him is almost totally nonverbal. In fact, we teach the students of psychotherapy to assume it as an operative fact. The psychotic is fully responsive to the inner experience of the therapist.

It's All
in the Family

20

History

A student called me one evening to arrange an appointment for his sister. He said she was "confused" about her marriage. She had been separated for two years and was considering psychotherapy as a means of working out how she really felt about obtaining a divorce. It became clear that he felt considerable urgency and wanted me to see her at his home which was a short drive from mine.

Upon my arrival he took me aside and told me that his sister had been hospitalized twice for a total period of about a year, and that she had had ECS treatments. Between hospitalizations she had seen a psychiatrist for individual therapy but had terminated shortly and to some extent blamed him for her second commitment and the shock treatment she received. The mother had a history of hospitalization and ECS; the father had died in a psychiatric ward.

It was quickly evident that the patient was suffering an acute psychotic episode. Her first words, spoken with a quiet terror, were: "You're not going to shock me, are you? I won't talk with you if you're going to shock me." I assured her that I would not and asked the brother and his wife to leave us for an hour.

The next hour and a quarter was a rambling, incoherent account of moral directives from God and her dead father, voices accusing her of being a prostitute, rejection by her brothers and sisters and later her husband, baby-snatching rings who were after her child, and so forth. Intermittently calm and extremely emotional, she would smile vacantly one moment and break into tears the next.

Piecing together scraps of her narrative, there emerged a picture of severe deprivation—both material and psychological—throughout her whole childhood. She was one of five brothers and two sisters in an immigrant family from a middle-Eastern culture in which women occupy a low position. She was constantly made aware of her inferior status, especially by her brothers and mother. A particularly traumatic event which reinforced her feelings of worthlessness was a seduction by one of her older brothers when she was 17. During her teens all members of the family ate alone. Each kept his or her food separately in the refrigerator, and there was constant bickering and accusations of theft of each others' food. Except for a few early memories of her father, she recounted not one incident which had the slightest show of mutual affection among the family members. It is noteworthy that in spite of this environment, she put herself through college.

Her recent past is a continuation of the pattern of rejection and deprivation. Her husband left her. Her brother committed her. She and her three-year-old daughter live in a small apartment with a younger brother and sister, who rail at her constantly, and an ambulatory schizophrenic mother.

Incident

At the end of this hour there seemed to be no satisfactory course of therapeutic action. The simplest and most expedient solution was to suggest that she be committed. But her two previous hospitalizations appeared to have done nothing constructive and a good deal that was destructive. I felt that a repetition of that experience and its probable consequence—a long series of commitments and remissions—simply must be avoided if any alternative offered the slightest hope. I could simply give her brother the names of several psychiatrists and suggest that she see one. But this, too, seemed out of the question. It was very clear that she had consented to see me only because her brother knew me and because I was a psychologist and therefore would not give her ECS. Furthermore, I did not feel that a psychiatric colleague would welcome the case any more than I. As for treating her individually myself, there were several factors about which I was concerned. First, as a psychologist I would obviously overstep an understood treatment prerogative by taking on an out-and-out psychotic with a hospital record. As much as I wished to help her, I thought of the possibility of my burgeoning private practice coming to an abrupt end should she act out with her child, husband, or any of the hated family members, the tremendous latent hostility that seethed in her. Second, her financial situation would not allow for a protracted period of therapy, even at a nominal fee. Finally, her attitudes toward her family were so fierce that it seemed unlikely that she would be able to work them through in relation to a therapist who might achieve significance for her only after a relatively long time.

The best course of action seemed to be an attempt to build on what resources existed in the family, namely, her brother and sister-in-law. I explained to them the conditions under which I would work with her. There must be at least one consultation with a psychiatrist, both as a medical and legal precaution. She would come for therapy three times a week with her brother and sister-in-law who would also participate. I explained in detail the psychological expectations in this arrangement—that they were to become sources of strength and support for her, that a great deal of vituperation would be directed at them, especially toward the brother, and that this "group therapy" would probably last at least from three to six months. In order to give them a foretaste of what they could expect, the four of us met for another hour. It worked very well. The client became much more rational and toward the end she and her brother embraced for the first time in many years. I asked them to think over the therapeutic plan and call the next day.

At this writing I have seen them for one month. The psychiatrist whom she consulted agreed that she was not homicidal or suicidal and also prescribed drugs as a supplement to psychotherapy. Therapy has not been without many critical moments, and although her general movement is positive, such things as one highly agitated hour, the intense "unreasonable" hatred and insulting behavior often directed at her brother and sister-in-law as well as the incessant demands she places on them, her "childish" refusal to take the prescribed drugs, and the several hours occupied with seemingly meaningless chatter often make the "co-therapists" very discouraged with, and rejecting of her. At such times I focus on a clarification of their feelings toward her, and also attempt to get them to see things from her point of view. In general, they have risen to the occasion far beyond my expectations.

Discussion

I would like to have some theoretical as well as practical comments on this group approach. Can the old resentments toward her brother be reduced enough to allow mutual affection to be felt? Or will those resentments stand in the way of psychotherapy? Is this too much to ask of persons without therapeutic training? I would especially value knowing if someone utilizes this approach in such critical cases and what are the results?

NATHAN ACKERMAN . . .

This incident confronts us with a challenge in mental health for which our community holds presently no adequate solution. It is the plaguing problem of how to care for a selected fraction of our psychotic citizens within the fold of the family and the community. This is a sad and pressing problem, continuously with us, and yet we are thus far unable to do much about it.

Let us honestly concede at the outset, that hospitals for the mentally ill serve first the interest of the community, and only secondarily the needs of the mentally ill. Persons who fall ill psychotically hold a certain critical nuisance value for family and community. This burden is peculiarly aggravated in our time owing to the smaller size of the average family and its increased social mobility. There is the trend of family members to seek satisfactions and meaningful associations outside the family in the larger community; each individual tends to go his own way. The traditional family function of nursing of the sick is now largely removed from the family to hospitals and clinics. For a variety of reasons having to do with change in the social pattern of family and community, the nuclear family is less able and less motivated to care for their own sick ones. This includes the question of caring for psychotic members of the family.

It is this social factor, among others, which has increased the demand for early hospital admission of mentally sick persons. To be sure, this more quickly relieves family and community of a harrowing burden; from the point of view of the patient, however, the story is a different one. He is exiled. He enters an isolated, timeless life behind walls in a strange institution which unfortunately offers little chance for nourishment of the healthy components of human relations. For many such patients it is the point of no return. The removal of the sick ones from the family fold is one sign of the times. It is a reflection of the utilitarian values which attach to our modern fast-living industrial community.

This critical incident in psychotherapy depicts the torturesome dilemma of a family with two such psychotic persons, a psychotic daughter and a psychotic mother, who make their home with one brother and his wife. In the description of the situation there is no mention of consideration of hospitalization of the psychotic mother. For the daughter, it is, of course, the easy prescription. It would relieve this small family of a terrible load but, as the therapist indicates, another hospitalization would have little to offer this young psychotic woman. With respect to the preservation of family life, there is intrinsic in such a human situation a deep value conflict. Should the young brother and his wife sacrifice the psychotic member of the family? Should they relieve themselves of this burden through hospitalization and pursue their own separate lives? Or, should they "care for their own"?

There is no easy answer for this dilemma. Regardless of the sincerity of the brother's feeling for the sick members of his family, he is impelled to consider his personal interests and those of his wife. Were they to have children, the burden would virtually be an impossible one. The decision of this young couple to try to help the psychotic sister within the family was possible only because they had no children.

In this instance the therapist elected to try to help this young psychotic girl through a form of group treatment of the family. This is a valiant effort in the face of almost insuperable difficulties. It is praiseworthy that this family expresses its love of the sick sister by trying to live through her illness with her. Up to the present there is little precedent for the attempt to treat a psychotic within the home in a manner which involves all members of the family in the patient's therapy. This is a complex but logical undertaking. A patient becomes psychotic within her family; it is appropriate to try to heal the psychotic illness within the family. It is a sorely needed level of intervention, but systematic research is required to determine the level of its potential effectiveness.

Such research is currently in progress in some parts of the country. There is the effort to treat schizophrenics together with the family group within the *National Institute of Mental Health*. There is also the *Boston Psychiatric Home Service* which endeavors to treat the relations of a psychotic person with family members, at first within the hospital while the patient is being prepared for discharge, and later, a continuation of the group approach to patient and family within the home. One is also reminded here of Dr. Querida's psychiatric services within the home in Amsterdam, Holland. There is also my own research in the problems of the mental health of the family. If this level of intervention proves valid and feasible, it holds the promise of relieving the excessive demand for new admissions to mental hospitals.

For many years this writer has been absorbed in exploring the possibilities of dealing with emotional and mental disturbances through evaluation and therapy of family relationships. This is briefly called family diagnosis and family therapy. Some aspects of this work have been published in a variety of journals. A systematic presentation of the entire problem appears in my recent book.[1]

In this particular case the prime value expressed by the therapist is the need of the family to value the patient, to accept, understand, and support her, despite her psychosis. He endeavors particularly to deal with the disturbed relations of the patient and her brother, to provide opportunity for catharsis of her wounded, embittered emotions. He guides the brother in ways of tolerating the patient's hostile abuse so as not to take these insults personally. This is all for the purpose of making possible an emotional reunion of sister and brother, a rediscovery of the old bond of affection between them.

There can be no question as to the appropriateness of this goal. On the other hand, there are numerous pitfalls due to the enormous personal investment which is required of family members. Are they willing? Can they really take the psychotic girl's abuse? And for how long? Can they mobilize in themselves that larger capacity for loving which would enable them to patiently await the long postponed reward of improvement in the patient's condition, and appreciation of her family? The home is turned into a nursing unit, a controlled therapeutic environment. The islands of residual health in the patient must be supported and nourished. A healthier image of self needs to be encouraged, to restore self-esteem. The emotional needs of the patient must be gratified within reason. The patient's conflicts require an avenue of expression within the context of family relations with the effort to find workable solutions. Finally, the patient's defenses against anxiety must be understood, and the more healthy of these must be supported by the family environment.

RUDOLF DREIKURS . . .

This incident is of interest because the therapist raises the question of "group therapy" with the whole family, or at least with several members of the family besides the patient. Such therapy with the "social atom" has

[1] Nathan W. Ackerman, *The Psychodynamics of Family Life: Diagnosis and Treatment of Family Relationships* (New York: Basic Books, 1958).

been frequently described. It is a standard procedure with many Adlerians. Mrs. Starr[2] described psychodrama with the social atom of the patient which we do almost routinely. A. A. Low[3] found discussion of the patient with the member's family in the patient's presence exceedingly helpful, and Meiers devised a technique of treating an inaccessible patient through members of his family.

The dynamic factors which makes such an approach effective are manifold. Naturally, previous resentments disappear when the patient and members of his family together discuss the patient's problems, and all participants get a better insight in each other's problems, as far as their relationship is concerned. In this sense, "Understanding is forgiving," at least very often.

The patient usually learns more from interpretation when these are not made to him directly, but to others in his presence.

In the treatment of borderline cases or psychotics, it seems to be necessary to limit explanations to one basic and most disturbing aspect of the patient's problems. With relatives being present, it is natural that the exploration of the patient's conflicts and problems will be limited and not cover as wide a range of problems as individual sessions generally entail. This is another reason why this form of procedure may be advisable for this kind of patient.

FAY KARPF . . .

We have here a case and incident which illustrate strikingly the recent tendency to regard the individual in therapy not merely as an individual basically in conflict with his environment, as has very largely been the practice the past couple of decades, but essentially as a family and group member in a distinctive sociocultural setting. The case under consideration is especially appropriate for illustration of this more integrated conception, and the interesting manner in which it is applied in a novel "group therapy" approach in an exceptionally difficult situation is highly suggestive of promising new areas for the extension of the usual view of group psychotherapy. In particular, problems having strong cultural implications, which have often proved resistant to individual therapy, offer promise of more fruitful handling in terms of the illustrated experimental approach.

In the usual handling of such problems, the patient is frequently left isolated and alienated from his natural social contacts and controls, with resultant feelings of guilt, loneliness, and worthlessness. In the present case, an attempt is made, whether deliberately or by necessity, to avoid these

[2] Adeline Starr, "Psychodrama within the Child's Social Atom," *Group Psychother.*, V (1953), pp. 222–25.

[3] A. A. Low, *Mental Health Through Will Training* (Boston: Christopher, 1952).

difficulties by securing for the patient cooperative and understanding support in her own family group, thus enabling her to bridge more constructively the immense gap between her restrictive cultural background and the free and easy life of the American college community.

It may be noted, incidentally, that the patient's parents may not have had the benefit of such easing of a difficult transition, and this may well have complicated their adjustment and their unhappy hospital careers. The patient herself was likewise initiated into this destructive pattern and it was only interrupted by the new therapeutic set-up. It would thus appear that, whatever the legalistic involvements may have been in the situation, the new treatment approach was a fortunate occurrence for the patient.

Since at the time of this report, the new therapeutic procedure had continued for only one month, the outcome remained uncertain even though the therapy seemed to be proceeding in a generally favorable direction. Accordingly, the therapist asks for comments on his approach and for confirming therapeutic experiences. This commentator can report the experimental use in specially selected cases of variations of the therapeutic set-up described and with decidedly satisfactory results in regard to (1) patient adjustment, (2) cooperation of family, (3) continuing therapeutic effect after formal therapy is terminated. It would seem worthwhile, therefore, to explore further the possible uses of likely family aids as "co-therapists," especially in the kind of cultural complicated situations illustrated in the present case and critical incident.

David Riesman . . .

The therapist's procedure here seems to me an exceptionally ingenious combination of psychodrama with "real" actors and the use of lay auxiliaries. Since the patient comes of an ethnic group (Polish, perhaps) in which virtually no understanding of therapeutic goals and methods could be expected, it seems especially sound not to alienate her entirely from her background by acculturating her to the therapist in lonely isolation, but rather to try to bring several members of her group along with her as psychotherapeutic fellow travellers. These fellow travellers may act, it seems to me, as they usually do in a "front" organization, namely to mediate between the hard core (in this case the patient) and the outside world (represented by the therapist).

Incidentally, the patient's reaction to shock therapy as a form of punishment for worthless women such as herself seems to me not necessarily delusional. I have heard of a state hospital in a backward area where the resident is asked in the morning by the visiting brass "Who *needs* shock today?"—that is, who misbehaved? In impatient use of shock in despair of milder measures, American culture seems to me to have shown its more mechanical and cavalierly melioristic side.

It is interesting to me that so very many of these incidents involve behavior by the therapist which was more active than his rules of the game had traditionally allowed—behavior, moreover, which apart from the rules was inherently more risky both in exposing the subjectivity of the therapist and in many cases in endangering a routinized plateau of conciliation between therapist and patient. If we ask why today therapy so often takes much longer than in the "classic" cases of Freud and his early disciples, one factor is no doubt (as I have indicated in some of my comments) the loss of the original shock value of verbal confrontation with reality or of an acceptance of people in a position of authority who would previously have denounced the patient for his or her "bad thoughts" and misbehavior. It is only in the residual superstitious strata that one can still find dramatic symptoms giving way to a dramatic cure. Many therapists have recognized this altered situation and have pleaded for more active therapeutic measures (among them Frieda Fromm-Reichmann, John Rosen, and the Gestalt therapists). Yet a good deal of what the sociologists call "pluralistic ignorance" would seem still to be operative among therapists if they select as critical those incidents in which they were markedly active and transcended the limitations in which they were schooled. It would not be surprising if therapists, too, need group therapy in the same sense that some of their patients do, namely to discover that they have all disobeyed the rules and can now form a union of sinners.

I would hope therefore that if a new volume of this sort is to be attempted, new problems on another level will emerge in addition to the ones dealt with here—problems in which the aim of the therapist goes beyond securing the patient's minimal adjustment or communication (and I am far from deprecating these aims)—that is, where the patient, cured of handicapping symptoms and gross character disorders, can face the ethical alternatives, reflected in his character structures, with which our society presents even its most privileged members. Here the problem facing the therapists would seem to me activity of another sort. They would no longer be facing patients with minimal cultural demands (for alcoholic sobriety in one case or sexual restraint in another) but with more complex valuational choices. Here ethical novelties may arise where it may not be enough either to draw on the moral capital we have all inherited which rules out grossly destructive and self-destructive behavior or even on the general mandate to the patient to "be himself" where choice remains within the range of socially acceptable behavior and is therefore free. To what extent can the therapist become an educator and a moral guide (as Erich Fromm has recommended)? Critical incidents in this area would seem to me to present less sharp but no less experimental dilemmas.

BESS SONDEL . . .

Indirect methods of therapy seem to me to be justifiable on the grounds of general acceptance of field theory of personality. Since therapeutic methods rely on the communication process, I venture the opinion that where a frontal attack on a problem may be highly threatening, indirection may be the preferred means by which to effect desired change in behavior.

It is conceded now that behavior is not an isolated phenomenon. As Dewey pointed out several decades ago, a habit is as much a part of the environment as it is a part of the human being. Sometimes it is much easier to manipulate the environment—social and physical—than to attempt to change the structure of an individual.

There are three ways of considering the disturbed personality in a field:

1. There is the inner self.

In the case of this patient, there is fear. There is tension. There is conflict without stabilizing values. There is disorder.

How can the therapist make order here?

The means of the therapist are limited to verbal and nonverbal communication. And these may fall upon a closed system.[4] Messages from the outside may, in other words, effect little change in the unstructured self.

2. There is the environment—social and physical.

It is in the nature of things that there are both order and disorder, and, because the patient is himself unstructured, he is incapable of distinguishing between the two.

What can the therapist do here?

It is sometimes possible for the therapist to manipulate the physical environment favorably. In this case, the therapist introduced aspects of the relevant social environment to effect change in his patient.

3. There is need for the individual to interact purposively with his world.

Here the individual must function constructively within the situation-as-a-whole. For the disturbed patient, this is an impossible task. For what is required here is that an organized self engage in cross organization with the relevant environment in order to transform it in the interest of a predetermined goal. Cross organization is structured change. Cross organization is planned change. Cross organization is the *use of change* in the interest of purpose. This is growth that flourishes on continuous reconstruction of the purposive self.

What can the therapist do here?

[4] See Charles Morris, *The Open Self* (Englewood Cliffs, N.J.: Prentice-Hall, Inc., 1948), and Kenneth E. Boulding, *The Image* (Ann Arbor: The University of Michigan Press, 1956).

In this case, the therapist introduced aspects of the relevant social environment into the therapeutic situation-as-a-whole. This amplified the field. The therapist could induce change in less disturbed individuals and observe the effects of this change on the patient, for any change in any one aspects of a human situation-as-a-whole must inevitably change every other (sentient) aspect of the human situation-as-a-whole. Observation of changes may be used as new information by which to evaluate strategy and correct procedures. This is, of course, the exercise of feedback.

In my opinion, the therapist proceeded intelligently because:

1. He introduced relevant aspects of the whole problematical situation;
2. He was able to observe the relationship between essential elements of the situation-as-a-whole;
3. He was able to observe possible causes of the disturbance of his patient; and
4. He was thus able to work directly and indirectly on his patient.

In any behavioral situation that involves communication, it has been my experience that a disturbed person is helped automatically by the realization that behavior is *behavior within a field*. This seems to help the individual look outward—and not hopelessly inward. This disperses guilt. This reinforces power. The individual is not alone. He is but part of his world. He is only one pole—but not a pawn.

Field theory of communication would seem to force the therapist to employ means that take him beyond the inner life of his patient.[5]

FREDERICK C. THORNE . . .

There are many very sick patients who can be helped by nonmedical therapists particularly when conventional psychiatric resources have been exhausted or unsuccessful. The psychologist in this case was wise to begin with a "group therapy" situation until he became reassured that the client's mental status would not deteriorate and that it was safe to continue. We have utilized the same device many times, usually finding that "group therapy" may be discontinued in favor of private individual therapy after one or two sessions. There are some dangers and disadvantages in having close relatives who are intimately involved in the client's neurotic disorder as members of the therapeutic group. While it may be desirable to start with a relative in the room, perhaps to reassure the family or to indulge the client who cannot part with the relative for a moment, usually more can be accomplished by having the group consist of strangers who may have

[5] See Bess Sondel, *Communication: A Field Theory* (Chicago: The University of Chicago Press, 1958).

similar problems but who are not emotionally involved with the client. While it may be desirable to have other family members gain insight organically by taking part in group therapy with a client, this advantage may be outweighed in the long run by making public details of the client's life which might better have remained private. While it is desirable for the therapist to protect himself, he should also be secure enough to take some personal risk in assuming clinical responsibilities which eventually may work out better for the client. The therapist is usually safe enough if he insists on psychiatric consultation and establishes a reputation among medical colleagues as being "sound."

Carl Whitaker . . .

For many years psychotherapy has limited itself by the tradition of a one-to-one relationship, actually set up as a research method. The fact that a family has grown up together indicates the depth of their mutual affective investment in each other. To say that hostility is strong between the members and affection merely available contradicts our knowledge of dynamics. They are equal. The problem is: How can we best help the patient develop a capacity to function interpersonally in such a way that she can fit into her social structure?

In this situation the social structure is culturally and psychologically sick. Naming the members of the family subculture as "co-therapists" seems a less accurate term than "group therapy of the family." Midelfort[6] uses members of the family as co-therapists. He takes the most usable family member as nurse to the patient and the most communicable family member as translator. The latter is usually a child and is in on each interview.

Our group has done work with couples on a somewhat similar basis and with cases as severe as the one reported. Some of this work has been done with two therapists and some with one. In a few cases two therapists have treated the entire family consisting of from four to six members. The process of therapy seems quite solid in many of these couples and families and fairly clear of transference and countertransference complications. The structural planning for therapy seems well done in this case. Family solidity will help, and the therapist can now keep the new family from reopening the illness.

The homeostatic stability of the family group is usable. Instead of merely saying, "The family made him sick," we say, "the family made him sick, and the family also kept him functional until last week when he went psychotic." We wonder if the family group is not easier to change than

---

[6] Christian F. Midelfort, *The Family in Psychotherapy* (New York: McGraw-Hill Book Co., Inc., 1957).

the psychological unit, just as the psychological unit is easier to change than the physiological. We plan for six months of weekly interviews with the family group. This should then eventuate in individual psychotherapy for the patient while the family or some other member may return for an occasional joint session. We have on occasion tried using a third staff person for the individual therapy, but this does not seem necessary.

"What Are You Hiding?"

21

History

A woman in her middle forties consulted me with the following complaints:

1. She always feels depressed.
2. She cannot enjoy life at all.
3. She has "awful" thoughts.

About the last one, it seems that when she sees a sharp instrument, such as a scissors, she feels an urge to kill her youngest child, a girl of ten. She is appalled by these horrible thoughts.

During exploratory discussions, it turns out that for the last several years, sexual relations with her husband have been relatively infrequent and usually unsatisfactory. She states repeatedly she neither misses sex nor is unhappy about the low frequency of mutual satisfaction. She claims never to have had extra- or pre-marital relations, nor any such thoughts.

Incident

After two months of therapy, during which period the patient unceasingly complained of severe emotional distress, which seemed almost apparent in her appearance, and after a good relationship with
the therapist was firmly established, the therapist asked point-blank
whether or not there was something in her life she had concealed,
which might disturb her. The reason for this request was the following: the patient gave the impression of being a perfectionist and was
extremely concerned with propriety and goodness, and never revealed anything derogatory about herself. The therapist believed
that the patient was consciously withholding something—probably a
sexual affair—which might have been related to her homicidal impulses. The patient denied, with great affectation of sincerity, anything whatsoever of any importance. The therapist did not accept this
statement and insisted to the patient that there must be something she
was withholding which she just had to reveal. The therapist made it
very clear that "This is your opportunity to get well; now is your
chance."

Finally, reluctantly, the patient admitted that there was something in her life, so shameful that she could not possibly discuss it. For
three interviews the content was whether or not the patient would
confess her sin. Finally, she told the following: at the age of six she
had been induced by another little girl to permit a dog to perform
cunnilingus on her. On and off throughout her life she had practiced
this perverted behavior, even after marriage, although she did deny
recent practice.

Immediately after these disclosures the patient obtained evident
relief from her depression. Besides, she showed a change of attitude
from a somewhat skeptical pose to one of reasonableness and was able
to accept the fact that her feelings of guilt for her perverted practices had generated these obsessions toward her daughter. It was explained that others also have committed sinful actions but are nevertheless able to accept themselves. The obsessive homicidal feelings
subsided slowly. Therapy is still going on, but on a more satisfactory
basis.

Discussion

The therapist reasoned somewhat as follows: This woman who is
suffering considerably both from general depression and obsessive
thoughts should be given immediate relief if possible. She is very

compulsive, a self-protecting kind of individual, and doubtlessly, if the therapy ever will be successful in helping her, she must be able to reveal certain guilt feelings, which must be behind these two manifestations of her sickness. After two months, there was no sign of any softening of her wall of self-protection, and the therapist felt: Maybe she will never get the courage to be honest with herself and me. Should one then, in the classical manner of a nonintervening therapist, permit this individual to go on perhaps for years, perhaps getting worse as the pressure strengthens, denying her guilt? But was there really something bothering her of which she was aware and which was causing these symptoms? Would forcing her to speak about matters that she did not want to, help her? The therapist gambled that there must be something, and that disclosure would help the immediate symptoms and permit the therapy to proceed more rapidly; Consequently, convinced that there *must* be something, the therapist did push and did insist until finally the disclosure came out.

It seems to me that the issue is one that involves ethics and values rather than technique or theory: How important is distress? Is it mandatory for a physician to reduce suffering at the expense of theory? Do apparently successful results justify unusual procedures? Had things turned out differently (that is, suppose the patient had left therapy), would my approach still have been justified when I felt morally certain that she was withholding something?

RUDOLF DREIKURS . . .

Here we have another example of a psychological shock treatment. Many of Freud's early analytic efforts brought results through the use of the discovery of a traumatic event, a discovery usually experienced as a shock. One must keep in mind that the therapist's ability to shock the patient is often the first attempt on his part to make an impression on the patient. The prevalent passivity and permissiveness is pleasantly interrupted when the therapist suddenly moves into action.

Here we see a patient unceasingly complaining for two months. One can easily assume that the patient got fed up with the procedure in which the therapist had nothing more to offer than to listen. After all, the patient was disturbed and wanted help. Now the therapist thought that he had a good idea when he assumed that the patient withheld something. Any patient who is given free reign in talking will only tell what she wants to tell, and not necessarily what is going on within her. Even free association, supposed to get to the depths of the unconscious, does not necessarily induce the patient to bring forth what really bothers her. This is then called resistance, which does not change the patient's reluctance or determination.

Here the therapist became insistent. And after he got the "confession" of the sex relationship with a dog, everything seems to proceed well, as if this confession would really form the turning point.

It is quite obvious what happened in the therapeutic procedure. The patient apparently was convinced that she was no good. A proper analysis of her life style and of her present field of action could have easily brought out these facts and offered sufficient basis for a discussion which may have led to a reconsideration of the patient's attitudes and convictions. But since such an educational procedure was apparently not attempted, it needed some other drastic experience to prompt a change in the patient.

We have no evidence whatsoever for the therapist's assumption that "her feelings of guilt for her perverted practices had generated these obsessions toward her daughter." It seems rather that the practices and the ensuing guilt feelings as well as the obsessions are concommitent symptoms of the same basic problem, namely, her conviction that she is no good. The therapist by his calm and undisturbed acceptance of her sinful deeds apparently helped her toward an assumption that perhaps she was not as bad as she thought she was. All the theoretical questions which the therapist raises seem to have, therefore, no connection with the incident which he reported. Where morals and values enter the picture is hard to detect, unless it is the withholding of moral judgment exhibited by the therapist, which, however, is essential for any therapy.

For this reason, we cannot accept either that his insistence was for the purposes of "immediate relief." It was rather his technique—and a not very skillful one for this—to get deeper into the problems of the patient, at least as she experienced them. Had he been able to win her confidence and induce her to open up more, he would not have needed such a shock treatment. Her "wall of self-protection" should not have stopped the therapist in his therapeutic effectiveness had he known how to deal with it more adequately. After all, don't most patients have a reluctance to show the therapist how bad they really are, while at the same time trying to convince him that they are utterly bad and hopeless?

This example shows the same deficiency in psychological procedures, once the trained and indoctrinated form of therapy proves inadequate. Such shock procedures are clumsy, in bad taste, and mostly cruel. In almost every case they are unnecessary. The therapist should know better ways of helping the patient to open up and to reveal himself.

ALBERT ELLIS . . .

This incident gives us another good example of how active intervention on the part of a courageous and competent therapist may lead to excellent results, where a more passive technique of psychotherapy might well have missed the boat entirely, or at best achieved results after much needless suffering on the part of the patient.

I am reminded by this incident of a similar case of my own. I was seeing a highly intelligent teacher who had urinary and defecatory symptoms which seemed to be closely related to her sexual problems, but she was loathe to discuss sexual issues and, in spite of my probing, she remained quite vague in this connection. She particularly insisted that she had never masturbated nor had any problem in relation to masturbation. I was most doubtful about this, but could not get any additional information with repeated questioning.

Feeling that she was definitely resisting, I determined to make an even more concerted frontal attack on her masturbatory feelings and actions. In spite of her insistence that she had never masturbated, I forced the issue and asked her if she knew what masturbation consisted of in females. She looked confused, so I said: "Masturbation in females is not usually like it is commonly supposed to be in so-called dirty jokes or conversational innuendo. Do you know how it's actually done?" She became quite flustered and finally blurted out: "Well, I've never used a candle, or anything like that." "No doubt you haven't," I persisted, "but masturbation in females very rarely consists of using a candle or anything like that. What it does consist of is utilizing some kind of friction, such as manual friction, on the external sex organs or the clitoris. Have you ever done anything like that? I'm sure you must have, since almost all girls do at one time or another. Maybe you pressed your legs together, or rubbed up against desks, or did things along that line. Can't you remember now?"

My patient suddenly blushed furiously and became completely mute for almost ten minutes. After that, slowly, and at my continued persistence, she indicated that she had been masturbating for years. It was then easy to show her that she had doubtlessly known all along what she had been doing, but had refused to acknowledge this fact by pretending that masturbation consisted only of inserting objects into the vagina. This meant that she must have been exceptionally guilty about continuing to masturbate; and her guilt was, at least in part, causing her defecatory and urinary symptoms. The patient quickly acknowledged this and began to improve considerably, whereas previously we had been able to effect virtually no movement.

It seems to me, therefore, that the therapist in this critical incident has done a fine job of forcing the issue and helping his patient overcome her sexual and general blocking. The one point on which I disagree with him is his feeling that the issue in question is one that involves ethics and values rather than technique or theory. I see little or no question of ethics in this particular instance, because it seems to me evident that the patient's distress is most important and that it is definitely mandatory for a psychotherapist to reduce human suffering at the expense of theory. Otherwise, he should remain a theoretician and not a practicing therapist.

The real question is, however: Assuming that the therapist's primary aim is that of reducing his patient's distress, should he, in any given case, try to reduce it as quickly as possible, and sometimes risk immediate but superficial "cure;" or should he, instead, concentrate on the deepest and most thoroughgoing type of "cure," even if this sometimes means leaving the patient temporarily in distress? This, it seems to me, is a matter of technique rather than ethics. My own feeling is that, if it were a matter of choice here, the choice should usually, though not always, be settled in favor of effecting a deep-seated instead of a quick improvement. Actually, however, I believe that in most instances getting at the patient's main problem as quickly as possible, and hence reducing his anxiety and tension, is the best possible, and often the only, method of achieving the most significant and lasting forms of improvement.

In other words, I do not feel that quick "cures" are necessarily superficial ones; but, on the contrary, that real improvement almost always follows the alleviation of painful symptoms and is often never achieved without such alleviation. Some of the most profound "cures" I have seen in my patient have been achieved very quickly; while many of my patients who are very slowly improved never reach the highest degree of integration and improvement.

I am consequently all in favor of getting to the heart of the patient's problems and symptomatology as quickly as possible, and of reducing his distress to a maximum degree in a minimum period of time. Occasionally, I find this procedure contraindicated, as some patients will quit therapy as soon as their presenting symptoms are ameliorated. But in the great majority of cases, relief of distress leads to a desire for permanent relief, and often is the only possible entree into profound personality reorganization. This is one of the main reasons why I find that highly active procedures, such as that employed in this critical incident, are often most beneficial and practical.

IAGO GALDSTON . . .

Perhaps the best way to initiate comment on this so-called critical incident is to consider the statement of "the issue" advanced by the therapist.

He affirms that the issue is one that involves "ethics and values rather than technique or theory." What is the ethics involved in this case? Seemingly, whether or not it is mandatory for a physician to reduce suffering at the expense of theory. Again, he inquires, does success justify unorthodox procedures? Finally, he asks, suppose that he had failed because of his procedure, equating failure to the patient's leaving therapy.

The therapist's problem in ethics seemingly reduces to this! Is it ethical to violate theory to achieve effective results? Surely there is no other ethics involved. Palpably then the therapist is cowed by "techniques and theory." Let us treat his queries in detail.

He asked: "How important is distress?" It is very important. It is that intrapsychic state which makes the patient aware that all is not well and that brings him under therapy.

It was taught by some of the older analysts, Freud and Ferenczi, that it was not wise to relieve a patient's distress before he gained insight. And yet, if the distress is overwhelming, it must, of course, be alleviated or else the patient is too disrupted to be available for therapy.

"Is it mandatory for a physician to reduce suffering at the expense of theory?" It *is* mandatory in the ultimate sense that a physician reduces suffering "or what's a heaven for?" But the judicious physician, one who is wise in the ways of therapy, will not reduce suffering at the expense of anything if suffering is contributory to the ultimate and fundamental recovery of the patient. As an aside: "at the expense of theory" is in effect a meaningless phrase. Again, "apparently successful results" justify nothing unless the appearances turn out to be valid, sound, and enduring.

One comment on the final query of the therapist: would his approach still have been justified had things turned out differently? The answer is simple: if, as Cromwell said, "by the bowels of Christ" the therapist thought himself to be right, then he *was* right, come hell or brimstone.

Now as to the case. The "infraction" of the therapist was only the beginning and not the end. That he broke through by his confrontation of the patient was all to the good. And that it led her to "confess her sin" was the "payoff." That she was able to accept her feelings of guilt in her perverse practices cleared some of the obstacles in the way to self-acceptance and interpersonal relations. All this, however, does not quite explain her obsession, and, more crucially, none of this dynamically explains why this woman persisted in her perverted behavior for so many years after her marriage. In other words, in the humble opinion of this commentator, the crux of the case lies not in her secrecy about her original sin, but rather in the dynamics of her persistent pursuit of the perverted practices, and her rejection of the normal heterosexual satisfaction nominally available to her in marriage.

VINCENT HERR . . .

The middle-aged lady in this case presents a fairly clear picture of exaggerated perfectionism resulting in obsessive compulsions. One might even argue that the motive for the extreme goodness-tendency might have been partially or wholly unrecognized and that it really was a need or desire to make amends for some subjectively evaluated wrong-doing.

Before commenting on the "ethical" issues that might be involved, with regard to forcing a confession from the client, this writer would like more information on the following points:

1. Did the lady, perhaps, remember too vaguely at the start of the treatment just what the circumstances of the childhood incident were? Perhaps, as often happens, she remembered only that it was very "disgraceful"? If so, then the fixation or return to the evil practice in the later years only served to add to her confusion, as to the real amount of guilt which she experienced in the initial childhood performance. If she had been really induced by others to perform the first act and excused herself on this account, then she probably excused subsequent acts on the same basis— somehow feeling that she was not to blame for the abnormal behavior— yet sensing all along that it might be interfering with the pursuit of normal outlets. This case is a familiar one for confessors, and leads to interesting forms of "conscience" which it would be too tedious to relate here. But this vague recollection of "guilty-not-guilty" serves to confuse many a doer-of-what-might-otherwise-be-considered the very good and perfect. Yet the person or client actually never fully knows whether it is right or not, in certain areas of behavior. As treatment went on, we suggest, not that the person began to accept herself as a wrong-doer, but that rather she accepted the fact that she would never know (or care much) whether the childhood incident was a sin or not.

2. It might be asked whether the woman was "unhappy" in her married life precisely because of the "guilt" or because she (as a consequence of the confusion) never related with people generally in a healthy way? The more she became at odds with people the more inadequate she became generally, and realizing this she set up a whole series of compensating mechanisms, such as the extreme striving after perfection and goodness on the surface.

3. It struck the present writer as very significant that the homicidal feelings should have been directed toward the *youngest* daughter. This feeling was probably a sign of her deeper feelings that this was her last chance to save another person (image of her former self) from a like misfortune, from being seduced into similar malpractices. Such displaced feelings often crop up in dealing with people who are perfectionists, and confessors sometimes at least learn to recognize them for what they are. Just why they should lead to such extreme forms of behavior as "killing" or being impelled to "kill" the one who is to be protected from evil might baffle the analyst as well as the confessor, but it certainly shows the plausibility of the account given above, namely that the client is on shaky ground with regard to her own

"responsible" acts generally, not knowing what really is or really is not right or wrong for her.

The therapist deserves highest praise for what is called "forcing" the confession. This writer has found no law or principle which would prevent counselors and therapists from *ever* acting in a very directive manner. What if the client had discontinued treatment after refusing to confess? Surely one of two things could have happened—the experience of confessors is generally that the person will come back later or will find someone else to whom to confess; or, as in the cases related in the literature, it might be supposed that the confession never would be made and that a life of suffering would be the lot of the patient. Whenever the confession is made to a competent and trusted friend, the result seems to be the same—namely, release from distress and tension, and a gradual return to better human relations generally.

Obviously a priest-counselor could expatiate upon this case, but the present writer cannot help thinking of an old adage in medicine: cure like with like. This patient most probably was led into her present difficulties because she thought she had been "forced" into the original act. The therapist in the case also used a sort of "force," knowing that the patient was not too clear in her own mind about the difference between being induced to act by outside forces, and deliberately accepting herself and her acts with a feeling of true responsibility for some of them at least. It is also likely that a rather prolonged period of patient treatment will usually be needed, in order to re-educate a person in this matter of distinguishing between "accepting an act as his own," and just drifting along with circumstances. If the recent Vienna School has a quicker way to produce this effect, priests and priest-counselors would be most willing to give it a try.

O. HOBART MOWRER . . .

The material here reported reminds one of Freud's papers, "Analysis terminable and interminable,"[1] in which he asked whether or not there was any conceivable means by which analysis, which is usually "a lengthy business," might be "shortened," or "speeded up." He tells of some of the expedients undertaken both by himself and by others, without success; and then, brave man that he was, he even goes on to comment on the disappointing frequency with which apparently full-length analysis fails to give permanently satisfactory results. One cannot escape the feeling that the author of the present report is coming straight to the heart of at least one of the common causes of both the discouragingly protracted and, even then, often unproductive nature of analysis.

[1] Sigmund Freud, *Collected Papers* (London: Hogarth Press, 1950), Vol. V.

Although the therapist expresses a becoming uncertainty about the justifiability of the procedure followed in this case, it is noteworthy that there was apparently no thought in his mind about an excessively severe superego or *false* guilt. Instead, he acted squarely upon the assumption that this woman had done something really wrong and was continuing to conceal it. The reported sequence of events fully supported this premise and justified the therapeutic approach dictated thereby.

How many months or years of suffering were bypassed by this bold stroke can only be guessed; but the gain, in this respect, however substantial, carries a sobering implication. The whole procedure reminds one of religious confession, with the perhaps disquieting intimation that the secular—and avowedly scientific—approach to such matters may be in the process of self-liquidation.

What one misses in the present report, following the dramatic confession, is any suggestion of what steps were taken to help the patient repair the loss of self-esteem which the confession presumably entailed. It is true, of course, that she could now think of herself as a more *honest* person than she had previously been; but her sexually perverse behavior was also now more of a reality, in one sense, than it was prior to its admission. Can it be that one of the next steps in secular therapy will be the institution of penance and good works? The present report says that the patient, despite the relief experienced following the confession, is still in therapy. Who knows but that, by an appropriate program of redemptive action, another major shortcut might not also be achieved? Indirect reports indicate that at the Menninger Foundation, in Topeka, depressed patients are sometimes given "menial," but useful, tasks to do on the assumption that their guilt can be thus expiated more rapidly and more realistically than by self-administered psychological suffering.[2] Also, Scher[3] and Peffer *et al.*[4] have recently reported on the therapeutic value of meaningful, socially valued work in schizophrenia. Perhaps a synthesis between two long-discordant approaches is in the making here.

CARL ROGERS . . .

As I read the account of this incident, I realize that I would have handled it in a somewhat different fashion. Let me assume that the background events in therapy have been as described in this incident. I have had a very distressed client who for two months or more has never said any-

[2] H. Whitman, "Keeping Our Sanity," *Weekend Magazine,* VII (1957), 2 ff.

[3] J. M. Scher, "Schizophrenia and Task Orientation: An Experimental Study of a Structured Ward Setting," *AMA Arch. Neurol. Psychiat.* (1957).

[4] P. A. Peffer, *et al.,* "Member-Employee Program—A New Approach to the Rehabilitation of the Chronic Mental Patient," mimeographed, V. A. Hospital, Brockton, Massachusetts (1957).

thing negative in regard to herself. If this occurred, I am sure that the feeling would arise in me that she was not talking about the things that really disturbed her. If and when such feelings occur in me and are strong enough to begin to interfere with my listening to and understanding the client, then I voice them.

The point where I would differ with this therapist is that I see no advantages in making a statement about this other person. When I made a statement about another person, it can only be something which I suspect is true, but which I cannot possibly know. For me to tell another person "You are withholding something from me," is offensive to me. It seems to imply a God-like omniscience which I do not feel. I am saying something which I cannot *know* to be a fact, and hence it involves a certain amount of falsehood. All that I know to be fact is what I know to be true in me. Consequently, in a situation of this kind, it is quite likely that I might tell my client something of this sort: "I find myself hardly able to listen to what you're saying because I find myself feeling that this isn't all, that the important things are not being said." When I put it this way, simply voicing my own feelings, it leaves the client entirely free to take whatever stand or hold whatever attitude she wishes. From the picture given of this client, she would probably have replied that she *was* telling me all. I would quite genuinely be willing to accept this as her attitude, but if at a later time the same feeling arose again in me, I would again express it. I am sure that in the long run she would come to express her own fear and reluctance to share her painful past experiences, and to express her feelings about these experiences. I like my way of handling it because then I can feel completely real in the relationship at all points. I do not feel that I have been playing a role or expressing something that is slightly false.

To reveal such feelings in a relationship is not a "gimmick" on the part of the therapist, and I am sure that what I am saying can easily be misunderstood or misused. Let me describe a little further how it seems to me. I think of it as listening to myself. I am listening to my client and trying to understand the subtleties and feelings which are going on in him. If I am completely integrated in this, then this is all I hear when I listen to myself; there is nothing in me at this point except the desire to understand. But if in listening to myself I find some other feeling rising in me with a sufficient strength that it interferes with my listening and understanding, then I have discovered that it is worth expressing this feeling in the relationship. I would also point out that my response in these situations is not what I think about the client, but is rather an expression of a feeling which I find rising in me.

This is again an instance in which therapy can be the meeting of two persons. It is my hypothesis that when this relationship on my part consists of acceptance and empathy, then movement is most rapid; but when these are not my real attitudes, then whatever is real in me is more important than playing a role of acceptance or empathy. I feel that to listen to oneself accurately and to be "that which one truly is" in the relationship with the client is one of the most difficult and demanding tasks that I know. Almost inevitably we slip off into playing roles or going through the motions of being a therapist rather than being real. Yet, to the extent that we can achieve this sensitive integration in our meeting of this other separate person, we are therapists.

FREDERICK C. THORNE . . .

Probing may be indicated therapeutically when other clinical evidence indicates the existence of repressed material which is nearing the surface. However, in our opinion, it should never be done coercively as by insisting that something is wrong and the client *must* tell what is bothering her. We prefer to approach the sensitive area indirectly, introducing tangential interpretations, and insisting gently that as long as symptoms persist there must be something deeper to uncover. We use the analogy of buried cities which are progressively uncovered layer by layer. We reassure the client that it is not necessary for him to dig for material actively but simply to allow thoughts to come to the surface passively. If more active probing is necessary, we always follow up whatever material is uncovered to insure that the client is reacting in a healthy manner to it and to institute any further therapeutic measures as may be indicated.

We have learned not to be too disturbed by a client's immediate reacting to probing with intense negative emotions. It is not the immediate reaction but the long term effects which are important. Although the client may react with alarm, anxiety, resentment, embarrassment, hostility, or excitement initially, after the first shock has worked off and the newly conscious facts assimilated, the client usually comes to accept the truth and even be very thankful for the new insights. Much depends upon the tactfulness with which probing is done. Instead of blunt questions such as "Are you homosexual?" more indirect approaches such as "Are you satisfied with your sex?" or "Have you ever wanted to be of the opposite sex?" or "Have sexual feelings toward people of your own sex bothered you?" usually will be better accepted.

In our experience, there are only a relatively few topics concerning which caution must be followed in probing too fast. Obviously, many areas are relatively insensitive and probing there does little damage. Tabooed feelings such as homosexuality, incest, hostile impulses, and so forth, may be most difficult to assimilate into the self-concept and are more delicate to handle. In general, we use caution in probing or presenting any new insights which might seriously threaten the client's self-concepts and ego-structure. However, probing even in these sensitive areas may be accomplished if the therapist has good enough rapport with the client to carry him over difficult periods of reorientation.

An indirect way of probing is to inform the client that as long as he continues to have symptoms such as anxiety, there must be something beneath it which has not been uncovered yet. The client is requested to just allow his mind to free associate or just drift until new material comes up. Using the analogy of buried cities, we tell the client that as one layer of forgotten or repressed experiences is uncovered another begins to come to the surface just beneath it. This method stimulates the client to bring up new material, and usually even the deepest material will come to the surface with indirect probing.

There is always the question of whether such material is actually repressed or whether the client is embarrassed to discuss it openly. We have seen many cases in which a client might deny completely the existence of homosexual trends early in therapy, only to admit it later when he feels safe and accepted no matter what happens. Many clients are dimly aware of what is the matter but may require more or less active probing to admit the truth openly.

Incidentally, we have always been critical of research which bases too many conclusions on the client's immediate reaction to any part of therapy. It may take several days or weeks before the true, long-term reaction appears because of the fact that assimilation and reorganization is a slow process. We assume that the immediate process of psychotherapy may be unpleasant or painful to the client, and we advise him that such feelings usually indicate that we are in fact dealing with material which is important. Probing can be diagnostically important if it merely elicits telltale emotional reactions which give clues to sensitive areas.

CARL WHITAKER . . .

Central to any discussion of this incident is the statement, "After a good relationship has been firmly established." With a competent, professional, experienced, and personally mature therapist, arrival at the point thus indicated makes possible a greatly increased freedom from the usual patterns of social interaction.

Not only is this excellent move justified, but continued withholding of the therapist's interpersonal pain relating to the patient would be dishonest and an evidence of poor faith. The "getting worse" is actually loss of affect for the therapist who has proven he doesn't believe in the patient and therefore doesn't believe in himself. Persistent avoidance of the therapist's own feelings response would be as affected as the patient's denial and would

only increase the separation between them. To keep quiet and wait is as
dishonest as a misstatement. With added experience a therapist should
be less tied to psychiatric tradition. Psychiatric tradition has been preoccupied with the problems of developing a symbolic relationship. To continue first phase patterns of behavior after the therapist is in the stage of
direct give-and-take is a countertransference problem in the therapist. If
we assume the maturity of the therapist, we can assume that his impulse
to vary techniques is based on the feelings he has for the patient and not
on his own pathology.

   The integrity of the therapist is more vital to protect than the continuity
of the therapeutic process or even the integrity of the patient. Sometimes
our technical approach to therapy can become as puritannical as teaching a
medical student that he must not do a vaginal since it might make the girl
feel immoral.

Cinderella

and the Actress

22

History

This was the thirty-sixth meeting of a group of neurotic women. Mrs. Henry had sought treatment because since 1938 she had been through "tortures of the worst punishment in the form of the most obsessive thoughts anyone could have." She had obsessive preoccupations with death, sex, and other matters, in addition to compulsive rituals that seriously interfered with her activities. On certain days she could not bathe or attend to other aspects of personal hygiene. She felt compelled most of the time to wear old ragged clothes, to pick trash from the streets or out of garbage cans, and to go through elaborate rituals while walking. She presented herself at her initial interview wearing a plain black dress and no makeup. Her hair was stringy and unkempt, and her legs were bare and covered with dirt. She talked rapidly and incessantly, describing in minute detail her obsessions, compulsions, and the lengthy psychiatric treatment, including hospitalization, she had received so far, obviously with little benefit.

She was the oldest of four daughters of an alcoholic, emotionally unstable father and a rigid, quietly domineering mother. As she grew up she became increasingly concerned over her father's withdrawal from her and her mother's favoritism for one of her sisters, but she was little aware of her own hostile feelings, especially toward her mother. She had been increasingly avoided by her friends and spent much time with her mother who had become a "nervous wreck" worrying about her. Through her prolonged contact with psychiatrists she had developed exceptional facility in describing her difficulties in psychiatric jargon that tended to obscure her real feelings. Group therapy was offered to her in the hope that she might have helpful emotional experiences through it. Those seemed unlikely to occur in individual treatment because she had become so routinized in it.

Mrs. Henry soon came into open conflict with Mrs. Carnes, who grew increasingly irritated at her constant attempts to hold the floor, attract the doctor's attention, and belittle the importance of other patients' problems as compared with her own. This behavior was in striking contrast to her professed feelings of inadequacy and of consideration for others. Mrs. Carnes, an actress, had sought treatment for almost intolerable feelings of impending disaster that prevented her from performing before other people. She also feared that she was contaminating objects around her, thereby harming others. She lived with her authoritarian mother who constantly criticized her and overtly favored her older sister. This patient had received seven months of individual treatment at weekly intervals from the doctor conducting the group. She had grown so dependent on the doctor that she was unable to express any negative feelings toward him for fear of losing his support. She felt particularly threatened by Mrs. Henry's attempts to monopolize the doctor's attention and after an initial period of self-control began to criticize her for talking too much and for being unable to control her compulsions. Other members tacitly supported these attacks by not coming to Mrs. Henry's aid. They also tended to avoid her company outside the group meetings. Mrs. Henry felt that the therapist's permissive attitude toward Mrs. Carnes represented antagonism toward herself. The tension between these two patients persisted for many group sessions. Mrs. Henry gradually began to talk less and so became more acceptable to the others, but she showed no change of symptoms.

The thirty-sixth meeting was attended by Mrs. Henry, Mrs.

Carnes, and Mrs. Light. A good portion of the time was devoted to casual conversation led by Mrs. Carnes, who described in detail her artistic interests and achievements. Mrs. Henry remained restlessly silent for the most part, occasionally making rather pertinent comments without resorting to her old pattern of interrupting and taking the floor herself.

Incident

Mrs. Carnes, annoyed at Mrs. Henry's remarks, suddenly told her to "Keep quiet and don't talk so much!" The doctor, aware of the inappropriateness of Mrs. Carnes' attack, asked her what she was annoyed about. Mrs. Carnes burst into tears and told Mrs. Henry that she resented her because of her unattractive appearance and could not stand being around her. Mrs. Carnes then abruptly walked out of the room. The therapist, somewhat startled by this development, decided to go after her and ask her to return, so that things could be threshed out, hoping in this way to give her support while at the same time implying disapproval of her behavior. She came back and remained silent for the rest of the meeting, which continued to be laden with tension.

Mrs. Henry was absent from the next meeting for the first time. The therapist wrote her a note telling her that the group and he had missed her and inviting her to come for an individual interview after the next group meeting. Mrs. Henry came to the next meeting. To everyone's astonishment she wore a colorful dress, was carefully made-up, and had a permanent wave. She seemed cheerful and proudly announced that she had been absent the week before because she had an appointment to apply for a job. The other members seemed perceptibly more cordial and relaxed than before. In the individual interview Mrs. Henry told how elated she felt when Mrs. Light had told her after the meeting that the attack by Mrs. Carnes had been totally unjustified. She also had the feeling that the therapist was on her side for the first time and contrasted his behavior with that of her mother who always sided with the favorite sister, whether she was right or wrong. "I never realized how mad I was at my mother for preferring my sister to me." In this connection the doctor inquired how she felt when he asked Mrs. Carnes to return. She replied that this was reassuring to her because she felt that he would do the same for her (which he had by writing her after her absence from the next meeting).

Discussion

Mrs. Henry's tendency to monopolize the conversation had been repeatedly criticized by Mrs. Carnes during the earlier group meetings. Mrs. Henry felt, with some justification, that the doctor as well as the group supported Mrs. Carnes in her attacks. When she gradually became less talkative the group as well as the doctor accepted her more, which in turn stimulated Mrs. Carnes' feelings of rivalry toward her. When she was again attacked by Mrs. Carnes, this time without justification, she felt promptly supported by the doctor as well as by another group member. This was different from the situation at home where mother always sided with her favorite daughter. To make sure of the doctors's attitude, the patient stayed away from the next meeting—a very rebellious act for this obsessive person. Instead of reprimanding her, the doctor let her know that he and the group had missed her. It is noteworthy that, until this event, the patient had no conscious awareness of hostile feelings toward her mother or rivalry with her sister. After this emotional experience, she no longer felt herself to be as much in the role of Cinderella, as shown by her improved appearance. Mrs. Carnes showed beneficial effects also. For the first time she rebelled against the therapist by running out of the meeting, but in contrast to mother he did not rebuke her. As she became more assertive with the therapist, she began to be less competitive with the other group members.

NATHAN ACKERMAN . . .

We are here presented with an incident of critical rivalry between two women patients in a therapeutic group of neurotic women; the rivalry resolves itself in a way seemingly favorable to both patients. It is important at the outset to make clear that the account of this particular incident appears deceptively simple. There is more than meets the eye in this therapeutic drama; it is a situation of great complexity.

Reading between the lines, I must infer the existence of a number of overlapping problems which are not adequately defined. One is a question of the depth and relative malignancy of Mrs. Henry's illness. We are told that this is a group of neurotic women. I cannot avoid some doubt and skepticism that Mrs. Henry is an uncomplicated psychoneurotic. There may be an underlying schizoid pathology in this patient. She has a history of severe incapacitating obsessions and a period of hospitalization. Her behavior verges on the bizarre. It is stretching the limits of the concept of neurosis quite far to encompass a person who does not bathe, and comes to therapeutic sessions with legs bare and covered with dirt. The obsessional manifestations may serve to obscure a basic tendency to schizoid pathology. It is well known clinically that some cases diagnosed as severe neurosis are really schizotypes. Paul Hoch popularized the concept that pervasive neurotic disorders, "pan-neuroses," often turn out finally to be cases of schizophrenia. For this group of cases, he introduced the term, pseudo-psychoneurotic schizophrenia.

Of course, it is hazardous to diagnose patients from afar. Nonetheless, in this case, it is valid to raise here a question of differential diagnosis. If there is a schizoid factor in Mrs. Henry, she must have sufficient preservation of her social self to benefit from a therapeutic group.

A second problem which makes interpretation of the incident more complicated is the dearth of data regarding the role of the other members of this women's therapeutic group. Unfortunately the description of the group situation offers no picture of the level of participation of the other female patients. These women seem to be treated as shadowy figures. What is highlighted sharply in this account is the competitive contest between Mrs. Henry and Mrs. Carnes for the favored interest of the doctor, that is, it is a case of two women fighting over one man. If we are to examine the significance of the reported behavior of these two women within the context of the group, we ought to have at least a minimal definition of the dynamics of the group as a whole. In particular, we need to know the role relations of the other women with the doctor and in turn, his attitude toward them.

The third problem is a component of underlying similarity in the conflicts of Mrs. Henry and Mrs. Carnes. In a sense, they suffer from the same disease. They have in common a component of disturbed, conflicted feeling which pertains to the symbolic use of dirt and contamination. Both women have a critically damaged self-esteem. Both of them have suffered rejection and degradation at the hands of their mothers. Both are obsessed with the theme of guilt and punishment. One might say that they share between them a profound layer of sadomasochistic distortion.

There are also significant differences. At the manifest level of behavior, the two women are differently oriented to punishment. Mrs. Henry mainly punishes and degrades herself, while Mrs. Carnes assaults and insults others. Beneath the surface, they are each laden with guilt and have a need to incite punishment. In terms of their overt group roles, Mrs. Henry's and

Mrs. Carnes' personalities form a complementary pair insofar as Mrs. Henry provokes punishment while Mrs. Carnes hands it out, even though she fears retaliation. The component of complementarity in their overt role adaptation in the group provides the possibility that they might usefully treat one another. At the manifest level Mrs. Carnes vehemently denies a common bond with Mrs. Henry, and overasserts her difference. The competitiveness covers an underlying need for one another's acceptance. The therapist has partly the responsibility to help them to understand the way in which they are alike, and suffer from the same debasement of self-worth. The superficial aspects of competition might conceivably be turned into a relation of mutual, compassionate understanding.

In group therapy, as contrasted to individual psychotherapy, the patient is provided with no immunity against a personalized, aggressive attack. The attacks of one patient upon another in a group are sometimes primitively brutal. Mrs. Carnes' attack on Mrs. Henry is violent, but contains in it a concealed defense, a denial of her own sense of degradation.

A fourth problem is the countertransference of the male doctor. The therapist hints at his difficulty in being fair to both women; in other words, he experiences the dilemma of how to cut the piece of cheese exactly in two equal parts. In this connection, one wonders: does the doctor subtly though passively encourage the jealousy between the two women by sicking the two women on one another? As long as they continue fighting over him, neither can succeed in possessing him.

In the beginning Mrs. Henry seems coercively to monopolize the doctor's attentions. Her compulsive talking is a way of asserting exclusive possession of the therapist. Yet, at the same time, she is forcing her dirt in everyone's face. This is a familiar testing device. In effect it signifies: "If you love me, you must prove it by loving me at my worst—love me, love my dirt; love me, love my dog." The motivational elements contained in such behavior are twofold: a coercive demand for attention and protective services from the parent and at the same time, a disguised, vindictive reproach of the parent. Mrs. Henry coerces the doctor's attention while at the same time avenging herself by forcing her dirt into his face. Mrs. Henry's history reveals rejection by both parents. Mrs. Henry forced attention from her mother; she worried her to the point of making her a "nervous wreck." It is not clear to what extent in the transference the male doctor was a mother substitute or a father substitute.

The rival woman, Mrs. Carnes, is an actress. She reflects her actress personality in the group through her exhibitionistic role. She vies with Mrs. Henry for the lead part. She is impelled to captivate the male doctor. For Mrs. Carnes this is, dynamically speaking, an antidote for the wound she sustained in being degradated by her mother. Therefore, the way to hurt her mother or any rival female, the path of vengeance, is to steal the man from the other woman. This urge evokes guilt and fear of retaliation. In the case of Mrs. Carnes there is a significant question which remains unanswered in the story. Was she better looking? Was she more attractive physically and sexually than Mrs. Henry? Presumably she was, but the doctor says nothing about this. This is significantly by omission. Was the doctor not conscious of a difference in sexual attractiveness between the two women, and if so, was he not influenced thereby in his dealing with them?

As the situation unfolds Mrs. Carnes proceeds to shut Mrs. Henry's mouth. The competitive conflict rages for many sessions. Since hate and love are two sides of the same coin, is it not logical to guess that Mrs. Carnes in attacking Mrs. Henry was showing a special interest in her. Mrs. Carnes' aversion may conceal an unconscious fascination and attraction to Mrs. Henry. Mrs. Henry in turn reacts to the attack by washing off her dirt and making herself more attractive. Did she dress up to please the male doctor or the other woman? Do not each of these women in their twisted hostile way seek reconciliation with a mother figure?

With regard to transference patterns, it might look as though the doctor represented predominantly a mother figure for Mrs. Henry, and rather more of a father figure for Mrs. Carnes. But Mrs. Carnes was also mother to Mrs. Henry.

The basic emotional problem for both women patients is damaged self-esteem. Each of these women seeks to repair this by winning affirmation of personal worth from other persons. It is not clear, however, at what levels they seek to be accepted by the therapist; as a child or as a woman. At the child level, they both behave as though they were motivated by the conviction that there is not enough love for two children, only for one. This implies something amiss with the way in which the parent shows love. It takes for granted that the therapist, as parent, has not enough love to go around. The challenge in such a situation is to use the group so as to correct the neurotic misconception that if one child has love, the other child has nothing. A parent who is able to love in a good way has enough love for both children. The other aspect of the problem, the search for love in the role of woman and the need of a man, is not sufficiently clarified. The conflicts at this level do not achieve clear definition. It is as if for each of these women the rival is emotionally more important even than the man. The worth of the man is measured by the violence of the struggle between the two women rather than by the intrinsic value of the man himself. In other words, the man gains value only so far as he is wanted by the other woman. Each of the women fears being robbed. The man becomes a prizeworthy catch only if he is craved by the rival.

Rudolf Dreikurs . . .

This report of group sessions indicates that the events described in the incident are rather puzzling to the therapist who seems not quite able to understand what actually went on. His explanations of the events are not shared by this reviewer. There is little evidence for any understanding of the conflict between the two members of the group and of the movement of each, besides the recognition of the strong feelings of jealousy for each other.

Both patients seem to be suffering from an obsessive compulsive neurosis. They are typical examples of this disorder and clearly show the characteristic overambition, pronounced good intentions, and covered-up hostility. The description of the first patient clearly indicates her perverted overambition. She had been through "the worst punishment" and had "the most obsessive thoughts anyone could have." Her behavior showed to which extent she tried to be "the worst," wearing old ragged clothes, picking up trash and garbage; and her whole attire including her dirtiness was an ostentatious display of "badness and lowness." Her passive and negative power could be seen in her ability to make her mother "a nervous wreck." No doubt, group therapy can be exceedingly helpful for such a patient. But we could not agree that individual treatment, if properly carried out, could not provide "helpful emotional experiences" for her, although we must admit that the treatment of an obsessive compulsive neurotic requires skills and modes of interaction for which most psychotherapists are not trained.

Her opponent in the group also attempted to be first, and with similarly ineffectual methods. Most severe compulsive neurotics can't stand the claim of another one to be worse than they are. But this contest became quite evident. One claimed to be low, the other to be dangerous, by contaminating objects and harming others. Her way of dominating others through weakness was evidenced by her apparent dependency on the doctor while actually putting him into her service. The poor therapist was the victim of a contest of two passively dominating women to keep him busy with them, each interpreting permissiveness to the other as favoritism. It was obvious that the first patient, Mrs. Henry, lost out in this contest because her opponent's means of control were more acceptable to the group—and the therapist. There is no evidence in this report that the therapist understood this conflict or did anything to resolve it.

Then finally the blow came. It is not to the credit of the therapist that he was not instrumental in bringing it about, but rather the passive onlooker in a decisive battle. The crisis came about when Mrs. Carnes overplayed her cards and basked in the glory of her victory over Mrs. Henry. She was showing off "her artistic interests and achievements" while Mrs. Henry was cowed into silence with very feeble efforts to assert herself. But even that was too much for the winner, Mrs. Carnes. And here she made her fatal mistake of trying to subdue her even further. At this point she lost her favorable position and the doctor took a stand against her, thereby turning her victory into a defeat. She admitted this defeat openly by bursting into tears and leaving the scene. It is pathetic how the therapist who apparently had no idea of what went on between the two women admits innocently that he was "somewhat startled by this development." No wonder he could not understand the effect of this episode on Mrs. Henry.

For the first time in probably a long period she had experienced a success in a useful and socially accepted way: her socially successful competitor was defeated. It was apparently this fact which made her now switch back from the useless to the useful side, getting well dressed and well groomed. Now she was ready to give up the glory of her torture and seek importance in useful means, even looking for a job. Her reference to the jealousy of her sister because of the preference of her mother is another admission that she had to be first, be it by being good or bad, a fact which probably would come out clearly in her past history had the therapist made efforts to get these facts. It can be well assumed that even in her contest with her sister there were many ways that she won out against her assumption of constant defeat. We can doubt very much the therapist's belief that she never was aware of her rivalry with her sister. This probably was the cornerstone of her whole personality structure.

Wladimir Eliasberg . . .

In this case, an ingrained obsessive-compulsive neurotic changes abruptly—apparently immediately sloughing off her obsession, becoming normal. The therapist goes to some length to make understood the psychodynamics of the session immediately preceding the change. Essentially, the patient was rebuked by a competitor in the group, but she was made to feel that the doctor was on her side. This, it is implied, was quite different from the home situation, where the mother always sided with a favored older sister. This experience is given as an explanation for the rapid change. But is this the answer?

We are still in the dark about the psychodynamics of revelation to conversion, or to put it in a more pedestrian manner about what causes a change to click. However, few therapists would attribute conversion to revelation alone: to something that happened immediately preceding the event of change. Saulus did not become Paulus only through the apparition. Hamlet did not obtain his character solely because his father's ghost spoke to him.

Our curiosity is aroused by what may have happened throughout the session before the change occurred. The patient kept asking the doctor:

"Why didn't you tell me that all the time?" The doctor *had* told her that all the time; but there had been no free affinity to take hold of the truth.

There is another kind of sudden social reaction which offers a comparison: traumatic neuroses subsequent to accidents. The neurosis is characterized by suddenness of the event, by rapid disturbances of psychological functions, revival of archaic patterns. But one can not overlook the dispositional factors, such as congenital-habitual dispositions, chronic needs for security, integrity of body and mind, and most important the social-psychological background.

These underlying dispositional factors must not be neglected in the face of the suddenness of the event, as described in this incident. We would want to understand that evidently the untidyness, the self-neglect, the wearing of unbecoming clothing are an arrangement. She is saying: "You don't like me? I shall then make myself more unlikeable." But gradually, through the session, the patient begins to understand that this arrangement will not work. It is almost as though she came to this conclusion: If I want to be liked I must make myself likeable; if I want to be loved then I must look lovely." There can be no doubt that the final click in the change is only a last dramatic moment in the long process of rearranging a well-established set-up.

The therapist makes a point that the individual treatment might not have achieved this regrouping because the patient was too accustomed to psychiatric terminology. The therapist is quite right in this. Psychiatric vocabulary is often an inhibitory factor. The patient clings to it, juggles it, and tells the therapist contemptuously that he knows everything, but that this knowledge does not help. Group treatment brings in various new factors, and among them is a fresh linguistic approach; and in this case, competition for love. If these are understood in addition to the slow underlying build-up, we begin to have a dynamic understanding of these cases.

My remarks are a criticism of any implication that the change can be attributed to itself: that the incident in itself is an explanation. The finger that pulls the trigger does not "cause" the shot: this event is only the "triggering" of the consequence; but much more went on before.

J. W. Klapman . . .

Perhaps of even greater interest than the incident within this case is the statement of the whole, because to me it clearly gives indication of a massive fact: that some procedures in psychotherapy are more naturally effective than others, a matter which appears to have caused very little speculation and perhaps hardly any research. In what other branch of medicine do we have a routine procedure for all ills? The very concept of a panacea would be considered charlatanism in somatic medicine, and yet experienced and conscientious therapists plant themselves behind a desk ready to dispense words for all that ails all patients, or in the case of the phenomeno-logical psychotherapists to listen, either actively or passively. And so, to me the real meaning of this case, what makes it of critical importance, is that while the patient had had "protracted contact with psychiatrists" and had "developed exceptional facility in describing her difficulties in psy-chiatric jargon," apparently all this individual treatment had been to no avail. I am reminded, perhaps unkindly, of a cartoon I saw once, probably in the New Yorker, of a witch doctor prancing about a patient while the onlooking father tells the sorrowing mother, "After all, we are doing all that science knows."

However, we psychotherapists owe ourselves, our professions, our pa-tients, and science the obligation to be keen observers, and not to let any significant observation pass by without pondering its ultimate meaning, looking for hypotheses to explain the inexplicable: and so, still keeping to the larger issue, I see that the patient did improve from group psycho-therapy, and that an apparently necessary element in her therapy was the behavior of another member of the group—a woman who strongly dis-approved of the patient's appearance and behavior.

A last comment before we penetrate to the incident itself. It is a com-mon principle of medicine that treatment is contingent on diagnosis, and if so, it may well be that certain types of problems have their obscure origins in certain constellations of human interactions, and that it might be possible to attempt to diagnose in advance those problems which cannot be brought to satisfactory solution in particular ways. I believe that the greatest possi-ble advance could be made in this arcane area if some central clearing house could be established so that psychotherapists could report certain basic data about patients (who could be anonymous) and that periodic statements of a follow-up nature could be provided research students, who could then perhaps begin to weave the net of certainty from the random threads of knowledge. From the mass of observations of isolated therapists perhaps patterns of understanding might develop, and so we might, for ex-ample, learn that every case that had similarity to the one reported here was cured by group and unaffected by individual psychotherapy. But enough of these general remarks, and to the situation itself.

Imbued as we are with certain implicit and explicit conceptions of psychotherapy, which include in them a type of reaction to the patient which denies the individuality of the therapist, the behavior of Mrs. Carnes might well seem antitherapeutic. Does not a patient need understanding, consideration, acceptance? How could Mrs. Carnes' bitter words help poor Mrs. Henry with all her problems? Evidently, she feels as though she is dirt already; what can further heaping of verbal garbage do to help her? And what of the other members of the group? They "tacitly supported" Mrs.

Carnes' attacks by not defending Mrs. Henry. Where is Christian love? And what of the therapist? Why does he not interfere? Why does he not explain how the patients should react to Mrs. Henry?

The reason is that all of these individuals naturally did what was right, and this occurred probably because the greater wisdom of the group, the ineffable rightness of the many, took over the situation in an atmosphere where a feeling of security existed. Where else would Mrs. Carnes have stood for Mrs. Henry's behavior? In any other social situation she would well have kept her remarks to herself, and would have talked about Mrs. Henry when Mrs. Henry was not present. But here, in the group therapy atmosphere, Mrs. Carnes finally acts out her aggression, and possibly this act of this woman "who had grown so dependent on the doctor for fear of losing his support" was critical for her too: she learned that she could successfully express her repressed ideas, and later—miraculously—that perhaps she had been instrumental in helping Mrs. Henry.

And so, in the realest sense of the word, Mrs. Henry's therapist was not the only accredited person in the group—all of the members were, especially Mrs. Carnes.

Now, there are several mysteries in this incident. The first is that Mrs. Carnes finally expressed herself in the thirty-sixth meeting after Mrs. Henry had apparently changed her formerly unpleasant behavior. Mrs. Carnes, in a flood of emotion, cries only because Mrs. Henry is unattractive in her appearance. What can all this mean? Why is Mrs. Carnes, after being in this group presumably for many months, so upset that she actually leaves the room and comes back only when the therapist asks her to return, but remains uncommunicative? At this point I am wondering about Mrs. Carnes' behavior. We don't really know too much about Mrs. Carnes, but is it not possible to assume that possibly Mrs. Carnes realizes unconsciously that now is the time to attack Mrs. Henry—for her own good? As fanciful as this may seem, this writer is convinced of the wisdom of people who are untutored in psychotherapy, and I have frequently marveled how wise even a lobotomized schizophrenic can be, seeing and evaluating things that appear correct to me only after the fact. And so, I would insist on the hypothesis that Mrs. Carnes' outburst came at precisely the right time, at just the moment when Mrs. Henry needed this treatment, and that it was intuitively timed.

The second mystery, which I believe I can better understand, is the connection between this outburst, aggressive and negative as it seemed to be, and the miraculous result it had. We learn that Mrs. Henry missed the next meeting. Surely this meant that she had reacted negatively to Mrs. Carnes' intemperate and destructive outburst. "Oh, Mrs. Carnes," I can imagine the therapist feeling, "could you not have contained yourself? Now, all is lost with Mrs. Henry. She never missed a session before, and now you have caused perhaps irreparable damage to another human being." Perhaps it was for this reason the therapist wrote to Mrs. Henry. And then she appeared, and "wore a colorful dress, was carefully made-up, and had a permanent wave." And she "seemed cheerful and proudly announced that she had been absent the week before because she had an appointment to apply for a job." Surely this instantaneous change was a miracle, but what is the reason?

Whether we can trust the patient's introspections is doubtful. I do believe that perhaps there was something to her arguing that the therapist's behavior in siding with her had helped her to realize "how mad I was at my mother for preferring my sister to me," but I believe that the truly more important element was the recreation of the family situation, with Mrs. Carnes representing possibly the rejecting mother and the preferred older sister, and that in Mrs. Henry winning the battle over Mrs. Carnes, (I made her cry! I made her cry!) may have signaled a victory for a never discontinued battle within her. And also, perhaps, Mrs. Henry perceived Mrs. Carnes' distress as a truly loving act, one in which real consideration and emotion are shown—not, mind you, at Mrs. Henry's obnoxious behavior, but rather to Mrs. Henry's own self-degradation as shown by her unattractive dress.

I am, therefore, attempting to second-guess, and so cannot accept the therapist's own discussion at the end of the case as the reason for Mrs. Henry's recall to life, except to aver that it could be supporting. The crux of the therapy, I am convinced, had its locus in the other patient, who undoubtedly was concommittantly helped, rather than in the therapist. I am highly gratified to notice, on looking over the record once again, that the contributor of this incident mentions, "Mrs. Carnes showed beneficial effects, also."

ASHLEY MONTAGU . . .

I wonder what may be the "true" reason for the progress in this case. Perhaps the comments that follow delve beneath the surface of these interactions, but I would be the last to assert that my assumptions and reconstructions are accurate. Each of us sees reality in terms of his past experiences, our unique global apperception of subjective truth.

Mrs. Henry felt rejected by her world. Her father had abandoned her psychologically by his retreat from life—her mother had pushed her away in favor of a younger sister—and she came to view herself symbolically as less than dirt beneath her feet, a living piece of garbage. Her symptoms of not washing, making herself unattractive, were all consistent expressions of her self-regard—she wore the badge of her essence for all to see. But at the same time we can be sure she was desperately signalling, like a shipwrecked mariner on an inhospitable ocean, for attention—for love and consideration which had been denied her, and which she so urgently needed. This craving for attention was signaled not only by her manner of appearance, and also by her going to psychiatrists, but mostly by her compulsive talking. I have found that talkativeness is one of the most constant symptoms of starvation for love.

The group became her family. The therapist was the mother, the other members were her "sisters." Mrs. Carnes then represented the favored younger sister with whom the other sisters had sided—against Mrs. Henry. The therapist's permissive attitude to Mrs. Carnes simply confirmed in Mrs. Henry's distorted perceptions that the world was all of a piece—and that once again others were preferred over her, that once again she was rejected. The blow to Mrs. Henry, when Mrs. Carnes attacked her, was heightened and enhanced when it appeared *after* Mrs. Henry had quieted down, had become more acceptable to her sisters: and thus, was even more a confirmation of the unfair cruelty of life.

This situation seems now to have been the critical incident in Mrs. Henry's life. Had it been handled with indifference or perhaps in any other manner than the way it was handled, Mrs. Henry would once again have felt left out and let down by life. She remained away to see what would happen, whether anyone would notice her absence and whether anyone would care. To her amazed delight she noticed that her substitute mother, the therapist, and her sister surrogates *did* care. She was no longer rejected, no longer unfairly treated, no longer the "unclean" one. The behavior of the therapist was not the behavior of the mother. And at this moment she realized how "mad" she had become at the mother for preferring the sisters. She felt reassured by the group's demonstration of interest, and in the continuing accepting situation. Previously, people had been at the same time hostile and indifferent; now they showed love and consideration. A step had been taken in the right direction. Further progress would then depend on the consistency of the group's treatment along the lines indicated.

This case brings into high relief several important matters. First is the utmost value, in cases of this sort, of the therapeutic necessity of a group situation. The re-enactment of the family experience in the group situation could only have occurred in the midst of others, and was a reality substitute for her past which closeted interviews with a therapist could not establish. Often what a patient may need is not direction, guidance, or explanation which may not penetrate beneath the superficial level of the intellect, but rather something which goes deeper, to the essence of the personality.

The next matter is the tremendous importance of love. If love is not enough, then neither is understanding. But the simultaneous combination of both reinforces either and may provide a dynamism beneath whose surgent power even Mrs. Henry's long-lasting distortion of reality and her firmly entrenched perceptions of herself had to yield.

I believe that the therapist's action in going beyond the more conventional and limited conception of therapy being confined solely within the group—that is to say, to attempt to reach out to this desperately unhappy woman by writing to her—is a tribute to the therapist's wisdom in realizing that this extra investment in Mrs. Henry could be the straw that would break the camel's back—to recall Mrs. Henry back to life.

J. L. MORENO . . .

The crux of the incident occurred when Mrs. Carnes burst into tears, told Mrs. Henry that she resented her, and then abruptly walked out of the room.

It is a point of the highest involvement, externally, between them, in the momentary action *in situ*, and internally, in each of them in reference to many corresponding situations in the past or future. The therapist should not let such an opportunity go by without making a direct attack upon the syndrome, unless there is a contraindication or some good reason to hope that a better opportunity will break in the course of action. The therapist may not "know" what the actual dynamics of the syndrome are, and he may never know anything about it unless he undertakes an exploratory operation like a surgeon would. In the course of the operation he hopes to find where, topologically, and what, dynamically, the trouble is. In this moment, therefore, the psychotherapist has the indication to step in. He could step in at four points in time, which means acting within the rush of a few seconds.

The first moment (A) is when Mrs. Carnes burst into tears and told off Mrs. Henry. At this moment he coud have stepped in himself or as an *auxiliary ego*. By *doubling* Mrs. Henry she may be provoked to respond to Mrs. Carnes, verbally or in action. If he could get Mrs. Henry into the production, other techniques such as *role reversal* and *soliloquy* might be used to get into the relationship of both before the incident develops any further. But let us imagine that he lets this first potential indication pass.

He has a second moment (B) when Mrs. Carnes walks out of the room. This moment may indicate fruitful intervention for theoretical as well as for therapeutic reasons. Instead of merely going after her and asking her to return, displaying his approval or disapproval in a paternal way, he could have turned the walking out process into a psychodramatic scene.

A third moment (C) is when the protagonist came back and remained silent. At a time of comparative relaxation of both protagonists, the tension of the entire group could have been mobilized in favor of a structured psychodramatic session, so to speak, trying to tap the wound before the warmup was dispersed.

A fourth opportunity (D) for intervention came up in the next meeting, when Mrs. Henry was absent. There and then, with the help of the entire group, the relationship between Mrs. Carnes and the absent Mrs. Henry, represented by one or more auxiliary egos, could have been worked out, the therapeutic session developing into a "training" and "rehearsal" session as to what to expect from Mrs. Henry and how the relationship between the two protagonists could be adjusted, using Mrs. Carnes, the aggressor, as her own therapist and as the therapist of the other.

These four indications for intervention should bring out on different levels of depth the dynamic meaning of their conflict and its direction, past and future. If the indication in moment A had been used, it might have mobilized the spontaneity of the entire group against the "aggressor," by having them come to Mrs. Henry's rescue in the midst of the outburst. This might have resulted in a frustrated anxiety in Mrs. Carnes, turning her towards the therapist for help against the group which would not permit her to complete her anger against Mrs. Henry. She left the room after her job was done, and she felt ashamed and annoyed; she may have been caught in the middle of warming up her anger. Her spontaneous urge to explode her anger may have been greater than her anxiety to escape the group and run away. She might have stood there stubbornly to bring her expression of hostility to a finale. It is like somebody who has a good erection and is engaged with a female partner in a sexual intercourse when, in this moment of greatest physical and emotional involvement, a group of voyeurs suddenly step in. Similarly, the group of patients facing the argument between Mrs. Carnes and Mrs. Henry can be considered as voyeurs and intervening intruders. Caught *in flagranti* in such a moment, the warmup and spontaneity manifesting itself in the sexual act may be more precious to the sexual actors than the anxiety and shame to stop the act or leave the room. They want to continue and finish the sexual act. If in such a moment the therapist steps in, halts the group from aggression against Mrs. Carnes, and gives her a chance, so to speak, to finish her act, he may turn a rudimentary session productive.

This is *one* possible alternative. There are many other alternatives which depend upon the *composition* of the group (only women, only men, or a mixed group), the sociometric position of the two protagonists in the group, and many other factors. The dynamics of the incident cannot be divorced from the dynamics of the structure of the group and the immediate milieu.

The therapeutic objective of the session may be simple and clear, but the ways to attain it are numerous and unpredictable on paper.

In Grandmother's Image

23

History

A 33-year-old woman asked her physician to refer her to a psychiatrist because of her fear of "going insane." To the male psychiatrist, she admitted her fear of killing her four-year-old adopted daughter, but did not amplify. There were references to an extremely unhappy childhood, but the severe anxiety and agitation blocked communication. The psychiatrist referred the patient for extended psychotherapy with his associate, a woman psychologist.

In the ensuing psychotherapy, decisions had to be made regarding the degree and kind of therapeutic activity. The patient had grown up with an unusually punitive, depriving, and dominating grandmother who hated men and was separated from her own husband, but who favored the patient's older brother in all ways calculated to arouse frustration and jealousy in the patient. The patient seemed to have incorporated much of the grandmother's dominating and hostile personality. In therapy, after the initial working-through of disorganizing anxiety, she maintained very active control of every therapeutic hour, apparently needing to keep the therapist passive except for soliciting support of her child-rearing methods. She had attended an adult education project in which nursery care for children was accompanied by group discussions of child-parent problems. From this she had derived an excellent understanding of parent-child relationships which, combined with awareness of her own childhood unhappiness, produced very constructive maternal patterns. The genuineness of her insights was confirmed by the spontaneity and creativity of the child, whose adjustment was also facilitated by a very gentle and understanding adoptive father, the patient's husband. Nevertheless, it seemed evident that the patient also felt, toward the child, intense but suppressed hostility, which was kept inactive and unexplored by the reaction-formation of the "good-mother-role," for which she solicited therapeutic reinforcement. The therapist therefore saw a choice between, on the one hand, actively supporting the good-mother defense and remaining relatively passive otherwise, or, on the other hand, interpreting to the patient the defensive nature of her "good-mother-role" and helping her to face the underlying hostility. The therapist's decision to work on the level chosen by the patient was based partially on the Rorschach, which revealed an inadequate ego-structure and such pathological indicators as a pure C response, "blood."

During months of this reintegrative work, the therapist sensed a growing negative transference, which also remained inaccessible to exploration. Clarifying clues were provided by the patient's content, which moved gradually from preoccupation with the daughter to the patient's own early experiences. During the preschool period she had lost first her father, through her parents' divorce, and then her mother, who remarried and moved to another state, leaving the patient and her brother with the maternal grandmother. The grandmother emphasized her sacrifice in caring for the patient and kept her under control through threats of an orphange. The patient's attempts at self-expression were used by the grandmother as an excuse for deprivation and humiliating punishment. Nevertheless, the grandmother was the patient's source of security; and, as an adult, she remained bound by a sense of obligation and unconsciously obedient to the grandmother's dictate: "Never trust or depend on anyone."

The grandmother's dictate that the patient should always love her mother became particularly confusing after the mother's return during the patient's adolescence. Instead of the hoped-for love, the patient received viciously expressed hatred from the mother, who apparently saw the patient as a rival for the grandmother's favor. During these severely traumatic years, the patient's mother called her "crazy" and threatened her with an "asylum."

Incident

As the patient talked of these experiences, she became more wary of the therapist and began to cancel appointments. It was over the telephone that she stated her decision to terminate. The therapist had to make an on-the-spot decision whether to influence the patient's decision or simply to accept it. Because the patient manifested such an urgent need to "escape," the therapist remained passive, other than telling the patient she was welcome to return at any time.

It was almost a year later that the patient voluntarily returned to the same therapist. Her greatly increased receptivity to help seemed related to the regression that had occurred. During the first therapy, she had regained the lost ability to drive a car; but this was again lost, and the patient was now unable even to leave the house without her husband. Her use of alcohol was also getting out of control. On the positive side of the ledger, the patient seemed to have used the interim period to work through some of the transference, for her fear and distrust of the therapist were definitely diminished.

The rather sudden deaths of her husband's parents and oldest brother, early in the second therapy, stimulated reactivation of old defenses as she actively worked with her husband on family affairs. She would overextend herself beyond the point of exhaustion, and then act out her hostility and feelings of persecution. This time the therapist actively interpreted defenses, and this led to a revelation of the original incentive for therapy. In great turmoil, the patient brought a dream in which she felt great anger toward her daughter, beat her, and saw blood everywhere. She then revealed that, before seeking therapy the first time, she had in fact lost control and had beaten her daughter unmercifully, leaving the child severely bruised. It was now possible to begin exploration of the patient's hatred and jealousy of her child. The therapist's sympathetic and nonjudgmental acceptance provided a basis for positive feelings, which the patient expressed toward the therapist. She then became able gradually to verbalize her hatred and fear of the therapist as the rejecting mother who would bring about her permanent imprisonment in a mental hospital. Therapeutic progress was greatly facilitated by this communication.

Discussion

There is currently steady progression in the production of deeply significant material, and the patient continues to be able to examine her ambivalences toward the therapist, toward her child, and others. She is now deeply involved in her therapy, and occasionally reminds the therapist that she has years of therapeutic work ahead. However, she suffers intensely and is, at times, overwhelmed by doubt and despair. At home, she continues in a regressed state, sleeping much of the time, unable to assume her old responsibilities, and limited in her living by deep-seated phobias. She speaks of how she has changed from a jumpy and sharply aggressive woman to a calm and subdued one. She says she likes this change but is not yet used to it. In therapy she relates much like a young child. The therapist feels optimistic about the eventual outcome but wonders if a different therapeutic approach might have achieved as much at less cost to the patient.

RUDOLF DREIKURS . . .

Comment on, and evaluation of, this incident is greatly hampered by the completely different frame of reference of the reporter and this reviewer. A great many statements are difficult to assess from my point of view. I have never experienced a situation where "severe anxiety and agitation blocked communication," as reported in the first paragraph. There was always one point of departure where understanding and communication was possible. The term "initial working-through of disorganizing anxiety" is meaningless to me. I do not recognize any "disorganizing" anxiety since every anxiety has meaning and function and is usually well organized if one understands its *purpose*. It is difficult for me to perceive how a patient could maintain "very active control of every therapeutic hour." I have never experienced such a predicament. A patient may want to keep me passive, but does that mean that I have to submit to such a desire? From my frame of reference this is bad therapeutic procedure; but I understand well that it is perfectly acceptable in different orientations.

I see no evidence for the therapist's assumption of evident and intense but suppressed hostility which the patient felt toward her child. Why is her "good-mother-role" considered a reaction-formation when the child showed spontaneity, creativity, and adjustment? If there was any "underlying hostility" which would establish "the defensive nature of her good-mother-role," the therapist failed in my opinion to give the evidence.

The most striking remark is the report that the therapist sensed a growing negative transference "which remained inaccessible to exploration." The use of such labels seems to becloud the problem. Terms like "negative transference" and "resistance" are used whenever the relationship between therapist and patient deteriorate; then the therapist, often not knowing what to do, may blame the patient for the unfavorable development. Actually, such situations usually occur when the goals of the therapist and of the patient clash or diverge. A careful investigation could clarify such divergences and lead to some agreement. Here the therapist received "clues" from the patient's early experience leading to the conclusions that she could not trust or depend on anyone. This may be so; but there is no report of the therapist's effort to overcome the patient's distrust. Is it possible that the "growing negative transference" came from the patient's feeling that she did not get any help during the "months of this reintegrative work"? After all, she came because of her fear of "going insane," and for "soliciting the support of her child-rearing methods," if I understand the therapist's report. What has the therapist done to satisfy this desire? We don't know; but from her report we cannot see what she has done in either regard. Is it possible that the patient may have become "more wary of the therapist and began to cancel appointments" because she felt that she did not get help in what she wanted, and not because the discussion of her childhood made her break up the therapy due to growing "resistance"? Considering this possibility, the therapist may not have been so certain that this attitude of the patient manifested "an urgent need to escape." Only a therapist who does not constantly scrutinize his own role is inclined to blame every therapeutic impasse on the patient, calling it negative transference, resistance, or here "escape." In my opinion, it was a grave mistake to accept passively the patient's "decision" to quit without exploring her dissatisfaction with the treatment.

In this sense, the therapist seems to be partly responsible for the worsening condition of the patient during the following year. I fail to understand why the deterioration is called regression. To what has the patient regressed in not leaving the house without her husband, or in beginning to drink too much? This seems a loose use of the word "regression." It can only mean here that the patient got worse. And because she now was determined to get help, the therapist interprets this as indicating that she had "used the interim period to work through some of the transference." It seems obvious that such concepts and terms do not do justice to the real issue and prevent the therapist from understanding what apparently took place. We can see that the patient was less resistant. But was it really that "her fear and distrust of the therapist were disminished," since we did not have any evidence for this assumption by the therapist? Or was it, perhaps, that the patient now suffered so much that she wanted help at all costs, and had overcome her anger and dissatisfaction with her therapist in one year of increasing suffering and discomfort? Such considerations seem not to have occurred to the therapist who is apparently satisfied with the simple labels of "transference" and "resistance."

The therapist seems to be highly satisfied with "the second therapy" and even optimistic about the outcome. This reviewer cannot share this evaluation. He agrees that "a different therapeutic approach might have achieved as much at less cost to the patient," as the therapist cautiously suggests; another approach may even have prevented the gradual worsening of the situation and the bad condition in which the patient finds herself in the "incident."

I do not know which defenses the therapist "actively interpreted," nor do I agree with what she considered "the original incentive for therapy." According to the therapist, it was the patient's hatred and jealousy of her child. Such questionable interpretations of dynamics are understandable if one explores the unconscious and not the actual movements of the patient. Without having the necessary information about the patient's early childhood, I am in no position to be certain of her goals in life. The data which the therapist reports brings only the material of what others had done to the patient during her childhood, as if she had been a passive recipient of the actions of father, mother, and grandmother, and not an active participant in the interaction with all of these. We do not know what her methods of response were. But there seems to be sufficient evidence that her main goal in life was *to be good*. Only if she could be good, would she have a place. The therapist may consider this a "defense." The question is, defense against what? From the theoretical frame of reference of the therapist we can assume that she meant defense against her own hostility, against her guilt and hatred. From our point of view, it may be called defense against social humiliation and rejection. Actually such desire to be "good" can be regarded not as a defense but as a means to find a place, although not a very safe one. Because as soon as the patient cannot be as good as she thinks she ought to be, she is bound to get into trouble. And that apparently happened to her, particularly in regard to her daughter. It seems that she actually was a good mother. According to the therapist "she had derived an excellent understanding of parent-child relationships which . . . produced very constructive maternal patterns." The "genuiness of her insight" was recognized. But then she got into trouble because contemporary relationships between parents and children make it almost impossible to avoid clashes and conflicts. And this patient, with her high standards, was apparently unable to face her anger toward and her defeat by her child. The ensuing incidental "hostility" with which she could not deal was accentuated by the therapist's assumption of a deep underlying hostility in the patient. Instead of helping her to see that one could get angry and hostile without being "bad," the approach of the therapist made this badness worse by considering it an integral part of her nature. No wonder that the patient, now under treatment for considerable time, "suffers intensely and is, at times, overwhelmed by doubt and despair," continuing in a "regressed state," unable to assume her responsibilities and plagued by "deep-seated phobias." True enough, she renounced her desire to be good, stopped being jumpy and aggressive, and became calm and subdued. This is a small comfort in a state of complete demoralization, which in my opinion can be directly attributed to this form of treatment.

The crucial moment was the dream in which the patient "felt great anger toward her daughter, beat her, and saw blood everywhere." Then she revealed that she had—before she started her first treatment—"lost control and had beaten her daughter unmercifully, leaving the child severely bruised." To begin with, it indicates, in my opinion, a deficiency of a therapeutic approach, if such important material comes out only after prolonged treatment, here only in the "second therapy." A therapist who can win the patient's confidence and explore the patient's thoughts and actions might have been able to get this material in the first few interviews. Because, after all, that was the patient's original desire for therapy, and apparently the basis for her fear of becoming insane. One usually does not need a dream years after the beginning of therapy to solicit such a crucial occurrence. If anything, this fact alone justifies doubts about the approach used by this therapist.

To make it worse, the therapist fell for the patient's mistaken assumption. Instead of helping her to see that losing control does not make her a bad mother or woman, the therapist used both dream and incident to fortify the patient's mistaken self-evaluation by exploring further "the patient's hatred and jealousy of her child." Regardless of how much the therapist may credit herself with "sympathetic and nonjudgmental acceptance," it is she who emphasizes what the patient erroneously is afraid of, namely, that she is no good if she once permits herself to lose control and beat her daughter. This is probably the worst thing one can do to this woman—and the therapist did it. I cannot see how such a therapeutic attitude can bring any good results. From what is presented in this report, I could not share the therapist's optimism about the eventual therapeutic success.

ALBERT ELLIS . . .

I fully share what seem to be the therapist's misgivings about the approach employed in this case. My feeling is that, from the start, the therapist was unduly intimidated by the patient's symptoms and by her Rorschach responses. Pathological indicators such as shown by this patient are seen in innumerable individuals who come for therapy; and if they are always to be taken as signs that the therapist must tread exceptionally easy and use highly passive approaches, little progress in individual cases, and in the theory and practice of psychotherapeutic technique, is likely to be made.

My own feeling is that the "growing negative transference" which occurred during the patient's first therapy experience was caused not so much by the traumatic experiences which she was talking about in the therapy but largely by the therapist's passive, almost negative attitude toward these experiences. The patient, like so many patients who relate these kinds of experiences, was mutely begging the therapist, as it were, to help change her attitudes toward these early traumatic events; to help her gain a positive, constructive philosophy which would enable her to surrender her early fears of losing her mother's approval or "going crazy." The therapist, instead of rising to this challenge, kept passively letting the patient ventilate her feelings which, by itself, rarely leads to changed attitudes toward such feelings. Naturally, under these circumstances, the patient began to get more instead of less disturbed, and to retreat from therapy.

At this point, when the patient wanted to withdraw, the therapist should have sensed the error of her procedure and taken a much more active stand. But, still intimidated by the patient's symptoms and Rorschach, and still adhering much too rigidly to passivity, she interpreted the patient's need to escape from her as a need to escape from *therapy*. Only by sheer luck, in my estimation, did the patient subsequently return for treatment and begin to work through some of her problems. In the great majority of cases where patients leave therapy as this one did, they never return; and the fact that this one, quite exceptionally, did return, is no good reason, in my estimation, to sustain the approach employed.

It is notable that, in the course of the second set of therapeutic sessions, when "the therapist actively interpreted defenses . . . this led to a revelation of the original incentive for therapy." I am willing to wager that active interpretation during the first series of sessions would have had the same result; and that this, added to an active attack on the patient's early-inculcated attitudes involving her dire need to be loved and her guilt about her feelings for mother and grandmother, would have brought equally good therapeutic results at much less cost to the patient.

J. McV. Hunt . . .

I am inclined to believe that the fact that this patient asked to be referred to a psychiatrist because of her fear of "going insane," and that she admitted to the male psychiatrist her fear of killing her four-year-old adopted daughter were clues indicating that it might have been wiser to have chosen the alternative of interpreting to the patient the defensive nature of her "good-mother-role" and helping her to face the underlying hostility. The fact that this patient recognized her own hostility implies that she was more ready than the therapist thought to examine her own hostilities and the reasons for them. It was probably unfortunate in this case that the therapist was a woman instead of a man. The hate deriving from the mistreatment by the patient's mother and grandmother very likely generalized to all women to a greater degree than it generalized to all men. In fact, the client brings this out directly, according to the report, after her return for further therapy. Probably, one can now say that the evidence was at hand with which to make the decision in terms of conflict theory. The mother's fear of killing her daughter implies great hostility, and her combination of understanding and usual performance of the "good-mother-role" implies that this reaction formation can be maintained only at great cost and by bolting up the tendency for hostility to produce anxiety. This argument is based upon Miller's[1] conflict theory in which hostility in this instance is the approach response, and this hostility has been held in check by its tendency to produce cues conditioned to anxiety responses which in turn inhibit hostility.

As hostility mounts in strength, anxiety must also mount in strength to hold back this hostility. The ultimate theoretical outcome of continuing to strengthen the anxiety would be some kind of immobilization or a definite anxiety hysteria, probably coupled with occasional instances in which the hostility would break through and, once it had broken through, produce intense guilt. With the theoretical outcome of this kind of conflict being something very much like a psychosis, the risk of gently interpreting the role of good-mother as a defense combined with the expectation that the patient herself has sometimes been hurt by other people might well have overcome the suspicion she had of the passive therapist as she moved herself toward discussion of her mother's and grandmother's roles. The pure C response ("blood") in the Rorschach may not have any relevance to the individual's general status but only represent the relatively temporary dynamics of her situation in relation to her child. This candid report, and this question so honestly and candidly put forward by the therapist, can only lead a similarly honest commentator to note that hindsight is a

[1] Neil E. Miller, "Experimental Studies of Conflict," in *Personality and the Behavior Disorders,* J. McV. Hunt (ed.) (New York: The Ronald Press, 1944).

lot better than foresight. On the other hand, perhaps if therapists would think more often of their client as a person in a situation rather than as a static personality with a set of relatively permanent dynamics, it would facilitate confidence in looking carefully at the clues that are put forward at the opening of therapy. This woman was asking for help, she had recognized her own limitations in dealing with her own hostilities. Should not these have been dealt with as directly as possible?

J. W. KLAPMAN . . .

What happened in this instance is certainly far from clear. The reconstruction must, perforce, be highly speculative.

What was the reason the patient dominated the interviews in the first span of the therapy? It appears that she had identified with her mother and grandmother out of fear of the aggressor. With this identification there was probably much guilt feeling and much ambivalence, and her so completely dominating the therapeutic interviews may have been a desperate attempt to escape the realization of guilt by hyperactivity.

It may be assumed that in the first series of treatments the therapist's passivity aroused the patient's doubt and hostility in two ways. First, there was no referee in the intense ambivalence and conflict she was undergoing at the time; second, the patient may have placed the therapist in the position of the superego. "I am dominating; I am cruel and unjust to my child. I am taking up all of the time in the interview. Why don't you stop me? Why don't you make it possible for me to feel toward my adopted child the way a mother should feel, instead of the compulsive way I am doing, and just as my mother and grandmother did to me?"

Compulsively she may also have repeated another pattern—the jealousy toward the child over the likelihood of being displaced in the husband's affections. All these fears and compulsions she knows to be chimerical, but cannot rid herself of her deeply-buried affects. It is conceivable that the therapist's greater direct intervention might have meant greater ego support, which would have tended to eliminate the negative transference, possibly with an emergence of a positive relationship and without any break in the therapy.

There is no certainty in these formulations. No doubt she had worked on her problems and conflicts in the interval between treatment, but there are signs that she has capitulated. There are signs of a beginning disintegration of the ego and lessening of the defenses. Though this hypothesis may be entirely wrong, it is tenable that the regression signifies a resolution of the conflict by withdrawal from the problem. Some of the therapist's statements seem to suggest it, for example: "However, she suffers intensely [probably as seen in the therapy session, where she mobilizes her last remaining resources] and she is, at times, overwhelmed by doubt and despair. At home she continues in a regressed state, sleeping much of the time, unable to assume her old responsibilities and limited in her living by deep-seated phobias. She speaks of how she has changed from a jumpy and sharply aggressive woman to a calm and subdued one."

Apparently the therapist is now the sole remaining lifeline.

I may seem to be giving a very alarmist construction, but in my opinion the therapist has need to think and feel deeply in order to try to fend off a frank and outright schizophrenic breakdown.

RUTH MUNROE . . .

This patient certainly needed heavy reinforcement of the good-mother defense pattern, in view of the probable diagnosis of a severe hysteria, with possibilities of psychotic decompensation. Direct bringing to consciousness of underlying hostility to the child might well have been shattering. Yet the patient must have been aware of the hostility (she told the male psychiatrist in the initial interview of her fear of killing the child) and probably could not find a "real" support in mere reassurance. Her hostility needed acceptance also.

As the patient moved toward consideration of her own early experience, further complications probably arose. Despite the severe deprivation and cruelty of her childhood, one may guess even from the structure of the neurosis that some positive identification with the mother and grandmother had taken place. Indeed the absent mother had quite possibly been idealized and internalized; the "sacrifices" of the grandmother must have been accepted partly as an adult model of value. As the patient became vividly aware of the actual hostility of these figures, two consequences are likely: (1) the underlying trust which enabled her to accept support from the therapist is undermined by the severe rejection now re-experienced in course of therapy, and (2) the deep identifications with the maternal figures approach consciousness. In condemning these people she also condemns herself and whatever constructive aspects of her personality are related to this early period.

Passive support is no longer feasible. The therapist is willy-nilly caught in the intrapsychic drama of the patient's reliving. Support of the patient's hostility to the parental figures now means to the patient shared condemnation of those traits in herself which are like the parents'. As she penetrates the falsity of the "good" aspects of her parents' behavior, she is very likely to begin to penetrate the falsity of her own behavior toward her child. Moreover, the therapeutic release of hostility generally endangers her tenuous defenses unless it can somehow be absorbed and redirected by the therapist. Retrospective justification is not enough. The patient is going beyond the defenses supported by the therapist, and is very likely to withdraw in a mixture of fear and contempt.

This therapist must have offered a firmer basis for the relationship than mere "support," since the patient returned after her problems had become more crystallized and proceeded to courageous work on her defenses with good results. Could the process have been made less painful and prolonged?

Such patients tend toward dramatic symptoms, and it may be that the actual experience of overt failure of her defenses was a *necessary* preamble to their examination. I would, however, like to suggest the systematic conscious use of what I shall call an "intellectualizing" technique in such a case—after the initial panic has subsided, tapering off as the patient is able to move toward more direct therapy, but never entirely lost sight of as a means available both for reassurance and for gentle prodding ahead.

Every school tends to consider theorizing with the patient and psychological discussion of other people's problems as alien to true therapy. In many schools therapy is understood as essentially the transference relationship without even the intellectualization ascribed—not altogether correctly—to the Freudian concept of "insight." There is, however, an increasing emphasis on what several schools call "working through." Although the emotional shift is the primary and necessary condition of any true therapy, the patient needs help in understanding how his attitudes and behavior are affected in the many facets of his actual living.

I hope that my proposal of a conscious "intellectualizing technique" will not be seen as an abrogation of the fundamental principles of therapy developed over the years, a naive substitution of better intellectualization for better feeling in the patient. On the contrary, this is the most obvious *danger* of the approach, to be guarded against. I propose it as a *tool* for use in the development and control of the transference. The tool must be used with care, because it is surprisingly sharp for many patients, perhaps for all if used as a tool instead of a helpless giving-in to intellectualizing defenses. It can also be used protectively to intimate, to build up new defenses, above all to share the ego resources of the therapist very directly with the patient.

The technique might be especially suitable for this patient, since she responded well to a course on child rearing. She would be likely to enjoy discussing other people's problems and psychological principles. My suggestion is that "incidental" discussion of this apparently objective nature be encouraged in an atmosphere of *sharing* psychological understanding with the patient. She may be subtly complimented on her insight. The therapeutic aim, however, is to introduce sympathetic acceptance of the patient's own problems by constant mild interpretation of these "others," so far as possible leading the patient to "spontaneous" insight into the *defensive* meaning of "bad" behavior.

As the patient moves toward reliving her own childhood she should have direct support of her self-pity, resentment, and growing insight into how badly she was mistreated. She may be told that she is entitled to more hostility than she shows, that she had developed remarkably well despite the early handicaps. "Interesting case of constructive growth"—and here the therapist should be able to smile *with* the patient in looking at her as a "case." With this sort of background, patient and therapist can work together at understanding the parental figures—their defenses as well as their bad behavior; how "good" things about them as well as her own strength helped the patient mature.

In such a setting, I think, the patient can proceed to work on her own defenses, underlying hostilities, and so forth with a strengthened ego. The strength is not really "intellectual." It remains 90 per cent transference, and 10 per cent "bucking up." The therapist has, however, concretely demonstrated acceptance of the patient's real problems repeatedly, although covertly. With all the force of the transference she has set a new ego model for the patient's self acceptance. Storms are inevitable, but the therapist has many concrete instances to fall back on in brief comment for purposes of reassurance as to her own benign acceptance of such problems, and in addition, reminders that the patient has accepted them in "others." Why is she so hard on herself? Provided the joint "intellectualized" background stays firm, one may even gently taunt the patient with inconsistency. Does her strength of understanding stop when she looks at herself? One may also remind her that the essence of therapy is real feeling. Her present distress is the real thing at last, hard but valuable. Probably she should let herself go a bit, since she knows she has the resources not to go too far. She should phone the therapist at any time. Arrangements may be made for extra hours. Emphasis should be laid less on desperate need than on "this is your chance to *really* solve the problems that bothered you; I am proud of your courage; we know your basic strength," and so forth—a bit dramatic as the patient becomes dramatic, but steady reiteration that this is a phase she can and must work through.

Cautionary remarks. The "intellectualizing technique" must always be seen as a tool of the transference, not as an end in itself. Nor is it mere padding, an inert ingredient of the therapy. The therapist must be constantly aware of the probability that the patient will partly identify with the "others" or the general principles discussed. *All* such discussion must, therefore, be kept essentially benign as to potential outcome; if this is impossible regarding some types of illness the patient inquires about—deteriorating schizophrenia, psychopathy, and so forth—the symptoms should be stated with such exaggerated sharpness as to forestall identification. Premature tentative identifications may be handled by the comment "You feel like that sometimes? I'm not surprised. Most people do, but . . . ." continuing with more distant discussion until a sufficient backlog of transference has been established. (For essentially stable patients the followup may be more direct, though protected by "theoretical generalization," sometimes cutting through secondary defenses rapidly without the risk of the sharply personal comment.)

Patients come to talk about themselves and should, of course, be encouraged to do so. "Intellectualization" should never be forced upon them. Nevertheless almost all patients want the therapist to "tell them something," and many want pronouncements on "others." These natural demands may be answered therapeutically as above with an apparent directness *essentially tailored to prepare the patient for self insight.* The only excuse for discussion really distant from the patient's problem is the brake upon insights which might swamp the patient. The therapist should develop a sharp nose for red herrings, and above all guard against being beguiled into mere chatter about his own interests. If necessary the patient may be cheerfully reminded that "after all we are here to talk about *you.*" If necessary, the therapist may gently prod toward self-identification. "Why are you so interested? Is your question a statement about your *own* fears?"

Modification is necessary for the dyed-in-the-wool intellectualizers. They come supplied with a large stock of herrings. It is usually possible to establish rather quickly *with* the patient the fact that he "intellectualizes" and use this joint recognition for an agreement to "no debate." It requires no great tact to make this request a positive flattery and to reinforce it by saying occasionally, "You're probably right. I hadn't thought of that," *almost* always ending with the wish that "We can go into a real *discussion* once we're through with this therapy business, but I mustn't be tempted away from our basic agreement. We both know how important it is."

It is still important to establish very concretely the therapist's accepting position in general theory and *re* "others" by the same technique as above, but with more emphasis on the tentativeness of any given idea. For these patients especially it is the "acceptance" rather than the idea that counts, and the basic transference should be to the mind that sees complications, but is not lost among them. A few dazzling interpretations— chosen when the therapist happens to be sure of his ground—may supply the respect necessary to such patients before they can trust an authoritative unsureness.

Yet these patients are stymied unless one can bring strong feeling into the therapeutic session. Perhaps one may proceed something like this: "It seems to me that what bothers you is this . . . [a very direct, deliberately disturbing interpretation]. I may be wrong altogether, and certainly there are other factors. I hope this really hurts you—*that's what we need.* Try to be honest about the 'hurt,' and to figure out *what* hurt. I *may* think you're still intellectualizing and tell you so, but we'll have more to work on." One may also ask them to report any sharp feelings of *happiness* or a new sense of relaxation. Then one must be very gentle in interpretation. Such patients are as sensitive as those discussed above; their defenses are even more important to them. They need both shock and support, the therapist as gadfly, sometimes as goad, and also the therapist who *essentially* approves the kind of person the patient is trying to be, with whom he can identify on the constructive levels of "intellectualization."

A corollary of "not forcing intellectualization on the patient" is its contraindication for patients of very limited intelligence or education. They also often want to know what is wrong with them and their neighbors. They easily become confused, however, not only by our big words but also by the essentially complex concepts behind them. Any mixture of black and white tends to be construed as ignorance, indecision, or disloyalty. The slightest effort to explain the "good side" of a person the patient hates is likely to mean only that the therapist has gone over to the enemy, and a move like this can be risked only after the patient has already begun to shift. (There are exceptions, of course, especially when the problem is lack of education.)

At the opposite pole of this dimension stand the highly intelligent patients, well trained in other professions or business, but scornful or badly misinformed about psychological "intellectualizations" here suggested. The tentativeness of the therapist means that he doesn't know his business; "theoretical" statements lead to challenging debate and to resentment when the therapist cuts short an intellectualistic argument distant from the patient's problem. Far from encouraging the approach here recommended, the therapist should try hard to avoid it until (or unless) the patient shows some glimmer of "our" kind of understanding. Even then the therapist must be cautious, and prepare the patient for refusal to continue a discussion which becomes argumentative. "I would like to hear more of your position, but we'll have to wait till this therapy is over. My ideas may be wrong, but it's not our *ideas* that are going to help you handle your problems." One must sometimes, I think, express rather definite authority as *therapist*, and turn to appreciative analysis of why the patient finds this difficult. "Any intelligent person resents dismissal of a logically sound position, but suppose we concentrate on why this position is so important to *you*." The answer may lead to specific revelations, or to some cautious examination of such general trends as intellectualizing as a defense, the need to be right, and so forth.

Moreover, the therapeutic release of hostility generally endangers her or individuals—niggers, kikes, wops, Catholics, imperialist capitalists, commies, bosses, and so forth, down to particualr people hated or loved profoundly and irrationally. Such "prejudices" must be bypassed as a rule. I think they should be used *only* for dramatic impact when the "intellectualizing technique" is in successful operation and the patient seems to need an extra, but relatively impersonal prod. The therapist should be aware of the fact that he endangers the whole transference to his therapeutic ego if he prematurely accepts anything that is to the patient profoundly unacceptable. He must be careful not to discuss such "others" sympathetically until the patient is ready. He can meet active attack on them with at most the mild comment: "Well, these people are human beings too."[2]

It is impossible to generalize about extremely self-absorbed patients: psychotics, psychopaths, panic states, and so forth. Obviously there can be no such sustained "intellectualizing technique" as the one suggested for the patient here under consideration; but brief, carefully pointed, so-called "intellectual" comments may be very useful. As I was writing this article a "Freudian" analyst asked rather apologetically if I would undertake repeated testing of a patient—primarily on *intellectual functions.* The diagnosis was probably an atypical schizophrenia with marked manic symptoms. He had begun what he called a "pedagogic" approach and had the impression that the patient was "thinking better" and that this improvement would be dynamically related to his total functioning. In discussion of the general problem, he brought up instances from varieties of syndromes more severely pathological than my own experience as therapist includes. I was especially pleased by his feeling that carefully used "intellectualizations" do not preclude movement toward a classical psychoanalytic approach when this seems desirable.

In summary, an "intellectualizing technique" has been suggested as a tool of the transference in suitable cases. (That is, brief "theoretical" comments and discussion of other people.) In the present instance the therapist might have offered indirectly important support to the patient against unacknowledged conflicts, and strengthened her ego through shared and practiced understanding as a background for direct confrontation of her own problems.

2 Unless the therapist is openly identified with the despised groups in a way the patient may discover. For example, Dr. Munroe cannot allow full assumption of anti-Semitism on her part since the patient may run into a book written with her first husband, Dr. Levy. Such discoveries invite distrust. It is better to say, "I don't happen to share your feelings on this point, but it doesn't seem important in our discussion of your problems,"—continuing only on the patient's initiative. The way should be kept open for easy return when and if the question becomes significant. It may be very helpful *eventually* either in therapy or in that education toward a more liberal humanism which most of us consider a valid aim in treatment, however secondary to the immediate therapeutic goal.

"Intellectualization" is not an end in itself and should never be forced on the patient. Apparently "objective," it should be definitely oriented toward the patient's problems. It is a very sharp tool to be used with care lest it cut too deep or become blunted by too much irrelevant discussion, distant from the main issues of therapy.

Modifications and contraindications were suggested.

It is proposed only for psychotherapy, of course, and is considered as incidental to the deeper insights and transference reactions utilized by any dynamic school. With suitable care it probably facilitates rather than precludes more direct approaches, not excluding full psychoanalysis.

CARL ROGERS . . .

As I read this case material, it seems to me that my aims would in many ways be similar to those of this therapist. At least it would be my hope that the client could eventually come to live with her "good mother" feelings and also with her hostilities and hatreds. I would not find it necessary to know the pattern of her history in advance, nor would I need to make a decision as to whether to support her "good mother role" or to interpret her defenses.

Without, then, any of these diagnostic formulations, I would have endeavored simply to understand sensitively and to accept fully her frightening impulses to kill her child. I believe that this is the most supportive thing which I can do, but it means support for the person, not for her hostile impulses or her good ones. One reason for feeling comfortable about an empathic acceptance of her desires to kill her child is that I feel quite securely that she would not make any drastic moves of this sort while she was in a relationship where she could express such feelings.

We do not know, of course, quite why this client broke off her therapy. In my own work when a client breaks off in the middle of therapy like this, I wonder whether I have been completely acceptant of all the feelings she has had, or whether in some way I have been pushing her toward insights or understandings which I perceive as a goal but which she may not be ready for. I cannot help but wonder if this might have occurred in the present instance. A therapist who had to make an initial choice to use interpretation of a somewhat confronting nature would probably have used some such interpretations in spite of a conscious decision not to do so. If such interpretations were used, then certainly they would add to the anxiety and fright which the client would feel as she gets more and more deeply into her confusing and upsetting feelings about her early family life.

Certainly in the one attitude which the therapist specifically mentions, I would have endeavored fully to perceive her feeling that she can "never trust or depend on anyone." I would have been alert to any expression of this which seemed to be directed toward the therapist, and if such indications were present I would have responded with the general reaction that "quite possibly you feel toward me, too, that you can't trust or depend on anyone."

It would be my hope and perhaps my expectation that if I was sensitive enough in receiving all her feelings, this would support her through the darkest moments of therapy; but if through my error or perhaps through other causes she broke off therapy in the same way that she did in this incident, then I believe I would have reacted in these ways. When she called over the phone to terminate therapy, I would not have remained passive but I would have expressed to her my feelings that if she clearly wished to terminate, then I would fully accept and respect that decision. It is very likely that I would have told her that I would, however, save our next appointment hour free of any other engagements so that if she wished to use it, she could come in.

If she did not appear for this appointment, then I would have searched my own feelings to know as precisely as possible how I, myself, felt about her termination. I would then write her a letter expressing the feelings that existed in me in regard to her termination. I would not call her up on the phone because this seems to demand a response, and I would genuinely feel that she did not need to respond unless she wished to do so. I do not, of course, know precisely what my feelings would be in this situation, but it is probable that I would feel regret; that I would feel some concern that perhaps I had failed to be of help to her; that I would like to be of help to her; that I would wish her to be free to leave if that was her decision; that I would be pleased to have her return to work further with herself if that was her desire. I would try to express these feelings in this letter as freely and straightforwardly as possible.

If actually I found myself feeling quite anxious about what she might do without therapy, then it is likely that I would express this to her. I would probably say that I felt uneasy about her termination of therapy, that for my own peace of mind I would like her to return for one interview which would be *my* interview. There would be no charge for this since I was asking for it. I would simply wish to make use of this interview to be sure that it was clear in her own feelings whether or not she wished to terminate, and whether or not there was anything I might do which would enable her to obtain help she could use.

It may be noted that what I would be trying to do in such a letter would be to express the feelings that exist in myself. I would not be attempting to make any judgment about her. I feel that such judgments are not an expression of my own feelings but a projection of them. I would simply be writing the letter to make quite sure that I was saying as transparently as possible, "These are the feelings that exist in me. I want you to know in making your own choice about whether or not to continue therapy that I have no desire to hold you in therapy or to cause you to arrive at any given decision. I only hope that your decision will be made with some awareness of my feelings as well as yours."

I feel that such an exchange would be a real meeting of persons and that the reality in me would be coming in contact with the reality in her. This I believe is the essence of therapy both at usual times and at critical times.

If and when she returned, whether immediately or at any later date, my attempt would again be to be with her in her experiences, to be a genuine companion to her as she searched through and experienced the many disturbing and conflicting and denied aspects of her feelings.

I hope that what I have written about this is as far removed as possible from the "expertese" which makes solemn judgments about such incidents on the basis of the expert knowledge of the therapist as against the lack of insight of the client. I hope that, on the contrary, what I have said sounds like the attempt on my part to keep the relationship real, straight-forward, transparent, and deep. I am thinking of it and would hope to deal with it simply as a human relationship which it was important to maintain.

Summary

24

For this chapter the consultants' comments were analyzed to determine the major issues of each case. Following a brief summary of each critical incident the reader will find comparsions of the consultants' opinions on these major issues.

Case 1: "Don't Give Me Up!"

Tom, a 25-year-old prisoner with 13 years of correctional institutionalization, was admitted into group therapy but later expelled because of disruptive behavior. He pleaded with the therapist for help and was taken in individual therapy, evaluated by both as unsuccessful upon termination at the tenth session. Four months later Tom returned with an account of a conversion experience. Ten more individual sessions were held during which, again, little apparent progress was made. He rejoined the group and remained a year. With friendly social assistance from the therapist, Tom made a very good adjustment after release from prison.

Should Tom have been removed from the group? According to Thompson, removing Tom was correct. This move, in combination with the offer of individual help, established a climate which permitted later development. Frankl agrees removal was proper because Tom was disruptive. A therapeutic group cannot tolerate a person who will not abide by the basic rules of the group. Snyder argues that the therapist should have removed Tom even earlier. His failure to do so probably stemmed from inexperience and countertransference attitudes. Wolff says group therapy should not have been attempted with Tom, whose special problems disrupted the group. Herr points out that although there are difficulties in choosing between the welfare of the many and that of the individual, there often may be alternate solutions, as in this case.

Some consultants feel that Tom's expulsion was a crucial confrontation. Whitaker believes that Tom and the therapist were in a power struggle, and that therapeutic regression was induced when Tom lost. Riesman feels that Tom saw the therapist as a person to be exploited (presumably, therefore, a person who could not be significant) but in learning he was wrong, altered his views of reality. Blake thinks Tom felt that to accept authority was synonymous with admitting inadequacy—and that the massive rejection by society (imprisonment), peers, and therapist forced him to alter this attitude.

The therapist's reaction to Tom's plea, "If you give me up, then there is no hope for me," was another critical juncture. Hilgard says it was fortunate the therapist was equal to the demand, for Tom might never again have allowed himself to trust a human being enough to induce change. Sondel's semantical analysis of the plea reveals Tom's desire to remain in the group and in relationship with the therapist. Riesman says Tom's plea may have hidden a hope that the therapist would abandon him and thereby confirm his "perceptual map" of reality; but the therapist's offer to help confronted Tom with data he could not cynically misinterpret. According to Mowrer, Tom threw himself on the therapist's mercy and the therapist's powerful altruistic feelings led him to make a personal sacrifice for Tom. Mowrer commends the therapist for not analyzing away these feelings as mere "countertransference." Whitaker argues that in successful therapy the therapist himself must have the courage to grow; where the therapist fears growth and change, the patient dares not change. Herr takes a similar point of view. Therapy may become just a game, or the therapist may become hardened to the uniqueness and inherent value of the person. Tom's plea forced the therapist to grow, to realize that he was a humble instrumentality of larger forces. Wolff and Frankl see this encounter as an important moment of existential relationship or spiritual intimacy which set the stage for the later conversion experience.

Most of the consultants agree that the relationship between Tom and the therapist was essential to the success of therapy. According to Mowrer, a major factor was the therapist's respect for Tom, expressed in his statement that the "worst" people are often the "best." He also emphasizes the therapist's willingness to do some actual good for the patient as an example of a growing belief in psychotherapy that realistically deserved *gratitude* can be therapeutically effective.

Herr points out St. Paul's dictum that salvation cannot be obtained by faith alone, that good works are necessary. The therapist's concrete evidence of faith and love was irrefutable evidence to Tom that his former conception of life was false. For Sorokin, too, the critical factor was real concern, friendship, or altruistic love. He believes this to be true of all psychotherapeutic change. Snyder points out the therapist's inexperience in not recognizing the countertransference. He sees strong mutual affective interests, transference and countertransference, as the heart of therapy. It was Tom's recognition of the therapist's love that allowed him to change. Wolff seems close to Snyder's view. He says the friendship experience promoted the self-healing transformation. The unconscious contact of existential elements, the deep human contact, gave support through which restructuring could take place. Riesman and Frankl both see the "human encounter" as crucial. For Riesman, the therapist's willingness to be flexible conveyed to Tom the fact that he could matter to someone. Porter also believes that this flexibility was important, along with the therapist's positive feelings of altruism and respect. Thompson says Tom sensed a genuine interest, especially when, instead of rejecting him, the therapist took him on as an individual case. Thorne, similarly, attributes therapeutic efficacy to the therapist's belief in Tom. For Whitaker, the friendship or love element was unessential. It was, rather, the sheer genuineness of the relationship which was important. Hilgard and Sondel both see the relationship as having allowed Tom to identify with a figure of positive influence. For Hilgard, the therapist embodied the same socially conforming "good" values as had Tom's grandfather, and these suppressed values became reactivated. Sondel says the relationship gave Tom, a high-level person, a chance to identify with another high-level person. Blake lays practically no emphasis upon the relationship, except to point out the potency of rejection, even by a loving therapist.

The conversion gives rise to several interpretations. Herr and Frankl explain it in religious terms. For Herr unhappiness results from evil obscuring the basic good in man. The therapist reawakened Tom's consciousness of good—love, regard, hope, and so forth—and the conversion was a glimpse of the new life. Frankl sees the conversion as a "re-version," a return to "religio"—to previously repressed religiosity. Hillgard's explanation is similar. He says the conversion was the resolution of ambivalence which brought to the fore a well-integrated value system (conforming personality resulting from early identification with the grandfather) held in abeyance by a superimposed value system. Conversion is a dramatic occasion providing commitment to change. Thompson and Thorne view the conversion as a culmination or spontaneous fruition of the therapeutic process. Mowrer says the conversion was a foretaste of what life could mean, and he believes that much more should be known about the phenomenon. Wolff seems to attribute the frequent occurrence of conversion experiences to the kind of human contact inherent in "existential psychotherapy." Both Riesman and Frankl describe it as a reaction to a human encounter. Whitaker sees the cure as resulting from *bilateral* transference, and conversion, which is a word implying hysterical, cannot be used in connection with cure. The conversion was merely a sort of therapeutic psychosis which resulted when Tom permitted himself, for the first time in his life, to use fantasy for fantasy satisfaction in the place of using reality (acting out) for fantasy satisfaction. Snyder, too, explains the conversion in terms of transference and countertransference; but, he also expresses it in simpler terms: it resulted from Tom's realization that the therapist loved him. Blake's interpretation is almost directly opposed; the conversion is a reaction to the sudden realization that he has gone "beyond the point of no return" in unacceptability.

Some general observations on psychotherapy. Thompson says more psychopaths might be rehabilitated if more similarly dedicated therapists were available. Herr warns that people in the helping professions are likely to become hardened and lose sight of the person behind the problems. Porter finds therapists too provincial, poverty-stricken in concepts, and too willing to stake therapeutic success on a single rigid approach such as interpretation, reflection, and so forth. Riesman, too, argues for flexibility. Formula-grounded therapists cannot confront certain patients with behavior novel enough to challenge them to change their distorted "perceptual map" of the social environment. Sorokin sees in the case an example of the therapeutic influence of group affiliation in rehabilitation, a factor he says is given insufficient attention by many therapists. Thorne says that, contrary to the nondirective position, directive action may have long-term positive results even though it has short-term disruptive effects. Mowrer sees it as an example of therapy which goes beyond the traditional psycho-analytical approach revolving around transference, the therapeutic possibilities of which, he believes, have been pretty well exhausted. Frankl says that accounts like this make possible the extension of psychotherapy to the spiritual dimension.

Many consultants feel the therapist was technically inept, but his desire to help and his courage to respond with genuine feelings more than compensated for his inexperience. Blake is the only consultant to suggest that two person therapy may not have been necessary, that Tom's agonizing reappraisal of himself may have been brought about by the simultaneous massive rejection by society, his peers, and the therapist.

Case 2: "Behave Yourself!"

A 27-year-old girl whose behavioral problem was sexual promiscuity was treated by a passive approach to avoid meeting dependency needs.

There was little behavioral improvement throughout two years of therapy. After the patient went on a sexual binge, the therapist suddenly got tough and ordered her to stop. The patient seemed relieved, accepted responsibility for improving her behavior, and also became more active in her own therapy.

The major issue is the therapist's sudden authoritarian prohibition of sexual misbehavior after two years of permissiveness.

All consultants agree that authoritarian treatment is sometimes appropriate and that in this case it served a good end. Frankl believes the authoritative influence was not an issue since the therapist merely verbalized what the patient already knew. Klapman feels the therapist's injunction freed the patient from the thralldom of the mother's influence and gave her a chance to exercise her own will and judgment. Without the mediation by the therapist, the patient's internal conflict might have resulted in a schizophrenic withdrawal. Thorne says there are many cases where insight is achieved, but where no progress in behavior occurs. Such impasses often require confrontation of the patient with the discrepancy. Aldrich and, to some extent, Herr and Frankl believe the patient may have interpreted the therapist's passivity as sanction for her promiscuous sexual behavior. Aldrich, however, does not approve of the abruptness of the change in approach—the patient might have seen it as a betrayal. Ellis, too, although agreeing that intervention is often desirable, feels the abrupt change was too risky. Herr is most explicit that such interventions must be made at the discretion of the therapist, but that he has the duty to protect not only the interests of the patient but also the interests of society.

Klapman sees the injunction against authoritarianism as a sacred cow, inherited from psychoanalysis, which has become a therapeutic phobia and obsession. Frankl criticizes the nonevaluative, nonjudgmental approach as a characteristic of Anglo-Saxon psychotherapy, and, he says, such an approach is more likely to imply judgment than is interference. Thorne believes the passivity a product of an untenable principle of nondirective theory, that directiveness will always be resisted. On the contrary, he says, such passive handling may cause a loss of respect for the therapist and subsequent withdrawal by the patient. For Herr, the decision to let the patient chart his own course involves grave ethical considerations. Although he does not prohibit such a procedure, he points out that different cases involve different degrees of responsibility on the part of the patient; and therapists who espouse blanket independence for the patient may overlook these ethical considerations.

There is general agreement that under some circumstances the therapist should intervene with outright prohibitions and take a strong stand with reference to the patient's behavior. When to do this, and how, are matters which call for great sensitivity and judgement.

Case 3: On a Saturday Afternoon

Joan, a 19-year-old college freshman, previously diagnosed on the basis of a Rorschach as schizophrenic, was treated along client-centered lines after consultation with a psychiatrist. Although usually late, Joan arrived punctually for her fourteenth appointment. Because she was obviously distressed, the therapist offered to extend the interview. After an hour and a half the therapist mentioned the time. A half hour later he did so again. She was visibly disturbed each time, and because of her disturbed behavior the therapist began to make interpretations. Joan then told of incestuous relations with her father. After this confession she relaxed. The session lasted a total of three hours.

Was time handled correctly? Aldrich and Snyder criticize the time handling. With firmly structured time limits, says Aldrich, the patient can pace himself. Snyder feels an unknown termination point is threatening to patient and therapist, and, except in special emergencies, a therapist can give of himself more freely when he knows when the session will end.

For Dreikurs the time factor was not well utilized. A firm limit could have precipitated the crisis and when one was finally set, it did encourage the patient to tell what she had to tell. Karpf and Whitaker feel the patient's recurrent tardiness called for earlier intervention; but both, along with Frank, approve of extending the time. Karpf and Frank add that the therapist's reasons for offering more time should have been made clear to the patient. Rogers feels it was fortunate that the therapist could extend the time when he saw how disturbed the client was, but he adds that if the therapist had not felt comfortable about doing so, it would have been unwise. He is confident that the expressed material would have emerged eventually. Porter and Munroe compliment the therapist on his flexibility and lack of slavish adherence to rules. Thorne and Frankl believe the therapist was right to extend the time in view of the changed circumstances.

Was the therapist seductive? Dreikurs sees no seductive interplay, only indecision. Aldrich sees seduction, but feels the therapist was too inexperienced to recognize it or realize its implications. Mowrer agrees seduction may have occurred. Munroe says borderline paranoid patients are likely to project "rejection," "seduction," and so forth, out of proportion to the therapist's actual behavior and so extreme caution is required with them. Porter looks at the therapist's behavior through Joan's eyes and finds it highly seductive. Snyder believes the unlimited time was seductive. Frank and Whitaker think the story of incest with her father reflected the patient's conflicting sexual feelings about the therapist. Whitaker believes the account was an invitation to the therapist to seduce her. Frank regards the incident as a covert sexual encounter on the parts of both patient and therapist.

Reflection or interpretation? Porter distinguishes between reflection and interpretation. What matters is the therapist's *intent,* not his *words.* If his response aims at furthering his own understanding of what the client is communicating, that is reflection; if his aim is to communicate to the client what the client's words mean, that is interpretation. Rogers takes issue with identifying "merely reflecting" with the client-centered approach. The true client-centered response is empathic acceptance, the effort to feel in oneself what the client is feeling and to communicate that understanding. Complete empathic understanding is impossible, but the *desire* to understand is the important factor. Thorne agrees with Porter and Rogers that interpreting was unwise here since the patient was under sufficient stress to unburden herself without external stimulation; a sympathetic listener was all that was needed. Snyder, Munroe, and Dreikurs recommend gentle or modified interpretation. Snyder believes the patient was too disturbed for abrupt interpretation of transference elements, but that gentler interpretation might have helped. Dreikurs feels the patient came prepared to express herself and that gentle probing and coaxing at the start would have accomplished with less trauma and more speed what the belated interpretation did. Munroe contends that insight alone would have had little value because of the patient's weak ego structure. She recommends a more educational approach where, within the context of a supportive, encouraging relationship, gentle interpretations are coupled with suggested generalizations to external reality. Whitaker says interpretations or reflections would have been mere verbal smoke screens in this case; the depth of the relationship far outweighed matters of technical competence. Frankl sees both interpretation and reflection as inadequate since they are aimed at elucidating complexes and symptoms. Such is not the main task of psychotherapy; it is reorientation of the patient to the meaning and value of life—helping her find her own "will-to-meaning." Mowrer also regards interpretation and reflection as insufficient. The guilt that makes people ill, contrary to the working assumption of Freud and his followers, is not always false guilt, but may be based on actual transgression. Therefore, self-acceptance through confession is not enough; a program of positive action may be needed.

How well was the case handled? Thorne feels it would have been safer to refer the patient to a more experienced therapist, preferably a psychiatrist; but, as in this case, it often is not possible. Fortunately the therapist stumbled upon the right procedure, which was to allow the patient to ventilate her feelings. Aldrich states that the diagnosis of paranoid schizophrenia implies the likelihood of dangerous behavior and that it is essential that a psychiatrist participate more fully to insure appropriate medical and legal safeguards. He also points out that a Rorschach diagnosis is insufficient. Snyder raises the question of whether or not a clinic solely ultilizing client-centered methods should treat outright psychotics, since there is not yet enough evidence that the approach is suitable for such cases. Frankl disagrees that the patient was schizophrenic or that the office episode was a psychotic break. Karpf, too, seems doubtful as to the diagnosis of schizophrenia, but asks why, in view of the diagnosis, the patient was not referred to a psychiatrist for treatment. Porter likes the therapist's evident respect for the patient and his willingness to depart from client-centered tradition. He says the therapist, far from being in-decisive, was very decisive in acting out his willingness to give completely of his time. Rogers commends the therapist for his ability to be transparent to his own feelings and to follow their dictates, factors he sees as essential to therapeutic change. Whitaker, too, praises this genuineness as being the most important element in the therapist's approach. Mowrer, Porter, and Munroe praise the therapist's humanity and sincere desire to help.

Case 4: "Hold Me! Hold Me!"

A patient confronted by the possibility of a uterine carcinoma arrived trembling and desperate. The therapist touched her head, and the patient clutched the therapist and sobbed. After a few minutes the patient relaxed.

The therapist feels this is an illustration of the psychological union that provides soil for growth. However, she questions the appropriateness of the physical contact, though it seemed necessary as part of a bridge.

Munroe entirely agrees with the therapist's position that the patient needed direct psychological union with a strong, loving person. Rogers feels that the therapist had much to offer: deep feelings of warmth and acceptance, which were transparent to herself. For Klapman, the therapist was an anchor point in the patient's terrible isolation. Riesman believes the patient pulled herself together in order not to let the therapist down.

Thorne and Dreikurs, though generally approving of the therapist's warmth and encouragement, agree that little was accomplished thera-peutically by the "psychological union." Dreikurs says the patient gained no insight or reorientation in her view that no beneficient forces exist, but merely enlisted the therapist as a new source of the strength she needed to fight the world singlehandedly. Thorne says she simply utilized her usual defense, that is, open admission of weakness and throwing herself upon the other person's mercy in order to gain sympathy and support.

All consultants support the therapist's view that physical contact was permissible and helpful. Riesman believes the more primitive physical contact was especially important in view of the patient's lower-class origin and consequent difficulty with abstract concepts. Rogers thinks the physical contact was all right, so long as the therapist was genuinely comfortable with it. Dreikurs believes it fortified the intense communication and expressed warmth, sympathy, and involvement. Munroe feels that physical contact is desirable, even necessary, in reaching some psychotics; and, although approving in this instance, adds that after such a major deviation from the usual rule, the therapist should take stock and readjust the relationship. Thorne believes physical contact should be very limited, preferring soothing words in such emergencies. Needs for dependency should be reflected nondirectively. Allowing the client to achieve support through physical intimacy weakens his attempt to unify himself independently. Thorne agrees with Munroe that such deviations call for very prompt stock-taking and readjustment by the therapist.

Opinions on the interpretation of God are varied. Dreikurs sees no significant interpretation to the patient, largely because the therapist is unaware of the true dynamics of the case. Nothing was added by the interpretation, says Rogers; it was merely an expression about which the therapist could have no primary knowledge, as she does about her feelings. There would have been more meaning to empathically living through the patient's fears with her. Riesman likes the therapist's ability to transcend her own viewpoint (obvious in her words "unrealistic turning to God") and to reinterpret the patient's theistic striving in a way which gave her strength. Munroe believes the patient was brought back to the reality problem through the tactful interpretation of God. She sees this interplay as a very good example of her "intellectualizing technique" and believes it played an important part in the patient's recovery and maintenance of control.

There are some isolated observations of considerable interest. Klapman points out that the very hypersensitivity that makes life hazardous to such a person also makes her much more amenable to the beneficial elements of therapy. Munroe, though firmly opposed to the Reichian approach in general, is interested in the possibilities of direct attack on the "body armor" and believes physical contact may some day become a feasible adjunct in some situations. Riesman, a sociologist, is struck by the quiet courage displayed by the therapists who, time after time, must face such violent upheavals in the client or patient with little more than themselves as tools. Rogers feels the order of events in the crisis is reversed; it was the client's perception of the therapist's fear which precipitated the psychotic break, not vice versa. Although there is no doubt that heredity, constitutional makeup, and chemical factors have a part in the predisposition to psychosis, psychologically a psychosis occurs only when human relationships break down.

Case 5: Socratic Therapy

The patient, a 27-year-old male, displayed ruminations, scrupulosity, perfectionism, and depressed spells. At one session he arrived in a depressed mood and was handled by an inductive approach to generalization through dialogue, by which his mood was strikingly transformed. The therapist says the procedure exemplifies the "Socratic method," the importance of dealing with the "on-going" situation rather than with historical factors, and the ego support derived from self-discovery by patients.

How useful is the procedure? Ellis is enthusiastic about the Socratic approach and states that under the name *rational therapy* he often uses a very similar method. Psychotherapy has neglected direct attempts to demonstrate, by examining the patient's basic assumptions, that his present irrational and illogical ways of behaving are wrong. The less efficacious interpretive technique shows the patient only how symptomatic attitudes and behaviors were originally acquired. Mowrer is encouraged by another instance of psychotherapists' willingness to try new, unorthodox techniques. Specifically, he believes this technique illustrates the possibility that changes in behavior may often necessarily precede insight rather than follow it. Munroe regards the Socratic method as an example of her "intellectualizing" approach. She approves, but cautions that depressed spells may be very complex, masking psychosis or acute mood disturbances, and hence this technique should be used sparingly. She prefers a broader sharing of understandings, utilizing the transference. Thorne believes the treatment and results are only symptomatic. Also, as does Munroe, he regards this patient as only mildly disturbed. The Socratic method would be almost useless, or even dangerous, where the client was deeply disturbed, since there would not be enough control over impulses to utilize the instruction. Porter disapproves of the method and feels that a nondirective approach would have obtained the same good results. Riesman indicates a danger of permissive therapy in which a myth of individual nonresponsibility may arise. A vigorous, intellectual, logical approach like this one seems preferable for some patients.

Should the emphasis be on the present or the past? Mower says that dwelling upon and blaming the past may deprive the patient of hope for his own responsibility and, therefore, the possibility of self-directed change. Porter readily agrees that little can be accomplished by dealing with "ghosts" from the past. The past can be dealt with effectively, however, with the client-centered procedure of emphasizing *present* feelings about the past. Ellis approves of the emphasis upon the present. He believes that with concentration on the irrational thinking of the patient in the here and now most problems of psychotherapy will be solved.

What is the importance of self-discovery? Munroe agrees heartily that self-discovery is a "valid and realistic" ego boosting, but she stresses the importance of its occurring within a transference relationship. The value of self-discovery, according to Porter, is a central tenet of client-centered therapy. What puzzles him is why other therapists, once hitting upon this concept, do not try to order their therapeutic behavior more fully around efforts to promote self-discovery and abandon efforts to teach.

Case 6: "I Love You, Doctor"

The patient, a beautiful widow of 21, confessed her attraction for the therapist, who attempted to explain the attraction as derived from transference. When the patient convinced him that her sentiments were real, the therapist suggested she go to someone else for treatment. She accepted the suggestion, but when the therapist gave her information about himself to the effect that he might not be as desirable a mate as she had imagined, the patient changed her mind and stayed in therapy, which then proceeded successfully.

The therapist feels that many "transferences" have clear-cut reality bases and, in such cases, to insist that classic transference exists is to force a false interpretation of the situation. He says this should be recognized as a problem.

Why do patients fall in love with their therapists? All consultants agree that this commonly occurs. Mowrer feels that, although reality factors may have been involved in this case, too often this is not so and other explanations must be found. If the patient can seduce and corrupt authority, he discredits the therapy and is relieved of the necessity of going through with it. An alternate explanation is that the patients simply are attempting to regenerate meaning, if only briefly, in otherwise empty lives by experiencing themselves more vividly in the sexual act. Riesman says in our culture a visit to the doctor is often a form of social mobility. The professional man appeals to women on a soap-opera-glamor level; but, also, on a quite realistic basis. Dreikurs feels there are often very real factors in the patient's attraction to the therapist—the relationship is probably better than any the patient has ever had. But there are also neurotic elements operating. Only a pessimistic attitude reflecting eventual unhappiness in marriage would permit a patient to disregard the red light in the therapeutic relationship. Such attractions may indicate the patient's intention to fall for the wrong mate to prove the correctness of the underlying pessimism. In another explanation Dreikurs says the patient attempts to deprive the therapist of his role by making an ordinary man of him. It is a way of resisting therapy by negating the therapist's influence. Frank bases his explanation on the patient's pervasive demoralization. Her misperception of others (in this case the therapist) is an attempt to protect herself from feelings of failure. Aldrich feels that the patient's seductiveness was an expression of hostility and that the therapist was probably showing his own hostility through counterseductiveness. Thompson states that falling in love with the therapist occurs more frequently with female patients because of cultural factors. The patient sees the therapist as a safe bet for marriage. Unlike Mowrer, Thompson feels that in such cases the therapist always has shown some personal response to the patient, even though it may have been unconscious and very slight. Galdston disagrees that there is any reality basis, in this case, but sees the patient's vigorous, aggressive, and domineering pursuit as part of her fundamental neurotic pattern.

How well was this case handled? Aldrich is disappointed in the therapist and sees his lengthy dissertation to the patient as hostile counterseduction which frightened the patient. She remained in therapy not because of the flimsy reorientation to the true state of affairs, but because she needed help so badly and because his abandoning the role of counterseducer reassured her. Frank says that trust is the basis for therapeutic readjustment, and that trust is based on accurate as well as distorted perceptions. The mature therapist will acknowledge accurate perceptions, accept the accompanying feelings whether good or bad, and, where the feelings cannot be resolved, refer the patient to another therapist. Munroe feels the reality factors were dealt with and then the transference elements were understood. Dreikurs and Aldrich say the therapist missed an opportunity to analyze and interpret the patient's behavior.

Several consultants deplore the fact that therapists too often use "transference" as a refuge from dealing with their own feelings, either alone or openly with the patient. Thompson believes the analysis of many an attractive woman comes to grief when the therapist, guilty because of his own thoughts, does not dare to deal directly with the situation, but talks about transference while, at the same time, behind his professional mask he continues to enjoy the sight and presence of the patient. Riesman points out that the frequent attempt of therapists to hide behind the concept of transference throws the emphasis upon the past and thereby prevents patients from dealing with the more painful present, further obfuscating and alienating patients from their own feelings. Galdston commends the therapist's questioning the classical sham and humbug of the analyst's pose as a psychic castrate. He agrees with the therapist, and others, that where the patient's attachment derives from reality it should be recognized and used constructively.

Mowrer cites evidence that the psychoanalytic dictum to avoid imposing values upon the patient is impossible. Furthermore, it may not even be desirable. Perhaps there are values we can legitimately exchange for the patient's old ones. If so, the therapeutic problem is how to get the patient to accept such alternative values.

Case 7: "Don't Help Jim Read"

A therapist hypothesized that Jim, a 12-year-old boy, was unconsciously using poor reading to gain his mother's attention, and that the mother's need to feel needed contributed to the reading problem. He decided to "trick" the mother out of her "helping" pattern by getting her to withhold all help for two weeks and to indicate to the boy that learning to read was his own problem. Jim's reading improved markedly. The therapist then confessed his "duplicity" to the mother.

The therapist asks several questions regarding the correctness of his hypothesis and the ethical justification of his procedure.

Was duplicity necessary or desirable? Herr says that there might have been even greater risk if the mother had known of the dynamics; Riesman says favorable results partially vindicate the therapist; and Sondel says the hypothesis was reasonable. However, arguments against the procedure are much stronger and are presented by all the other consultants. Aldrich, Hilgard, and Hunt feel duplicity was unnecessary. Some factor, possibly the mother's insight into the problem, must have already changed, otherwise she would not have been able to follow instructions. Blake and Karpf feel strongly that the approach was unwise. Blake says the basic problem between mother and son was not changed through manipulation and that it is likely to come out in other forms. Karpf agrees with Blake that although short-term results were good, long-term effects may be bad. She says such arbitrary handling is hazardous, especially the abrupt removal of support from an exceptionally dependent child. Both Hunt and Karpf present reasoning upon which the therapist might have elected courses of action other than duplicity. If his hypothesis about the mother's need to keep Jim a baby were correct, she could not have followed instructions and could have obstructed Jim's progress in various other ways. If his hypothesis about the mother's need were wrong, then she would have accepted the explanation of the effects of her overconcern, and both she and her son might have been better prepared for such a drastic change. Furthermore, if the mother needed more therapy (which she most certainly would if the therapist's hypothesis were correct), he had fostered mistrust on her part and at least partially closed the door to future therapeutic help for her.

What is the ethical status of the therapist's procedure? Herr finds no reputable code of ethics which binds a person, professional or otherwise, to tell all his motivations. The point is especially true in this case because of the uncertainty involved. Sondel sees the question of ethics as superfluous. One cannot talk about ends justifying means unless there are specific ends and specific operational means; not the case here. She points out the question must have arisen from the therapist's inner conflicts. A therapist who is fully patient-directed never entertains such thoughts as "duplicity," "trick," and "confession." Aldrich, too, believes the therapist's ethical doubts arise from internal confusion. If his therapeutic morality excluded deception, he might well be ashamed, but not guilty and called upon to confess. Herr says the anxiety may have proceeded from the therapist's taking on total responsibility for the cure, rather than from lying to the mother. Riesman feels that, although there was some ethical approbrium in using the same controlling tactics with the mother that she used with Jim, the therapist's ultimate aim of liberating both Jim and the mother from dependence on experts vindicates him. Blake feels that no ethical problem is involved in such approaches so long as the client is aware that psychotherapy in the ordinary sense is not being administered, and knows that forces of which he is unaware are being manipulated with the aim of a positive outcome. To Karpf, the question in this case seems more one of judgment and viewpoint than ethics. If one believes in authoritarian types of therapy, the therapist's procedure was justified, assuming that his judgment was correct; if one does not believe in an authoritarian approach, he was not justified. However, she adds that psychotherapeutic techniques involve the individual's basic rights. Too much manipulation can put the therapist in a dictator's role which is not appropriate in a democratic society.

What theoretical issues are involved? Aldrich says the reading failure was prolonged, not caused, by the mother's attention, and that this is an example of effective treatment directed at secondary gains. For Hunt, the case illustrates the technique of manipulating social motives and social stimuli which produce them. Blake points out that the approach was not psychotherapy but psychodynamic engineering. The results came from instruction or manipulation and lack the hallmarks of therapeutic growth. Hilgard finds the case important because reading problems have been so resistant to clear solutions. A complete psychology of learning must recognize the psychodynamic context with its basic implication that there may be obstacles to learning which the learner, although consciously wishing to learn, cannot overcome.

Case 8: All Alone by the Telephone

The patient, a foreign girl, was living in a rented room in a strange city, knowing only one family friend and the therapist. For weeks during treatment she was despondent and withdrawn, but kept appointments regularly. During one session, she talked about suicide. The next day she missed her appointment. The therapist feared she might commit suicide; nevertheless, he decided to avoid being drawn into her net of domination by waiting and doing nothing. The patient called later, giving a palpably false excuse, and the missed appointment was not discussed further. Three months after leaving therapy, which terminated soon after the incident, the patient wrote: "I have never hated anyone so much as I hate you. Because I know now that I have only one way before me: to get well." Three years later she visited the therapist and confirmed that his actions gave her the feeling she was understood.

What was the main factor in the patient's change? Klapman says the patient realized the therapist really understood her; but, she also saw that he was not having any of this self-defeating behavior. The healthy part of her personality insisted that the therapist was right, and she had to get well. Porter says that although the therapist's attitudes toward her decision not to come were actually manipulative, he demonstrated a kind of respect by not intervening and thereby bestowed upon her a rare gift: the realization that she could be responsible for herself. Karpf thinks other factors, such as the American relative, may have contributed to the change, but it was heavily influenced by the early establishment of a significant relationship. Herr sees the effective element as a combination of a delicate balance of appreciation and understanding with feelings of confidence in a favorable outcome. Wolff says the patient's basic experience was to be abandoned, disliked, and made to feel worthless. The therapist conveyed the fact that an important person trusted, understood, and believed in her. Dreikurs grants that the friendly feelings and respect were important, but much more important was the therapist's refusal to be intimidated, thereby becoming a match for her.

How should a therapist deal with possible suicide? Herr says that the ethics of nonintervention have been discussed by moralists and ethicians, usually to no avail. There are no concrete answers as to what to do in such situations. However, he points out that the effects of "not permitting" and "scolding" are well known to be bad, whereas understanding and trust often bring good results. Karpf takes an opposite view. Most therapists would probably prefer a more active approach where there is a possibility of suicide and work out any repercussions in the course of therapy. However, she does not give any indication of just what should be done.

How was the therapist's over-all handling of the case? Klapman feels the therapist displayed penetrating understanding of the dynamics and that the patient was handled with finesse. Wolff, Herr, and Porter are generally approving, though Porter would like to see less emphasis upon what techniques to use and more emphasis upon genuinely respecting the patient. Both Karpf and Dreikurs feel the case was too risky to treat under the circumstances. Dreikurs is especially concerned about taking on a person who did not have even enough trust to give the therapist her address. At least this fear should have been worked out before continuing therapy.

Karpf wonders why the therapist did not explore with the patient her true reasons for missing the appointment.

There are several general observations on therapy. Dreikurs points out that doing the unexpected sometimes is good, especially where the therapist is on the run or cornered; it deprives the patient of his systematic (but mostly unconscious) scheming procedure. However, shock techniques are best used only in deteriorating relationships. Their effect on a good relationship may be poor. Klapman feels the patient, although self-defeating and resistant, always has a healthy part of the personality that longs for understanding and rescue from his situation. Porter believes that everyone has independency needs as well as those for dependency. Is it not likely that "feeding" independency needs through respect and nonintervention will make those needs grow and become predominant in behavior, just as feeding dependency needs seems to make them grow. Wolff says provocations of the therapist are rooted in resistance and transference. Those due to resistance challenge the therapist's initiative; those due to transference challenge his emotional relations. However, in cases of "existential isolation," such as this was, the therapist may have to prove his "humanness" in order to establish an effective relationship. Herr says it would be a real scientific contribution if it could be shown how a person becomes endowed with a conviction of his own worth and gains the determination to pursue worthwhile goals when no one else in the world seems to find any good in him. Karpf regards this case as a triumph of brief therapy, in which a strong relationship continued to have a significant, beneficial effect on the patient's life in spite of its brief duration.

Case 9: "I'll Kill You If You Leave Me!"

A woman patient, the main support of an irresponsible husband and three teen-age children, wanted a divorce. The husband threatened to kill her and the children if she went through with the plan. The therapist, after discussing the matter with both of them, became convinced that the husband was a dangerous paranoid. Unless the husband would consent to psychiatric treatment, the therapist could do nothing but advise legal aid for the wife. The husband refused, and effective legal aid proved impossible. Later, after threatening to shoot the wife, the husband killed himself.

How well did the therapist handle the situation? Hunt, Klapman, and Mowrer commend the therapist. Hunt especially liked the fact that he checked on the story by interviewing the husband and took into consideration the whole family's welfare. Therapists too often take responsibility only for the patient. Klapman says the case could not have been better handled. Mowrer states the management of the case is somewhat of a model. However, Thorne and Eliasberg feel the therapist should have called in a psychiatrist. Eliasberg would ask for an accurate diagnosis; and Thorne would question whether the husband should not have been institutionalized. However, some consultants doubt the wisdom of forced institutionalization, and some question whether or not the husband's treatment was neglected. Klapman says the slight behavior improvement after a few interviews showed there was a healthy part to the husband's personality. Dreikurs and Eliasberg say the therapist should have probed for homosexual tendencies, or for doubts about his masculinity. In addition, Dreikurs would have concentrated on freeing the wife from fear, since fear could only increase her danger. Mowrer says the husband's lifelong history of "sins of omission" made it difficult for him to change, but that the therapist should have tried.

Why did the husband kill himself? According to the story as told by the wife and substantiated by the evidence, the husband threatened to kill his wife, but suddenly turned the gun on himself. Dreikurs, Klapman, and Hunt agree that the reason for the suicide must have been the wife's sudden acceptance of her fate, although they interpret differently the husband's reaction. Dreikurs says when she did not care any more, the husband lost his power over her. There was then no longer any sense in threatening her. Hunt says the husband was a narcissistic failure and that his wife was his most immediately frustrating object. Her abject submission to his death threat both satisfied his need to harm her and suddenly intensified his own self-deprecation. Klapman's view is almost identical. The husband's life was built about grandiose heroic aims, which increasingly were shown to be futile. His wife's wish to leave him was the greatest evidence of his failure. To kill her, with apparent justification, would have removed the reminder of his inadequacy. Her sudden capitulation brought about an agonizing moment of insight and in his despair at what he saw, he destroyed himself.

What are the legal considerations? Thorne believes such cases should be referred immediately to a psychiatrist or a physician empowered to institute commitment procedures, or to legal authority. Klapman comments that if the husband had been committed, he would probably have been given only perfunctory treatment and then released. His delusions about his wife would have been given objective confirmation and his homicidal tendencies would have been increased. Thompson comments that at present there is no adequate way of protecting anyone from the destructive behavior of paranoids, who, when the occasion demands, can appear deceptively normal. She says it is criminal to ask a lay jury or a judge without psychiatric training to make final decisions about the sanity of a potential killer. Hunt, Eliasberg, Mowrer, and Thompson call for closer cooperation between the courts and the professions concerned with such cases. Hunt asks that psychologists, social workers, and psychiatrists try to cast diagnostic statements into predictive terms instead of the dynamic form limited to what goes on within individuals. Without predictive statements, which can be shown to have statistical validity, society will not change its laws so that the freedom of individuals can be restricted before they commit tragic acts.

Case 10: Client-centered Hypnosis?

A prisoner, who referred himself for therapy, was treated for about a year by means of client-centered therapy. Good progress was noted, but due to external reasons, therapy was about to end. The patient protested that there was something "which had to come out" but which failed to appear during several more sessions. The therapist used hypnosis, which brought forth the memory of a childhood "murder." This seemed to relieve the patient, and he made a good adjustment upon release from prison.

What was the value of hypnosis in this case and as a general therapeutic technique? Frankl states the aim of psychotherapy is to educate the patient toward self-reliability and responsibility. Hypnosis may limit the freedom and responsibility of the patient. However, in this case it was the only thing that worked. Ellis, too, feels that hypnosis does little to enhance the patient's self-confidence, but he disagrees with the therapist's contention that it should not be used in therapy, since in some cases it can be very valuable. He also sees it as a useful diagnostic tool. Galdston feels the hypnosis was important only because it demonstrated the therapist's interest and willingness actively to help the patient. Blake believes the repressed material would have been brought to light eventually, whether by the client-centered technique, an interpretive method, or hypnosis. Eliasberg, Blake and Galdston believe the patient's development depended upon therapeutic factors other than the hypnotic treatment.

It is wise to use procedures which depart from a consistent frame of reference? Here Porter takes the field against the others. Porter's essential message is that a systematic position requires that the therapist keep to it, since only by being consistent can he test his theory. Jumping about gives him no information, and apparent failure with one procedure and success with another does not tell him whether or not keeping to the original premise would have succeeded. The client-centered point of view is best conceived as a series of hypotheses which can be established as laws only by testing them fully. He implies that the primary motivation of client-centered therapists is the understanding of therapy, which, of course, is not inconsistent with helping patients. Aldrich and Eliasberg react exactly opposite to Porter. Using one technique stubbornly is like giving penicillin to all patients with fevers or always amputating the left leg, regardless of the illness. The therapist's task is to help the patient; and rigid adherence to any theory or procedure is incorrect. Ellis regards the therapist's departure from his theory as sound. Galdston points out that some cases require a "therapist centered" approach. Frankl says that any system of psychotherapy must give way when the patient's welfare is at stake.

Case 11: Hans Finds a Father

A 60-year-old male of German origin, self-referred to a state hospital, was diagnosed as "psychoneurosis-mixed—prognosis, poor." He was regarded by the staff as an intelligent, dependent, demanding, and hostile person who had "found a home" in the hospital. After four months of therapy, during which the patient manipulated the situation with psychiatric jargon, was frequently late for appointments, and generally abusive and complaining, the therapist finally lost his temper and spoke angrily—quite differently from his prior passively accepting manner. The therapy took a decided turn for the better and eventually the patient made a good adjustment outside of the hospital.

Why did this outburst produce good results? According to Dreikurs, the patient was a spoiled child who got into a power contest with whomever opposed him. He had successfully impressed the therapist into his "service," but when the therapist finally showed strength, the patient backed down. The therapist's aggressive behavior was interpreted as implying genuine appreciation and respect. Frank points out that tyrannical German fathers may express interest and affection in ways which Americans regard as showing hostility. The patient needed to feel that the helpgiver was strong, and therefore the therapist's initial politeness was perceived as weakness and lack of interest. When the therapist was openly critical, the patient accepted him as a person who could help. Frankl says that under all circumstances the patient is entitled to compassion; however, certain situations call for expression of emotional value judgments or even explicit condemnation of a patient's actions. Persons have a right to be punished as well as rewarded. Universal forgiveness is in reality a degradation of a patient or a criminal. The therapist's aggressiveness indicated a willingness to meet the patient on a man-to-man level and proved to the patient that he was considered seriously as a person who should be ready to take responsibility.

Galdston, Thorne, Ellis, and Klapman are opposed to the use of non-directive or permissive techniques with such patients. Galdston says patients of this type, often from Germanic backgrounds, are not suitable for classical or active analysis but require guidance in addition to pressing and uncovering therapy. Thorne feels that nondirective handling puts such patients in complete control. They must be shocked, so that an inner conflict is created, and then they will take a good look at themselves. He points out that shock has to be handled selectively for it may backfire. Ellis feels this is an example of a patient who had developed iron-clad rationalizations to explain his illness and must be made to take a more negative attitude toward his behavior. Mild-mannered propaganda is likely to be ineffective in changing such attitudes. Although not always recommended, sometimes the therapist must use shock techniques to get through the patient's systemized delusions. Klapman says a psychoanalytically trained, passive therapist is nothing but an inanimate sounding board for such patients. The explosion cut across façades—the superficial gyrations of the patient and the polite, disdainful, unconscious attitude of the therapist—and created conditions for a meeting of the minds and feelings so that the healthy part of the patient's personality could utilize help. Wolff believes that unconscious communication was established by the blowup. The patient's attitude had mobilized the therapist's needs for assertion and dominance which facilitated the patient's projection of a "tyrannical father," but the therapist's expressed interest produced a feeling that *this* father figure accepted him as a person.

Whitaker and Rogers take the position that the early relationship had been false in that the therapist had acted a role. Only when the therapist took off his mask did the relationship become honest. Whitaker indicates the therapist actually became a patient for a time. Rogers reiterates that in therapy there is no substitute for genuineness of relationship. At least one person in the therapeutic situation must be thoroughly integrated—aware of his feelings and willing to express them. Only when the therapist brings in his whole self can therapy really proceed. When this therapist became genuinely angry he was no longer playing a role, as he had been before with his apparent permissiveness. Anger and annoyance were not necessarily the most therapeutic feelings to have. Had the therapist been genuinely comfortable and completely accepting of the patient's hostile and critical attitudes, therapy would have moved forward just as fast, and probably faster. However, so long as the therapist did not possess such accepting attitudes, it was important for him to express the attitudes he did have.

Case 12: Rescue at the Cliff-House

A beautiful girl of 22, recently divorced, developed a severe depression. She was hospitalized and treated with 20 electroshocks. After this treatment she was advised to seek "emotional counseling." She began psychotherapy but was aggressive towards the therapist, late for appointments, and made the therapist an "unwilling referee" between herself and her father. The therapist structured limits of their relationship in detail in an attempt to prevent her from exploiting him. One evening shortly thereafter, the patient telephoned from an isolated cliff house where her lover had abandoned her without funds or transportation. The therapist, after some consideration of what to do, picked up the patient and drove her home. Following this incident, the patient stopped her hypomanic behavior, kept within therapeutic limits, and developed a good relationship with a young man. She became, however, more dependent upon the therapist and her parents.

Was the therapist wise to rescue the patient? Snyder and Thorne disapprove. Snyder points out that immediately after going to great lengths to structure limits, the therapist complied with the patient's first demands. Instead of helping her to find acceptable ways of living, he let her become dependent on him. Snyder feels there is no theoretical justification for actions which lead to the therapist assuming a submissive role. Thorne believes most situations of this sort can best be handled by nondirective responses or telephone suggestions. In the occasional case where such a procedure will not be enough, the therapist should have available dependable consultants to insure professional protection for himself and proper care for the patient. Thorne admits the therapist had to do something, but he should have been accompanied by a physician or a chaperon to insure against attempted seduction by the patient or misinterpretation of his behavior.

On the other hand, Ackerman believes the therapist's actions "saved the day." He is critical of the therapist for doing so little. The therapist was confused—hesitant to leave his barricaded position as an office therapist. Psychotherapy with a mature adult is one thing, but the therapist in this case was dealing with a patient scarcely out of adolescence and trapped in a pathologically warped pattern of family interaction. He had to provide protection. Wolff feels that acts of friendship can interfere with transference. However, insistence upon a therapeutically neutral atmosphere, as Freud's recommendation of independence from the patient can be interpreted, may be harmful. Neutrality can be perceived as rejection, thereby supporting a patient's feeling of existential isolation. In this case, the transference received depth. The tyrannical interference of the father was replaced by the helpful assistance of the therapist. The positive turn of therapy resulted from this humane act.

Klapman approves of the therapist's actions; but he is not sure they really turned the tide. The girl was in an iron-bound impasse, torn between her desire to pursue her own goals and her desire to retain her parents' affection. A compromise represents capitulation, which might be death to her personality. The flash of insight over the incident may prove to be help-ful, but it also may herald a complete breakdown.

Riesman sees the therapist as troubled by his violation of the norms of passivity. Why did the therapist not think of some alternative course of action, such as sending a taxi? Riesman believes that when a therapist can see only several unpalatable alternatives he may be limited in his perspec-tive and should refer the patient to someone else, who, though also limited, may have blind spots not so detrimental in the particular case. Ideally, of course, a therapist should have a behavioral repertoire flexible enough to confront the patient with various facets of himself.

Mowrer believes that by returning good for evil the therapist *showed* the patient her inferiority in a compelling manner. He sees in such con-crete social acts a tendency to abrogate established therapeutic concepts and practice. Relatedness, through such acts, may be more important than the release of repressed instinctual forces through expert interpretations. He says the time is approaching when a whole new theoretical structure will be needed to deal with such manifest realities.

Case 13: Science and the Soothsayer

A woman of 35 complained that she was frequently seized with the desire to grab a kitchen knife and run it through her husband and children. She had just left her husband because she feared she might carry out these thoughts. The therapist spent two sessions getting a history, but by the third interview the patient was remarkably improved, had rejoined her husband, and wished to terminate therapy. The therapist believes that he had unwittingly absolved her from a five-and-a-half-year-old post-hyp-notic command of a fortune teller.

Was the woman affected by a post-hypnotic command? This explana-tion is rejected by virtually every consultant. Hilgard says that when a magical belief is inculcated, there may develop a "saga" which helps per-petuate the belief. The fortune teller's prophesy was not a post-hypnotic suggestion, but rather a controlling belief with a target date. The frighten-ing nature of her fantasies made her ready to relinquish the belief on the therapist's suggestion. Snyder says the therapist's labored explanation is not in accord with the best scientific findings on hypnosis. The events approximate the typical cure of the highly suggestable obsessive. Galdston says the patient was the victim of an affirmation which operated as an en-during suggestion. The therapist was simply a shaman who cast out the evil spirit. Blake believes the patient's reaction to the fortune teller evi-dences her dependency upon authority. The therapist was in a position to exercise influence on her feelings and behavior through his position. Ellis says the patient was originally indoctrinated with faith in fortune tellers. The respected therapist effectively depropagandized her of this faith, and thereby relieved her of the fortune teller's prophesy. Ackerman attributes the cure to transference elements.

The incident raises several theoretical points. Ellis says that virtually all disturbed behavior in adults is caused by some original illogical, inappropriate, or superstitious suggestion. These suggestions are internalized, acted upon, and "reconfirmed" over and over. A therapist may use several kinds of countersuggestion (acceptance, permissiveness, analysis of transference relations, frank suggestion, advice, and so forth) to undermine the long-standing, pernicious, suggestive influences. Hilgard feels magical thinking is far more widespread in our country than is generally believed; he points out that there are nearly twice as many "water witches" as psychologists. Galdston says suggestion enters into every therapeutic contact and that its use should be conscious and deliberate, for if the therapist tries to eliminate it, it will enter in ways not always beneficial to therapy. Blake points out that "authority" can operate in ways so subtle that the therapist is completely unaware of its influence.

How well did the therapist handle the case? Several consultants feel the therapist handled the situation poorly, primarily because he did nothing to encourage the patient to work on a more permanent adjustment. Blake says this was not therapy, but psychodynamic engineering. The patient achieved no insight or problem-solving skills and was just as susceptible to the exertion of authority when she left as when she came. Hilgard says that a belief changed by faith can easily change again. The therapist should have helped modify the belief through more realistic processes, such as helping the patient to learn to gather evidence to make rational judgments. Snyder feels it would have been better to tell the patient in the third interview that she was not really improved, but only hoped to escape the painful work of psychotherapy. Ackerman says therapists should be grateful when patients are relieved of emotional suffering, but it is regrettable that this therapist did not lay the basis for continued treatment.

Case 14: Christmas with Mother

A young woman college senior was obsessed with the thought of cutting her mother's throat. She confided in her psychology instructor, who interpreted her problem as an underlying hatred of her mother. The girl strongly denied the interpretation, insisting that her mother was good. The instructor then changed his tack and pointed out what an ungrateful girl she must be for having such thoughts. The student then angrily denounced her mother for much of the session. She left shortly thereafter for Christmas vacation. On her return, the therapist learned the obsessive thoughts had disappeared, and that the girl had been openly hostile to her mother for the first time in her life.

How well did the therapist handle the case? Thorne sees the therapist's actions as an example of what *not* to do in directive psychotherapy. It was fortunate that the client reacted so well under the highly explosive conditions created by the therapist. More sensitive handling was indicated. The girl's hostility could have been bled off, rather than allowed to erupt against her mother. Thorne believes every effort should be made to keep clients from losing control with significant others.

Karpf says the therapist was incautious when he knew so little about the girl. He left her with an overtly hostile attitude toward the mother without any attempt to give her real insight. Instead, he should have tried to build up a sound relationship between the girl and her mother. Wolff says the approach, although successful, could very easily have produced anxieties and depression, or even psychosis. The girl and her mother should have been advised of the need for regualr psychotherapy, in which the structure of the girl's fantasy should have been approached slowly and systematically.

Munroe is generally sympathetic with the therapist's approach, but wonders if it might have been done without an overt "attack." Unless a person is fully committed to therapy, hostile phrases should be avoided. In a short-term, semi-informal relationship like this, it is best to leave the person with positive verbal tags to remember. Munroe feels also that insufficient attention was given the mother-daughter relationship, and that not enough consideration was given to further psychotherapy to help the girl with deeper problems.

Hilgard feels the therapist had a sensitive grasp of the underlying dynamics and that his actions were well calculated to get the student to restructure her perceptions of her relationships with her mother. Frank believes the therapist strengthened the girl's self-confidence by alleviating her fear that she was crazy, through giving her a plausible explanation for her obsessive thought, and by accepting her hostile feelings. This increased self-confidence, coupled with her emotional involvement, brought about rapid attitudinal changes which, fortunately, could be tested almost immediately with the mother. Ellis enthusiastically endorses the therapist's direct attack on the patient's false perceptual system.

The incident raises several theoretical points. Ellis is convinced resistance is often a healthy reaction to a therapist's poor technique. However, where resistance is genuine, therapists are usually too squeamish about direct approaches. The therapist is stronger and better trained and so there should be relatively few instances where, in the long run, the therapist's strength and knowledge cannot overcome the patient's neurotic or even psychotic resistance. To be intimidated by resistance is to take a nontherapeutic and often an antitherapeutic attitude. Munroe points out that in handling a rebellious patient the therapist must be careful to support mature strivings as well as the rebellion, otherwise the therapist will find himself repudiated by the patient.

Where there is interpersonal strife, Thorne believes in keeping the participants separated until the client can handle his emotions. In rare cases people may have to be separated for life if the unhealthy chains of interpersonal feeling are to be broken up.

Wolff says that a therapy of fantasy, as was this case, should always be preceded by an analysis of the structure of the fantasy in terms of behavior and perception in order to decide on the therapeutic approach. Hilgard sees in the incident a reminder that the problem of fantasy production has not been well integrated into contemporary psychology despite projective techniques and psychoanalytic interpretations. Karpf says the incident points up the problem of the exact goals of psychotherapy. She feels this question should be given more systematic consideration.

Case 15: The Therapist Was a Demon

Homer was a 40-year-old prisoner, convicted of fraud. After about 18 sessions of nondirective therapy, the therapist concluded that Homer was a scheming, suspicious, hypocritical person who was merely attempting to manipulate therapy to his own ends. In the twenty-first session, after being repeatedly asked to give an evaluation, the therapist told Homer in very harsh terms exactly what he thought of him and then terminated the session. Later, therapy was resumed and proceeded satisfactorily.

How did the therapist's sudden shift bring about the change? Mowrer comments that in his new approach the therapist showed his concern for the patient. Homer was given one of the most remarkable experiences a person can have, that someone who was in no utilitarian way dependent upon him was willing to exert himself and make sacrifices on his behalf. Thus, Homer was forced to look at the kind of person he was. Riesman sees Homer as casehardened. His shell was cracked by the intelligent and pertinent shock technique. Hunt believes that change may come about only when the client is in emotional distress. The therapist's emotional involvement brought about sufficient disruption in Homer to cause change. Snyder comments that it was a true transference-countertransference situation, the patient acting out his needs for punishment and forgiveness, the therapist acting out his sadistic needs through being a fair but punishing father. The outburst permitted just the relationship Homer needed:

a guilt-expiating dependency on a strong but loving authority figure. Rogers does not feel the verbal shock was the effective aspect. Both client and therapist were hiding their true feelings behind façades. After the therapist's blowup, he was free to express his own feelings and there ensued a real existential encounter between two persons, which is the heart of therapy.

How well did the therapist handle the case? Only Riesman takes no issue with the therapist. Mowrer, Hunt, Rogers, Galdston, and Thorne call for earlier and less extreme measures. Mowrer says the therapist might have picked on the patient along the way. Hunt believes the therapist could have expressed the same feelings little by little without a sudden outburst on the twenty-first interview. Rogers comments that he would have expressed his feelings as they occurred to him. Furthermore, he would not have called the client names, but would have stuck to statements about which he had firsthand knowledge, his own feelings. Galdston says the case called for gentler handling. Thorne says a more experienced therapist could have got the same results by confronting the client with the basic issues after the first two or three sessions. Also, verbal shock should always be administered in an objective, impersonal manner or the client may be antagonized permanently. Snyder says the case was a near failure, saved only accidentally by the therapist's righteous indignation. Had the procedure been planned and understood by the therapist, it could have been accomplished more economically. Hunt states that this was not nondirective therapy as he understands Rogers to mean it, since the therapist began with the attitude that Homer was not much good and that therapy probably would fail.

What general issues are raised? Mowrer says the case illustrates the basic importance of genuine *concern*, and questions therapy conducted on a payment basis. Perhaps the best therapists would be "amateurs" who made their living in other ways. He also asks how anger can get results, in the face of the Freudian dictum to remain uninvolved. Does the therapist in some sense have to suffer and sacrifice in order to achieve a moral advantage that is uniquely powerful therapeutically? Hunt asks if emotional involvement by the therapist is perhaps necessary in certain cases in order to arouse enough discomfort in the client for him to want to change. Galdston, Thorne, and Riesman raise questions about nondirective therapy. Galdston says its limitations are many and stringent. The only patient who can profit from nondirective therapy is one who is therapeutically active and resourceful, capable of scanning deeply and broadly his past, present, and projected goals. Where deprivation is an important factor in the pathology, there is likely to be little profit from nondirective therapy or from the free association of classical psychoanalysis. Thorne takes a similar position. Certain clients will waste hours talking about insignificant matters. Directive psychotherapy must be used to obtain results. Riesman says that for verbal, college-trained persons, clever in deceit, nondirective therapy may present a new kind of "feminine" passivity to be victimized. However, he says that in the hands of a saint (he ". . . thinks of Rogers as something of a secular saint") this method of nonviolence may get through to many otherwise casehardened persons. Snyder and Rogers both indicate that therapy can never be effective when the therapist is forcing himself to maintain a role which is inharmonious with his true feelings.

Case 16: "Go Plumb to Hell!"

The patient, a man in his late twenties, was regarded by the therapist as "a first-class stinker." He persisted in aggressive and offensive negativism until finally the therapist told him he could "go plumb to hell." The patient subsequently had four dreams, in one of which he was in hell. He then became cooperative and responsive.

What reasons account for the apparent change after telling the patient off? Dreikurs feels the therapist originally was intimidated and unable to handle the patient, who did not respect him. When the therapist showed a little spunk, the patient was impressed and became cooperative. Klapman says the therapist demonstrated that he had always been aware of the patient's true measure and thereby exploded the patient's false self-concept. Ackerman states the therapist had been inappropriately permissive. His outburst informed the patient that he supported certain basic human values and required that the patient also attempt to live up to those values. Thompson says it was a false relationship. The therapist thought he should like the patient even though he could not. The beneficial effect of telling the patient off was due to the elimination of insincerity in the therapeutic relationship. According to Blake, the patient was merely engineered into being "good" by the stern attitude of the therapist, which acted to reinforce the patient's superego.

How well was the case handled? Ellis is the only consultant who gives unqualified support to the therapist. He feels the situation was handled wisely and courageously. Dreikurs says the therapist was poorly trained or he could have been firm without so much aggression. Klapman approves, but warns that this kind of procedure does not always work. Ackerman says that if the therapist had understood his position better, and if the intrinsic value conflicts were more clearly defined, there would have been no need to tell the patient to go to hell. Thompson approves of the therapist's move to get himself out of the trap he had got into, but it would have been much better if he had been outspoken from the beginning about the problems of the therapy. Blake sees no therapeutic change because there was no significant increase in insight or problem-solving skill. The therapist merely forced the patient to be good. More maturity of adjustment would have come from the patient's understanding his need to "be bad" than from reinforcing the obligation to "be good."

There are several general issues discussed. Ellis believes that the use of well-aimed, well-timed harsh language by therapists is more widely called for. Dreikurs says that many therapists, trained in permissive techniques, function well until action, decision, or definite steps are necessary. Then they are at a loss. If resourceful, such therapists usually devise a variety of shock treatments, but with better training it would be unnecessary to resort to them. Ackerman and Thompson also condemn certain kinds of permissiveness. Ackerman says the ethos of permissiveness in psychotherapy is misunderstood. The therapist can respect the patient for his basic worth as a human being, but he is not called upon to be fond of the sick, distorted, injurious aspects of the patient's personality. Rather than helping to cure, inappropriate permissiveness toward this kind of perversion in human relationships passively accentuates the illness. Thompson points out that only a sincere relationship between patient and therapist can produce lasting results. The therapist who is tolerant and accepting under all circumstances does not really help the patient because he has undertaken a God-like pose which he cannot maintain with complete sincerity.

Case 17: "Get Well—or Else"

Although thoroughly reliable and conscientious on the job, the personal life of a 27-year-old single nurse was characterized by imprudent acting-out behavior. After about two years of group and individual therapy, she got involved in a drunken sexual affair which might have had serious consequences for her career. The therapist forbade her to behave that way in the future and threatened to hospitalize her if she did not act within socially acceptable bounds. The patient markedly improved her behavior thereafter, and also seemed to make appropriate attitudinal changes.

How did the therapist's personal reaction to the patient's behavior bring about change? According to Karpf, the therapist gave expression to the same reactions and was caught up in the same moral indignation which the patient associated with her old life. The therapist and the group provided a unified set of values by reactivating her old controls. Frank says the therapist showed real respect by attacking the deviant behavior as unworthy of the patient. This raised her self-esteem. Thorne believes the patient was demoralized about the apparent impossibility of getting married and was bogging deeper and deeper in self-defeating behavior. The therapist's action heightened the contrast between what the patient professed to want to be and what she really was, thereby creating a therapeutic conflict which she could resolve only by being consistent with her professed goals. Wolff feels that the patient had a "dependency neurosis" and by means of alcohol and sexual promiscuity was trying to escape seeing herself. The therapist acted out a paternal superego role in order to force the patient to confront the implications of her behavior. Whitaker says the change from professional to personal in the quality of the therapeutic relationship made the difference between a therapeutic impasse and a growthful experience. The therapist showed emotional involvement which was both personal and mature, and she had enough belief in the patient to demand maturity from her. This gave the patient a new perspective from which to readjust her own integration.

Several consultants take issue with the handling of the case. Frank questions the wisdom of the therapist's showing doubts about taking an authoritarian role. Karpf says the therapist's joke reveals attitudes of sexual competition with the patient. She also questions the whole supportive-permissive approach used for so long with this patient. What was needed was a more integrative approach to help build up a positive outlook on life and to help replace or repair the guiding values she had partially discarded. Thorne would prefer a gradual reconditioning program aimed at securing a strong self-concept around which the patient would be taught to behave more consistently. The therapist needed a more positive program and more patience. He disagrees with taking punitive or disciplinary action in this case since the behavior was not truly antisocial, but only symptomatic. Wolff feels the therapist abused her role by threatening the patient with hospitalization.

The incident gives rise to several general comments on therapy. Frank points out that a direct attack on unworthy behavior often seems to raise a patient's self-esteem, whereas permissiveness or interpretation seems to convey that the therapist does not expect much of the patient, thereby further damaging self-esteem.

In his discussion of confessions on the part of the therapist, Frank says that "breast-beating" during the initial phases of group or individual therapy is likely to undermine the patient's faith in the therapist, but sharing one's problems after the relationship is firmly established may have the salutory effect of showing the therapist's common humanity with the patient. However, he warns against relating problems in a way which undermines the patient's confidence in his ability to handle his own emotional difficulties.

On the issue of directive control, Thorne believes that unless acting-

out has a definite antisocial consequence it should be regarded as symptomatic behavior. At most, the patient should be shown the practical limits
of behavior which can be tolerated in the therapeutic situation. Wolff
feels that conditions have to be imposed on certain types of patients, such
as psychotics, drug addicts, and psychopaths. However, therapists should
not assume power over the patient's existence through the use of threats.
It deprives the patient of his existential sovereignty. Therapists, teachers,
and parents must never transcend their rights to the point where their
behavior includes the danger of crushing individuality.

Case 18: It's Difficult to Treat a Friend

Because he was a social acquaintance, the therapist took a 29-year-old
male as a patient on an exploratory basis at a nominal fee. After three
months of unsatisfactory progress the patient wanted to terminate. At
this point the therapist disclosed information about the patient which
indicated his behavior was leading him into serious trouble. The patient
was frightened and continued therapy, which the therapist then structured
on a more realistic basis.

Should a therapist treat friends or social acquaintances? Dreikurs believes a therapist can not only treat acquaintances successfully, but even
friends and relatives. It is necessary only for the therapist to regard therapy
as a learning procedure rather than as a peculiar emotional relationship
specific only for therapy, and for both therapist and patient to have mutual
respect and common goals. Ackerman says complete openness is the
cornerstone of psychotherapy. Friendship creates special problems in
therapy, but they can be solved if therapist and patient can eliminate the
insincerity present in most casual relationships.

Ellis takes a more cautious view. There are advantages in treating
acquaintances because the therapist knows the patient better, is presumably strongly motivated to help, and may gain rapport more easily. However, the disadvantages—evasiveness, countertransference problems, embarrassing involvements with mutually-known third parties, and the
reluctance the patient may feel to quit or transfer—outweigh the advantages, except in rare circumstances. Snyder says that doing therapy with
a friend is like doing a "favor." Neither person is fully free to exercise critical judgment; the therapy is therefore hampered. Snyder makes the additional point that help requested from a friend may be a sign of initial
resistance to therapy.

*Was it advisable to confront the patient with knowledge gained from
outside sources?* Ellis believes that confrontation with social facts is fre-

quently called for, but must be done judiciously. Thorne favors gathering evidence about the client's behavior from independent outside sources. But the client should be confronted with reality in small doses; the therapist should attempt to balance unpleasant topics by "sugaring off" the interview so the client is left with a predominance of positive feelings. Although a client may be pained by the existence of such common knowledge, psychotherapy often has to be painful; fear of hurting should not deter the therapist.

Riesman says that supplying information revealed to the patient his precarious position in his sociometric network and gave him a sense that he was real and that the therapist was real. Sondel feels the patient had deluded himself with incorrect signs. When the therapist confronted him with the social facts, the patient was enabled to really see his problem and begin to work on it. Riesman observes that providing a challenge to patients from the emancipated social strata requires a different orientation than Freud had with his early patients. Psychotherapists have for so long had to fight the Philistines who insist on "hard reality" that they have a disinclination to adopt a realistic position even though it may be called for in acquainting an indulged person with disturbing "reality."

Snyder cautions that while in some cases confrontation may be beneficial, in other cases the patient might retreat from therapy, or even be further damaged in his functioning in life.

How well was the case handled? According to Dreikurs, the relationship was mismanaged from the start and the therapist used a clumsy, brutal shock procedure to get out of the impasse. Worse, the therapist used the old stock in trade, "resistance," as an excuse for his inability to win and maintain the patient's cooperation. Ackerman feels that, in spite of the case's avowed exploratory nature, the therapist seemed to push the patient to stay in therapy and then used confrontation in a retaliatory manner—punishing the patient for his stubbornness. He intimidated the patient into submission to his therapeutic powers. This resulted from conducting therapy without honesty. If the patient was resistant, so was the therapist, who held back certain knowledge until the incident.

Snyder says the therapist should not have taken the client in the first place, knowing how resistant he was. Having taken him, however, the therapist then cheapened the significance of his service by offering therapy for a nominal fee. In addition, there was plenty of advance information that the client would try to "bluff his way through" unless he were required to be absolutely honest from the beginning. Admitting these initial errors, Snyder thinks the therapist salvaged the situation in the most feasible manner by assuming a nontherapeutic position, apprising the client of his true situation, and then offering to resume therapy.

Case 19: Love Was Enough

Nine years after hospitalization for a psychosis which included delusional paranoia and catatonia, a white male in his early thirties discussed the role played in his recovery by a female Negro attendant who gave him special loving care. After improvement he saw the attendant and found her to be quite different from the way he remembered her.

What factors induced recovery? According to Ackerman, the aide's love for the patient saved his life. Her sincere, warm, steady ministering to his needs challenged his paranoid misconception that he had no chance for life or love. He was inspired to live for her. Whitaker says it was contact with the aide's maturity, her capacity to give and to love, which saved the patient. Despite his condition, he was able to perceive her maturity since the psychotic is fully responsive to the inner experience of persons to whom he is relating. Both Ackerman and Whitaker feel that at the reunion the depth and truth of the relationship was obscured by cultural stereotypes and other barriers to perception. Sondel says that each person communicated something intimately associated with values at deep levels of their personalities and that this hastened recovery. Hunt believes the aide's personal interest created the impression that the patient was of value to someone. Herr feels the aide satisfied the patient's need for affection, attention, or respect. However, he adds that the patient had "tentatively accepted the psychiatrist's disagreement with his delusional beliefs," and this may have prepared the way for improvement.

Frank is somewhat skeptical of the patient's account since memories are so strongly influenced by present motivations. The patient may have credited the colored aide in order to make sense of his recovery and to please the therapist to whom he was recounting the experience. However, assuming the account to be true, Frank believes the patient had regressed to an infantile state where he became accessible to a primitive mothering approach. Also, he may have been more able to accept the aide's good intentions as genuine because he identified her as a member of a persecuted minority, which he felt himself to be. Frank suggests additional contributing factors. The hospital's total program may have influenced his recovery. Also, life-threats often produce remissions in schizophrenics; the patient's concurrent severe physical illness may have mobilized curative forces.

What are the implications of this incident for the treatment of psychotics? Hunt says that genuine personal interest on the part of ward personnel may be of major importance in treatment. If milieu therapy is ever to be more widely adopted, experiments are needed to test this notion. Ackerman says the care of psychotics cannot be mechanized. Architecture and technical facilities cannot replace brains, but, even more important, brains cannot replace heart—warm, kindly, interpersonal intimacy is indispensable to recovery. Both Ackerman and Frank state that these humane ingredients are not developed by professional training. The right *kind* of people, with warmth and a sense of dedication, can inspire the contagion of hope and faith. Whitaker comments that this case may help us develop respect for maturity and deep feelings in the therapist. Countertransference is crucial, but investigation is needed to determine when it is damaging and when growthful. Whitaker and Herr both feel there is a degree of health in the psychotic. Whitaker believes this is often ignored.

Much of the comment centers around nonverbal communication. Frank says that patients who are too disorganized to interpret words correctly may still respond appropriately to physical contact. Sondel and Whitaker believe that communication between psychotics and others is almost totally nonverbal. Sondel points out that this adds responsibility to the therapist since his values are communicated over and beyond the literal significance of his words. Whitaker believes the psychotic's perception of interpersonal reality is exceptionally acute. Hunt feels that the subtle cues of interpersonal communication evident in this case have thus far escaped systematic organization in psychological theory.

Case 20: It's All in the Family

A young divorced woman with two previous hospitalizations for psychotic conditions was seen for the first time in her home. Despite her highly disorganized state, the therapist thought it unwise to return her to the hospital against her wishes. Conventional out-patient treatment was out of the question. The client's brother and sister-in-law agreed to escort her to and from the therapist's office. They were also to act as "co-therapists" on the assumption that they might become sources of emotional support for her.

Is this approach practical? Ackerman, Dreikurs, Thorne, Whitaker, and Karpf state that they have successfully used similar procedures. Ackerman argues that since people become psychotic in families, it is only logical to treat them in families. There is no question as to the appropriateness of the therapist's goals; the question is whether or not the family is equal to the demands. Dreikurs points out two advantages of "family therapy." First, the patient usually learns more from interpretations made to others in his presence. Second, in working with a borderline or psychotic case it is wiser to limit explanations to the most disturbing aspect of the patient's problem. With relatives present, the exploration of the patient's conflict will not cover so wide a range as in individual therapy. Whitaker believes the method helps a patient develop the capacity to function in his own social structure. The homeostatic stability of the group is usable. It may even be easier to change a total family than an individual. Ackerman and Karpf point out that psychotic patients are usually isolated and alienated from natural social contacts which might offer nourishment. The present approach is the reverse of the usual procedures, which foster isolation.

Although the procedure has advantages, Thorne believes a therapeutic group is better made up of strangers, otherwise the client may have to live down details long after he is well. He also says that regular individual therapy should be instituted as soon as possible.

What are the psychotherapeutic implications? Sondel says a disturbed patient is always helped by the realization that his behavior is part of a field. It helps him look outward instead of hopelessly inward. A field theory of communications would force a therapist to employ means that take him beyond the inner life of his patient. Ackerman sees in the method a challenge to the plaguing problem of how to care for a selected fraction of psychotics within the family or community. Karpf sees the method as suggesting to therapists that they explore further the use of family aides as "co-therapists."

Riesman believes that this and many other incidents reflect, on the one hand, therapists' needs to confront their present day, sophisticated patients with more active therapeutic techniques; and, on the other hand, their fear of doing so because of the traditional passive, verbal approach which, in Freud's day, worked very well. Therapists ought to get together, admit they are all sinners, and then proceed to openly develop techniques more suitable to present day practice. Riesman also makes the observation that psychotherapists seem mostly concerned with minimal adjustment. He hopes that there will be another study in which the incidents concern more complex valuational choices.

Case 21: "What Are You Hiding?"

A woman in her middle forties who suffered from depressed spells and homicidal impulses toward her youngest daughter was asked point-blank by her therapist, who suspected deliberate withholding, whether or not she was concealing something important. The patient at first denied this, then disclosed a long-standing sexual perversion with dogs. The patient was immediately relieved of her depression, and therapy improved.

The therapist feels that it was important to relieve the patient of her distress, but questions the wisdom of his method.

How well was the case handled? What alternative approaches were indicated? Dreikurs, Rogers, and, to a lesser degree, Thorne disapprove of the approach. Dreikurs does not accept the claim that a forced confession was necessary for immediate relief. It was simply an unskillful technique for getting to the patient's deeper problems. All patients are reluctant to reveal how bad they really are, while at the same time they try to convince the therapist that they are utterly bad and hopeless. Had the therapist been able to win the patient's confidence and induce her to open up, such a shock procedure, which is "clumsy, in bad taste, and cruel," would not have been needed. Roger's criticism is gentler, but no less definite. The therapist, by assuming specific attitudes, feelings, or knowledge in clients, asserts a God-like omniscience inimical to therapy. He cannot possibly know what is going on inside the client. He can only know what is going on within himself, and it is his own feelings which he can and should express. Thorne, critical of the bluntness of handling, feels that gentle, cautious probing was indicated. It is a mistake to coerce clients.

Ellis, Herr, Galdston, Mowrer, and Whitaker approve of the way the problem was handled. Ellis calls it a "fine job," and favors getting to the heart of a patient's problem as quickly as possible. Herr says the therapist deserves highest praise for forcing the "confession." Like was cured with like; the patient was forced into the practice and forced out of it. Although she might have refused to confess and discontinued treatment, she would probably have returned or confessed to someone else later. Galdston states the therapist's confrontation broke through and cleared the way for self-acceptance and better interpersonal relations. Mowrer feels that the therapist's bold stroke went to the heart of what might otherwise have necessitated protracted and perhaps unsuccessful therapy. However, he criticises the lack of constructive steps to help the patient regain self-esteem. Whitaker approves of the therapist's breaking with the tradition of keeping psychotherapy a symbolic relationship by putting it on a give-and-take basis. He and Thorne both point out that a great deal more freedom is possible after rapport has been established.

Dreikurs, Galdston and Herr add that the patient's perverted practice hid some more basic problems and that these would have to be worked through.

What is the therapist's responsibility in alleviating distress? Galdston says that Freud and Ferenczi taught that it was unwise to relieve distress before the patient gains insight; but he points out that if distress is overwhelming, it must be alleviated since the patient is too disrupted to utilize psychotherapy. Herr and Galdston feel it is mandatory to reduce suffering, even at the expense of theory. However, Thorne, Ellis, and Galdston add that distress should not be relieved if suffering is necessary for long-term recovery.

Ellis believes that getting at the patient's main problem as soon as possible (and hence reducing anxiety quickly) is usually the only method of achieving lasting improvement. Many patients who improve slowly never reach the highest degree of integration.

Was the therapist's procedure unethical? Ellis says no ethical issue was involved; it was a matter of technique and theory. Galdston says essentially the same thing, adding that the therapist was cowed by the dicta of technique and theory. Herr knows of no ethical law or principle which *ever* prevents counselors from acting in a very directive manner.

Some theoretical notions. Thorne states that the efficacy of therapeutic techniques cannot be judged by clients' immediate reactions since it may be weeks or months before assimilation and reorganization take place. Rogers and Whitaker agree that the therapist should not withhold his own feelings when it interferes with the genuineness of the relationship. Rogers reiterates that when acceptance and empathy are real, they promote the most rapid growth. But if the therapist cannot genuinely feel accepting and empathic, he had better express his true attitudes. Whitaker states that it is vital to protect the therapist's integrity even at the expense of the therapeutic process or the integrity of the patient. The case reminds Mowrer of a religious confession, especially since real rather than false guilt was involved. But real transgressions are very often at the bottom of psychological disturbances. Secular therapy might profitably follow the religious course of penance and good works. A short cut was achieved in this case through confession; an appropriate course of redemptive action might have achieved another. Mowrer intimates that the secular, scientific approach to real guilt may be in the process of self-liquidation.

Case 22: Cinderella and the Actress

Mrs. Henry and Mrs. Carnes were mutually antagonistic members of a therapy group. During the thirty-sixth interview Mrs. Carnes attacked Mrs. Henry for her dirtiness and then walked out. The therapist followed and asked her to return. Mrs. Henry missed the next meeting, and the therapist wrote inviting her back. She returned much improved in outward appearance and stated she had applied for a job. The incident had given her new insight into her Cinderella relationship with her mother and sister.

How well did the therapist handle the case? With the exception of Montagu, all consultants are critical of the therapist. Ackerman believes the therapist misdiagnosed the severity of Mrs. Henry's condition and feels she probably had a schizoid personality. Also, the therapist did not seem to realize that two women suffering from severely damaged self-esteem were fighting over him, and he did nothing to clarify what was going on. He may even have subtly encouraged the rivalry. Dreikurs, too, feels the therapist did not understand what was happening. As does Ackerman, Dreikurs believes the therapist was a victim of a power contest between the two women and that he acted like a passive observer, having little recognition of his role. Klapman also sees the therapist as a passive observer and feels he took initiative only when he wrote Mrs. Henry after her absence from the group. The real therapists were the other patients. Moreno is quite critical of the therapist for his passivity and indicates four points where he could have profitably intervened, but did not.

Only Montagu reacts in a positive manner to the therapist's behavior. Writing to Mrs. Henry turned the tide. The extra investment the therapist made was crucial in recalling her to life.

What brought about the abrupt change in Mrs. Henry? Klapman is convinced the locus of therapy was in the other patients and not the therapist. The family situation was recreated with Mrs. Carnes representing the rejecting mother and the preferred sister. When Mrs. Henry won her victory over Mrs. Carnes, it was a signal for a victory within herself. Also, from a different point of view, Mrs. Carnes' attack may be seen as an intuitively well-timed act of love or interest. Mrs. Henry may have reacted to it as such.

Dreikurs, who sees the women in a power contest, believes Mrs. Carnes went too far in her assault, and that when the therapist and the other patients took Mrs. Henry's part, Mrs. Carnes was defeated. For the first time, Mrs. Henry experienced success in a socially acceptable way. This victory caused her improvement. She no longer needed to cling to her useless behavior, but could seek approval through socially acceptable behavior.

Ackerman sees the two women struggling in a sado-masochistic encounter. Each sought reconciliation with her mother. Their outward competitiveness covered underlying needs for each other's acceptance. Mrs. Carnes' attack may have been perceived by Mrs. Henry as a special interest in her. Mrs. Henry's change was an attempt to please either the therapist or Mrs. Carnes.

Montagu, who sees Mrs. Henry as a love-starved person, believes the group experience was a reliving of her former life—the group representing the family in which she held a low status. The therapist was the mother, and the other patients were her sisters. The group's acceptance of her verboseness was the first step in changing her estimate of her own worth. The final change occurred when, after staying away to find out if anyone cared, she learned that she mattered to the therapist and to the other patients.

Eliasberg feels that the incident was not a crucial factor. It was only a final point in a long series of contributing incidents and must be seen as a culmination and not an explanation.

Case 23: In Grandmother's Image

A 33-year-old woman feared she might go insane or kill her daughter. Her hostility was kept inactive and unexplored by the reaction-formation of a "good-mother" role. The therapist chose to actively support the patient's good-mother beliefs and otherwise remain passive, rather than interpret her defenses. This choice was based partly on Rorschach signs indicating inadequate ego structure. An "inaccessable negative transference" developed and the patient finally terminated therapy by telephone. The therapist did not try to influence her to remain in therapy. The patient returned a year later. This time her hatred and jealousy of her child were explored with the therapist, who was sympathetic and nonjudgmental. Therapy improved steadily.

How well was the case handled? All consultants agree that the therapist was too passive. Klapman says passivity fostered doubt and hostility, partly because the patient's domination of the therapist reinforced her feelings about dominating her child. More intervention would have meant more ego support, and hence less negative transference and a more positive relationship. Ellis and Dreikurs also believe the therapist's passivity fostered the poor relationship, and they favor early active interpretation. They feel the therapist unwittingly rejected the patient's plea for help. Dreikurs adds that the passive approach let the patient believe the therapist supported her erroneous conclusions about herself. Hunt believes the patient interpreted the therapist's passivity as criticism, not acceptance. There was a hostility-anxiety spiral which could have been prevented by early "gentle" interpretation. Munroe feels that passive support was inadequate in view of the weakness of the good-mother defense pattern and the strength of the latent hostility. Rogers believes the therapist's passivity was not genuine—that she strongly desired to direct the client toward preconceived goals. Her inadvertent expression of these desires frightened the client away from therapy.

There are several opinions about the desirability of interpretation. Dreikurs, Ellis, and Klapman favor early, active interpretation and believe it would have prevented termination. However, Dreikurs thoroughly disagrees with the therapist's formulation of the dynamics operating and therefore implies disagreement with any interpretations which were or might have been made. Ellis feels that this therapist, along with many others, was too intimidated by pathological signs in the projective tests.

Hunt agrees with the above consultants in that he recommends early interpretation, but he suggests a less vigorous approach. Gentle interpretation would have overcome the patient's suspicion and provided a source of support as she worked through her hostility-anxiety conflict.

Munroe believes the patient had insufficient ego strength to support direct interpretations and suggests a sharing-learning type of interpretation through which the patient could have translated insight about "others" into insight about herself. The sharing part of the approach would have built a positive, supportive relationship conducive to and helpful in the more painful emotional changes which must follow. She cautions that her "intellectualizing technique" does not supplant emotional change, the major aim of therapy, but does follow a shift in some schools of psychotherapy toward "working through," that is, learning how one's attitudes and behaviors are affected by different facets of everyday life.

Rogers feels that interpretations are undesirable. However, if a therapist holds interpretive thoughts, they will be communicated, probably more detrimentally than if openly expressed. The problem is not to interpret the client's subjective world and behavior, but rather to interpret one's own feelings and attitudes at critical junctures in therapy and to be able to express these feelings as transparently as possible to the client, thereby allowing ". . . a real meeting of persons . . . the reality in me coming in contact with the reality in her." He suggests several steps which might have been taken when the client terminated. Rather than remaining passive when the client telephoned, he would have made it very clear that he respected her decision, but that he would save her next appointment in case she wished to use it. If she did not, he would have searched for his own feelings about the termination and then tried to express them as openly and straightforwardly as possible in a letter. He would have offered one further interview which would be *his* (no fee) to give both the client and him an opportunity mutually to clarify their feelings.

Index

387